Business and Society

Business and Society

Managing Corporate Social Impact

George C. Sawyer

Hofstra University

HOUGHTON MIFFLIN COMPANY   Boston

Dallas   Geneva, Illinois   Hopewell, New Jersey

Palo Alto   London

To Margo

Printed in the U.S.A.

Library of Congress Catalog Card Number: 78-69570

ISBN: 0-395-26541-X

Contents

Preface

The controversy over social responsibility has provoked a literature rapidly increasing in volume and diversity. Yet no treatment of this subject from the viewpoint of corporate management has seemed sufficiently action-oriented to merit widespread application. In this book, the search has been for a conceptual framework from which practical guidelines for management action could be developed. This has led to an integration of concepts necessary to provide such a framework and to the development of tentative management guidelines for a business operating according to these concepts.

The broad area of corporate responsibility and conscience was approached with some temerity because of the scope of past efforts. Yet, as reflected in the literature, the necessary unification of management concepts has not led in the past to objective operating guidelines for responsible business corporations. This need exists, and the present work is an attempt to fill a portion of that need.

The analysis of corporate social impact is presented here as (1) a newly defined portion of the total sphere of corporate management, (2) an area where corporate self-interest seems to call for earlier and more complete balancing of these impacts, and (3) a part of the management process in any well-managed, profit-seeking corporation.

The primary purpose of this book is for use as a text in that area of the business school curriculum that aids students in understanding the broad scope of the relationship between the corporation and society. The book moves from the wealth of pre-existing concepts to the social balance frame-work of this analysis, and from the social balance concept of avoiding social cost to a consideration of the impact of business corporations on the various components of society with which they interact.

The discussion of impacts begins with specific instances in which corpo-rations have faced social and environmental problems whose dimensions help make the application of the proposed guidelines real and relevant. These examples are presented as a prelude to analysis that provides a basis for generalizing about the process of managing responsibly. To aid the reader in dealing with the underlying concepts (for example, social balance), a brief list of important terms is included at the end of the book. Also, an index is provided to aid in locating topics and concepts.

In acknowledging my indebtedness to others, I must first cite Peter Drucker, whose broad view of managers and the business enterprise both shaped my ideas and challenged me to build on the foundations thus laid. Acknowledgement should also be made to Robert Kavesh and Herman Krooss, whose friendly challenges stimulated me to organize and articulate my ideas more clearly; Harold Lazarus, who encouraged the present work in its critical initial stages; and my wife, Margo, who shared in the pain and frustration as a group of ideas were molded into an organized work. I would also like to thank Professors Rogene Buchholz, University of Minnesota; Dennis W. Callaghan and Robert A. Comerford, both of the University of Rhode Island; William C. Pavord, Indiana University East; Daryl G. Mitton of San Diego State University; Charles N. Kaufman, University of South Dako-ta; Edison E. Easton of Oregon State University; and Thomas R. Webb of Dalton-Dalton-Little-Newport for their assistance in reviewing the manu-script. Built and refined from this base, the present work will have accom-plished its purpose well if it leads to further discussion of the social balance and social impact concepts and to the trial and further evolution of operating guidelines for socially responsible management.

G. C. S.

To the Instructor

This text is concerned with the symbiotic relationship between a corporation or other large organization and the surrounding society. The importance of such an area of study is beyond question. Moreover, the poorly defined and understood nature of this critical relationship further justifies its consideration as a separate area. The rate of evolution and development of the social systems and controls required for a successful industrial society has lagged far behind industrial progress, causing great suffering and trauma. This has reached the point that society has now finally begun to give attention to specific social and environmental stresses caused by corporate and organizational actions. The underlying principles of an acceptable business-society relationship have begun to emerge, but the specific requirements will continue to shift for the foreseeable future as society's regulations and preferences continue their rapid evolution.

Thus, there is an urgent need for managers and all others interested in corporate conduct to obtain a sufficient grasp of the underlying principles to allow them to deal with the shifting requirements as new problems and rules emerge. A part of the practice of effective management is the management of the social impact of corporate or organizational decisions. Those interested in large organizations—their management, their governance, their potential, and their limitations—need a working understanding of the options and techniques by which their social impact can be managed.

Various courses focus on this area; each is somewhat unique because the subject matter deals with many questions for which there are no specific answers. Instead the emphasis is on defining the general standards that will determine potential answers and decisions and relating those standards to the accumulated body of knowledge about society's regulations and desires and corporate practice. The focus therefore is on guiding principles and on their application to specific cases in the past, present, and future.

Using the Text

This text is designed to relate current industrial practice to a theoretical foundation that can become a guide for such practice in the future. After a brief summary of relevant elements of economics, industrial development, and management history, the discussion focuses on a framework for the management of corporate social impact. This is then summarized into guidelines for the emerging field. The various corporate social impact issues are illustrated by specific examples, selected to show particular elements in the organization-society relationship. These examples can be made more valuable by contrast with similar elements in the current flow of corporate events.

An enjoyable and effective instructional pattern for developing an understanding of the relationship between business and society can be based on current material brought in by students. As the course progresses, each student is assigned to find one or more news or magazine articles describing a current organization-society issue of the type treated in a reading assignment. The clippings are submitted together with a few lines of commentary explaining how they relate to the issues in the assigned chapter. In opening the class discussion on that topic, students are asked to report on the events described in their clippings, with key words noted on the chalkboard. Almost invariably the diversity of the current issues reported is such that, as the discussion relates them to each other under the instructor's guidance, the conceptual framework of the chapter emerges.

This approach serves several worthwhile purposes. First, it relates the course specifically and immediately to the current corporate world, consequently increasing the relevance of the material. Second, it provides specific issues against which to test the course concepts and experience in relating them to changing requirements. Third, it increases student interest through their direct participation. Fourth, this approach frees the instructor from much of the need for routine lecture preparation, requiring instead a high-level, free-form skill as a discussion leader.

Fruitful sources of current reports on issues are daily papers such as *The New York Times* and the *Wall Street Journal,* news magazines such as *Business Week,* and more specialized publications ranging from the *Sierra Club Bulletin* and *National Geographic* to internal corporate sources. In most cases little effort is required to obtain the clipping material, and the task helps the student keep the focus of the course in mind in the course of normal activities. In addition, this approach leads students to see new dimensions—such as the use of resources, employment, and the impact on the community and society as a whole—in current headlines concerning pollution, energy, or nuclear power.

On the instructor's side, it is necessary to record this flow of materials from the students to insure compliance with the assignment. The normal practice is to grade this material only in terms of its fulfillment of the assignment; that is, relevant material with intelligent comments about its relationship to the topic fulfills the assignment completely.

Most instructors will require a term paper or other similar written work, and the discussion linked into current events issue by issue provides a convenient and stimulating source of ideas for topics. The instructor may wish to extend this discussion to the point of class presentation of some of the better term papers. Thus the development of ideas is further reinforced by additional related investigation and analysis of the selected subject material.

While there are few absolutes in this field, the existence of the course assumes that corporations have some degree of accountability for their actions. Once this is granted (whether the student does or does not agree fully with every element of the text) the analytical framework, the balancing of actions, and potential accountability can provide the necessary basis for developing an understanding of corporate social impacts that must precede improvement in this particular dimension of effective management in the future.

A major part of the course grade can be based on the written work submitted plus the caliber and extent of participation in class discussion. Where formal examinations and quizzes are also to be used, the author's experience suggests the use of essay questions aimed at testing student ability to intelligently understand and apply the suggested analytical framework. Questions can test understanding by asking for a paragraph on the potential meaning and application of one of the suggested guidelines for management action. Or a question can outline a hypothetical situation in an organization and ask the student to discuss the managerial decision alternatives in terms of their social impact and the degree of need for avoiding or balancing this impact. The questions at the end of each chapter are intended for oral or written discussion, but they are also a convenient source of quiz questions if testing seems necessary to insure careful reading and study of the text.

Supplemental Materials

The text treats the background to the industrial present only briefly, and some instructors may wish to extend this with supplemental readings. Massive quantities of material are available. A few examples: for economic history, Robert Heilbroner's *The Worldly Philosophers* is an interesting and readable starting point; for business history, Miriam Beard's *History of Business* is recommended; for a more current background, the contrast between John Kenneth Galbraith's *American Capitalism* and Milton Friedman's *Freedom and Capitalism* makes a good subject for student analysis. Also, an assortment of good case and readings books are available, such as William Greenwood's *Readings in Business and Society* (third edition, also published by Houghton Mifflin); some instructors may wish to ask for further exploration of a particular area or to use contemporary cases from a case book rather than from current events as suggested above.

Conclusion

This text deals with a most urgent and important subject; no business student can be considered well equipped without some understanding of the principles governing the relationship between corporations, or other large organizations, and the surrounding society. This text is aimed at aiding the development of such an understanding, as the principles governing this relationship begin to emerge more and more clearly. The guidelines summarized at chapter ends attempt to initiate the formulation of these principles in a concrete form. Your comments and suggestions are most welcome.

This book embodies a unique pattern of dealing with the subject matter and the issues. The author has found this approach effective and interesting for the student and instructor, and it has made the course a rewarding professional experience. May others find it similarly rewarding.

G. C. S.

Introduction

"None of our institutions exists by itself and is an end in itself. Every one is an organ of our society and exists for the sake of society. Business is no exception. Free enterprise cannot be justified as being good for business. It can be justified only as being good for society." [1]

This book is devoted to the theme that corporate social impact can and must be better understood and managed. The text presents an analytical framework and a set of tentative operating guidelines designed to make this management process effective. But such guidelines are of use only when a given management chooses to apply them. For the management of any specific corporation, two questions exist: (1) Why bother? and (2) What if the corporation can't quite follow the guidelines?

There are many reasons for attempting to manage corporate social impact, including the notable public antagonism toward corporations generated by both injury and misunderstanding, the increasing imposition of limiting regulations and bureaucracies, and the escalating attacks on corporations by consumer and public advocates. Without effective corporate initiatives, there is every reason to expect that the pressure of these forces will continue to increase, even to the point of reducing the efficiency and output of the economic system.

To permit continued degradation of the corporate operating environment is not sound stewardship of corporate assets. Management can no longer

---

[1]Peter F. Drucker, *Management: Tasks, Responsibilities, Practices,* (New York: Harper & Row, 1973), p. 41.

afford to ignore society and its demands. There is a clear need for an effort to manage corporate social impact, and many managements have already undertaken some sort of program to meet these demands.

What happens if management, in spite of good intentions, cannot balance its corporate social impact? The question is complex but the elements of the answer are clear. If a corporation cannot maintain a social balance, it will create social costs. In the past society paid little attention to social costs, but it is far more aware of them in the present. If society discovers that a corporation is creating social costs, it will question corporate actions sharply. Unsatisfactory answers will bring anger and agitation. Sooner or later, depending on when political power can be mobilized, this anger over the creation of social costs will bring regulation or reprisal to stop the offense.

Once such a sequence has begun, the outcome seems inevitable; but the sequence of events need never begin. It is based on an assumption of antagonism between society and the corporation. If a corporation permits itself to be seen as an antagonist of society, social response by regulation or reprisal is clearly invited. The alternative is an open relationship in which society sees the need to work out the social cost problem in partnership with the corporation.

Thus, for example, public funding has sometimes eased the strain on a business unable to find the capital needed to build waste treatment facilities. Congress proceeded slowly to force the closing of unsafe Appalachian coal mines, allowing management the time to find the means to comply with essential federal safety regulations. In the first instance, a degree of public subsidy was approved to aid management; in the second instance, a period of delay was allowed for management compliance. The need in both cases was to eliminate social cost, but society was willing to join in a cooperative effort to help find a solution to the problem causing the social cost.

In the long run, management has no choice but to balance its corporate social impacts; any such impacts that lead to social costs will not be permitted. But in the short run, a corporation seriously intent on avoiding social cost and able to demonstrate a "good faith" effort often can gain time or even assistance, so that the long-term necessity weighs less ominously in the present. "We try harder" should become the corporate motto both in managing corporate social impact and in striving to achieve a corporate social balance.

Free Enterprise and the Management of Corporate Social Impact

Adam Smith visualized a profit-oriented trading and industrial society in which the sum of the self-interested strivings of individuals equaled the common good of the whole. This appealing vision fitted closely to the pattern of the time and the temper of the western world; it became the economic driving force for the industrial revolution and the free enterprise society of the nineteenth and twentieth centuries. However, as industries have grown and technology has spread, the shortcomings of this philosophy have been manifested in the growth of legislation and regulation controlling

business behavior and in the clamor over the lack of corporate social responsibility.

The largest single deficiency in Adam Smith's vision was his failure to see
that the individual's profit from a given transaction is not the same as
society's profit, and that social costs constitute the greatest part of this
difference. The sum of the businesses' profits cannot be equal to the
common good if massive costs are left to be borne by society.

The theme in this book is that corporations can no longer safely leave
social costs for society to pay. Such a process is becoming unacceptable. At
some point in the future all corporations will be required to maintain a social
balance in which no social costs are created unless society has explicitly
agreed to absorb those costs, thus subsidizing the operation to a certain
extent.

The point in time where a social balance will be required in all areas of
corporate social impact is still far away. In the following analysis, a number
of the proposed operating guidelines are somewhat speculative because
society has not yet clarified its standards. In other areas, guidelines are
clearer because recent legislation has defined society's requirements; in
these areas, only routine enforcement is now required to bring laggards into
compliance. The demand for a social balance is coming, but not everywhere
at the same rate, as some social cost issues come to public attention before
others.

The argument here is that corporate social impact must be managed
because it is too important and explosive an area to leave unmanaged.
Further, the management of corporate social impact must be directed toward minimizing confrontation with society. This means minimizing social
costs, particularly in areas of current social sensitivity. This is an urgent
short-term corporate self-interest.

The long-term self-interest of a corporation (as presented here) is to
manage its corporate social impact in order to achieve a social balance
immediately wherever this is possible and to present and defend a constructive program that moves the firm towards a balance in areas where social
costs are still being incurred. To do less would seem unwise.

Also, corporate long-term self-interest dictates that the social mechanisms
that regulate corporate behavior be adjusted to require that a social balance
be achieved. This will take time, since society's standards are imperfect, but
the potential rewards are large. If the industrial system as a whole can begin
to achieve a reasonable balance with society rather than burdening it with
leftover costs, the principal reasons for the pervasive public distrust of
corporations will begin to fade.

The free enterprise system is continually under attack. Many in our society clamor for regulation aimed toward the social control of corporations, or
even state ownership, as the only means of solving today's problems.
Instead, by beginning to truly pay the full costs of industrial operation and
achieve a social balance for the first time, the industrial system can begin to
return to Adam Smith's vision of a world where the sum of individual
self-interests equals the public good.

This cannot be done in the absence of social control, but neither can it be done under the present regulatory structures. As argued here, society's governance processes need to be redesigned. These processes should be altered to control more lightly but more surely and clearly in the public interest. It is in the corporate interest to encourage more intelligent and thorough governance, as well as to manage its own social impacts well enough to eliminate social costs.

Achieving better governance and a social balance will resolve the confrontation between corporation and society and create an environment in which enterprise can be free once more. Such an achievement will also allow businesses to be more efficient and effective in the production of goods and services, establishing the highest national level of living that sound management of the environment and of the available resources allows. From sound management of corporate social impact can come substantial progress towards a less regulated free-enterprise society. This book outlines a framework for the analysis of corporate social impact and tentative guidelines for managing this impact as a means to such progress.

The Plan of the Book

This book is divided into five parts that deal with major facets of the subject in a context intended to create an integrated flow from introduction to conclusion. Part One introduces the concept of social responsibility. An initial profile of the issues illustrates many of the stresses that arise between business and society. The evolution of the economic system and of the industrial society that has grown up with it provides the historical background for today's confrontation over the proper role of the corporation and the nature of its responsibility to society.

Part Two considers tools for measuring corporate impact on society, beginning with the problem of social costs and the development of the social audit concept. Next, the concept of a social balance between business and society is introduced, and the potential relationship of such a balance to the social capital of that society is discussed. This leads to the outline of a social balance analysis.

Part Three applies this analysis to the areas directly affected by the firm's operation—products and their consequences, the firm's use of resources, and the neighborhood effects from its operation. Part Four carries this analysis into the societywide impact areas, dealing with the ways in which a corporation affects society and conversely the ways society influences and controls the behavior of the corporation.

Part Five summarizes major considerations facing management in a changing world as it deals with social issues, social impact, and social balance within a context of the economic and social survival of the firm. Conclusions from the earlier parts of the book are summarized, and a tentative set of guidelines is advanced for use by management as it struggles with these turbulent and sometimes contradictory forces.

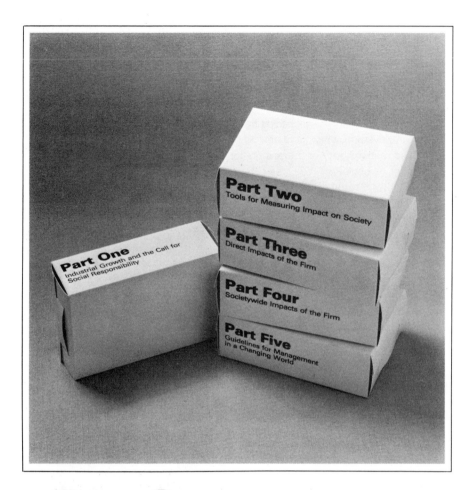

Part One
Industrial Growth and the Call for Social Responsibility

Part One provides background for the issues that have developed between industry and society and examines the nature of the institutions and value systems underlying these issues.

Chapter 1 introduces the social responsibility issue with a brief overview of its origins and evolution, while Chapter 2 gives examples of corporate impact on society. In presenting both positive and negative impacts, these examples illustrate how a corporation can earn criticism and praise simultaneously from society for different aspects of its actions. Also, these actions exemplify the major categories of corporate social impact that will be examined later in the book.

1

Chapter 3 reviews a few of the themes in economic history on which modern institutions are based, such as private property and the corporation, and the evolution of the business firm within the context of modern industrial society. In Chapter 4 this discussion is expanded to include the various aspects of growth and economic development processes, the accompanying value systems, and the resulting changes in the workplace. All this information is preliminary to characterizing the role of the business leader in molding the system, which is, in turn, a necessary prelude to later consideration of the responsibility of the corporation and its leaders for the corporate impact on society.

Chapter 5 returns to the issue of social responsibility, outlining its history and evolution and also its relationship to the profit concept. This examination raises questions about the most appropriate way to define and assess costs during the calculation of corporate profits, in preparation for examining various types of tools for measuring corporate social impact in Part Two.

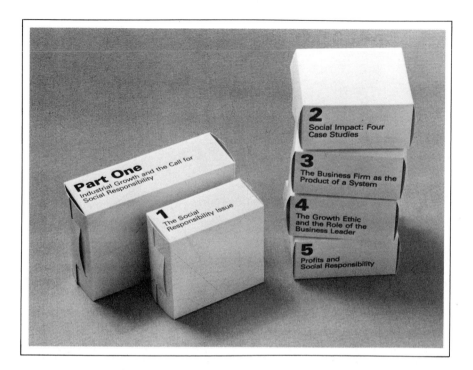

1
The Social Responsibility Issue

The concept of business responsibility to society was not considered when the first factories were established, in part because, prior to that time , no institution in society had demonstrated the power necessary for independent action potentially detrimental to society as a whole. From the beginning industry had such power, but its effects were neither anticipated nor clearly recognized as the industrial system grew. Only recently has the social responsibility issue come to the fore. Chapter 1 briefly profiles its emergence.

The manager is the dynamic, life-giving element in every business. . . . The three jobs of management: Managing a business, managing managers, and managing worker and work. . . .[1]

PETER F. DRUCKER

Social Responsibility: A New Management Task

In the two decades since Drucker's landmark analysis of the three tasks of management, another management task has been receiving growing attention. Some describe this task as managing the business environment; others speak of managing the environmental pressures or the social responsibility of business. Regardless of the terminology used, it is clear that there has been a shift both in the emphasis placed on the different tasks and in the nature of the work of many managers. The result of this shift on the validity of Drucker's division of the jobs of management is to add a new dimension to business that broadens all the tasks of management. Now, more than ever before, a good manager is expected to include a social or environmental component in the performance of Drucker's three tasks. Among the factors responsible for this new emphasis are the cumulative impact of the accelerating rate of change in our industrial society and the reaction of society to both the sweet and bitter fruits of unparalleled industrial growth.

The Rate of Change

Perhaps the most fundamental impact on our society is from technological and social change. By 1800 change had already reached a rate unparalleled in human history, and this rate has been accelerating ever since.

Anthropologists tell us that much of the origin of human culture lies in the survival mechanisms that evolved in primitive tribes. The ability to communicate enabled primitive peoples to carry forward the wisdom gained and adapt it gradually as conditions changed. The store of culture was one of the most valuable assets of any tribe since it endowed children with a knowledge of successful survival techniques that became richer and more valuable with each generation.

Pressures against hasty change in these techniques were great since this store of

---

[1]Peter F. Drucker, *The Practice of Management* (New York: Harper & Brothers, 1953), pp. 1, 16.

wisdom was precious to the individual as well as to the community. The social mechanism of most tribes provided a high degree of insulation against all but carefully considered change. The respected wisdom and effective governance lay with the elders, usually the grandparents. Children, taught by their parents, learned chiefly those values approved and accepted by the elders. Thus, the continual pressure toward change from the young was moderated by the collective experience and values of the two older generations. Throughout most of human history, the rate of change in both environment and technology remained slow enough to be accommodated within this three-generation span.

With the start of active world exploration by European adventurers during and after the Renaissance, more powerful forces of change were set in motion. As trade grew, the cumulative effects of mercantilism began to change lifestyles and customs.[2] New goods became available, labor shifted to trade-related occupations, and significant new technologies were employed. For example, the transition in agriculture from small farming to sheep raising in England was a direct result of the increasing demand for wool for the textile trade. This important agricultural development led to enclosure of the land, displacement of masses of peasants, and major changes in rural English society.

Nonetheless, the mercantilist era represented only the beginning of industrial growth. In the environment that mercantilism created, many advances in production technology were made. Use of spinning wheels, steam machines, and steam engines increased, and assorted metal-working and related fabricating processes began to spread. First, locomotives and steamships and, then, automobiles changed the transportation system. Industrialization meant factory jobs rather than farm jobs for many and new types of goods for all. With progress in transportation, communication became more rapid. Canals, railroads, and highways were built; the telegraph, telephone, radio, and television were introduced; and numerous types of lights and electrical appliances were the result of the commercial development of electric power.

The old system of inheriting values from the elders weakened because much of society, particularly the younger generation, readily accepted the new values and affluence produced by the new technology. This rapid change in values cannot be accommodated within the traditional system spanning three generations. Thus concern is now being directed to the increasing generation gap between contemporary parents and the children to whom they wish to impart their values. Human culture is evolving in a new and untested way, by a method and with a speed beyond the precedent of the tried and true, slow evolution of the past.

The rapid change and its dramatic impact have received a great deal of attention. The classic treatment of the subject is given by Alvin Toffler in his book, *Future Shock*.[3] Toffler contends that the cultural impact of the rate of change has a substantial shock value, which has continued to intensify. He expresses considerable

---

[2]For a further discussion of mercantilism (an economic philosophy based on profits from trade), see Chapter 3.
[3]Alvin Toffler, *Future Shock* (New York: Random House, 1970).

concern about whether the fabric of society can survive the stress that the increasing shock of moving forward into the future represents.

One element contributing to the intensity of this stress is the lack of appropriate social control mechanisms to apply to social problems. Society's control mechanisms have tended to evolve slowly, with due wisdom and after the fact. Since problems did not appear rapidly in the past, this time lag was not serious. In the present, however, industrial progress has caught us unprepared in that we have not anticipated the rules and customs necessitated by the various new developments. For example, there were no traffic laws for automobiles before traffic accidents posed serious hazards and no regulations governing discriminatory pricing of transportation services until the railroads developed such pricing to a fine art. In the absence of rules, some industries have been free to exercise license in their behavior, as in the robber baron era. Thus, certain developments have led to hasty improvisation of regulations and controls that have not been thoroughly considered or evaluated. Now management faces the stresses and strains of this rapid growth as a restless society questions how today's problems arose and who is going to solve them.

The Impact of Industrial Success

By the 1930s the major climax of the Industrial Revolution in the United States had been realized in the transition to mass production of consumer goods and then to a more service-oriented economy. With the rising standard of living, the United States became a society in which most of the members were affluent—at least in comparison to older standards—and were able to own automobiles, radios, and other products of industrial success.

This surge to affluence is familiar enough now so that the public entrancement with new gadgets no longer prevents the asking of other questions about their impact. As consumers have become more sophisticated, the ability to mass-produce merchandise has ceased to be an automatic route to success or public approval. The public has learned that big organizations are powerful compared to any individual and that they sometimes abuse their power. All products are not perfect, all complaints are not answered, and occasionally outright fraud and deception are practiced. The public's feeling of warmth toward industry has changed to one of watchfulness, in which any big, powerful organization is suspect. Consequently, public action groups, such as the Nader group or the American Civil Liberties Union, are now welcomed uncritically by a large segment of the population that assumes that a little agitation is needed to keep the system honest.

At the same time that the American people have been developing this new reaction to bigness, the accumulation of wastes and tailings from rapid industrial development has begun to reach critical levels. Environmental pollution has been accompanied by equally serious industrial and social waste. Slums that grew up long ago in most large cities received a degree of acceptance because they represented the first home of those immigrants who went on to move out into society in the next generation. No longer is this true. Since the 1930s slum populations have stabilized and expanded; generation after generation continues in the same environment, and the children have little opportunity to break out of the pattern. The American people have found it necessary to attempt explicit social remedies for the problems posed by slums and many other social conditions. The very act of intervention in social problems is foreign to the earlier tradition of this country. The decision to aim major public programs at the various social and ecological ills is a significant change in past attitudes.

In another important change in past attitudes, the public has moved more and more toward taking the ready availability of industrial goods for granted. Mass production is no longer new. Now the public is asking searching questions about the directions that industrial progress and business value systems will take. Business corporations find that their great achievements of the past have faded out of public memory. The foremost question today has become: What have you done to me and my environment?

Defining the Social Responsibility Problem

It is not surprising that the rapid rate of change in our industrial world has created not only new cultural and social attitudes but also the need for a new set of relationships between the business firm and the surrounding society. Primarily, the requirement is for a more comprehensive framework for the business-society interaction. This framework must be defined in terms that are fundamental enough to endure in the face of change. In other words, the definition must be built on basic concepts about the nature of the industrial system so that new rules and regulations at each stage of change can be absorbed or even anticipated more easily and so that the necessary adaptations of corporate behavior will fit within the boundaries of the relationships already defined.

Frequently, public statements about the relationship between business and society deal with the many dimensions of the responsibility of the business community for the welfare of society. Howard Bowen's *Social Responsibilities of the Businessman* is now over twenty-five years old,[4] and, in the time since its publication the subject of social responsibility has provoked an expanding literature on what business does to and owes to society.

The business firm is an economic entity whose purpose is to supply desired goods and services to society. It must generate a profit to survive because that is the intrinsic nature of the institution. There is an economic necessity—in terms of sound management of the national resources—for insisting on good economic performance from each productive unit. Where this practice does not result in a profit, any losses must be kept within the range of an economically justifiable level of subsidy or else society is in danger of dissipating its resources. How the profits may be used or who will own them constitute another issue, but the basic requirement that economic activity yield predictable and acceptable economic results seems to be almost inescapable in the management of any modern economy. However, any consideration of the nature of profit raises other questions. Those who have had a first brush

---

[4]Howard R. Bowen, *Social Responsibilities of the Businessman* (New York: Harper & Brothers, 1953).

Figure 1.1   Profit as a Residual Term

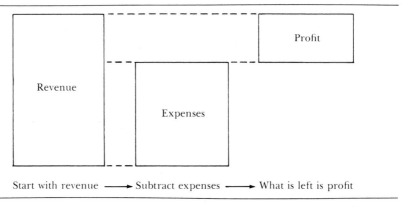

Start with revenue ⟶ Subtract expenses ⟶ What is left is profit

with economics are aware that profit is defined as a residual term. A business receives income, pays expenses and taxes, and counts the difference as profit (see Figure 1.1).

Unfortunately, there are substantial subtleties in profit accounting. As soon as accountants began to do profit accounting carefully, they faced the question of how to deal with the declining value of the productive assets on which a particular economic process is based. The answer lay with the concept of depreciation, in which a certain amount is charged as a current expense annually to provide for either the repayment of the capital originally invested in the productive assets or their timely replacement if that is deemed appropriate. Depreciation charges, however, are not cash charges. They are legal, but hypothetical, asset transfers and do not represent actual money payments as do other items on the income statement. Thus, the calculation of a business's profits involves more than just current cash payments and receipts. It must also include noncash depreciation charges whose size may vary according to the choice among the various depreciation schedules that the accounting profession and the Internal Revenue Service will accept.

In the time since the industrial system began to operate, not only depreciation and other noncash charges but also new types of cash expenses have found their way into the cost sheet. For instance, initially manufacturers did not make any provisions for vacations or pensions or for any of the other conventional benefit items. Now, of course, they do, and the fringe-benefit package has become a very significant entry in the expense statements of most firms, either reducing the residual profits or raising the prices by a corresponding amount. Another expense item that has become common is the cost of waste treatment or pollution control. Now most businesses incur considerable waste disposal expenses, whereas there were few or no disposal expenses in the earlier days of the system.

This need to pay to reduce pollution raises the question of social and environmental costs. Some pollution costs and certain pension costs (for example, the costs for care of retired people) have existed since the beginning of industry but were formerly borne by other parts of society rather than by the business firm. The industrial system in its rapid growth found many circumstances where its impact on society was unanticipated or at least unregulated. Thus, industry was able to operate without accounting for or dealing with important social costs, such as pension or pollution costs, which were left for the public to bear. This policy has now provoked a strong reaction from society.

A recurring theme in analyzing the way a business relates to its surrounding society in its different areas of impact is that business has an inherent management self-interest in minimizing the social costs caused by the impact of its actions. In most cases where there have been extensive social costs caused by a corporation, society has tended to curb business actions with corrective or punitive legislation that not only requires the absorption of the costs in question but also restricts management freedom in that area. Now some of the more progressive managements are attempting to reduce social costs in areas that might lead to similar confrontations with society in the future.

A major theme of this book is that much of the social responsibility issue has arisen over the problem of uncompensated social costs. Many of the cries for responsible action could have been quieted if the firms involved had simply paid the full costs of their operations in the first place. This does not cover the entire social responsibility issue, however. The book will fully explore the issue's needs and limits, including cases where social responsibility claims reach beyond the boundaries of social cost since effective management of corporate social impact requires their consideration.

Summary

This chapter has briefly reviewed the origin of the socioeconomic changes in which the corporate social impact and corporate social responsibility issues now facing corporate management are based. The evolution of modern society and the impact of successful industrial development have created great stresses and strains. This situation has brought new dimensions to the tasks of managers and has emphasized the need for management to reappraise the way that a business enterprise relates to social demands. These unprecedented demands are grounded in social ills and can no longer be turned aside. Society is requiring an accountability and will not accept past customs, rules, or sanctions as justification for the problems of today. The perspective offered in this introduction is preliminary to a more detailed analysis of the social responsibility problem and of the way that a well-run enterprise must relate to the issues in the surrounding society.

Questions for Analysis and Discussion

1. What is your definition of the social responsibility of a business firm? Does it make any difference whether the firm is large or small?

2. From your own experience, give examples of the way that a culture protects

and preserves its traditional value systems. To what extent is this still a valuable trait for society to have? To what extent would it be better if each generation formed its own value systems without considering the beliefs and values of preceding generations?

3. In terms of their impact on your own life, what are the most important technological developments since the Industrial Revolution? List two developments that have had positive impacts and two developments that have had negative impacts on your life. What could have been done to reduce or avoid the negative impacts?

4. How do you view the role of profit in our society? Who should be concerned about the amount of profit that is generated?

5. The chapter speaks of charges, other than actual cash payments, that change the amount of profit a business reports. Review the annual reports of several corporations for examples of such charges.

For Further Information

Bowen, Howard R. *Social Responsibilities of the Businessman.* New York: Harper & Brothers, 1953.

Drucker, Peter F. *The Practice of Management.* New York: Harper & Brothers, 1953.

Nader, Ralph, and Green, Mark J. eds. *Corporate Power in America.* New York: Grossman, 1973.

Ogburn, William Fielding. *Social Change.* New York: Viking Press, 1922.

Toffler, Alvin. *Future Shock.* New York: Random House, 1970.

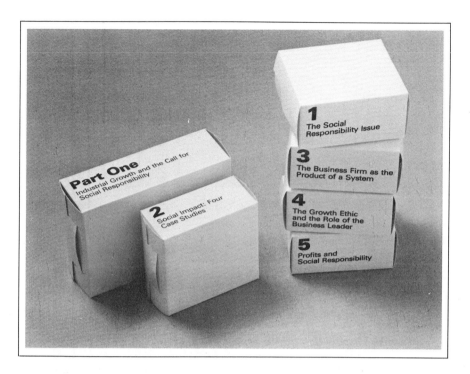

2
Social Impact: Four Case Studies

In the rush for expansion of the country and its industrial system, many of the consequences of this development were neglected. For the most part, contemporary society consented to the neglect. The pattern of treatment of the environment, of employees, and of communities that developed had its roots in historical acceptance, even though many of the aspects of this pattern would not be accepted under today's standards. This chapter seeks to illustrate some of the adjustments that corporations have faced in conforming to the changing standards of society and to examine some of the impacts of corporate and social actions as this adjustment process has evolved.

The duty of corporations is to take account of their impact on society.[1]

MARY GARDINER JONES

In the early 1950s the Wabash River in the vicinity of Terre Haute, Indiana, had been degraded by its burden of raw sewage, acid mine wastes, and various industrial discharges. It had become a muddy sewer that welcomed the purification of spring floods and made a sorry comparison to the neglected remnants of a once attractive riverfront park. This park was a memorial to Paul Dresser, a native son whose song, "Banks of the Wabash," was inspired by what had been a romantic and beautiful river.

Among the riverbank industries located downstream from the park was the Commercial Solvents Corporation. At the outfall from the Commercial Solvents penicillin plant, the discharge of filter cake and other solids created a distinct sandbar in the river; the fermentation operators commented on the way this bar would shift with the level of the river and the pattern of its currents. True, these solids were relatively harmless, except for making bad odors as they fermented on the river bottom, because the spent solvents and acid process wastes were swept off downstream by the current.

This pollution seemed to cause no real local concern. The most frequent comment in the penicillin plant was about the competitive disadvantage that was suffered by the Charles Pfizer Company, whose antibiotic processing was located inland as a result of the purchase of the old Vigo ordinance plant. The Pfizer wastes had no outlet except into Honey Creek, a small Wabash tributary that had been so quickly overburdened with process wastes that Pfizer was forced to install treatment facilities for them. Commercial Solvents had been more fortunate.[2]

It is hard to understand how such practices could ever have been acceptable because times and public attitudes have changed. Now such practices are no longer acceptable, and the point of view that permitted them is scarcely comprehensible.

Early in the growth and development of the United States, conservation of its resources seemed to be the least pressing of many problems. Professor Krooss has commented on the appropriateness of the play on words inherent in the frontier

---

[1]Mary Gardiner Jones (Commissioner, Federal Trade Commission), speech to the National Association of Concerned Business Students, New York, 1973.

[2]This information is based on discussions with Commercial Solvents employees and Terre Haute residents.

expression "they wanted to get there in the worst way."[3] Rapid development was given a national importance that made the rate of progress much more urgent than any concern for the reckless way in which the material wealth of the country was utilized. The public saw no need to look to the future, nor did many of its leaders—"Why should I do anything for posterity: What has posterity done for me?"[4] This attitude persisted almost until the present time in some quarters. By now its consequences have provoked a great public outcry.

> We behave as if we were the last generation to inhabit the earth. . . . Men, unknowingly, and whether for good or ill appear to be making their last decision about human destiny.[5]

This country has moved rather quickly from a point at which the waste of resources was often justified as a necessary adjunct to rapid economic development to a point at which the mechanical extrapolation of present growth and pollution trends forecasts the end of our civilization within a relatively short span of time. Yet Brazil and other underdeveloped countries speak of inviting in polluting industries that have been displaced from other parts of the world to foster their own economic development, just as the United States and others did in the past.[6]

Not long ago the grossest sort of pollution and misuse of resources was accepted casually in the United States provided that no obtrusive public health hazard appeared. Since much of the industrial system grew up with the acceptance of such practices, they became implicit in industrial economics and were incorporated in the design of plant facilities. Today the rapid change in society's rules for the business use of resources is disturbing the business community and raising issues with the surrounding society.

The problem extends far beyond the waste of physical resources—serious as that is—to the major waste of human resources that occurs when people's lives are warped and frustrated by the actions of the industries that support them. The first example selected for this chapter shows the impact on a community of a plant closing that was triggered by the inability of the Olin Corporation to meet Virginia's new pollution standards. The discussion will then be extended to cases raising broader questions about the use of resources and to the impact of these resource decisions on the people with whom a responsible corporation must balance its interactions.

The Olin Chemical Company and Saltville, Virginia

Whether businesses can afford the cost of controlling pollution—and whether dependent communities dare to require this control—have become central issues

---

[3]Herman E. Krooss, lectures at New York University Graduate School of Business, 1965–1966.

[4]Speaker of the House Joseph Cannon in the early 1900s, as quoted by Herman E. Krooss in *American Economic Development: The Progress of Business Civilization*, 2d ed. (Englewood Cliffs, N.J.: Prentice-Hall, 1965), p. 17.

[5]*The Last Whole Earth Catalog* (Menlo Park, Calif.: Portola Institute, 1971), pp. 17, 4.

[6]*New York Times*, 13 February 1972.

almost every time public pressure has brought industry to the point of making a significant pollution control expenditure. In many cases the issue subsides again as money is spent, waste treatment is improved, industry readjusts to the economics of a new cost structure, and community life continues functioning smoothly.

However, this was not the case in the little Virginia town of Saltville. Here an Appalachian community had grown up around plants built and expanded by what is now the Olin Chemical Company. Then the principal process units began to grow old. Public awareness of pollution problems grew. The state of Virginia pressed for effluent improvements that Olin found difficult to effect. First the soda ash plant was shut down, then the chlorine-caustic plant, and finally the remaining minor processes were discontinued. Olin turned the town services and utilities over to the community and departed, leaving the town without any major employer.

As concern about the environment increased, Virginia had begun to adopt and apply stricter standards. The Olin soda ash plant was discharging more waste materials into the North Holston River than these standards would permit; therefore,

> On April 7–8, 1970, the State Water Control Board adopted revised water quality standards.
>
> As a part of its program for the implementation of the standards, the Board directed each industry . . . to submit a program and schedule for providing such facilities as were necessary to meet the new standards. This Board directive was transmitted to the Olin Corporation by letter of May 7, 1970.
>
> . . . Olin chose to bring this case to a quick termination by requesting an informal appearance before the Board at its meeting on July 7, 1970, to announce that, since there is no known method for treating the wastes, the only alternative to a clean stream would be to shut down the plant. The company's decision to close the plant was accompanied by a request that the Board permit the plant shut down to be a phasing out operation over a $2^{1}/_{2}$-year period, with final termination on December 31, 1972.
>
> Realizing that this represents a drastic means for the elimination of a pollution problem, the Board unanimously approved the proposed gradual phasing out, which will permit, hopefully, Olin to move into the area processing operations of a non-polluting nature, and thus to absorb some of the displaced personnel, and to seek transfer of any other displaced personnel to other operations elsewhere.
>
> While we are happy that this thorny problem will now be solved, we regret that it had to be done in a way that will undoubtedly cause considerable economic repercussion in the area over which the plant has influence.[7]

Thus, the state's application of regulatory pressure led to an early decision by Olin to accept the standards and to the subsequent decision to enforce them and close

---

[7]Letter from Millard H. Robbins, Jr., Director, Pollution Abatement Division, Commonwealth of Virginia, State Water Control Board, to Jack H. Newcombe, Washington Bureau Chief of *Life* magazine, 18 January 1971.

down the soda ash plant. The actual closing came slightly less than one year later. Olin encouraged its other plants to offer relocation opportunities to the displaced employees and made arrangements for special retirement and severance benefits for those who stayed in Saltville.[8]

Separate but simultaneous examination of other pollution problems led to serious concern about mercury, which was being used in the chlorine-caustic process and being discharged with the plant wastes.

> From the time this process was first installed in the early 1950's, until recently, about 60 lbs. of mercury found its way with the waste waters from the plant to the North Fork of the Holston River. According to our analyses the mercury content of the river ranged between less than 0.5 and 1.9 parts per billion.
>
> As soon as the significance of mercury as a stream pollutant came to the attention of Olin, the company instituted a crash program for reducing mercury losses. At this time, the discharge of mercury is less than 0.125 lbs. per day, and Olin has plans for the replacement of the electrolytic chlorine-caustic process with another process that will eliminate the use of mercury entirely.
>
> When analyses of fish from the North Holston showed concentrations of mercury up to 3.0 ppm, ... the State Health Commissioner ... issued an emergency order restricting the taking of fish from the river.[9]

At first Olin discussed installation of a new process that did not use mercury and obtained initial approvals.[10] After further study Olin found that conversion to another process was not feasible, and the entire chlorine-caustic operation was shut down.[11] In 1960 this plant employed 1,500; in 1970, 800; after the cleanup was completed, about 100.[12] The search for new industries had not yet been successful, and the remaining Olin operations soon closed.

Life magazine ran a profile of the parting between Olin and Saltville.[13] Apparently this relationship had been solid and friendly. The people were disappointed but not bitter as the company left; the company dealt generously in its settlements with the town. Between the *Life* magazine article and the corporate press releases, a simple story emerges.

Saltville and Olin had a long-term relationship with mutual support and interdependence. The *Life* reporters found little rancor against the company, which had

---

[8]*Olin Public Relations Press Release,* 15 June 1971.

[9]Letter from A.H. Paessler, Executive Secretary, Commonwealth of Virginia, State Water Control Board, to Tucker St. M. Coleman, Gate City, Virginia, 28 April 1971.

[10]Ruling of State Water Control Board (Virginia), 14, 15 June 1971, minute 54 and attached 3 June 1971 memo of Larry G. Lawson.

[11]Letter from A.H. Paessler, Executive Secretary, Commonwealth of Virginia, State Water Control Board, to George C. Sawyer, 20 March 1972.

[12]Ward Worthy, "Saltville Rallies after Olin Shutdown," *Chemical and Engineering News,* 13 March 1972, pp. 7–9.

[13]"End of a Company Town: The People of Saltville, Va., Lose Their Plant to Pollution Laws," *Life,* 26 March 1971, pp. 37–45.

contributed a great deal to the development of the community. Now Olin was leaving; most of the employees were being laid off. The old plant that was involved had rising costs. Perhaps it would have been phased out within a few years. The immediate confrontation was over water pollution from the plant. Virginia wished to improve the quality of the environment and required that new standards be met. Olin studies showed that it was not economical to meet the new requirements; so Olin shut down the plant.

The last Olin process unit closed in 1972, and many of the former Olin employees now drive to jobs in other towns. The pain of losing the town's principal employer is no longer fresh, but discontinuing the operations did not end the pollution problems. Rain still leaches chloride salts from the muck ponds formerly used to settle wastes from the soda ash plant, and the mercury levels in the fish from the North Holston River have stayed above the safe limit. In 1976 the routine samplings of fish showed a sudden increase in mercury levels, possibly traceable to activity at the site where the old chlorine-caustic plant had been located before being razed. Subsequent investigation showed indications of metallic mercury around the old plant site and muck ponds. Mercury vapor was detected in sufficient amounts to require further sampling to determine whether levels dangerous to health might be reached in warm weather.[14]

Both Olin and the state started an investigation of all available alternatives for keeping the chlorides, and especially the mercury, from reaching the river. However, the long-term nature of the problem was obvious. Five years after the plant's closing, mercury levels had not fallen enough for the ban on eating the fish to be lifted. Even if contamination leaking from the old plant site could be prevented entirely, the levels of mercury already present in the North Holston River system are probably sufficient to keep the mercury levels in the fish dangerously high for many years to come.

Olin closed a relatively old, high-cost plant. The community was the loser; while Olin attempted to deal fairly with individual employees (in terms of severance, retirement, and opportunity for transfer elsewhere), it had not entirely succeeded in cushioning the impact of its shutdown on the community as a whole.

In a similar situation duPont found it possible to install a new process for the manufacture of a different type of product and was thus able to employ the labor force displaced by the shutdown of an obsolete plant.[15] Olin, however, had not found an alternative that was feasible. Although Olin had aided the community in its search for new industries to provide employment for the displaced Olin work force, the search was not productive.

Olin also was the loser, when the value of a strong relationship with a community furnishing 1500 employees is considered. While it is difficult to estimate this value, the potential saving in labor costs, as well as in turnover and community expenses, is significant in comparison to the costs of developing a similar relationship in a new community.

---

[14]Summarized from copies of June–December 1976 correspondence of A.E. Paessler, Assistant Executive Secretary, Commonwealth of Virginia, State Water Control Board.

[15]See Chapter 13.

Olin had shown a concern for its customers, and the timing of the actual shutdown of the plants was related to the accommodation of their needs for a continuing supply of material. Likewise, the company's expression of concern for its share of the Saltville community and for its impact on community life was commendable. However, in its own internal planning, Olin had not come up with a process for a new Saltville plant.

Insufficient information is available to permit a definitive evaluation of the major social costs resulting from Olin's shutdown of the Saltville plants. These social costs would seem to arise from the lack of alternative opportunities to use the employee potential or to find other employers for the workers that were displaced in an already depressed region. In addition, Olin created the long-term mercury pollution of the North Holston River. The underlying issues here include (1) the burden of applying new waste treatment standards to old plants and (2) the unresolved and controversial question of whether corporations like Olin can be expected to anticipate the obsolescence of plants and processes by planning for the development of alternative opportunities for employees and community.

International Paper Company Versus the Environment

The paper industry has been under great public pressure because so many paper mills have caused water pollution. In addition, this industry is heavily dependent on the forest resources of the United States. As the industry adjusts to new pollution standards and discovers new uses for its landholdings, it also faces a complex new set of social problems.

The experiences of the International Paper Company serve to illustrate the social impact of land development and pollution, new techniques in forest management, and corporate community programs. This example also shows how society can evaluate the separate facets of a corporation in different ways, depending on the social impact of each facet's operations.

The paper industry regards environmental concerns as an extension of its own self-interest.

> The nature of its business gives the paper industry strong practical reasons for pursuing policies consistent with the findings of ecologists and conservationists. Its very life depends on the continual renewal of its raw material source, the forests, and on an abundant supply of good quality water, without which paper could not be manufactured. Good air is important to the industry not only because of its bearing on the nation's quality of life but specifically because mill personnel and their families share the desire of the communities in which they live for clean air. Self-interest and social responsibility thus point in the same direction, and the industry's efforts for the environment have paralleled public concern.[16]

---

[16]"The Paper Industry's Part in Protecting the Environment," (New York: American Paper Institute, 1970), pp. 17–18.

While International Paper shares this attitude about social responsibility, it has not hesitated to explore the development of its landholdings.

> The president and chief executive, Edward B. Hinman . . . announced formation of an executive advisory committee . . . as a step toward "plans for more intensive development of the company's assets and business." Hinman was not talking just about paper mills and machines. More significantly, he was referring to the enormous assets represented by I.P.'s great landholdings—except for the U.S. Government, I.P. is the largest landowner in the U.S.[17]

I.P. presented its land development program to its stockholders as follows:

> The timberlands acquired by I.P. over the years to support its paper and lumber manufacturing operations have become one of its most important assets. But land is not a static asset—its highest and best use is subject to continual change. These changes, basically the result of population and economic expansion, reflect the growth of urban and suburban communities, highway extensions and the development of industrial or recreational facilities in formerly rural areas. Any of these factors may radically change the value and best use of a given forest area.
>
> A systematic review of our landholdings has been undertaken designed to identify those lands which are more valuable for uses other than growing trees.
>
> Your Company is aware of the opportunities which exist for companies having expertise in the field of real estate development for recreational, residential, commercial and industrial uses.
>
> In the fall of 1968, I.P. made an important first step in this field. It acquired American Central Corporation of Lansing, Michigan. This company has an impressive and profitable ten-year record of selecting, planning and developing leisure-home communities—a business with growth potential resulting from recent changes in work habits, family mobility and age patterns of our population.[18]

In the summer of 1969 American Central began to build in Stratton, Vermont, a rural township with a ski resort. Sixty percent of the township was owned by International Paper. According to Richard Klein's account, in 1968 Stratton had only 94 vacation homes yielding a little over $6,000 in taxes, and 23,000 acres of timberland ripe for vacation development. When bulldozers began clearing in Stratton, the local alarm reached the governor, who telegraphed the president of I.P. to find out what was planned. A local officer of I.P. finally presented the development plan for Stratton to a state commission in June 1969. In this plan water supply and

---

[17]Eleanore Carruth, "International Paper Sees the Forest Through the Trees," *Fortune* 79, No. 3 (March 1960): 105 ff.

[18]*International Paper 1968 Annual Report,* p. 29.

sewage disposal were to be handled individually by each lot owner, no building restrictions were proposed, and no open space was reserved except for certain very steep areas. Vermont's concern grew.

> Tiny Stratton was unequal to the task of controlling the mammoth IPC combine. One commissioner said that the company was able to hire all the lawyers around and had even invited local selectmen to go on the company's payroll as consultants. One local conservationist reported that he was warned to get out of the way or he'd be run over when he tried to take pictures of operating bulldozers; but he hired a plane and took his photographs from the air. According to people who attended the meeting, the pictures show a hunk of land cut by roads from bottom to top, with virtually no thought of water flow or other ecological considerations.
>
> . . . [The] special assistant to the governor . . . in a report to the governor . . . concluded that if American Central were to develop in Stratton as it has been developing in New Hampshire, Vermont should not allow it. . . .
>
> On July 25, Stratton residents finally learned that much of the township would soon become a community of one-acre lots—10 percent down and seven years to pay. . . . It didn't allay their fears to be told that any jump in school-age population would be the concern of the local school board, that the township would double or triple its population in a few years, that 12 miles of roadways are being built for the town to take care of, or that expansion is virtually certain within the next three to five years.[19]

Perhaps Vermont should have instituted controls on land development earlier, but I.P. made the problem urgent. The corporation appeared to show little understanding or concern for the profound impact of its development on Stratton and on that portion of the state of Vermont.

For the communities in which its mills are located and in which its employees live, International Paper expressed a great concern.

> It is increasingly evident that the corporation that is to grow and prosper in the coming years will be one that demonstrates a sincere regard for the needs and opinions of its communities. International Paper Company has long recognized that this concern must rank very high among its corporate responsibilities. In this special section we indicate some of the many forms this concern takes—on the part of the Company and the thousands of I.P. men and women, who are the Company, in all the communities where we operate.[20]

The 1969 annual report then goes on to describe a most attractive corporate

---

[19]Excerpted and reprinted, with permission, from "Green Mountains, Green Money," by Richard M. Klein, *Natural History* Magazine, March 1970, pp. 20, 22. Copyright © The American Museum of Natural History, 1970.

[20] *International Paper 1969 Annual Report,* p. 17.

program, starting with the corporate concern for air and water quality and the plan to continue to upgrade I.P.'s operations as a necessary cost of continuing to do business. The report then turns to the beauty of the managed forest and describes the steps that I.P. has taken to share the use of its forest lands with the public. This position fits well with the discussion in the previous year's report of the program to develop new and superior types of trees to increase the productivity of the forest resources that I.P. manages.

The 1969 annual report also presents a comprehensive program to aid education in the areas where it operates. It mentions specific assistance to twenty-seven school systems through the International Paper Company Foundation and also details extensive involvement in a variety of other regional and community activities. The company's concern for the environment was expressed in this way:

> There is a growing realization that our natural environment is being taxed beyond its inherent power to restore itself. All of us—individual citizens, industry, agriculture, communities, state and Federal agencies—contribute to this burden. International Paper believes that the aspirations of our society can be met, that the pollution of our environment can be controlled and that the vital quality of the basic resources we all share in common can be maintained within the framework of our economy. International Paper is dedicated to its commitment to do its part as an industrial citizen to achieve this goal.
>
> We are applying modern technology in many ways to this Company-wide effort, which is progressing at an accelerated pace.
>
> At the new Ticonderoga mill we are installing one of the most efficient paper mill waste-treatment systems in all of North America.[21]

Meanwhile, others saw I.P. waste discharges in a very different light.

> The company has been under fire from both Vermont and New York because of a paper mill at Ticonderoga, New York, at the lower end of Lake Champlain. This mill has for many years made a cesspool of the adjacent segment of the lake. A new plant may reduce insults to the eye and nose, not to mention the lake, but pending its completion, sulfite sludge keeps pouring into the water. International Paper's local reputation as a conservation-minded organization is minimal.[22]

I.P. had addressed its problems and built a beautiful new mill at Ticonderoga.

> When I.P. held an open house at the end of October to show off its spanking new $76 million, 650-tons/day odor-free pulp and paper mill at Ticonderoga, N.Y., more than 15,000 visitors . . . jammed the highways. . . .

---

[21]Ibid., p. 9.
[22]Excerpted and reprinted, with permission, from "Green Mountains, Green Money" by Richard M. Klein, *Natural History* Magazine, March 1970, pp. 18–19, Copyright © The American Museum of Natural History, 1970.

The new mill replaces one built in 1878 that was the subject of heated debate over pollution problems, which has carried to the Supreme Court in a still-pending suit between New York and Vermont.

More than $5 million has been spent on pollution control for the new unit to eliminate the characteristic kraft-mill odor and to produce a treated effluent that is practically color free and not harmful to Lake Champlain.[23]

Meanwhile, the furor over past pollution continued. As Vermont Senator Aiken stated it:

At the southern end of the lake near Ticonderoga, N.Y., Lake Champlain has been seriously polluted by discharges from a large paper mill. The sludge deposited over many years now covers some 300 acres which is 12 feet deep at some points. The paper mill is now closed and a new larger mill has been built and is operating several miles further north on the lake. This sludge has been the subject of controversy for a number of years. The residents on the Vermont side of the lake in that area have found the water to be unfit for swimming and fishing. Air pollution blowing across the lake from the old millsite has been extremely offensive at times.[24]

This concern over the sludge beds and the pollution it represented led to a major court action to force a cleanup.

The state of Vermont is requesting U.S. Supreme Court action to force the state of New York and the International Paper Co. to remove the accumulated decaying sludge from the bed of Lake Champlain. According to Sen. George D. Aiken (R.—Vt.), the Corps of Engineers estimates that $4–$5 million is needed to clean up the lake. Also, Vermont is considering action against the Corps for issuing a discharge permit without calling a hearing.[25]

It should be emphasized that International Paper has held a special kind of responsibility because of its ownership and management of such an important portion of the nation's forest resources and, further, because of its wide utilization of the products from this land. A big old company with firm roots in the past, I.P. has seemed to realize the potential of modern forest management. Through its dynamic forest program, it might be on the threshold of achieving some of the types of gains in productivity that similar techniques have brought to shorter cycle agriculture; both the company and the nation will benefit.

In the employee-community relationships that relate to its established mills and forests, I.P. has assembled a good record. However, in its attempts to become a dynamic company, International Paper may not have administered all its programs

---

[23]"The Pulp Mill Doesn't Smell," *Chemical Week*, 1 December 1971, p. 41.
[24]Senator George D. Aiken (Vermont), *Congressional Record*, 2 November 1971, S17422.
[25]"Vermont Seeks Legal Aid in Lake Champlain Cleanup," *Environmental Science & Technology*, January 1972, p. 102.

with the same understanding and concern that it has claimed for its handling of pine forests and employee communities. The real estate development subsidiary was portrayed as having little concern for the public welfare.

In the matter of its waste treatment problems and the troubles that Lake Champlain suffered as a result of the operation of the Fort Ticonderoga plant, International Paper showed its roots in the past even more clearly. To some extent, the competitive economics of these older mills depended on the absence of waste treatment, and the cost of redesigning a marginal mill to meet reasonable pollution standards has often proved prohibitive. In many ways the situation with I.P.'s Fort Ticonderoga plant parallels that of the Olin soda ash plant discussed earlier in the chapter. However, International Paper did not leave the area in which it had been involved. After some years of local pressure and concern, I.P. resolved the problem by closing the obsolete mill and building a modern new plant not far away.

This situation with the old mill resembled that of the Commercial Solvents penicillin plant (cited earlier) that depended on the nearby waterway to flush away its discharges. However, the Wabash River has the advantage of being frequently purged by floods that could scour and disperse the antibiotic wastes. Lake Champlain is a rather quiet body of water with no natural mechanism for carrying away sediments. Thus, the shallow bay on which the old I.P. mill operated for so many years has been filled steadily by accumulated paper wastes.

The build-up of this sludge over many years calls to mind the comment quoted earlier that we sometimes act as if there were no more generations to come and no need to leave resources for the future. A parallel can be made with the Reserve Mining project that has been slowly filling one corner of Lake Superior with mine tailings. Both Reserve Mining and International Paper can claim valid precedent in the type of resource management policies that were accepted by the public in the past, perhaps as recently as the time when their respective mills were built or modernized.

In the case of International Paper and Lake Champlain, however, the fact that the company has now ceased filling the lake with fermenting paper fibers is not enough. I.P. has been pressured to clean up the accumulated mess as part of its abandonment of the old mill site. This requirement to remedy past damage is a new development. The request is basically fair, except that social or governmental obligations to share in the expense may have been created. To the extent that I.P. committed a wrong and was caught, there is justification for making it bear the burden of the cleanup. To the extent that society is requiring retroactive correction of abuses that were formerly accepted practices in industrial conduct (as appears to be the case), society should share in the burden of the cleanup. In the actual resolution of the legal proceedings between the states, Vermont won recognition of its rights, but without requiring removal of the sludge deposits.

Maine Clean Fuels: The Proposed Searsport Refinery

As the industrial pollution issue has come more and more to the public's attention, various states and communities have defined stricter statutory control over new as well as existing plants. This control has even extended to the point of blocking new plant construction in some cases. One of the most interesting examples of this trend is the turmoil and controversy over whether the state of Maine should permit oil refineries on its coast, although it desperately needs both the new industry and the cheaper, cleaner fuel oil that would be produced.

For several years now, the state of Maine has been in an uproar over the efforts of some oil companies to sponsor a substantial piece of business in the state. The companies' proposals envisage large refinery complexes and deep-water ports able to accommodate the great new supertankers. Not too long ago, such proposals would have been received enthusiastically and uncritically just about any place in the U.S., and their sponsors would have been hailed as heroes of economic growth.

. . . Maine possesses virtually the only natural harbors in the eastern U.S. with water a hundred or more feet deep. This resource had no special value until a few years ago, when oil tankers began to outgrow such traditional harbors as those in upper Delaware Bay.

. . . Maine is a relatively poor state today, with an economy well below the national average. It is heavily dependent on lumber, paper, shoes, farming, fish, and tourism, industries that on the whole offer little promise of expansion. The state has no special love of the oil business, but oil offers the only present prospect of a substantial new industry. Governor Curtis recently put the case for new industry forcefully: "Right now 7.6 percent of the population of Maine are unemployed. In Washington County it's 12.7 percent. You can't sustain rates like that, and an excessive number of our people are underemployed besides. That erodes your tax dollar. You can't plow the roads, keep the schools open. . . . The only answer for Maine is to try to develop industry that's compatible with the environment."

What gives point to these arguments is the great and relatively unspoiled beauty of the Maine coast—an area almost as vivid in the national imagination as the Grand Canyon and Yellowstone Park, and even more prized than these wonders by generations of artists and writers. Although the coast above Portland is only a few hours' drive from centers of eastern population, the industrial revolution has as yet scarcely reached it. The danger of an oil spill from a supertanker is very much on the minds of state-of-Mainers. . . .

At the time the first oil proposals were made in 1968, the state had no effective laws that would restrict or control oil development in order to protect the environment. But in 1969 the state legislature came under strong pressure to enact some such laws, and it did so in February 1970. For one thing, the state created an independent State Environmental Improvement Commission with authority to veto industrial sites. When a company nowadays selects a site for an industrial plant, it must apply to the commission for a permit before it can break ground.

. . . the principal issues had centered on the Machias area. But in February an enterprise called Maine Clean Fuels filed a proposal with the Environmental Improvement Commission for a 200,000-barrel-a-day refinery at Searsport, seventy-five miles west of Machias.

The company, a subsidiary of Fuel Desulphurization, Inc., is headed by David Scoll, a promoter who had been in search of a refinery site on the east coast since 1968, when he had received 100,000 special import tickets. These tickets—the number was later raised to 150,000—would allow the company to import high-sulphur residual oil and refine it further in the U.S. until it had a 1 percent or less sulphur content. (Residual fuel can be freely imported, but refiners without tickets are not allowed to process it further in the U.S.) In giving Scoll the tickets, the Interior Department was moved by a desire to make available more low-sulphur residual oil; a low sulphur content means less pollution. Ironically, however, Scoll has been opposed by environmentalists at the sites where he has tried to locate his refinery. After considerable struggle, his project has been rejected by the town councils at Riverhead on Long Island and at South Portland, Maine.

It was against this background that Scoll filed for permission to build a desulphurization refinery and supertanker terminal at Searsport, right in Penobscot Bay. For some, this proposal seemed a far greater outrage than any of those put forward in the Machias area. Penobscot Bay is a haven for thousands of vacationers and others seeking serenity in nature and has been a special retreat for wealthy eastern families for about a century.

The issue of the Searsport site is now before the Environmental Improvement Commission for decision. The issue is whether Scoll's project would be "located in such a manner to have a minimal adverse impact on the natural environment of (its) surroundings." The standards to be applied are obviously broad. The E.I.C. will have to consider how the players involved value the environment, and this is a not inconsiderable job in view of the fact that some of the values—for example, money, aesthetics, ecological worries—seem to be incommensurable. The problem of melding such values into a single over-all value has never been fully resolved.

From the beginning, the nub of the issue has not changed. The state has been trying at every point to find a procedure that would release the forces of economic development while giving protection to those who might suffer harm from it.

The job the state is trying to do raises the most fundamental questions—about its physical environment, its present economic activity and needs, and its way of life. The state will have to determine the net gain, if any, from a deal to bring oil in. The achievement of these aims will have to mean that each group in Maine is satisfied that it cannot do better. And while not every group may be satisfied with the justice of the arrangement, each might have to accept its lot. Any such political solution would be viable only if the arrangement reflected a stable economic solution.[26]

Maine Clean Fuels had applied to build a refinery on Sears Island, near Searsport.

---

[26]John MacDonald, "Oil and the Environment: The View from Maine," *Fortune* 83, no. 4 (April 1971): 84 ff.

After a public hearing, the Environmental Improvement Commission rejected the application.[27]

The Maine Clean Fuels decision, which was appealed, is interesting for several reasons. First of all, it represents change in public standards in its most dynamic form. When the proposal was first made that a major refinery be located in Maine, the state had no laws to regulate such a development. Since the first proposal in 1967 and during the period when major issues over the necessary oil import quotas were being resolved, the state passed laws and created the Environmental Improvement Commission to enforce them. The Maine Clean Fuels proposal represented a studied attempt to gain approval of the first application processed by a new commission enforcing new laws.

The environment in which this application was received was not typical for that of a depressed area badly needing industrial development, as Maine, in fact, did and still does. The environmentalists' concern was so great as to mobilize opposition from many people who shared this concern for the well-being of the Maine coast. Maine Clean Fuels approached this difficult environment after careful preparation and with the hope that the sincerity of its attempt to meet environmental standards would permit an open discussion of any ways that the Commission might suggest to improve the application. However, the rejection of the application showed a very categoric and uncompromising attitude toward a corporate invader, rather than an open spirit of negotiation between a needed industry and a community anxious for responsible new employers.

> The Maine Clean Fuels decision by the Environmental Improvement Commission has been criticized as being the result of a political process, rather than the result of a regulatory hearing impartially comparing an application with the legal requirements established by the state legislature. The appeal of the decision went before the Maine Supreme Court. In its brief Maine Clean Fuels again committed itself to meet or exceed all legal emission standards and sought to define its obligations and performance requirements so carefully that simple justice would leave the court no alternative but to direct for approval.[28]

The failure of the Environmental Improvement Commission to follow a normal regulatory role (as Mr. Scoll saw it) is an important phenomenon. It may be that the EIC decision reflected the will of the people; certainly, it is consistent with the desires of those interested enough to speak out. Yet it appeared to go far beyond the law that was enacted only the year before. From the legislation of conditions under which a refinery could enter, many people had moved on to support the position that there should be no refinery regardless of economic need. While the people of Maine

---

[27]"The Complete Text of the EIC-Maine Clean Fuels Decision," *Island Advantages* (Deer Isle, Maine), 30 July 1971.

[28]This is a summary of a discussion with Mr. David Scoll, President of Fuel Desulphurization and Maine Clean Fuels, 14 March 1972.

are free to actually legislate against all coastal refineries, they have not yet done so. And while the Maine Clean Fuels case dragged on in the courts until the oil situation had changed and this proposal was dropped, other refinery proposals have taken its place.

Recently, the emphasis has shifted farther east to Machias and to Eastport, as the drama in which the Maine Clean Fuels Searsport proposal was only a chapter continues to unfold. The Pittston proposal for a refinery at Eastport has seemed to be the most active and most viable. Pittston, unlike its predecessors, has won an approval from state authorities. However, other approvals are necessary, including a Canadian approval of the route through which the tankers must pass; gaining this approval is now viewed as unlikely.

All these confrontations involve the same issues concerning the risks and rewards of industrial development in such a physically poor and environmentally rich area as the Maine coast. The Maine Clean Fuels story was far from the first attempt at such development, and the later proposals and maneuverings that narrowly failed to gain approval for a refinery at Machiasport fill an interesting book by Peter Bradford called *Fragile Structures*. Whether or not Pittston finally succeeds at Eastport, the story will not end until society has reached a consensus on how to balance the needs for petroleum, the best technology for handling it, and the risks to the environment. Meanwhile, the Maine Clean Fuels episode serves to define and illustrate the issues that are held in common by this series of Maine refinery proposals and by proposals for industrial development of shore land and wilderness areas everywhere.

For almost the first time, an area was willing to sacrifice its own economic gain because of potential hazards to the environment. The community would accept nothing on faith from Maine Clean Fuels. First, it insisted on very stringent guarantees before permitting a new industry to enter. Then, when the guarantees were offered, it looked for ways to refuse the industry entirely. This same spirit has barred coastal industrial installations in some mid-Atlantic areas;[29] it also caused Dow Chemical Company to abandon its proposal for a major chemical complex in California in 1977 because of difficulties in determining and satisfying environmental requirements. In the future many development plans may have to undergo the kind of scrutiny that faced the Maine Clean Fuels proposal.

American Can Company reports a happier outcome in a similar situation:

> Political leaders, the press, and the public have acclaimed our new paper mill at Halsey, Oregon, as "the cleanest mill in North America." This mill utilized breakthrough technology for the treating of both air and water discharges, and we believe it will be a model for every new pulp mill built in the future. We are proud of Halsey, but our motives were not entirely altruistic. We wanted a mill in Oregon, but Oregon did not want another polluter. We had to convince the state authorities that the mill we would build would respect the environment of that beautiful state.
>
> There is a sequel to this story. Halsey may be the cleanest mill in North

---

[29]Sally Lindsay, "Showdown on Delaware Bay: An Interview with Governor Russell W. Peterson (Delaware)," *Saturday Review,* 18 March 1972, pp. 34–39.

America, but it is far, far from the most profitable. Pollution-control equipment drove our capital costs to levels unrecoverable by efficiency. The public talks pollution, but they buy price. We compete against polluters who have not yet been forced to match our standards.[30]

Note that the new mill was approved as meeting local standards, although American Can reported being at a disadvantage in competing with those who continued to pollute. However, the company and the community agreed on a basis for continued industrial development. Whether this spirit of cooperation or that of opposition to development that Maine Clean Fuels encountered will prevail is going to be important in shaping the industrial future of large areas of the United States.

American Can Leaves the City

When a corporation shifts its resources, then its employees, suppliers, and community are put in the position of either following along or losing whatever advantage the relationship represented. Along with the authority that permits such a resource shift goes a responsibility to balance any resulting social costs.

One of the most complex types of resource shifts is the relocation of a corporate headquarters because it involves a large group of people, most of whom have to move to a different environment.

While corporations move both in and out of large cities, the trend seems to be generally toward exodus. American Can carried out a smooth and successful move from New York City to suburban Connecticut. Its experience illustrates some of the relocation problems. A 1969 newsletter to its employees expresses the elements involved in terms of a personal equation.

> *It's your move:* A year from now, the new headquarters building in Greenwich will be completed. Almost four years of careful planning will have gone into preparation for the big move. Next week, to put the planning into more personal perspective, a survey, covering all headquarters people and conducted by representatives of each department, will get underway.
>
> The survey-interview will spell out newly-developed policies designed to encourage everyone to STAY with American by going to Greenwich. This STAY bulletin will help you prepare for the interview. Take it home; read it carefully; talk it over with your family. You will then be in a better position to view the move in terms of 'what does this mean to me?' If you haven't made up your mind, this information may help you to do so. If you have, you may want to tell the interviewer what additional information and assistance you will want to help you plan further for the move.
>
> *STAY means go:* The survey will make one thing clear; American Can wants every headquarters employee to continue his or her employment with the

---

[30]Judd H. Alexander, Vice President, Environmental Affairs, American Can Company, "The Four Corporate Challenges in the Environmental Age," speech before the White House Seminar on the Environment, Washington, D.C., 26 March 1971.

company at the new site. To make the transition as attractive as possible, several assistance programs have been worked out. They are all designed to get you to try Greenwich, in the belief that working conditions and job opportunities will be such that you will want to stay.

Relocation policy: The Corporate Headquarters Relocation Policy is offered to any headquarters employee who by moving, can improve his or her state or local income tax position or decrease commutation time by 30% (with some reasonable restrictions on those people already living in Greenwich and nearby Connecticut towns). The moving policy is spelled out in a booklet obtainable in the Relocation Office at 100 Park Avenue. For those who need financial aid in the sometimes critical period between closing dates on two houses, the Treasurer's Department will arrange for short-term, low-interest loans. In addition, certain lending institutions have indicated that American Can people would get preferential consideration on mortgage applications.

Incentive bonus: This policy has been developed to encourage those who may not want to move, to try commuting from their present residence. . . . Here is how the plan operates: On March 3, 1969, a 'Stay Account' was opened for each eligible employee. Each week, a credit will be entered into his or her account in an amount determined by length of accredited service as of March 1, 1970. As a result of this build-up of credit, those people actually working at Greenwich four weeks after the official moving date for their department will receive a check for the amount due them.[31]

In 1971 an American Can executive reviewed the history of the move.

A projection of the expected future growth of the company indicated that a sales increase of at least 50 per cent could be expected by 1975, calling for a sizeable increase in the headquarters staff.

It became obvious, early in the game, that with 2,000 people under one roof, a basic requirement was equity, in the form of ownership of the building.

We had to move quickly, since the lease on our New York headquarters location would expire in April of 1970.

We tried, unsuccessfully, to buy 100 Park Avenue, where as the 35-story building's major tenant, we housed about 1,200 people.

A number of situations in New York City, ranging from the construction of our own building to several counter proposals made by the city government, were carefully considered.

When none of them proved feasible, we were headed for the suburbs.

Toward the end of 1966 we narrowed the field and took options on property in northern New Jersey, Westchester County and Connecticut. Our first-choice location was 154 acres in the northwest corner of the Town of

---

[31] *STAY* (Specifics to Assist You) *A Headquarters News Letter Supplement,* American Can Company, 26 March 1969.

Greenwich, with an adjoining 27 acres in New York State. Accordingly, we obtained an option to purchase the land, subject to the requirements of the Town of Greenwich and to the best interests of all neighboring communities.

A scale model was made to demonstrate in three dimensions not only the aesthetic values to be built into the headquarters complex but to show what the entire headquarters complex would look like in relation to the immediate terrain and to the neighbors.

One of the most stringent requirements laid down by the Greenwich community, and a condition we heartily agreed with, was that our new corporate headquarters would not destroy or materially alter the natural beauty of the area.

When we were planning the use of the 154 acres we now own in Connecticut, we made every effort to insure the natural beauty of the terrain.

Our buildings were designed to rise no higher than tree-top level. They are barely visible from Interstate Highway 684 that borders the southern edge of the property. And since all our parking facilities are underground—where 1,700 automobiles can be garaged—there are no open parking lots.

Furthermore, we put in perpetual trust 45 of those acres for the Greenwich Conservancy so that this area could remain a wildlife sanctuary.

All of American Can's traffic is taken off local roads as quickly as possible by a sweeping four-lane highway that enters and serves its own property. The corporation has built its own sewage disposal plant. Water comes from its own wells. Neighborhood views are unspoiled. Recessed windows are of gray glass, with muted incandescent lighting to keep the building from being a beacon at night.

We clearly recognized the need to integrate the corporate entity with the most progressive, social aspects of the community. To take this step successfully, any corporation must concern itself with the wishes and the needs of the people of the community. When your own people move into a given area, they become part of the people of that community.

From one of our detailed studies we knew where our employees lived and how they got to and from work. We found them equally distributed throughout the metropolitan area. Thus, a move in any direction would require a substantial number of relocations. Thus, a highly important factor was the development of the company's moving policy.

This policy was extended across the board to our headquarters employees, from chairman to janitor. The total cost of the move, including all such miscellaneous items as legal fees and allowances for rugs, drapes and the like, was borne by the company. Furthermore, we did not impose the traditional restriction of minimum number of miles from the headquarters site as a condition for application of the policy.

Provisions were made for the equitable disposition of houses from which people were moving to new locations. At our former headquarters in New York, an office had been established to offer assistance to employees who were planning to move.

We published a Headquarters Newsletter which reported all details of the relocation project, dispelled rumors by reporting the facts, and did everything possible to condition our people to the realities of the relocation process. This newsletter was mailed regularly to our employees at their homes.

We ran free buses for our employees from Manhattan and surrounding areas for three months. We had two Family Days, before and after construction of headquarters. We had representatives of realtors, rental agencies and builders from the Connecticut area visit our New York headquarters several times to answer employee questions. We had a filmstrip made that described the communities surrounding Greenwich. We had lending institution representatives give lectures to employees about housing, mortgage money, points and other related subjects. We had a Stay Bonus program in which we paid bonuses to employees after they came to Connecticut and worked here for four weeks, the bonuses ranging from $500 to $2,500 depending on length of service. We published an Apartment Hunters Guide and a Starter Kit, the latter familiarizing employees with the new headquarters and its services.

We had phenomenal success in retaining employees in the move. Much of it was due to advance planning. We lost less than 10 percent of our work force in the move.

For the benefit of the residents of the Greenwich area, many of whom understandably were concerned with the influx of corporations in the area, we conducted a series of meetings with civic, service, and community organizations. At these meetings we reported the construction progress of the headquarters, responded to questions, dispelled rumors and made clear the company's concern both on the corporate and the individual levels, with Greenwich, Fairfield County and the State of Connecticut.

Also, we were in almost daily contact with the press and radio—with full and complete disclosure of the project.[32]

In reviewing the reasons for corporate movement of headquarters, O'Meara has listed taxes in the suburbs, availability of the necessary space, difficulties with commuting, and concern about the hazards of living and working in the cities.[33]

In a broad sense, of course, American Can did not leave the metropolitan area but only the island of Manhattan. It continues the active role of a major corporation with its headquarters in the metropolitan region. But because of the anomalies of state boundaries and subdivision of geographical units, American Can has, in fact, moved to an area where its employees pay less city and state income taxes, and its own tax and expense levels are reduced by the relocation.

In terms of the social aspects of a relocation of this type, neither American Can's finished products nor its routine use of physical resources is significantly involved

---

[32]Leonard A. Britzke, Vice President, Corporate Engineering, American Can Company, "The Human Aspects of a Corporate Move," address before the Chamber of Commerce, New Canaan, Conn., 8 March 1971.

[33]J. Roger O'Meara, *Corporate Moves to the Suburbs,* (New York: Conference Board, 1972).

since only the corporate headquarters moved. The primary impact areas were the communities (new and old), the employee group, and all of those doing business with or depending on the corporate headquarters.

For the employee group the primary problem was relocation. American Can seems to have run a careful and well-conceived relocation program. Ample notice was given and specific planning for the relocation preceded the actual physical move by over a year. A sincere effort was made to aid in personal planning considerations and to cushion the financial burden of relocation. The company made very clear that it really wanted the entire work force to move with it. Where other corporations have been accused of disregarding employee interests, causing hardship through quick or frequent relocations, or even structuring a move deliberately to eliminate sections of the executive group or the work force, American Can seems to have planned a thorough and conscientious program for a smooth relocation.

The business firms that supplied products or services to the American Can corporate headquarters were affected as the headquarters moved to Greenwich; some New York City ties were broken and some Connecticut ties were established. Again, the advance notice and careful planning of the move allowed the other firms involved at least as much time to adjust as is normal when customers or markets change in a competitive world.

The impact on the several local communities does raise some special issues, however. The city of New York (or, more specifically, the island of Manhattan) lost a large business. Despite the advance warning, social costs may have resulted from the relocation. The city lost the tax revenue from the incomes of the American Can payroll. A large block of office space was vacated. The demand for subways and other city services was cut by some small fraction due to the shift in the commuting pattern of some American Can employees and the relocation of others. Since only a few employees actually lived in Manhattan, the loss was felt least at the level of community job needs.

Greenwich and the surrounding communities gained a business, its taxes, and its participation and support in community affairs. The intent of the local regulatory authorities was to require a facility that would be attractive and appropriate for the location and that would not disrupt or place great demands on local services. Since it was in the interest of American Can to construct such a facility, suburban Connecticut and nearby New York undoubtedly benefited by the transfer.

Furthermore, American Can became an active participant in Greenwich and a number of other suburban communities. This is worthy of comment since corporations in the city of New York often find that their attempts to participate in city affairs are unrewarding; they are unable to see any influence or impact of their actions. Thus, the change in attitude in a smaller suburban community—or series of communities—is very noticeable. Some corporations consider this increased participation in and responsibility for the community to be very rewarding and to represent an advantage in the shift from the inner city. Others prefer the anonymity of the city where nonparticipation escapes notice.

If the American Can move is regarded as a shift from one location to another within the greater New York metropolitan area, then no social costs to the greater community can fairly be attributed. Because the greater New York area has no overall organization or government, both the city and state of New York have lost revenue to Connecticut. Yet it is hard to criticize American Can or any other corporation for taking advantage of the subtleties of taxation and geography to locate itself favorably. Thus, based on the published facts, the American Can relocation has worked out satisfactorily from the standpoint of employees, other business firms, and the community at an overall level, although causing a shift of tax revenue between local governments in the community.

American Can has completed its move, and the succeeding adjustments have also been concluded for the most part. Greenwich, which strongly desires to keep its suburban residential character, has refused subsequent proposals for headquarters relocations. The location of American Can on the periphery of the village, where there was minimum direct traffic or visual impact, presented less of a threat to the community than the later Xerox proposal, which called for a more visible, central headquarters structure. Xerox withdrew in the face of strong local opposition.

The American Can move represents both an example of a major relocation and an incident in the continuing process of corporations finding needs to relocate. AT&T has since moved a major unit from New York City to Basking Ridge, New Jersey, and Union Carbide has set in motion plans to move its corporate headquarters to Danbury, Connecticut. These relocations start with planning, continue through the relocation process, and then move into an adjustment phase as corporation, employees, and community adapt to the realities of the new relationships. Only then can the success and the social impact of the process be judged.

No shift of this sort occurs without pain. Inevitably, some employees will be disappointed by the new arrangements, although others will be pleased. Some local citizens will regret the admission of the new corporate neighbor. Since these pains seem not to have been intense for Greenwich, American Can, and its employees, the move can now be judged as having been successful, at least when the outward manifestations are considered.

Summary

These cases were included to illustrate the nature of some of the industry-society interactions that corporations must take into account in planning their actions. These examples must be regarded in a tentative and illustrative, rather than a definitive, light since only a sampling of the background facts is available. The purpose here is to highlight types of issues, as summarized in Figure 2.1, for their value in demonstrating corporate problems and alternatives and is not intended to pass judgment on any one corporation based on only a few published facts. The issues range from those concerning pollution and conservation to those concerning interrelations with the local community; they also cover the rights and responsibilities inherent in either establishing or moving a facility.

This review of events in the lives of several corporations and several communities has provided examples of specific problems that must be dealt with when a given organization interacts with its social environment. However, this interaction is also

Figure 2.1 Social Impact Examples

Examples	Issues
Olin Chemical and Saltville	Pollution versus plant closings
	Employer leaving community
International Paper versus the environment	Conservation of resources
	Land development
	Corporate community programs
	Rebuilding obsolete plants
	Remedy for past pollution
Maine Clean Fuels	What should be the controls on industrial development?
American Can relocates	Entering a new community
	Relocation of employees

influenced by the historical and cultural forces that have caused the corporation to evolve as it has. Next the origin and evolution of some of these forces will be discussed.

Questions for Analysis and Discussion

1. Figure 2.1 lists the following ten topics, which define some of the issues raised by the examples in the chapter:

Pollution versus plant closings
Employer leaving community
Conservation of resources
Land development
Corporate community programs
Rebuilding obsolete plants
Remedy for past pollution
Controls on industrial development
Entering a new community
Relocation of employees

Analyze the results of each of these issues in the light of the examples of corporate decisions and behavior that have been provided and others that you might know about.

2. What other issues caused by the social impact of corporate decisions do you find in the chapter?

For Further Information

Berg, Ivar, ed. *The Business of America.* New York: Harcourt, Brace & World, 1968.

Bradford, Peter Amory. *Fragile Structures: A Story of Oil Refineries, National Security, and the Coast of Maine.* New York: Harpers' Magazine Press, Harper & Row, 1975.

Krooss, Herman E. *American Economic Development,* 2d ed. Englewood Cliffs, N.J.: Prentice-Hall, 1966.

Osborn, Fairfield. *Our Plundered Planet.* Boston: Little, Brown, 1948.

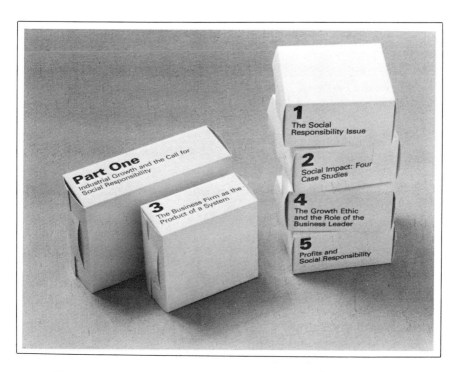

3
The Business Firm as the Product of a System

To a large extent, the modern business firm arose as the consequence of a rapid flow of cultural and institutional innovations. It arose as part of a change process, which will be examined in this chapter, to aid in defining both the present pressures on management and the possible future direction of social demands. One clear direction is toward requiring the corporation to take responsibility for the consequences of the actions it authorizes, even though this broad demand would raise many new issues and place new burdens on corporate management.

The purpose of a business . . . must lie . . . in society since a business enterprise is an organ of society. . . . [It is] the specific organ of growth, expansion and change. Business is the wealth-creating and wealth-producing organ of our society.[1]

PETER F. DRUCKER

The Evolution of Industrial Society

In many ways a business firm is shaped by outside forces. While a firm has its own management, business, and identity, the institutional form and the laws and customs that govern its operation are a product of its environment. To understand this environment and the ways in which it is changing, it is necessary to trace briefly the history of its development.

The origin of industrial society was from a premarket economy. At one point, society was based on hunting, fishing, and agriculture. Progress from a very primitive level finally led to a feudal economy and to a distinct degree of specialization of economic roles. With the division of labor and a need for new resources, the process of trading started by barter, initially; later money was adopted as a medium of exchange. Archaeologists have found records of extensive trade among primitive peoples, which is evidenced by the transportation of flint for arrowheads, for instance.[2] As trade continued to increase, the growth of commerce was guided by a body of economic doctrines called mercantilism.

Mercantilism

Mercantilism was a philosophy that regarded the national economy's trading aspect as being most important—a philosophy that did not acknowledge any creative potential in the economic process; one person's gain was another person's loss and one country gained at the expense of another country. Thus, a believer in mercantilism saw nations trading against each other in a struggle for supremacy.

Mercantilism was very important in Europe in the period when the feudal system was breaking down and nations were forming. The governments of France and

---

[1] Peter F. Drucker, *The Practice of Management* (New York: Harper & Brothers, 1954), pp. 37, 39, 386.

[2] Miriam Beard tells the story of this interesting period in Chapter 1 of her *History of Business*, 2 vols. (Ann Arbor, Mich.: Ann Arbor Paperbacks, University of Michigan Press, 1962).

England, in particular, made heavy use of mercantile theory. Consequently, they emphasized the acquisition of gold and the maintenance of a favorable balance of payments. The reliance on mercantilism led to some very interesting theories about the administration of colonies—for example, that colonies should not be permitted to trade with each other or with foreign countries—or that all trade should go through the mother country, yielding it a profit on every transaction. Colonies should not manufacture products—they should only produce raw materials; the mother country should perform the manufacturing because of the value that would be added to the product. When the resulting products were exported, this value was turned into gold.

Of course, this philosophy led England to create the net of regulations over its colonies that finally provoked the American Revolution. The British administration of the American colonies was a very careful and deliberate embodiment of mercantile theory, which formed the economic philosophy of the British government at that time. In many ways this philosophy was quite successful, but it did not recognize many things; as time passed, its shortcomings became manifest.

The Industrial Revolution

In the year 1776, which was also the year of the American Revolution, Adam Smith's *Wealth of Nations* was published. This was the first major economic text of the industrial world—the book that laid out the basic concepts of competition, free trade, and what later came to be called the laissez-faire economy. At the time Smith wrote as he did of the evils of the mercantile system, its inefficiencies were becoming increasingly obvious; yet no one had been able either to describe theoretically why it was wrong or to replace it.

Although people have attacked *Wealth of Nations* because "there was nothing original in it," Adam Smith made a very great contribution. He brought together in one place a cogent argument as to why mercantilist economics needed to be modernized, and he outlined the shape of a more workable system. He helped effect the changes in economic and political philosophy that accompanied and fostered the Industrial Revolution and also helped in causing this philosophy to crystallize in the now familiar pattern.

This major transition was predictable, at least in retrospect, since the whole foundation for Adam Smith's theory had developed over the previous several generations as the problems of British mercantilism had increased. The beginning of the Industrial Revolution was a crucial time because this revolution was a phenomenon that had been difficult to initiate. The problem of starting to build the first industries was remarkably hard because so many political and cultural thresholds needed to be crossed simultaneously before industrial development could take place.

Most of the European countries were still emerging from feudal control, and the hereditary interests of the aristocracy were in the lands and the power of armies. Because the aristocracy was largely rural and had little interest in manufacturing and commerce, the centers of development were the centers of trade—the cities. But there was great resistance to change in the cities; the guild system had been developed by the medieval artisan and held very tight control over work methods and the supply of labor for a given trade. The guilds controlled the number of apprentices that could be trained, what work methods each must learn, and the number of years that each must serve in apprenticeship to become an artisan of one kind or another. The guilds had created a very strong, change-resistant social structure. Thus, the guilds largely prevented change in the cities, while the rural power structure was disinterested in industry of any sort.

This was also a period of major religious upheaval. By this time the Protestant Reformation had reached its climax. The change in values represented by this reformation had a profound economic impact. A principal interpreter of this change was Max Weber in *The Protestant Ethic and Spirit of Capitalism*. Not everyone accepts the thesis of this very important book, but most accept the result that it identified, that is, the occurrence of a major shift away from the emphasis on nonmaterial religious values that was prevalent before the Renaissance. For some Protestant groups, worldly success became recognized as a token of divine favor. And for most of society, material gain became respectable. This social approval released large amounts of pent-up energy into the economic development process.

Since England happened to be less involved in the European political and religious wars because of its isolation from the Continent, the growth of mercantilism proceeded unchecked. An important part of the British merchant trade was in textiles. This led the British to discover the value of wool. As the textile trade grew, wool became very valuable. Under the village system in England then, most of the peasants did not own land. They lived by farming common ground that was owned by the local squires. The squires began to raise sheep when it became more profitable. A tremendous upheaval occurred as the commons were fenced in for sheep pastures because the peasants were then barred from the land that provided their livelihood and were left without any means of support.

At this time England had a welfare system that was well intended but poorly designed. It consisted primarily of a network of workhouses for the indigent. Money to support this system was raised by taxes on property. The large landholders and aristocracy were exempt, leaving a narrow tax base that included the small independent farmers. As the enclosure of the commons progressed, masses of displaced peasants were thrown into the welfare system. Taxes were raised repeatedly. The small farmers could not stand the burden of the taxation, began to lose their land, and were also thrown into the welfare system. With more peasants thrown into the welfare system by each rise in taxes to support the workhouses, very serious social unrest developed.[3]

The social troubles of the enclosure period did serve to provide a labor supply that was neither part of nor controlled by the rural or the urban social structure. These displaced peasants had no defined role in society, either under the guild control of work methods or the landed gentry's control of the rural communities. Hence this was available labor in England, where material gain was now respectable due to the Reformation and where Adam Smith and others had started a revolution in economic thinking. The textile trade was booming, more production of yarn and cloth was

---

[3]For a discussion of this enclosure period, see Karl Polanyi, *The Great Transformation* (New York: Rinehart & Company, 1957).

needed, and trading profits provided capital. As ideas came along for spinning machines and power looms and for steam engines to drive them, it became socially possible almost for the first time anywhere to build productive factories in the English countryside.

There had been impressive workshops in Italy during the Renaissance where hundreds of people were employed—but the laborers had used essentially the same work methods and had had about the same productivity as individuals working separately. In eighteenth-century England the potential for designing factories to increase productivity of labor and yield profits finally was demonstrated. Once labor-saving inventions were applied and productivity began to increase and generate profits, the resulting gains in economic wealth started a process that spread rapidly to other countries. The Industrial Revolution had begun, and both the modern business enterprise and its troubled environment were among the many consequences.

New Social Ills

The Industrial Revolution brought benefits, but also problems. New social ills were invented, to look at it in one way. The opportunity for growth and sudden awareness of new social ills is created, in part, by the manner of formation of our basic social institutions, many of which were reshaped by the changes originating with the Industrial Revolution. These changes are also reflected in our laws. Our basic law is the English common law, which, like most other legal codes, is formed and changed slowly. The basic mechanism of change is a succession of court decisions reinforced by legislative enactments.

This is a deliberate process, in which a case comes up for a decision and a precedent is established. Then another issue is tested, another decision is made, and things move forward, but slowly. These decisions are always based on actual, not anticipated, problems that have become so acute that they are brought to court. New laws rarely anticipate problems either. The nature of our system is such that there is a substantial lag between an actual occurrence in society and the point at which people get concerned enough to pass a law or bring a problem to court. Thus, there are very few rules for problems that have not yet occurred.

The child labor problem can serve to illustrate the slow development of this process. Before the Industrial Revolution in England, the peasant children worked. They were part of the economic basis of the small farm. They often worked at least as long and as hard as they did later in the factories, and sometimes their work was physically detrimental. However, once there were factories and it was possible to get an entire roomful of children tending looms, the actions of the textile industry focused attention on a problem that had existed for a long time without causing much concern. It became a social ill. The people of England suddenly became aware of what steady work under such conditions was doing to these children and began to pass child labor laws.

This process of creating social ills has recurred as the industrial system has developed. Repeatedly, society has become very upset about a condition that has existed almost forever (pollution is a good example) because it suddenly has reached acute levels. At a low level, environmental damage went largely unnoticed. When the level of the damage increased, the public noticed and became upset. And now we wonder why we did not have laws to stop pollution of streams a hundred years ago.

The rules that govern society lag because of the nature of the system. The codes and the patterns of the evolution of our culture were formed in an era when things changed much more slowly. One of the acute problems affecting the whole environment of the business enterprise is that rules have not been made for today's system, situation, and problems. Many of the things that the business system is doing wrong were not viewed as being wrong at some time in the past. Perhaps they should have been condemned then, but today we see things differently. Our society is dealing with a substantial change in the value systems that it applies to business conduct. Again and again, this book will trace these shifts in values and deal with the velocity of this change.

It is easy to lose sight of how much the country has really changed in the last fifty or thirty or ten years and how unusual this rate of change is when compared with other periods of human history. Our society is changing rapidly. We are suffering as a result of it. Yet perhaps we need to change much faster. The basic concept of *Future Shock* is that society can barely stand the stress of change, where this stress is from the shock of being carried into the changing future.[4] Nonetheless, the forces causing the change continued to accelerate, year by year.

Property Rights

Another example of change is the evolution of the private property concept. Once upon a time, all property belonged to the deities a particular tribe worshiped. At some later time, it became tribal property. With the evolution of nations, the property of the nation came to belong entirely to the king by divine right. This was the situation in medieval Europe.

Then the king began to parcel out property rights. Castles and landholdings were given to barons and nobles to ensure their loyalty and support. These nobles had possession of the properties, which could be removed at the king's pleasure, as they often were. As time passed, the nobles began to object. A confrontation in England between King John and his barons occurred because the barons wanted their rights spelled out more clearly. This action led to the signing of the Magna Carta. The gains made by the barons were followed by a further evolution in individual property rights, as the aristocracy succeeded in making the King's delegation of his rights clearer, more explicit, and less reversible. Where the issue at the time of King John was whether the earls and dukes could have rights to the property they were holding, it was eventually moved down to the question of whether an individual farmer could have property rights.

This evolution of the property concept proceeded to the point that any individual could own land and landholders could participate in the government as a matter of individual right. The concept finally became realized in England in the same period that the Industrial Revolution was gaining speed. For the first time, an individual who

---

[4]Alvin Toffler, *Future Shock* (New York: Random House, 1970).

was not of noble heritage could hold property and legally claim a right to it. "A man's home is his castle," as the English put it.

These ideas were carried to the English colonies and continued to evolve. In the United States the Fourteenth Amendment, which says that private property cannot be taken away without due process of law, was ratified in 1868, only then completing the legal process of establishing private property as a right. Private property had existed since colonial days, of course, but was not completely codified into law until 1868.

Because the right to individual property was still evolving, society had developed few controls over its use. Another characteristic of the processes of social change is that trends tend to overshoot, to carry a new thing too far beyond its intended areas of application. And since society tends not to have rules for problems that have not yet occurred, there is rarely any check on these excesses.

The age of the robber barons was a very bad period of business conduct. Many reasons for the public outcry involved abuses of private property rights in areas where society had not yet made rules. New laws were needed to control these abuses. Since this period came only a few generations after the right to private property had really become explicit, it would have been very surprising to find that there were good rules. As the rules were developed, they placed limits on private property rights.

Limits to Property

With the growth of wealth, with the fruits of the industrial system, and with the growing public belief in enlightened self-interest as the engine of public good through the business system, our society was carried along on a tide of enthusiasm. Adam Smith's ideas were important; they were offered at the right time. As Ricardo, Malthus, and many others in the succeeding generations of economists elaborated, developed, and carried forward Smith's doctrine, they named it *laissez faire* and extended it well beyond the limits that Smith had actually defined.[5]

By 1848 John Stuart Mill, in his *Principles of Political Economy,* had separated the process of producing wealth from the question of its distribution or, in other words, of who would receive the profit. This step was important, because it highlighted a divergence in political philosophies that remains as the largest single difference between Soviet and American capitalism. The difference is less in the production of wealth, which is managed by a corporation or its equivalent, than in the way profits are distributed and where the ownership is—with individuals and institutions here and with the government (society) in the communist and socialist countries.

Then, about 1875 William Graham Sumner took Smith's ideas, incorporated some ideas from Spencer and some ideas from Darwin, and created *the gospel of wealth.* This theory provided a rationale for the extension of the free enterprise idea to include almost anything a businessperson or business corporation might do that did not directly violate a law. Economically, it was the survival of the fittest, the

---

[5]The French term *laissez faire* literally means "to allow (people) to do."

unchecked aggressive individual pursuit of wealth for the common good.[6] Sumner's gospel presented a justification for the unlimited use of private property.

But what was happening to private property? As soon as people began to extend the use of their property rights and explore the boundaries of the actions that the absolute right to a piece of land permitted, society began to abridge the extension of those rights. An area that received attention in this regard, for instance, was that of riparian law, the law involving rivers. As soon as one landowner shut off the flow of water through the mill pond on property that was rightfully owned, a neighbor downstream could object to the lack of water that resulted. Eventually, a code developed to define what property owners could and could not do with the water flowing through their land.

Again and again this kind of development has occurred in different areas; the scope of application of a property right has been extended until it becomes an exploitation and an abuse of others' rights, whereupon it is curtailed by society. These abridgments of the rights to private property have developed rapidly. For instance, the whole idea of zoning is that some more or less remote social body can decide how an individual is allowed to use property—whether for residence, for industry, or not at all. In some cases zoning can specify that an owner must plant certain kinds of shade trees and replace them if they die.

These are very substantial abridgements of the private property concept. Yet it seems to be necessary to have some restrictions on use of private property in order for a modern country to function. For example, the right of eminent domain permits taking of land for public purposes, such as the building of a road, in spite of the property owner's objections. Such an abridgment of property rights is often necessary for a public purpose. And although these abridgments have been developing rapidly, they have not kept pace with the times because of the basic tendency of cultural control mechanisms to lag behind change.

Adaptability of the Economic System

As Sumner was talking about the gospel of wealth, the United States was experiencing a very major growth of business enterprises and large business institutions. Adam Smith had not been concerned with big corporations as we know them. He spoke of monopolies and corporations in terms of the British East India Company, which was semigovernmental, semipolitical, and very strongly monopolistic. No industries in the modern sense yet existed. By the time that the country had U.S. Steel, the Pennsylvania Railroad, and Standard Oil, the United States had developed a different kind of economy. The early rules no longer had appropriate applications. Not only had the business firms changed, but the economic system had also changed in the course of its evolution and development.

In evaluating change within the economic system it is helpful to consider that

---

[6]For an interesting book on this period, see Robert M. McCloskey, *American Conservatism in the Age of Enterprise* (New York: Harper Torchbooks, Harper & Row, 1951).

some expected the system to fail long ago. Some of the reasons why it has not failed are demonstrated in its evolution and its power to adapt.

Marx and Revolution

The self-destruction of capitalism has been freely predicted by serious and perceptive critics, starting with Karl Marx. Besides his obvious association with communism, Marx made great contributions as an economic historian. He did the first serious analysis of the pattern of development of a factory society—a deterministic analysis of the way the industrial system was developing.

Although Marx came originally from Germany, much of his writing was done in England after he had been exiled from the continent. Primarily, he based his analysis on the events in England in the days when the Industrial Revolution was well underway and when England was beginning to become the first industrial power. His major analytical work was *Das Kapital,* whose first volume was published in 1878.

Marx saw the forces that had been turned loose by the emergence of the business enterprise as causing very serious strains in society. He saw a class of owners and managers, the capitalists, acting in a pattern that was determined less by personal motives (he did not attack them as individuals) than by the economic forces that they both governed and were controlled by. And he saw a large mass of unskilled workers, the proletariat, who were being ground down under the system's pressure.

Marx observed the tremendous unrest in England and the acute social trauma that resulted from rapid industrialization. He projected that, as the historical forces continued to operate, the capitalist system would be destroyed by revolution. But the revolution that finally came was not in England. It was in Russia and when it came it did not fit the Marxian analysis. What Marx did not take into account was that social forces did not continue to act in the same way or in the direction dictated by their historical trend—the system changed.

Several important things upset the pattern. Probably the most important was the growth of the middle class. Instead of a two-class society composed primarily of a few capitalists who were opposed by a tremendous mass of unskilled laborers, the industrial countries began to develop a significant group of people in between; these were engineers, technicians, and middle management people. Also, some of the acute social problems did draw action; England in those years was conducting significant social reform. The right to vote was extended, legislation caused some improvement in working conditions, and the economic system adapted enough so that it was not destroyed by the forces that Marx had anticipated. Marx understood the system well, but he did not visualize how it would change as it matured and as new groups in society began to influence the law-making process.

Djilas and Modern Communism

A contemporary communist critic is a Yugoslav named Milovan Djilas. Djilas rose to prominence during World War II as a key member of the partisan group that Tito led. At one point, he was second in command of the Yugoslav state. More recently, he has been in and out of jail for writing books and articles that the Yugoslav government has not approved. *The New Class* is his analysis of the communist system.[7]

It is a pessimistic analysis, because Djilas wrote as a dedicated communist with a deep belief in the Marxian doctrines. He focused his book on the failure of the revolution to achieve its objectives. Marx had predicted the evolution toward a dictatorship of the proletariat. But instead of shifting from the rule of the dictators who organized the revolution to a stage where the workers could assume the responsibility for government, both Russia and Yugoslavia had developed a third and controlling group, the new class. This new elite class of administrators, engineers, technicians, and managers had taken over the economy and were running it increasingly in their own interest.

Djilas's analysis suggests the continuing parallel between the communist and free enterprise economic systems, as the evolution of both systems causes related changes in the respective industrial societies.

Veblen and Financial Control

Another prophet of doom was Thorstein Veblen, an American economist active at the beginning of the twentieth century. His book on absentee ownership concluded that the ultimate fate of the industrial system was to be run by "one big bank."[8] This prediction was based on his observation of the divorcement of technical knowledge, which had caused industrial growth, from financial power, which governed day-to-day operations. For example, Andrew Carnegie ran the Carnegie Steel Company as an efficient engine of production and then sold it to a group headed by J. P. Morgan that formed U.S. Steel. The management, which had been driving for economical steel production, changed to one that administered a dominant enterprise on the basis of good financial management and the principle of economic gain.

There was a shift of this sort in many industries. Veblen thought that this trend would go to its ultimate conclusion. The system would be totally strangled by the ability of interconnecting financial ties to choke off competition, run business in a way that was profitable but not productive, and basically stifle the economic growth of the country. When Veblen made these predictions, the Sherman Antitrust Act had not yet been enforced effectively, the major era of trust busting had not shown its potential, and the restrictions on holding companies and interlocking directorates were still to be triggered by the 1929 financial collapse.

Veblen was pessimistic about the future. But the severe threat that he saw affecting the future of the economic system has been averted. Of course, the country is not yet free from problems of nonproductive financial control. The process of preventing large private enterprises from restraining trade, stifling competition, or establishing monopolies has not been completed. However, the public regulatory process has largely controlled the particular set of private monopoly processes that Veblen thought would choke the country.

---

[7]Milovan Djilas, *The New Class* (New York: Frederick A. Praeger, 1957).

[8]Thorstein Veblen, *Absentee Ownership and Business Enterprise in Recent Times* (New York: Viking Press, 1938).

Schumpeter and Socialism

Another important thinker who foresaw the end of the free enterprise economic system as we know it was Joseph Schumpeter, an Austrian economist who came to the United States and did much of his writing here in the late 1930s and early 1940s. He wrote a major book called *Capitalism, Socialism and Democracy,* which outlines his views of the future.[9] Schumpeter, a strong proponent of a free enterprise system, felt that an inevitable erosion would take place because the success of free enterprise capitalism carried the seeds of a transition to socialism (state capitalism). This transition seemed to him to be beyond control. The reasons lay in the failures, both in fact and understanding, in the interface between the interests of the large business enterprises and the interests of the country. He envisioned the impact as occurring when a particular management took a step that would affect scarce resources or that would lead to a labor dispute and shut down a sector of the economy. He considered the actions of General Motors and other large corporations as sometimes not being in the best interest of the country and as being misunderstood in any case. He saw troubles and misunderstandings generating increased political pressure for changes in the system. A drift into socialism seemed to be the necessary and inevitable outcome of this evolution of the economic and political system.

The problems that troubled Schumpeter have developed along with the modern economy. Because the industrial system has grown, today's citizens have lost some of the independence of action that U.S. citizens had in the days when people lived on their own farms. By and large, individuals were self-sufficient and had minimum dependence on others, except perhaps their immediate neighbors and families. Now the country has moved into an era where every year there is less opportunity for self-sufficiency and more interdependence among people. If one of the major airlines does not fly, a mail strike occurs, utilities service is interrupted, or one of the big electric power grids fails, there is a massive impact on society. More and more, all parts of the economic and political systems must run in a certain coordination with each other in order for society to function. Schumpeter felt that society would have to solve this problem and that the politics of the problem would demand that government assume control over increasingly more of the private sector, even though a loss in efficiency might result.

In the thirty years since Schumpeter wrote his analysis, the country has made substantial progress in the development of the interrelationship between the public and private sectors, as the government has learned about regulation of private enterprise. From one standpoint, regulation restricts the freedom and reduces the ability of the firm as the owner of private property to do as it pleases with its own assets. In another sense, regulation is the overall function of governance, which is the government's job as a part of its duty in ensuring that the common good be a little bit better served. The United States has a regulated economy now, and the rapid growth of government regulation is one of the conspicuous trends. In some ways it is

---

[9]Joseph Schumpeter, *Capitalism, Socialism and Democracy* (New York: Harper Torchbooks, Harper & Row, 1950).

a good trend and in some ways a very bad one; but, in any event, it has tended to divert or defer the pressures that Schumpeter expected would cause a rapid transition to socialism. Because free enterprise is less free and more regulated, the pressures to socialize the system have been reduced.

This review of various critiques of the economic system serves to illustrate several points crucial to an understanding of the way in which the present industrial society is likely to evolve. In the first place, the economic system of the United States is not fixed in its nature. Within the broad framework called free enterprise capitalism, the system has developed rapidly since Adam Smith first characterized it in 1776. The changes have been rapid enough both to illustrate the dynamism of the process and to defeat the accurate historical projections of downfall made by Marx, Veblen, and Schumpeter. The changes continue and their pace even accelerates. It seems certain that the economic system will again be different within one or two more generations, whether the present system continues its successful evolution or finally changes in basic nature.

Examination of these critiques also shows the parallelism between the economics and the industrial evolution of politically different societies. For example, all industrial societies seem to generate a middle class with somewhat similar aspirations. The degree to which the free enterprise system is, in truth, superior to a socialist system depends at least partly on the ability of the free enterprise system to find means of governance that will be able to regulate and coordinate the efforts of the different sectors of a complex economy effectively in a manner superior to the central control typical of a socialist state.

Business Responsibility and Authority

The continuing evolution of the economic system brings new rules and restrictions on the operation of the business firm. One basic concept in this development of new rules is that society is beginning not only to react to past abuses but also to suggest that some responsibility accompany all authority. Where a business firm has the right to cause something to happen, society is frequently asking that the firm take responsibility for the consequences. The right to dump waste in a river means that the firm is responsible for what the refuse does to the stream. The right to build and sell motor cars may (or may not—society is still arguing about this) make General Motors responsible for what happens to the car body when it is discarded. Such a policy involves a long extension of responsibility, but there have been very serious proposals to tax automobile manufacturers or somehow make them responsible for the ultimate disposal of cars. The same logic is being applied to the plastic bottles and aluminum cans that are discarded in great numbers.

The right to do something—the authority to cause something to happen—this is a basic management prerogative. Given that a business operates and makes decisions and given the broad range of circumstances over which these decisions have impact, what is the extent and what are the consequences of this authority? A manufacturer who decides to put roasted nuts in a cellophane bag or in an aluminum can could then become responsible, based on the authority for making that decision, for the consequences of the aluminum can or piece of cellophane appearing in a park or in the garbage (see Figure 3.1). This degree of responsibility is not yet widely defined or accepted, but it is supported by a very strong trend in public thinking at the present.

Summary

One of the characteristics of our society is change. The institutions of this society are evolving. There are changes in private property concepts, rules governing business corporations, the nature of our markets, and employee rights. And the changes that have brought the social and economic system to the present do not simply stop. Social change processes have a velocity that carries them forward, and continuing effects flow from the initial adjustments to each change; for example, our society has not truly adjusted yet to the invention of the automobile. Society is still suffering with the consequences and impacts of this new mobility as it learns to live in a different way. The continuing adjustment involves new technological and social innovations,

Figure 3.1 Decisions and Consequences

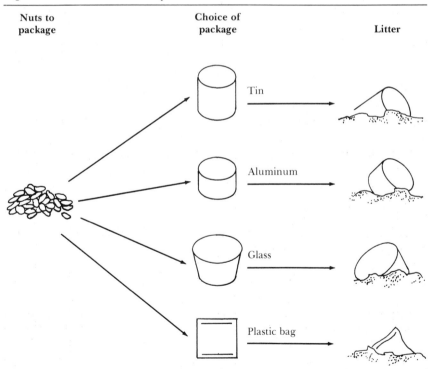

Nuts to package	**Choice of package**	**Litter**
	Tin	
	Aluminum	
	Glass	
	Plastic bag	

The corporate authority to choose the package brings some responsibility for the consequences.

each of which has its own impact and interacts with other major adjustments, such as those resulting from television and the growth of air transportation.

But as these changes go on, what direction will they take? While they will tend to remain somewhat static, there is no particular reason that each one should continue exactly in the line of its present momentum. There are choices ahead in major areas. In the case of the current concern about the automobile, it seems clear that the trend of momentum from the past will be deflected. What is not clear is whether our society will choose to restrict private transportation or whether it will invent a new form of propulsion that uses less energy and causes less pollution of the atmosphere. Realistically, it could do both.

The purpose here is to study these trends and alternatives, but not with hopes of discovering an absolute conclusion since the future is unpredictable. However, a great deal of benefit is gained in the analysis of what is most likely to happen or what the two or three most likely courses of action are because we can prepare a logical course of action instead of just stumbling into changes as they occur. Even though most individual trends have alternative paths, as in the case of the future of the automobile, they must fit within the basic developmental framework that forms an envelope around the process and whose general direction should be discoverable and predictable. A part of this general direction is toward a greater degree of social control over business activity, as manifested by the growth of regulation, on one hand, and by the demand for corporate response, which is called social responsibility, on the other. Both require further analysis to give each its proper place within the structure of a business corporation that is measured for profit performance.

The business firm, which is shaped by its environment, is also one of the forces that causes transition in the environment because society continues to respond to past changes and move toward new restrictions on business activity. This process of change in response to change continues, and business firms are constantly being shaped by an economic and social system that is, in turn, perpetually changing and generating other adjustments in social and competitive environments.

This chapter has summarized the evolution of private property and other key institutions and outlined the adaptations made by the economic system as industrial society has developed, reacted to abuses, and caused redirection of business and other energies. From this review emerges a pattern of restrictions and demands that emphasizes both the underlying primacy of social control and the likelihood that new restrictions on corporations will develop wherever adverse corporate impacts on society are detected. To a greater extent, society is asking that corporations assume responsibility for the consequences of any and all of their actions.

Questions for Analysis and Discussion

1. Analyze the concept of the development of new social ills. Select additional examples to use in illustrating and discussing this concept.

2. Choose a major new example of the rule-making process, such as a court

decision or a new law. Trace the interval of time that elapsed between the emergence of the issue as a matter of public concern and the actual rendering of a court decision or enactment of a law that affected the issue. Can you find any evidence that the rule-making processes in society are moving more rapidly than in the past?

3. Consider the process of society making new rules that reduce the freedom of property owners to use their property, for example, zoning laws. Find illustrations of this process and discuss the negative and positive aspects of the impact created by these rules.

4. Should a business be responsible for the impacts resulting from its actions? List some of the different types of corporate actions, their direct consequences, their secondary, indirect consequences, and the type of responsibility the corporation might be expected to exercise. Are there any impacts from corporate actions for which the corporation should not be held responsible?

5. Do you see the U.S. economic system as changing and evolving? What do you think might occur to change or stabilize the system?

6. How would you relate the benefits accrued from government control to the costs of this control? Discuss.

For Further Information

Beard, Miriam. *History of Business,* 2 vols. Ann Arbor, Mich.: Ann Arbor Paperbacks, University of Michigan Press, 1962.

Commons, John R. *Legal Foundations of Capitalism.* Madison, Wis.: University of Wisconsin Press, 1959.

Mantoux, Paul. *The Industrial Revolution in the 18th Century,* trans. Marjorie Vernon. New York: Harper & Row, 1961.

Marx, Karl. *Capital,* trans. Samuel Moore and Edward Aveling. New York: Modern Library G26, Random House, 1936.

Mill, John Stuart. *Principles of Political Economy.* New York: Colonial Press, 1900.

Polanyi, Karl. *The Great Transformation.* New York: Rinehart, 1957.

Schumpeter, Joseph. *Capitalism, Socialism, and Democracy,* 3rd ed. New York: Harper & Row, 1962.

Smith, Adam. *An Inquiry into the Nature and Causes of the Wealth of Nations.* Homewood, Ill.: Richard D. Irwin, 1963.

Veblen, Thorstein. *The Theory of the Business Enterprise.* New York: Mentor Books, 1953.

————. *The Portable Veblen.* New York: Viking Press, 1958.

Weber, Max. *General Economic History,* trans. Frank H. Knight. New York: Collier Books, 1961.

————. *The Protestant Ethic and the Spirit of Capitalism,* trans. Talcott Parsons. New York: Charles Scribner's Sons, 1958.

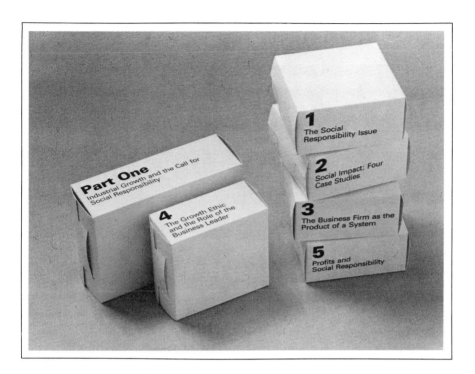

On the boxes in the image:

1 The Social Responsibility Issue

2 Social Impact: Four Case Studies

3 The Business Firm as the Product of a System

4 The Growth Ethic and the Role of the Business Leader

5 Profits and Social Responsibility

Part One Industrial Growth and the Call for Social Responsibility

4
The Growth Ethic and the Role of the Business Leader

Definition of the role of corporations, collectively, and of their leaders, individually, must precede any detailed consideration of corporate social impacts and responsibilities. To an extent, the individual firms are products of the system, as developed in the preceding chapter. The need is to clarify the degree to which the business leaders either are controlled by this system or act with an independence that engenders responsibility for the consequences of their actions.

This chapter deals first with the mechanisms of economic development. It begins by profiling several analyses of the way in which industry and the economy have developed, then suggests an integration of these analyses, and finally relates this integration to shifts in national value systems and the work environment. The purpose is to picture a national economic development process that is a product of the evolution of our culture but that is also under the guidance of the business leaders who shape each step as the process advances.

The power of a business leader to offer a new product or service that finds and directs an interest or a need and thereby brings growth and profits while changing society's habits and lifestyles is so subtle and pervasive that its wise use poses an awesome challenge.

GEORGE SAWYER

In considering the evolution and operation of our economic system, one finds that its past orientation toward growth emerges as a distinguishing characteristic. In the development of the system, the formalizing and institutionalizing of cultural processes have tended at each point to preserve the status quo, and innovation and new enterprise have been continuing sources of growth and change. The purpose of this chapter is to examine some insights into the nature of the process that represents the engine of this economic development and then to consider some of the other stresses in the workplace and the public forum that serve to define and constrain the role of the contemporary business administrator or entrepreneur.

Economic Change and Growth

The counterforce to regulation and bureaucracy is represented by innovation and the entrepreneur; innovation is the force of growth and change, and the entrepreneur is the agent who brings it about. The development of capitalism and the role of the entrepreneur have been closely linked. Many of the earlier entrepreneurs were viewed as heroic figures. Thus, the way in which several thinkers have regarded the entrepreneurial economic development process provides a useful background for considering elements in the public attitude toward business leaders and economic development today.

Evolution of Business Functions

N.S.B. Gras analyzed the growth of business firms some years ago in a book called *Business and Capitalism.*[1] The first form of capitalism Gras could identify he termed the *petty capitalist,* which included the door-to-door peddler, the singly owned

---

[1]N.S.B. Gras, *Business and Capitalism, An Introduction to Business History* (New York: Appleton-Century-Crofts, 1939).

business, and the small trader. With success and growth of trade, firms became larger and the *merchant capitalist* evolved. This was the head of a trading enterprise that had been brought to the scale of a large business and typically had a warehouse, a counting house, and many of its own ships. The large merchants of the colonial period in the United States exemplified this form of capitalism. From there the system evolved to create the *industrial capitalist*. This development first occurred when merchant capitalists found the need to manufacture some of the goods they sold and expanded into the establishment of manufacturing firms of all types as business volume continued to grow. Gras found that another shift took place as the system matured to something called the *finance capitalist*; this business emphasized entirely the financial side—banking, investment, and guidance of business management.

Most of the evolution that Gras described occurred over a span of time from the colonization of the New World to the U.S. Civil War, but of course the old forms did not go away as the newer forms of capitalism evolved. The individual businesses have changed with time, and yet today's economy contains frequent examples of all four types of capitalists. Now there is a greater tendency for the economy to depend on the equilibrium between industrial, merchant, and finance capitalists, thus placing the petty capitalists in a less influential and often derivative role. Sears, Roebuck & Company, in its role as merchant capitalist, develops markets for appliances often purchased from Whirlpool Corporation, in its role as industrial capitalist. Both of these businesses depend on a stable financial system and the ready availability of services from a variety of banks and other finance capitalist firms. The person who repairs appliances may function independently as a petty capitalist and consequently has a role that is at least partly defined by the nature of the appliances the companies such as Sears and Whirlpool make and sell.

Scope of the Entrepreneur

Another way of looking at the evolution of capitalism is by defining the role of the entrepreneur. Arthur Cole at Harvard took this approach and found that the first businesses were run by *empirical entrepreneurs,* business leaders that built businesses by trial, error, and intuition.[2] Next, as enterprises grew larger, they began to be run by a type of leader Cole called a *rational entrepreneur.* Andrew Carnegie was such a leader, one who had or drew on complete information about all functions and aspects of one business. These leaders were usually narrowly focused in one area and were often heavily production oriented. Cole said that the next step of progress was to the *cognitive entrepreneur,* the captain of industry with a broad knowledge of many fields. This type of entrepreneur was required to build a major firm such as GE, which has many different lines of products and types of operations. Thus, Cole characterized entrepreneurs by their method of operation as it related to the scope of their enterprises.

---

[2]Arthur H. Cole, "An Approach to the Study of Entrepreneurship," *Supplement to the Journal of Economic History,* vol. 6, 1946.

Structure Follows Strategy

Alfred DuPont Chandler wrote an important book called *Strategy and Structure*.[3] Its main theme is that the structure of a business (the way it is organized) is a direct result of the strategy that the business follows. In developing this concept, Chandler studied the way that the large decentralized business corporation had first originated. He found among the pioneer developers of this organizational form several of the present-day giants. GM, duPont, and Standard Oil, each from a different base of experience and each working independently on its own problems, had gone through trauma and trouble in working out a decentralized organization. While the three organizations differed and while each had reasons for these structural differences, they had evolved the same general theory of organization. Chandler found three stages in this corporate development; consideration of these stages offers another dimension to the present analysis.

Most of the businesses he studied seemed to have started as single-function, single-product firms, in which someone had an idea for a product and started a business to make and sell it. With growth and success, the normal line of development is toward an integration into other functions such as the manufacture of the parts and intermediate materials for that product. Thus, the trend is for a single-product firm to grow to a multifunction, single-product stage—to integrate vertically. Carnegie learned to make steel; presently, he was not only making steel rails but had purchased his own iron ore ships and iron mines. He integrated the functions of steel production from the mine almost to the consumer.

The next step in development, which most firms take if they continue their growth, is to go into other product lines. In other words, the typical large firm of today (duPont, GE, or GM) has many product lines and performs a number of different functions relative to those lines. GM not only makes and distributes cars, buses, diesel locomotives, and many other kinds of powered equipment but also makes the engines and many of the other components that go into them. So this pattern of shifting, diversifying, and decentralizing emerges as one of the basic characteristics of industrial growth. (See Figure 4.1.)

Figure 4.1   Evolution of Business and the Business Leader

Gras: Types of business leaders	Petty capitalist	→	Merchant capitalist	→	Industrial capitalist	→	Finance capitalist
Cole: Role of the entrepreneur	Empirical entrepreneur	→	Rational entrepreneur	→	Cognitive entrepreneur		
Chandler: Business strategy	Single functions, single product	→	Multifunction, single product	→	Multifunction, multiproduct		

Just as a complex statue changes as one walks around it, this evolution looks quite different from the three points of view.

---

[3]Alfred DuPont Chandler, *Strategy and Structure* (Garden City, N.Y.: Doubleday, 1962).

Waves of Innovation

Joseph Schumpeter also made a contribution in this area in *The Theory of Economic Development*, an important book in modern economics.[4] Central here is his insight that the basic source of profit in the industrial system is from innovation. He traced this concept through economic history and developed his case quite well. And in looking at the important innovations and their effects, he discovered that they have come in waves. A group of major discoveries occurs in one period and develops its economic impact, only to be followed by a lull in innovations, economic growth, and profits, which lasts until the next group of major innovations begins.

Steam power, a whole complex of spinning and weaving machines, and important developments in metal-working equipment occurred at about the same time. Another burst of innovation involved the development of railroads, steel, and related industries. A later wave has been identified with automobiles, electric utilities, and major advances in manufacture of machinery. A more recent group of innovations has included developments such as photocopying machines, transistors, and computers.

What relevance does Schumpeter's analysis have here? First, consider the implications of innovation as the major source of industrial profits. There are trading profits and monopoly profits, but these are likely to be transitory and subject to political intervention. Schumpeter argues convincingly that the major and fundamental source of profit is innovation. And profits are the fundamental source of economic renewal and growth as the industrial system continues to evolve.

In the real world also, as an innovation gets older, profits decrease because competitors enter and buyers find ways to erode the profit margin. A patent or other type of monopoly position, or a trading advantage, may slow this process, but only rarely for any significant span of time. From a wave of innovation should follow a wave of profitable industrial growth, as has been the pattern in the past and in the years since World War II. The interval between waves could involve periods in which innovations are less frequent, growth is slower, and business is less profitable.

At present, the management of an industrial economy is still far from a science. Today's art of economic management is primarily based on the dynamics of growth. We now depend on government manipulation of fiscal and monetary policy to keep the unemployment from going too high and to keep business from sinking too low. Traditional Keynesian economics and the many refinements of it that go into the modern theories of the management of the economy are largely based on stimulating growth to bring recovery. Population growth is less likely to increase economic growth in the future since birth rates have declined. If the country should have a period without economic growth (if we have no innovation or otherwise restrain growth), a new national economic management problem is created. There is a significant risk that our economists do not know how to manage an economy that is not growing.

It is not clear what the actual flow of innovations in the next few years will be; the

---

[4]Joseph Schumpeter, *The Theory of Economic Development,* trans. Redvers Opie (Oxford: Oxford University Press, 1961).

purpose here is merely to suggest the possibility of major overall forces pushing the economy up or weighing it down according to the rate of development and application of profitable innovations. This flow of discoveries can have a strong effect on the contemporary scene, regardless of how competent the business and economic managers may be.

Stages of Economic Growth

The fifth of these major viewpoints of the growth process is the one that Walter Rostow developed in his study of economic development.[5] He analyzed the experience of the existing industrial nations, searching for an underlying pattern useful for projecting future evolution of nations now seeking to accelerate their own economic development process. Rostow found five stages in this process. He said that development started in each case from a *traditional* society, that is, an established society that only changes slowly. In 1700 England was something like this, having a stable social structure that controlled the economic processes and showing no sign of rapid economic change.

As such a period approaches its end, a second stage called *precondition for takeoff* is entered. In this era commerce starts to expand, with the beginnings of industry and increasing strains on the established order. The third stage in Rostow's sequence is the *takeoff* stage, in which the economy begins to grow actively through rapid development of industry. Takeoff in the United States started about 1820 or 1830. Although the preconditions for takeoff existed in the colonial period, the rate of economic growth was actually very slow; rapid industrial growth occurred in the early to mid-nineteenth century.

The fourth stage Rostow called the *drive to maturity;* this is the continued growth of a large productive economic system. In this stage the major national effort is to produce. The value of the products are recognized, the public wants more goods, and the whole challenge is to produce as much as possible. The prototype for this period is the growth of the United States from the Civil War to the end of the century.

The next shift is from the emphasis on production to a fifth stage called the *age of high mass consumption*—the consumer goods period. In the 1930s the United States moved into this phase, which has been characterized by the development of advertising and national mass markets. The Russians seem to be moving into this period since they have also begun to develop national markets for consumer goods.

There is another stage that is neither identified in Rostow's analysis nor clearly characterized; some have called it a postindustrial stage. The need for characterizing this stage grows from the indications that the age of high mass consumption is being superceded by a more service-oriented economy that holds a somewhat different view toward industrial growth and consumer products. Current examples include the restrictions made on the kind of products that can be marketed and on advertising claims as well as the rethinking of our philosophy toward growth and development.

The pattern that Rostow has analyzed seems to apply to the past development of

---

[5]Walter W. Rostow, *Stages of Economic Growth.* (London: Cambridge University Press, 1960).

all the major industrial societies. This pattern probably will continue to have analogies in the case of developing countries, although some may move more rapidly into the later stages.

National Value Systems

David McClelland wrote a book called *The Achieving Society,* in which he studied the motivation of nations.[6] In looking for ways to study motivations objectively, he decided that the best mechanism was by measuring the motivational content of children's stories. He made a collection of children's stories of different nations and from different periods and analyzed the value systems that were being portrayed. At one extreme were the stories of well-behaved children playing quietly. At the other extreme were stories stressing the success ethic, with the killing of dragons, the capture of treasures, and the other rather fantastic themes that are scattered throughout tales for children. He did a content analysis of the stories from each of the countries where the information was available over an extended length of time and correlated the motivational content of the stories with those countries' gross national products in the succeeding years. The premise was that by looking at what was being taught to the children one could predict the rate of economic progress in that country when the children had grown up.

McClelland's data showed surprisingly good correlations. He found, for instance, that the very high motivation level in nineteenth-century English children's stories had dropped sharply about the time of World War I and that this correlated with the later decrease in the rate of economic growth in Britain.

McClelland then went on to explore ways of increasing achievement ambitions to promote individual success and national economic growth. One can argue about this part of it, which would depend on what each culture sees as a desirable result. Nonetheless, the basic concept is that people in different countries behave differently based on the motivation content of the value systems they are taught and that the economic performance of their countries differ as a result.

Today in the United States parents are not teaching their children the same things they used to teach them, or maybe they are not personally teaching them values as much as television is. However, the situation is changing, and younger people have accepted new values. According to surveys by Yankelovich and others, young people seem to be much less materialistic and value to a lesser extent the kind of success that their parents have suggested they seek. What kind of shift this will bring in our national aspirations years from now is less clear. From McClelland's data some drop in economic productivity would be suggested.

In tracing the origin of the Industrial Revolution, one finds that the shift in value systems accompanying the Reformation (the development of the Protestant ethic) was highlighted as a key causative factor in fostering economic growth. By looking at the rate of progress in different nations, one can easily confirm the conclusion that there are other things besides resources that explain economic progress. Germany rebuilt after World War II in a way that was faster than that of France or England; in

---

[6]David McClelland, *The Achieving Society* (New York: Van Nostrand, 1961).

this case it would seem that the important assets were a motivation and a level of skill in the people. The fact that most of the physical plant had been destroyed really made very little difference. With a favorable economic and political climate and American seed money, the Germans rebuilt at an amazing rate.

A similar situation existed in Japan, which also rebuilt with unusual speed. Today the Japanese seem to have a strong national success ethic. Various people have said that the national drive shifted from military conquest to economic conquest. In any case, the Japanese are doing well in the international markets. Even the reports of *Japan Chemical Week* to foreign readers capture something of the national competitive drive to excel in export performance.

As Israel continues to fight for survival and economic development, today's efforts seem to foreshadow emergence of the country as an important export power ten or twenty years from now. Certainly, there is a strong national drive for success. Since the Israeli market is not large enough to justify major basic industries unless most of the goods are exported, industries are being built with the premise that export markets must be found in Africa and elsewhere to compete with Japanese and German exports.

The point is that there is a differential here between countries. There are less aggressive countries than Germany, Japan, and Israel in material development, and there are cultures that do not prize material gain. In many ways these differences in national value systems are as important to the economic development equation as are the material resources of the country.

Before integrating the content of these various analyses, let us reconsider the process of economic development that has been intrinsic to the Industrial Revolution and to the continuing processes of economic growth. Historically, in a free economy this process has evolved around the role of the entrepreneur. Gras saw the shift in the role of the entrepreneur as new business forms became important. Cole looked at the use of tools and the breadth of knowledge that were applied as the entrepreneur expanded his horizons.

Chandler concentrated instead on the firm, observed the way that structure responded to changes in strategy, and found a systematic shift from the simple firm to the complex decentralized corporation. Schumpeter traced the source of profits to innovation and discovered its wavelike nature, with groups of innovations occurring together and pushing through the economic system with their impact. Rostow looked at the entire process of industrial development and identified the basic stages through which it moved. McClelland examined national motivation in an attempt to quantify and identify the cultural factors that govern objectives and thus tend to control the rate of progress with which an industrial system develops.

From the synthesis of these authors' ideas comes an interaction as all six patterns evolve together—with the economy developing from stage to stage, firms evolving with it, entrepreneurs changing function and roles in response to changes in the system and as a means to hurrying its evolution, and with overall cultural values modifying the driving force behind the whole. Since the evolution of the industrial system is the sum of the efforts of individual firms directed by individual management groups and carried out by individual employee groups, the operation of each individual business enterprise is both conditioned by the evolution of the system and incorporated as a part of the force for shaping it.

Changes in the Workplace

The economic development process is keyed into the premise that willing workers will accomplish the production of goods and services necessary for economic growth. However, the equation between work and willing workers is no longer quite so simple. Many changes have occurred and are still occurring in jobs and work, and at least three deserve discussion here. These are equality of opportunity, automation, and the demand for meaningful work.

The Demand for Meaningful Work

The Monitor Organization conducts an annual survey of U.S. public attitudes, values, lifestyles, and beliefs.[7] One of the clear-cut and rising trends reported over the last several years has been the increasing support of a value called the desire for meaningful work. Concurrently, there has been rising business and academic concern with the problem of job satisfaction. This problem has been highlighted as an issue in the labor troubles at GM's new Vega assembly plant in Lordstown, Ohio, and carried as a major theme through several important books, of which *Work in America* is perhaps the most notable.[8]

The industrial system is facing a crisis because of the workers' tendency to rebel against jobs that are boring and the workers' demands for jobs with some substance from which they can derive more satisfaction. When examined from a distance, the requests seem reasonable; several experiments in redesigning jobs to permit an individual to complete a major subassembly or to identify with a team that shares the entire assembly task have been quite successful. A key question is why this should gain attention only now, since many of the same jobs have been staffed with little complaint for years.

For an explanation, it is desirable to refer to basic motivation theory and, in particular, to the work of Abraham Maslow.[9] In his analysis of human needs and motivation, Maslow defined a hierarchy of needs. (See Figure 4.2.) The most basic

Figure 4.2   Maslow's Hierarchy of Needs

| Self-actualization |
| Ego needs |
| Social needs |
| Security needs |
| Physiological needs |

[7]The Yankelovich Monitor, Yankelovich, Skelly & White, Inc., New York, New York.

[8]U.S. Department of Health, Education, and Welfare, *Work in America: Report of a Special Task Force to the Secretary of Health, Education, and Welfare* (Cambridge, Mass.: MIT Press, 1973).

[9]Abraham Maslow, *Motivation and Personality* (New York: Harper & Row, 1954).

needs requiring satisfaction are the fundamental physiological needs, such as hunger and thirst. Then comes the need for security, for freedom from unusual jeopardy. On the third level are the social needs—the need to be part of a group and to have a place of acceptance in society. The fourth level includes ego needs—the desire to drive an expensive car, "keep up with the Joneses," and show affluence. On the fifth need level is self-actualization or self-fulfillment. At this level, the worker gains internal satisfaction from a job well done; the artisan or professional who has performed well achieves a sense of unusual accomplishment as an internal reward in addition to the recognition and payment that is received from others.

One of Maslow's fundamental points is that only the unfulfilled needs have any degree of motivational value. Thus, a starving person is motivated by the need for food to the exclusion of most other values, whereas the well-fed individual is not. Similarly, those who are secure in their jobs and their positions in society will look primarily to still higher motivations. While individual exceptions to this general motivational pattern do exist, it has considerable validity.

Maslow's hierarchy of needs relates to the demand for meaningful work indirectly in a very important way. In the first days of the Industrial Revolution in England, the work force consisted, to a large degree, of displaced peasants; these people had no place in society and little hope for the future. They faced real risks that extended to the possibility of starving to death if their jobs were taken away. From that time almost until the present, the risk of loss of job has been equated with a very real danger of loss of home and possessions and even of starvation. The value systems of our society have prized and recognized success and have tended to reject those who have met with failure and unemployment as not being worthy members of any community. Thus, the motivation to work has been closely linked with the first three need levels involving fulfillment of physiological needs, needs for security, and needs for a place in a social group.

In the Great Depression of the 1930s the United States began to address seriously the welfare problems created by both employment fluctuations and the changing character of the society. The Social Security Act represented a first major step in a continuing wave of welfare legislation, as emergency relief programs ripened into the social welfare and public assistance programs of today.

By and large, these programs have removed the risk of starvation from the poor in the United States. The exceptions that regrettably still exist affect only relatively small numbers of people; the majority of those in need are provided with food, shelter, and other public assistance. The thrust and intent of these programs is to permit a standard of living that is at least minimally adequate and allows for some dignity so that humiliation can be removed from the role of the welfare recipient. Furthermore, the social value systems have changed sufficiently to permit the welfare recipient a place in society, not only in the eyes of the welfare group but also in the eyes of many others with whom there may be reason to associate.

Throughout the social welfare process, the United States has been systematically removing the motivating value of the three lower levels of Maslow's hierarchy by providing for the physiological, security, and social needs of all of its citizens, whether or not they work. This change may well be in the direction of human progress, but it is bringing a problem in the workplace nonetheless. The timing of the eruption of this problem is probably related to several factors; a key factor seems to be the change in the proportion of workers who have personal memories of the Depression.

After all, young adults often tend to carry their value systems almost unchanged throughout the rest of their lives unless circumstances precipitate a re-evaluation. Most of the workers who experienced the Depression were shaped by it, particularly with respect to the insecurity of possible loss of job. The younger workers who did not experience the Depression tend to have value systems that are less conditioned by respect for traditional authority. As the number of these younger workers has increased and as they have begun to supplant their elders in positions of influence, the attack on traditional job design has become more strident. With no fear motivations stemming from the Depression and with the security of an increasingly effective welfare system, younger workers turn more often to the need for satisfying jobs and increase their demands for meaningful work as the alternative to not working at all.

Thus, it is apparent that the present cry for job satisfaction is an important movement that has only recently reached the threshold of effective public support. (See Figure 4.3.) This movement is not likely to disappear. Much of the routine work in U.S. industry, whether blue collar, clerical, or middle management, will have to be redefined and redesigned to persuade younger people to perform it. While the authorities agree that the human animal is happiest when deeply involved in meaningful activity and while they agree that work can be made sufficiently meaningful to capture these drives (largely the self-actualization drives), the present work situation in many industries cannot meet these tests.

This strident demand for meaningful work is somewhat blunted by weakness in the economy but remains as a long-term demand that must be met. Undoubtedly, the clamor will continue to rise until it is.

Affirmative Action and Equal Employment Opportunity

While good management calls for full utilization of all human resources regardless of race, creed, or color, cultural barriers have made this difficult. In the United States, as in most other countries, the cultural heritage contains sets and biases assigning social roles according to sex or color and providing barriers to association between different cultures or different subgroups within a culture. For example, the continuing turmoil in northern Ireland illustrates the depth of hatred and discrimination that has grown up between two groups with almost identical racial, linguistic, and cultural heritage; the religious difference provided the original schism.

Here in the United States the country is engaged in a serious effort to root such prejudices out of its employment practices and out of many other portions of society. This drive, which has had a turbulent history, has brought racial integration at least at the lower levels of most industrial plants. It is now focusing on equality of opportunity for advancement of minority groups and for both employment and advancement opportunities for women.

This drive has the support of federal law and of many activist groups representing both minorities and women. Using the existing statutes as affirmed by several Supreme Court decisions, its national position as an important purchaser of goods

Figure 4.3   Value Systems in the Work Force

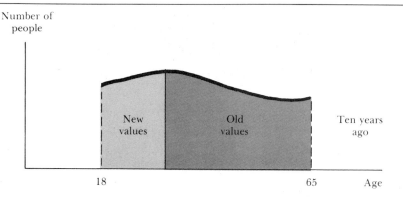

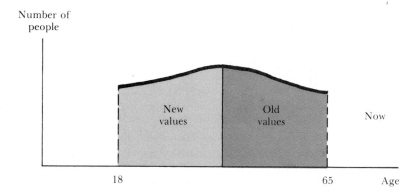

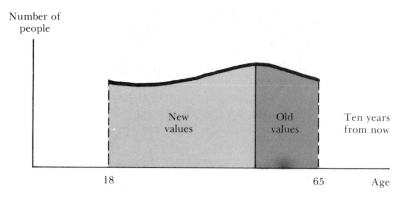

With time, the old values pass away.

and services, and its power as the overseer of all businesses engaged in interstate commerce, the federal government has requested affirmative action goals from each firm. These goals project the anticipated progress in the next several years in attaining a satisfactory balance of minority and female employees at all levels in business and in all types of jobs.

As pressure is applied to firms that lag in meeting these goals, additional turmoil can be expected. First, although the pattern for minority hiring and promotion has been established, continued enforcement pressure will be necessary in some areas to carry this pattern to a conclusion. Second, the adjustment in the social and cultural structure of management practices as women are given a share in management will be difficult in most management settings; the supply of qualified candidates is small for the need, and the program has already slackened in its early phases.

Managements have made goal commitments that are challenging to meet. Qualified job candidates must be found and trained, and this takes time. When the time has passed and the goals remain, the problem will be to find expedient ways to comply with the goals. If management begins to bypass qualified male candidates to promote less qualified female and minority candidates, other troubles will result; already incidents of this type have been reported. The reaction of those who are overlooked and their families is predictable and could bring intense disturbances in middle management ranks.

None of these problems affect the equity of the basic situation or the good management requirements for full use of human resources, but they may well have impact on many employment and promotion decisions in the next several years.

Automation

After World War II it seemed obvious that the technical progress during the war could be translated into changes in work methods that were so fundamental that a new term was even coined to describe them. Although the entire history of the Industrial Revolution has been one of rapid change in work methods and rapid increase in personal productivity, a discontinuity in this trend was predicted and named *automation*. A great surge forward in mechanization, automated control, and job displacement seemed assured.

Automation was heavily oversold, not in terms of its importance but in terms of its time of impact, particularly in the service industries. Steady progress has been obscured by the lack of dramatic change that had been predicted. Instead of a revolution, the evolution in both blue-collar and white-collar work methods has continued steadily and is still progressing as industry extends its use of new methods and of computers and the wide use of computer systems by the general public draws closer.

Automation remains as a major trend in the continuation of the improvement in work methods since the beginning of the Industrial Revolution, although improvement in productivity in the service areas is still lagging. Thus, this trend will continue to cause readjustments that must be absorbed and cushioned and to contribute to the overall increase in the national productivity and level of living.

With the demand for meaningful work tied to equality of opportunity requirements and to continued evolution of work methods, the need for top management attention and participation in the unfolding of these trends is clear. Not only is placement and promotion practice governed by new regulations, but the very structure of the work must also be replanned in many cases to provide a matching of its demands and rewards with the motivations of those who will perform the necessary labors.

The Business Leader: Role and Responsibility

As the primary directing force in the economic process, the business leader is frequently blamed for its failures, is sometimes awarded credit for its successes, and in either case is cast as a powerful influence. At other times, the economic, political, and governmental tides seem to treat the business leader as a pawn who is buffeted unmercifully; one has only to listen to the complaints of the business community to get a picture of the individual business leader as a cork bobbing helplessly on a sea of economic and political turmoil. Between these poles, where is the balance? Clearly, the answer conditions the degree to which the business leader can be held responsible for the results of business impacts on the surrounding world.

An indication of the way that individual executives have been related by society to the growth and prosperity of the business system is found in the way that business leaders have been portrayed in American fiction.[10] It is interesting that they have not been portrayed more often, considering their pivotal role. This omission is an important commentary that poses the question of why so few novelists have taken major business leaders as protagonists and studied the evolving facets of their careers. Obviously, business leadership is either not a subject that interests the reading public sufficiently or not an area that offers a fulfilling challenge to most novelists.

Nonetheless, there are a number of novels about business leaders, ranging from classic commentaries on the business system to more recent novels about individuals acting within the system, such as Frederick Wakeman's *The Hucksters* and Sloan Wilson's *The Man in the Gray Flannel Suit*. In *Babbitt* Sinclair Lewis pictured the sometimes pitiful struggles of a businessman trying to find a comfortable living within the confines of the business world. *Executive Suite* and *Cash McCall* (both by Cameron Hawley) give a more positive view of the role of the business leader, as do the Ayn Rand novels. Mark Twain's *A Connecticut Yankee in King Arthur's Court* portrays a very active entrepreneur, but not in an organizational context. Perhaps the best example of the leadership role is Frank Cowperwood, the titan of Drieser's famous trilogy *(The Financier, The Titan,* and *The Stoic)*. This figure created a business empire and manipulated it to his own ends; clearly, he placed himself above the system and used it for his own purposes.

Which is the more familiar role of the business leader, that of Cowperwood the

---

[10]For a more extensive analysis, see Henry Nash Smith, "The Search for a Capitalist Hero," in Earl F. Cheit, ed., *The Business Establishment* (New York: Wiley, 1964), pp. 77–112.

titan or of Babbitt the follower? A few contemporary examples may serve to show that both types exist.

Some of today's business leaders are active forces that are credited with shaping their environment. Such men as Harold Geneen of ITT, the electronics industry magnate H. Ross Perot, of Texas and Wall Street, and the automotive industry's Henry Ford II, who is a national figure among business leaders, appear to be able to shape their companies and their environments to a significant extent. On the passive side, even Ford and ITT must respond to a change in price legislation, social security taxation, or affirmative action regulations; in fact, the heads of many businesses, particularly the smaller ones, find it easiest to assume a passive role and complain about being buffeted by the system.

The truth, as usual, is at a point between the extremes. Any business and any business leader must live within the broad framework set by the laws and the state of the society. Yet innovations, which affect the fabric of the economy profoundly, only come to pass because various entrepreneurial business leaders see a potential, develop it, and reshape that sector of the economy as the innovation has its effect on the system.

A business leader must develop a basic pattern of operation within the established business system and therefore is at the system's mercy to that extent at least. The more imaginative and innovative leaders also have the opportunity to introduce new practices, new products, and new approaches to business problems; such applications, if successful, can reshape the boundaries within which that business must work. Examples vary, but include everything from Henry Ford's pattern-setting wage increase to five dollars per day in 1914 and Avon's successful development of door-to-door consumer sales to the creation of new consumer markets for aluminum foil via Reynolds Wrap and for plastic sheeting via Dow's Saran Wrap.

While natural progress in the building of the industrial system often has depended significantly on the imagination, ability, and charisma of individual business leaders, society's attitude toward and recognition of these leaders has changed. In the colonial and Revolutionary War era, business leaders such as Thomas Hancock and Stephen Girard were applauded as national heroes; their material success was interpreted as evidence of the magnitude of their virtue and of their contribution to society. Today few business leaders are able to tap any comparable reserve of public approval. Polaroid's Edwin Land, whose inventions and acumen gave the nation both a new type of camera and a major industrial company, is neither particularly well known nor respected outside his local area, except by fellow members of the business and scientific community.

The factors that caused so few novels to be built around the struggle of a protagonist who is a business leader would appear to relate to the lack of appeal of such struggles to the popular imagination, even in the earlier years when the accomplishments of a Cornelius Vanderbilt or Andrew Mellon attracted public acclaim. Now the basis for this acclaim has faded away and has been replaced by a widespread cynicism about the contribution and behavior of the business community. This significant change is reflected in the attitudes with which various public groups respond to problems or to overtures from business firms and business leaders.

Summary

One purpose of this review has been to establish the economic and historical importance of business leaders as catalysts in the past and future development of our society, which can be contrasted with the weakness of their public image, particularly in the present. While there is no disputing the role that the industrial system has had in building our society and the importance that the contributions of business leadership, both individually and collectively, have made to this past achievement, today's society is more aware of the unsolved industrial problems.

The workplace is slowly changing in response to society's demands for safe and meaningful work. Pollution is being curbed under the force of new public laws. Industrial practices ranging from illegal political campaign contributions to collusive pricing and unsupported advertising claims are under public pressure for reform. Society is pressing the business community in so many areas for proper compliance with proper standards of behavior that it is easier for the public to view business management as the natural opponent of all proper public causes. Examples of this view are far too prevalent.

The business leader has been and must continue to be the main director of the forces of growth and progress that constitute the national engine of economic development because this route is the one by which the development process moves forward and by which an individual firm can prosper. The incentives for success represent the best pattern yet devised for offsetting the risks and failures of a changing business environment. However, at the same time, the national attitude toward growth is changing. Population is beginning to stabilize, resources cannot be wasted, and the environment must be protected. Future growth will be more closely directed and controlled by society and will call for new and imaginative applications of modern technology. Economic growth could be stopped, but too many of today's industrial problems would remain unsolved. The role of the business leader is to continue to press forward in what is an increasingly difficult environment.

Corporate management and, in fact, the managements of all organizations are now faced with new challenges from society in an atmosphere that is skeptical and even cynical toward management's attempts to respond. Thus, business management's own understanding of its role is more imperative than in the past if these crucial relationships are to be successfully managed with the support of society.

One of the principal challenges presented to the business system is that it must become responsible if it is to merit society's support. This request is not frivolous, but the earnestness of the challenge does not provide specific details as to meaning or necessary response. Management's present role requires a working definition of its interrelationship with society and an understanding of the nature, cost, and implication of the many sorts of potential corporate responses. This book will turn next to an examination of the origin and nature of these demands for social responsibility in preparation for a later consideration of their justification and possible satisfaction.

This chapter has summarized several viewpoints of economic progress and development and suggested both their synthesis and their governance by the national value systems our culture has evolved. As these value systems develop, they are requiring a more fundamental organization of the workplace to provide motivation and a fairer, better use of human resources. These developments are occurring at a time in which society is increasingly challenging corporate impacts and in which the self-interest of business leaders is served by stimulating remedial action to avoid such confrontations.

Questions for Analysis and Discussion

1. Try to find an example of a company whose change in corporate strategy has resulted in an internal structural change (for example, a company may have shifted to a different organizational pattern).

2. Can you associate some major industrial innovations with the prosperity of a company? An industry? A country? Discuss.

3. If the value systems that are taught to children correlate with the economic productivity and general prosperity of the country, what will happen in the next thirty years in the United States? Will the desire for affluence and the good life be sufficient to maintain the living standard over this period of time? Or will Americans prefer to manage with less?

4. Do you see the demand for meaningful work as constituting an important issue in society? What will be the social impact of this attitude on business? Will it be greater in offices or in factories? Discuss.

5. Consider the statement: Only the unfulfilled needs motivate. If you agree with this statement, do you see it as being relevant to the relationship between a corporation and its employees? Discuss.

6. How serious are the stresses caused by full integration of women and minorities into business firms at all levels and in all job categories? Give examples. What can be done to ease the strain caused by this process?

7. Do you see the average business manager as being a controlling force or a functionary buffeted by the system? Illustrate.

8. What should business do now to rebuild its image and credibility with the public?

For Further Information

Chandler, Alfred Dupont. *Strategy and Structure*. Garden City, N.Y.: Doubleday, 1962.

Maslow, Abraham. *Motivation and Personality*. New York: Harper & Row, 1954.

"Public Images of the American Executive," Special Issue. *Journal of Contemporary Business* University of Washington, Autumn 1976.

Schumpeter, Joseph. *The Theory of Economic Development*, trans. Redvers Opie. Oxford: Oxford University Press, 1961.

U.S. Department of Health, Education, and Welfare. *Work in America: Report of a Special Task Force to the Secretary of Health, Education, and Welfare*. Cambridge, Mass.: MIT Press, 1973.

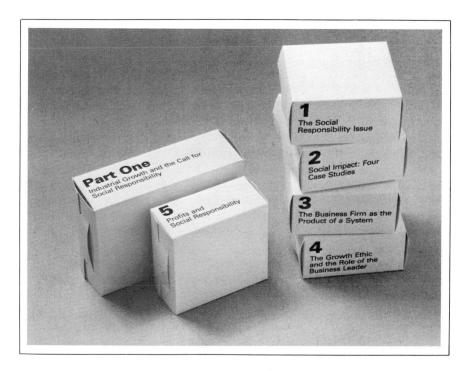

Part One — Industrial Growth and the Call for Social Responsibility

5 — Profits and Social Responsibility

1 The Social Responsibility Issue

2 Social Impact: Four Case Studies

3 The Business Firm as the Product of a System

4 The Growth Ethic and the Role of the Business Leader

5
Profits and Social Responsibility

The concept of corporate social responsibility has evolved over many years; a review of the evolution suggests some of the strengths and weaknesses of the concept's linkage to the economic purpose of the corporation. In a climate of change and with increasing pressure to cushion or ameliorate any negative consequences of corporate operations for society, popular support has been growing for the need to demand specific performance of corporate social responsibility in terms of one or more of its many definitions.

Both the amorphous nature of the corporate social responsibility concept and its broadening base of support are important considerations, and one of the tasks here is to relate them to guidelines that business leaders can apply to corporate management action. This chapter will provide some of the necessary background for that task.

An industrial revolution less than two hundred years old has allowed business to circumvent checks on power—and requirements of responsibility—as old as our civilization. . . . today's corporate responsibility movement is . . . an historical swing to recreate the social contract of power with responsibility, and as such may become the most important . . . reform of our time.[1]

NICHOLAS N. EBERSTADT

Emergence of the Social Responsibility Concept

As nationalism grew after the Renaissance, the new nation-states discovered that the proper pattern of commercial and economic ties served to unify and strengthen the state. Mercantilists sought to obtain this pattern through strict regulation of commerce and industry. Rather than relying on any sense of responsibility among traders and manufacturers, the mercantilists favored careful governmental control of all trade.

Adam Smith articulated and crystallized a growing opposition to mercantilism; in particular, he argued strongly for free trade and a legal framework within which individuals could follow their own self-interest. This was his famous doctrine of the invisible hand.[2]

Smith recognized the paramount obligation of the government to look after the general good and anticipated that the rights of private property might sometimes have to be sacrificed[3] and that government might have to provide aid to specific branches of commerce in the interests of advancing this general good.[4] Smith did not discuss any social responsibility of business but did define the freedom to pursue self-interest (and identified its relationship to the general good) as occurring within the framework of a nation that was governed by law and in which standards for moral conduct had been developed.[5] Thus, Smith's concept of free enterprise, which later became the prototype of the laissez-faire economic pattern, involved considerable

---

[1]Nicholas N. Eberstadt, "What History Tells Us about Corporate Responsibility," *Business and Society Review/Innovation* no. 7 (Autumn 1973): 76.

[2]Adam Smith, *An Inquiry into the Nature and Causes of the Wealth of Nations*, vol. 2 (Homewood, Ill.: Richard D. Irwin, 1963), p. 29.

[3]Ibid., pp. 136–137.

[4]Ibid., pp. 246–247.

[5]His first major work was devoted to the principles underlying this moral conduct: Adam Smith, *Theory of Moral Sentiments* (New York: Augustus M. Kelley, 1966).

economic freedom within a strong legal and moral framework and also permitted and acknowledged some governmental guidance of the economic system.

As the Industrial Revolution gained momentum, both companies and factories grew larger. Adam Smith had looked at individual self-interested business leaders and had judged the whole range of their competition to be not only healthy but also superior to monopoly control by the great trading companies. However, competition among larger enterprises began to have other implications. Variations of employment as business prosperity fluctuated caused shifts in the supply and demand for labor to which individual workers were not able to adjust. As the growth of factories continued, child labor practices, long hours, and bad working conditions reached a level of concentration and prominence that was sufficient to cause strong doubt that the profit-seeking self-interest of the business community always guaranteed the general good.

The type of competition that Smith had envisioned soon ceased to be representative. The very existence of large industrial empires brought a different kind of market. Combinations in restraint of trade resulted in new laws. While these laws controlled some of the worst abuses, they did not prevent the change to a new type of competitive environment.

Early Proponents

Among the thinkers who began to articulate a revised philosophy for the operation of a business was Henry Lawrence Gantt.

> With the increasing complexity in the modern business system (on which modern civilization depends) successful operation can be obtained only by following the lead of those who understand practically the controlling forces, and are willing to recognize their social responsibility in operating them.

John Maurice Clark put it this way:

> The world is familiar enough with the conception of social responsibilities. These do not need to be rediscovered. . . . But, the fact that a large part of them are business' responsibilities has not yet penetrated, and this fact does need to be brought home to a community in which businessmen and theoretical economics alike are still shadowed by the fading umbra of laissez-faire.[7]

As time passed, these concepts received more attention. Bowen contributed his summary and analysis. Because Bowen's book on social responsibilities was a pioneering analysis of the social responsibility problem, it served as a point of departure from which much of the later literature divided into two schools of thought.

---

[6]H. L. Gantt, *Organizing for Work* (New York: Harcourt, Brace & Howe, 1919), p. 105.
[7]J. M. Clark, "The Changing Basis of Economic Responsibility," *The Journal of Political Economy* 23, no. 3 (March 1916): 429.

The roots of both may be seen in the definitions on which Bowen based his work.

> The term *social responsibilities of businessmen* . . . refers to the obligation of businessmen to pursue those policies, to make those decisions, or to follow those lines of action which are desirable in terms of the objectives and values of our society.
>
> The term *doctrine of social responsibility* refers to the idea . . . that voluntary assumption of social responsibility by business is, or might be, the practical means to ameliorating economic problems and attaining more fully the economic goals we seek.[8]

Bowen's definition of social responsibilities leaves unclear the relationship between the obligations it represents and the economic obligations of business managers. The doctrine of social responsibility is normative and calls for voluntary assumption of the obligations that are ". . . desirable in terms of the objectives and values of our society." There is no qualification to indicate how these obligations are to be reconciled with the economic constraints on the business and no requirement that these obligations meet economic tests.

Current Interpretations

The conflict of priority between economic and noneconomic obligations is now represented by conflicting points of view about which type of obligation should be paramount in order for society's needs to be best served by the business system.

One point of view has developed a concept of business managers as trustees managing social assets in the interest of the whole. Within this framework, economics and the profit motive are important but not primary. The implication is that business must do well enough to survive, either through profit or subsidy; within this constraint, business will operate for the good of the whole, more or less regardless of immediate profits. Goyder has developed this concept and its potential application to industry in England.[9] His ideas have also provided the central orientation for a major seminar on social responsibility in India.[10]

The trusteeship concept involves a basic modification of the private enterprise system that most frequently calls for bringing broad representation of various social interests into the enterprise's board of directors and guiding the operation to satisfy public needs. This modification represents a compromise between private enterprise capitalism and state capitalism as it might be practiced in a socialist country. By maintaining the structure of private enterprise capitalism with representation of investors and stockholders and their participation in the decision-making process, the private nature of the business organization is partially retained. By giving other sectors of the interested public a major voice in the operation of the enterprise, a

---

[8]Howard R. Bowen, *Social Responsibilities of the Businessman* (New York: Harper & Brothers, 1953) p. 6.

[9]George Goyder, *The Responsible Company* (Oxford: Basil Blackford & Mott, 1951).

[10]India International Center, *Social Responsibilities of Business* (Bombay: Manaktalas, 1966).

basic socialistic focus, in terms of public control of a means of production, is assured. Many English, Indian, and also American writers have favored this approach, which supersedes the economics of business with a socially defined operating constraint.

The reaction against acknowledgment of any social responsibilities by business has been precipitated primarily by these various normative or trusteeship forms. Along with Friedman and others, Levitt has strongly stated the position of those who believe that business must operate under economic constraints or change its own basic nature; however, those in this school of thought do not favor such a change.[11] This approach does not directly deny social responsibility but insists that social responsibility cannot supersede the need for profits to fund an industrial society.

Examining the issue, one can recognize its implications. If business has basic responsibilities for the welfare of society, then management's authority to take the necessary action must be paired with the responsibility for discharging the action; any institution with such authority over the welfare of society not only forms a part of but ultimately must also be controlled by its government.

If business is responsible for ameliorating poverty and improving the conditions in an inner-city ghetto, for example, a meaningful program must be instituted to motivate the inhabitants of the ghetto area to change and redirect their lives. Good programs could offer incentives to the people who joined and an opportunity to participate in the planning and benefits. Eventually, however, there must be a level of social compulsion and control so that the plan will proceed as buildings are renovated or replaced and tenants are relocated. Even city governments and social welfare agencies have difficulty in making nonvoluntary portions of such programs run smoothly. So the concept that involves a private corporation taking this sort of direct social action will inevitably be repugnant to those directly affected. In federal, state, and city programs the cry is for community control to bring the program details under the direct guidance and approval of local leaders. Thus, if corporations attempt to take responsibilities in social action areas, they must attempt to exert authority in these areas to accomplish their responsibilities. And if corporations do this, they put themselves in the path of the local political forces, which must then either repel the corporate advance or bring the corporation under the direct control of the community so that it ceases to be a private business at all. Such social involvement is seen as being both intrinsically incompatible with private business and unnecessary where business is already under public ownership.

The Existence of the Corporation in Society

The specific problem that gives root to much of the discussion about social responsibility is the potential for a business in the course of its operation to cause hardship or damage to society or to individuals in such a way that costs are neither identified nor compensated by the business. Thus, the injury to a community that occurs when a major plant closes and the loss in value of a residential area that results from chemical plant odors are rarely compensated by the responsible

---

[11]Theodore Levitt, "The Dangers of Social Responsibility," *Harvard Business Review* 36, no. 5 (September–October 1958): 41–50.

industry. However, uncompensated losses or expenses experienced by society as a result of a business operation or the sale of a product are true economic costs of the responsible business. The nature of the underlying relationship between a business corporation and society tends to create a conflict if these costs go unrecognized in the long run.

The nature of this relationship stems from the origin and purpose of the corporate form of business. A private business corporation is chartered for the purpose of conducting a commercial enterprise; it is a legal entity with an economic purpose. From Chief Justice John Marshall's classic definition:

> A corporation is an artificial being, invisible, intangible, and existing only in contemplation of the law. Being the mere creature of the law, it possesses only those properties which the charter of its creation confers upon it. . . . Among the most important are immortality, and . . . individuality; properties, by which a perpetual succession of many persons are considered the same, and may act as a single individual.[12]

The opportunity for a group of people to create an artificial legal entity called a corporation is largely a function of laws that have been enacted since the Industrial Revolution. At one time the privilege of incorporation was rare and unusual. The nineteenth century was well advanced before a corporation could be formed in the United States without the passage of a specific law by a state legislature approving a charter for that corporation. Incorporation was made easier as the corporate form of business became more and more important to industrial progress. "The corporations were organized in the public interest of increasing the production of wealth more than could be done by separated individuals."[13]

Simple as it now is to form such an entity, this business form is only possible because of laws permitting the existence of corporations and defining their rights and duties. A business corporation has an economic purpose, however, and must make a profit to survive in the long run; one authority has said that the first duty of the corporation is to make a satisfactory profit.[14]

Underlying this necessary drive for profits is the fact that a corporation exists by the consent and sufferance of society. This consent is usually very passive, and the underlying social rights are often forgotten.[15] But these rights are valid, and corporate existence is dependent in the long run on the continuing public belief that society receives benefits from the existence and functioning of the corporate form: "The

---

[12]The Trustees of Dartmouth College v. Woodward, 4 Wheat. (U.S.) 518, 636 (1819).

[13]John R. Commons, *The Economics of Collective Action* (New York: Macmillan, 1951), p. 132.

[14]Peter F. Drucker, *The Practice of Management* (New York: Harper & Brothers, 1954), pp. 46–47.

[15]The President of McKesson & Robbins has said: "Some businessmen have not realized that the ultimate survival of private economic institutions must rest in the ability of such institutions to demonstrate clearly that they render society a greater service than could any alternative institutional framework." Herman C. Nolen, "Consultation: Are Profits and Social Responsibility Compatible?" *Business Horizons* 2, no. 2 (Summer 1959): 57.

business had its foundation in service, and as far as the community is concerned has no reason for existence except the service it can render."[16]

Irresponsible use of corporate power often infringes on the rights and privileges of other segments of society.[17] Where such infringement has become important in the eyes of the general public, corporate power has been restrained. Widespread rural anger channeled through the local Grange organizations led finally to restrictions on railroad power in many states. The resulting Granger laws in the states and the Interstate Commerce Commission Act at the federal level resulted directly from irresponsible use of railroad power. Abuses of the labor force through poor wages, hours, and working conditions led to child labor laws, limitations on the work week, and legislation establishing the rights of employees to unionize.

None of these legislative remedies occurred at the time that the abuse started; in all these instances the abuse of power occurred repeatedly and persisted to the point where public attention was finally aroused, political forces were stirred, and action resulted. In several cases the initial action was not effective. The Granger laws were declared unconstitutional and the first Interstate Commerce Commission was almost powerless, but public pressure continued until an effective law was passed to regulate the railroads. Sometimes such laws have had unanticipated effects. Because of the nature of the legislative process and of the processes by which public opinion brings political action, laws are not always well written. They may have unpredictable interpretations, carry punitive or vindictive overtones, or simply over-regulate in an area that has been neglected.

The general pattern seems to be that abuse of power (in this case corporate power) may go on for an indeterminate period of time until the interaction of public awareness and political forces is sufficient to effect corrective action. Some issues seem to go unnoticed for a long period of time; others are fanned to a white heat rapidly. Sometimes a slumbering issue provides an excellent vehicle for the ambitious public figure who can champion overdue reform and capture a ground swell of public sentiment.

Wherever corporate power is being abused in a systematic way, eventual termination of this abuse by public action seems certain, but the timing of that action is difficult to predict. On one hand, some issues grow slowly until people perceive an abuse to exist and then rebel against it; examples of such issues are air pollution and unsafe automobiles, which were previously considered to be inconsequential. On the other hand, the issue of mercury pollution of sea food brought immediate action in the United States and Canada.

Abuses of corporate power represent a failure to match the power to act, decide, and influence with the responsibility to use this power to promote the overall good of the firm and of the society that permits the firm to exist. By definition these abuses are infringements on the rights and privileges of others or of society as a whole. In a

---

[16]H. L. Gantt, *Organizing for Work* (New York: Harcourt, Brace and Howe, 1919), p. 5.

[17]Keith Davis has said that "social responsibilities of businessmen arise from the amount of social power they have. . . . Those who do not take responsibility for their power ultimately shall lose it." Keith Davis, "Understanding the Social Responsibility Puzzle," *Business Horizons* 10, no. 4 (Winter 1967): 48–49.

true economic sense, the abuses often represent costs that have not been recognized and attributed directly to a firm and that are left for society to bear.

Society has begun more and more to anticipate that corporations will abuse their powers. While corporations should act responsibly, activist groups expect that they will not and position themselves as watchdogs that maintain pressure and stand ready to pose a serious threat to corporate interests whenever the public interest seems to require such intervention. To some extent, these groups feel obliged to bully the corporation continually, whether or not there is cause; they must constantly re-establish their potential to curb corporate actions. As Ralph Nader put it: "Yes, I have a theory of power: that if it's going to be responsible, it has to be insecure; it has to have something to lose."[18]

Profits Versus Social Costs

In recent years this issue of social responsibility has intruded increasingly into the management processes of business corporations. The social responsibility of a business has been closely linked with its profits, but the virtue and the thrust of this linkage is controversial. The essence of the conflict in viewpoints is over the nature and priority of business profits. Profit has been a basic concept in our society for a long time.

> The material framework of modern civilization is the industrial system, and the directing force which animates this framework is business enterprise. To a greater extent than any other known phase of culture, modern Christendom takes its complexion from its economic organization. . . . Its characteristic features, and at the same time the forces by virtue of which it dominates modern culture, are the machine process and investment for a profit.[19]

Because of its role in governing the economic system, profit is a dominant characteristic of our industrial civilization.

> Profit discharges a function essential to the success if not the survival of any industrial society. The profitability must be the criteria of all responsible business decisions, whether the society is organized among free enterprise, socialist, fascist, or communist lines.[20]

While different societies have different arrangements for the ownership of capital and the use of business profits, the need for profit and its importance as a measuring standard is almost beyond argument. Thus, Friedman argued that the overwhelming

---

[18]Ralph Nader, as quoted by Eileen Shanahan in "Reformer Urges Business Change," *New York Times,* 24 January 1971. Copyright © 1971 by The New York Times Company. Reprinted by permission.

[19]Thorstein Veblen, *The Theory of Business Enterprise* (New York: Mentor, 1958), p. 7.

[20]Peter F. Drucker, "The Function of Profits," *Fortune* 39, no. 3 (March 1949): 110.

role of profit was (1) a guarantee of business survival for the benefit of dependent groups and (2) a contribution toward the overall functioning of the industrial economy. He made the achievement of profits the entire responsibility of the business.[21]

Friedman's statement drew this response from the President of the Bank of America:

> Just making a profit isn't enough by itself. . . . Either we choose intelligent evolution for the corporate enterprise, permitting it to be responsive to social challenges. Or we can expect something more drastic imposed by others.[22]

Clearly, profits are necessary, but the income statement may not tell the whole story. A Jones & Laughlin steel executive summarized as follows:

> Without a reasonable assurance of profits the businessman could not long continue as a businessman. But there is more to his responsibility than profits. Perhaps it can be summarized by saying that he has an obligation to keep alive and healthy the goose which lays the golden eggs.[23]

Drucker expressed the idea this way:

> The enterprise must operate at an adequate profit—this is its first social responsibility as well as its first duty toward itself and its workers.[24]

Profits are defined as the excess of returns over expenditures or, more commonly, as revenue less costs. Revenue or income is usually known, but the size of the resulting profit also depends on the costs that are subtracted. Although many costs are objectively measurable, others involve allocations that, by their very nature, may be somewhat arbitrary; examples are the depreciation allocation for replacement of capital and the depletion allowance for consumption of wasting assets. Other debits to society that may be caused by the firm, such as the social cost of a polluted stream, have no accepted profit value as yet and no imputed effect on the reported profits. Thus, the commonly accepted profit value can become somewhat uncertain when matched against such recognized but unvalued areas of cost.

It will be argued here that the uneasy relationship between social responsibility and

---

[21]Milton Friedman, "The Social Responsibility of Business Is to Increase Its Profits," *New York Times Magazine,* 13 September 1970; see also Milton Friedman, *Capitalism and Freedom* (Chicago: Phoenix Books, University of Chicago Press, 1962), pp. 133–136.

[22]A. W. Clausen, "The Corporate Evolution," speech before the Greater Los Angeles Chamber of Commerce, 1970–1971, Business Outlook Conference, Biltmore Hotel, Los Angeles, Calif., 20 October 1970, as printed by the Los Angeles Chamber of Commerce, pp. 13–15.

[23]Admiral Ben Moreell, "The Role of Business in American Social Progress," speech before the Indiana State Chamber of Commerce, Indianapolis, Ind., 1956, as printed by the Indiana State Chamber of Commerce, pp. 16–17.

[24]Peter F. Drucker, *The Practice of Management* (New York: Harper & Brothers, 1954), p. 271.

Figure 5.1 True versus Apparent Profit

Profits equal revenues less reported expenses; the difference appears to be *profit*.	Where corporate actions are injuring society, social costs could be subtracted in determining true profit.	Where new laws require compensation for injuries to society, expenses are increased and uncompensated social costs decreased; if the legislation is well written, true profits will be unchanged.

profit has its roots in the nature of the concepts of cost and, therefore, of profit. Profits are residual after costs. In addition to the direct and allocated costs that are now recognized by the accounting profession, another class of costs is truly attributable to the business enterprise. The costs that are not paid and are left for society to bear become social costs. Figure 5.1 suggests the potential shift from understated costs and overstated profits when social costs are ignored to a truer statement of cost when social costs are partially compensated.

One of the purposes of this work is to explore the extent to which such uncompensated costs are at the core of the need for more social responsibility. The purpose of such exploration and analysis is to develop guidelines for management action in the present and suggest the probable future evolution of these guidelines as laws are changed and new social standards develop.

The thrust of these guidelines is toward achieving a balance that must be maintained between the corporation and society in each major area of their interaction. This balance is required by the self-interest of both the corporation and society and, if maintained, tends to free the corporation from other constraints on economic performance so that profit-oriented and socially acceptable operating policies can again become congruent.

After all, the corporation is a powerful force with profound potential for having both good and bad impacts on the surrounding society, which, in turn, governs its operation. Thus, these many impacts need to be analyzed and understood to construct a basis for developing guidelines for wise, responsible management action.

Summary

The social responsibility concept evolved as the strains and frictions of an imperfect operation of the industrial system accumulated in society. The concept evolved out of efforts to define more clearly the relationship between corporation and society in the interest of the general welfare.

As social responsibility was defined, some translated the definition as a requirement for public intervention in management processes through trusteeship, public directors, or other steps in the direction of a more socialistic philosophy of capitalism. Others argued for retention of the private nature of private enterprise, which requires a continuing profit focus. However, since the profit calculation requires a definition of costs, a profit-focused organization could still be required to acknowledge social costs, and such costs are at the core of many of the strains and frictions that initiated the interest in social responsibility. This relationship between social costs and social responsibility will be explored at some length in the following chapters.

This chapter has reviewed the origins of both the social responsibility concept and the acceptability of the corporate form of business. While a corporation is an exclusively economic entity, its existence depends on receiving continuing approval from the rule-making society. Thus, the demands for social action from that same society cannot be lightly put aside even if they are incompatible with economic performance. Instead, they need to be translated into terms that are compatible with social needs and with the intrinsic nature and capabilities of the corporate form.

Questions for Analysis and Discussion

1. How do you reconcile profit motives with the pressures of business obligations to society? Consider Friedman's statement: "The social responsibility of business is to increase its profits." Do you agree? What exceptions, if any, should be made?

2. Assume that a business wishes to spend money on the betterment of the community and discuss how the management of the business could set out to achieve specific positive objectives without interfering in the community or its social processes or abridging the rights of any individual.

3. List as many of the different kinds of impacts from corporate action on society as you can. Discuss their relative significance. Which do you see as being proper? Which do you consider as representing abuses of corporate power?

4. Add to the list in question 3 any second- or third-order effects of the original actions that you have classified as proper, that is, any further impacts resulting from the impacts already listed.

5. Divide the list of impacts developed for question 4 into those for which the corporation should be responsible for the consequences and those for which it should not. Can you determine any useful boundary for the corporate responsibility?

For Further Information

Chamberlain, Neil. *The Limits of Corporate Responsibility.* New York: Basic Books, 1973.

Davis, Keith, and Blomstrom, Robert. *Business, Society and Environment,* 3rd ed. New York: McGraw-Hill, 1975.

Farmer, Richard N., and Pogue, W. Dickerson, *Corporate Social Responsibility.* Chicago: Science Research Associates, 1973.

Friedman, Milton. *Capitalism and Freedom.* Chicago: University of Chicago Press, 1962.

Goyder, George. *The Responsible Company.* Oxford: Basil, Blackford & Mott, 1951.

Greenwood, William T. *Issues in Business and Society,* 3rd ed. Boston: Houghton Mifflin, 1975.

Hay, Robert D., Gray, Edmund R., and Gates, James E. eds. *Business and Society.* Cincinnati, Ohio: Southwestern, 1976.

Kolasa, Blair. *Responsibility in Business.* Englewood Cliffs, N.J.: Prentice-Hall, 1972.

Kuhn, James W., and Berg, Ivar. *Values in a Business Society.* New York: Harcourt, Brace & World, 1968.

Luthans, Fred, and Hodgetts, Richard M. *Social Issues in Business.* New York: Macmillan, 1972.

McGuire, Joseph W. *Business and Society.* New York: McGraw-Hill, 1973.

Monsen, R. Joseph. *Business and the Changing Environment.* New York: McGraw-Hill, 1973.

Nicholson, Edward A., Litschert, Robert J., and Anthony, Willaim P. *Business Responsibility and Social Issues.* Columbus, Ohio: Charles E. Merrill, 1974.

Steiner, George A. *Business and Society,* 2d ed. New York: Random House, 1975.

Sturdivant, Frederick D. *Business and Society: A Managerial Approach.* Homewood, Ill.: Richard D. Irwin, 1977.

Walton, Scott D. *American Business and Its Environment.* New York: Macmillan, 1966.

Weidenbaum, Murray L. *Business, Government, and the Public.* Englewood Cliffs, N.J.: Prentice-Hall, 1977.

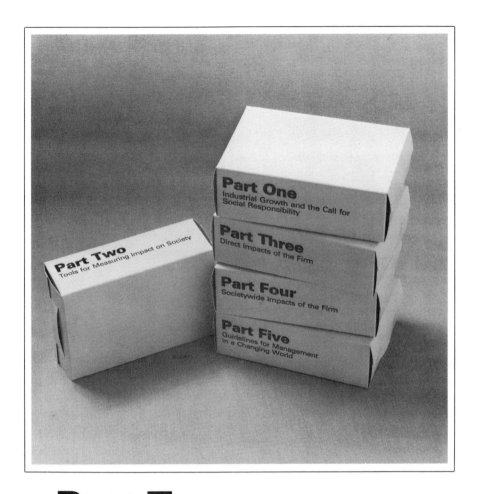

Part Two
Tools for Measuring Impact on Society

Part One briefly reviewed the background to and evolution of our industrial system, the manner in which the stress between business and society has risen to its present level, and the growing demand for "responsible management." A series of contemporary examples of the interaction between corporations and society suggested something of the scope of the corporate impact. Many of these impacts are favorable and reinforce the justification for society's encouragement of the corporate form, but far too many are unfavorable and need management to balance or ameliorate the impact and turn aside a disastrous confrontation with an increasingly angry society.

In presenting a few highlights of the economic and social evolution of industrial growth, Part One showed the individual business firm to be the product of an industrial system. While this system is under a degree of overall social control, its immediate course, industry by industry, can be greatly influenced by the individual imagination and enterprise of business leaders. In the past, their changing levels of ambition and entrepreneurship have correlated closely with the general level of industrial and economic growth.

The other purpose for the historical review was to delineate the change processes that are at work in society, influencing its relationships, value systems, lifestyles, and technologies. These are already changing at a rate unprecedented in recent human experience, and indications are that this rate is still accelerating. Clearly businesses exist within a dynamic society where economic and social forces are already meeting head-on the physical limitations of the environment. Thus the way that corporations cope with the stress between business and society should not only answer past and present problems. The generality and validity of a business's approach to corporate social impact must apply to the underlying relationship with society as well if the stress is not continually to escalate as new problems appear in the future.

Part Two moves on from this interface with the future to explore some of the concepts underlying the principal tools that are used to construct various solutions to the social responsibility problem.

Chapter 6 examines the social audit. Chapter 7 unfolds the concept of social balance as a state of operation in a business that avoids all untoward effects of the business on society. Chapter 8 reviews alternative analytical perspectives and defines the social viewpoint that is used in the discussions of corporate impact and social balance in Parts Three and Four.

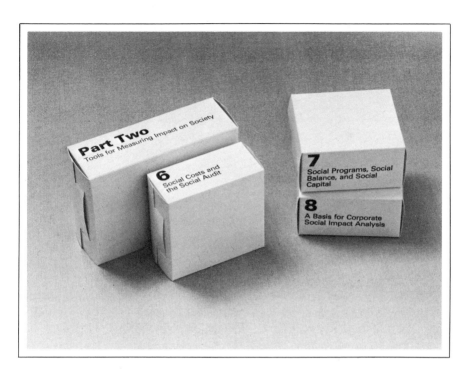

6
Social Costs and
the Social Audit

The concept of social cost is an important one. Several times in Part One it began to emerge as a central theme. Here its origin and development will be reviewed, and its relationship to corporate operations will be explored. The chapter will then examine some of the current efforts to deal with the measurement problems that are created when the possibility of social costs is acknowledged. The principal present effort is directed to the area of social audits. Two audits are presented as examples, together with a review of their concepts and limitations.

You may make money, yes, but you don't know what your efforts cost the community around you. If these costs were added to those costs, it might be that businesses very much in the black now would find themselves in the red—and vice versa.[1]

ADOLPH A. BERLE, JR.

Social Costs

Social costs of the type introduced in Chapter 5 measure the injuries to society that result from corporate action and may be indicative of a lack of social responsibility manifested by these corporations. The size and nature of such costs could become a useful basis for studying this dimension of corporate actions. Thus, it becomes important to consider social cost concepts and the problems accompanying their objective calculation.

Development of the Concept of Social Costs

The idea that identifiable social costs could result from corporate actions emerged only slowly as successive generations of economists struggled to delineate the relationship between individual businesses and society as a whole. In listing the proper grounds for public action to limit business conduct, J. M. Clark included the unpaid costs of industry.

> Such costs occur wherever there are interests which the general system of legal rights does not cover—interests which can be evaded without consent or compensation. Real estate values may be damaged as we have seen, by nuisances or merely by incongruous uses of the joining property. . . . Or the individual may, through sheer lack of bargaining power, be unable to translate his technical legal protection into actual economic protection of an effective sort. . . . In the broadest sense, any general evil resulting from industry has such diffused effects as to fall on innocent parties without compensation, and so comes under this principle. Damages of this sort also occur in the use of air and the ether, and the spread of infections and agricultural pests. The State has an interest in minimizing all such evils.[2]

[1]Adolph A. Berle, Jr., "Company Social Responsibility—Too Much or Not Enough," *Conference Board Record* 1, no. 4 (April 1964): 10.
[2]From p. 178, *Social Control of Business* by John Maurice Clark. Copyright © 1926, University of Chicago. Used with permission of McGraw-Hill Book Company.

Clark linked his list of grounds for public action with a similar list of John Stuart Mill, entitled "Grounds and Limits of Laissez-Faire." In 1848 Mill had dealt with many of the same problems, recognized some of the same necessities, and cited some of the same examples, for instance, the need for regulation of factory hours by the government, particularly in the case of women and children.[3] However, by 1926 Clark found the need to recognize much more explicitly the problem caused by these unpaid costs of industry because the continued development of the industrial economy had brought these issues to the surface in the years that had passed.

Another early exploration of the issues of social cost appeared in the work of Pigou. In *Economics of Welfare*, which was first published in 1920, he distinguishes between marginal *social* and marginal *private* net product. The marginal social net product is "the total net product of physical things or objective services due to the marginal increment of resources in any given use or place, no matter to whom any part of this product may accrue."[4]

His definition of the marginal private net product is the same except that it accrues "to the person responsible for investing resources there. In some conditions this is equal to, in some it is greater than, in others it is less than the marginal social net product."[5]

Although in this instance Pigou did not deal directly with costs, he recognized that the return to society from a given economic action could be different from the return to the individual responsible for that action. The present analysis is focusing on this type of difference, which is termed *social cost* in cases where society is left to bear costs that could more fairly be borne by the business responsible for them.

As an example of Pigou's distinction between the marginal social and private net product, consider the situation in which a company owns a hill of good building stone. The corporate decision to mine this stone and sell it for local construction will be based on the expectation that the added operation will return a profit, that is, that the marginal private net product will be positive. For the local society costs may arise from (1) the inconvenience caused by the noise and dust of blasting, (2) the damage to local roads caused by heavy trucking, and (3) the loss of a local resource (the hill) as it is consumed and finally disappears.

Since society receives benefits from the additional taxes and employment the operation of the quarry represents, as well as from the construction industry that the stone quarry supplies, the balance between additional costs and benefits is not clear without detailed study. However, the marginal social net product will be somewhat different, whether greater or less, than the direct increment of profits to the company operating the quarry. This balance is summarized in Figure 6.1.

The concept of unpaid costs of industry continued to evolve. Approximately two decades after Pigou's study, Bowen dealt with these costs explicitly.

> Costs in the usual sense involve the employment of factors which are capable of various alternative uses. The cost of using a factor is the most valuable alternate satisfaction that is sacrificed because of the fact that the resources

---

[3]John Stuart Mill, *Principles of Political Economy* (New York: Colonial Press, 1900), p. 464.
[4]A. C. Pigou, *The Economics of Welfare* 4th ed. (London: Macmillan, 1960), p. 134.
[5]Ibid., p. 135.

Figure 6.1   Social Versus Private Marginal Net Product

A corporation owns a hill of good building stone. It increases its profits by opening a quarry and beginning to mine and sell the stone.

What does this mean to the local society?

Benefits	Debits
New employment	Consumption of an irreplaceable resource (the hill)
New tax revenue	
Needed supplies for local construction	Loss of a feature of the local scenery
Additional work for the firms providing machinery, maintenance, and other business services to the quarry	Inconvenience from any blasting or dust
	Wear and tear on roads from heavy trucking

The balance is uncertain. Local factors will determine whether or not society benefits from the operation of the quarry. But the net effect on the total society will undoubtedly not be the same as the increase in profits to the corporation. The marginal private and marginal social net profit will not be the same.

---

are allocated to a particular purpose. In a price system, this cost is expressed as a price charged for a factor, the price of a product equal to its cost of production. There are certain other costs, however, which are not easily brought within the price system. These costs which we shall call *social costs*, result in the deterioration of the general environment (within which people live) rather than in the use of specific factors which can be priced.[6]

Bowen provides examples of social costs that occur in connection with both the production of a good and its consumption. In other words, production processes have sometimes been accompanied by uncompensated pollution, and consumption of goods has sometimes been accompanied by uncompensated injuries from faulty or dangerous products. Kapp, in the course of a careful examination of the same area, defines social costs as:

> . . . all direct and indirect losses sustained by third persons or the general public as a result of unrestrained economic activities. These social losses may take the form of damages to human health; they may find their expression in the destruction or deterioration of property values and the premature depletion of natural wealth. They may also be evidenced in an impairment of less tangible values.[7]

Kapp has surveyed the classical economists for an indication of their feeling toward social costs and has identified similiar concepts in the writings of Adam Smith and

---

[6]Howard R. Bowen, *Toward Social Economy* (New York: Rinehart, 1948), pp. 197–198.
[7]William K. Kapp, *Social Costs* (New York: Asia Publishing House, 1962), p. 13.

others.[8] He credits Sismondi with the first systematic recognition of other aspects of social cost concepts and cites Pigou, Hobson, J. M. Clark, Mitchell, and others as predecessors who recognized the nature and problem of social costs. Kapp summarizes in this way:

> The practical implications of social costs can be restated in general terms. Social costs are a common phenomenon within the system of business enterprise. Their neglect seriously interferes with the maximum efficiency in the uses of resources. For this reason, society must be prepared to translate social costs into private costs by political action.[9]

Kapp finds that the use of traditional economic theory based on traditional costs leads to a fictitious profit optimum for economic systems rather than the true profit optimum that can be only reached by including the appropriate social costs.

Interest in social costs is increasing and is being picked up in other countries. Also, these concepts are being applied to current problems under public discussion. Wright described the contemporary regulations as a subsidy of pollution.[10] Teller, among many others, called for changes in the tax laws to make pollution unprofitable by crediting compliance and taxing emissions.[11]

The Role of Social Costs

While a gap often exists between explicit business costs and the total costs to society for these actions, this gap did not begin to receive serious attention until relatively recently. Problems noted in the mid-nineteenth century or before began to be identified explicitly in the period of the 1920s. Indeed, the social cost concept seems to have evolved into an analytical tool only in the 1960s; the serious analysis of how to calculate and apply this cost concept has become an active area of contemporary research.

The concept of social cost represents a bridge between the theoretical economic system based on self-interest that dates back to the time of Adam Smith and the actual economic system that yields suboptimal results by leaving large areas of cost uncompensated and thereby puts them beyond the reach of the regulating mechanism of the market.

Adam Smith and the later economists who elaborated and defined his ideas created what came to be called *the world of laissez-faire* on the assumption that the general good could be best served by the unrestrained interplay of self-interested individuals or individual firms. This result was to be achieved under the guidance of the marketplace, with supply and demand setting prices and costs, and with the size of the resulting profits causing a continual shift of resources that would favor an increase in supplies and competition in the most profitable sectors.

---

[8]Ibid., p. 29.

[9]Ibid., p. 45.

[10]James O. B. Wright, "Pollution is Being Subsidized," *Chemical Engineering Progress* 65, no. 12 (December 1969): 6.

[11]A. J. Teller, "Should All Our Environmental Wastes Be Economic Wastes?" *Professional Engineer,* February 1970, pp. 24–27.

The lack of freedom in markets has been a problem with the laissez-faire concept from the beginning, and there is a continuing need for refinement of the governance of the free-market processes. However, between the antitrust laws and other explicit social interventions and the ability of entrepreneurs to find economic and technological alternatives to artificial market constraints, the long-term operation of market forces has been a sufficiently acceptable route to the general good. The social impact of improper cost calculations has been much more serious; despite the major economic distortions it has caused, it did not receive recognition until the recent interest in social costs began to develop.

The difficulty with the laissez-faire concepts lies in the assumption that private and public profit are the same, that is, that the operating conditions bringing maximum profit to the individual will bring maximum benefit to society. Only then can the sum of the individual efforts toward self-interest achieve the common good. This assumption was imperfect, unfortunately, and the distortions it has caused have grown steadily worse. Continued use of laissez-faire ideas requires repairing the elements in the economic system that permit costs to go unrecognized, profits to be erroneously calculated, and resources to be misallocated as a consequence.

In summary, if social costs are truly beyond the reach of the regulating mechanism of the market, then self-interest based on profit goals cannot be expected to compensate for them. One possible remedy is through measurement of and accountability for social costs; continued effort to develop and refine techniques for such measurements has become the focus of a number of substantial programs both in the accounting area and elsewhere.

Social Audits

If social costs result from the lack of corporate social responsibility, as can be inferred from the preceding discussion, then the social costs can be taken as a measure of the problems that the corporation must offset in order to properly discharge its social responsibility. With this interpretation, the possibilities for the measurement of these costs become increasingly important. At present, actual measurement of social cost is difficult and often rather subjective. To assign value to a human life or a lost limb, to the dislocation of a breadwinner who is laid off and cannot get other work, to the cost of a process that sheds dust and soot on the community, or to any other consequences of adverse corporate social impact is a difficult process. The value that results from such a calculation of injury is subject to much interpretation and debate. One approach to these measurement problems has been through the concept of a social audit.

> Just as businesses subject themselves to audits of their accounts by independent public-accountant firms, they might also subject themselves to periodic examination by independent outside experts who would evaluate the performance of the business from the social point of view. The social auditors would make an independent and disinterested appraisal of a company's policies regarding prices, wages, research and development, advertising, public relations, human relations, community relations employment stabiliza-

tion, etc. They would then submit a comprehensive report to the director and to the management with evaluation and recommendations.[12]

Bowen also suggested that the social audit concept be extended to include a separate review of the philanthropic activities of a given company.[13]

Bowen's social audit concept filled an obvious need. One development of this need was offered by Fred Blum, a management consultant who described a social auditing service.[14] However, this service was primarily an opinion survey rather than an objective evaluation of corporate operations and programs as Bowen had suggested. Otherwise, this interesting social audit concept received little public attention for many years.

The Need for Social Accounting

When the place of the individual firm in the overall economic and social fabric is examined, the same measurement issues also arise. The need for a system of social accounting has been suggested repeatedly. J. M. Clark put it this way:

> Social accounting is an unfamiliar conception, but the thing it describes has a very real existence. The principles of uncompensated costs, of unpaid services, of unused capacities and of conservation, all involve a revising of the market's reckoning of costs and values in the light of a fuller social accountancy.
>
> (a) Complete social accountancy would undertake to set a true social value on all the human values and costs of industry, revising the values set on them by the individuals concerned. In many cases, there is fairly solid ground for doing this, as we have seen in discussing the competence of the individual, although there will probably always be a margin of doubt and controversy in such social valuations.
>
> (b) A considerable measure of social accountancy is possible, using only the measure of things already found in the market, but really combining them so as to give a more complete picture than is found in books of any one concern. Here is not so much a question of finding the total income and outgo as of tracing the change due to any particular policy or transaction.[15]

This concept of social accounting as described by Clark is broad, but if properly and objectively defined, it would be an immense aid in determining the responsibility of individual businesses for social costs.

---

[12]Howard R. Bowen, *Social Responsibilities of the Businessman*, (New York: Harper & Brothers, 1953), p. 155.

[13]Howard R. Bowen, "Charity and the Corporation," *Management Record* 24, no. 2 (February 1962): 33.

[14]Fred Blum, "Social Audit of the Enterprise," *Harvard Business Review* 36, no. 2 (March–April 1958): 77–86.

[15]From pp. 180–181, *Social Control of Business* by John Maurice Clark. Copyright © 1926, University of Chicago. Used with permission of McGraw-Hill Book Company.

Other authors have seen the same need. Ansoff mentioned the need for social accounting. Elbing and Elbing called for a social balance sheet for the firm, and Gross covered this concept in macro terms in his discussion of social efficiency. Berle predicted that social accounting would be developed and routinely applied within the near future.[16] An Institute for the Future study group has restated the need for a social audit,[17] an affiliated consulting group has proposed a pilot project to the National Industrial Conference Board, a competitive consulting firm has set up a panel to attempt to audit its own performance, a corporate priorities service has proposed to measure the urgency of different social responsibility issues,[18] Abt Associates is offering a social audit assessing the cost-benefit tradeoffs in alternative social overhead expenditures,[19] and *Social Audit*, a quarterly journal, is gathering data on English corporations, largely without their consent.

The Social Audit as a Growing Force

In the resurgence of interest in the social audit, the concept has been carried beyond the threshold of business awareness. Today a number of U.S. corporations have decided that some variation of the social audit process is a desirable adjunct to their necessary confrontation of social issues.[20] A significant assortment of academic research and consulting groups are engaged in developing the tools and techniques that can permit this corporate interest to become an effective force.

More than a few corporations have attempted social audits for purposes of internal evaluation, for publication, or for both. Social audits that have been published include those from the Bank of America, Eastern Gas & Fuel Associates, and the First National Bank of Minneapolis.

Academic groups, such as those at Harvard and the University of Pittsburgh, have begun active research on the social audit process; numbers of corporate clients have welcomed their assistance in establishing and developing the application of the social audit to their own particular organizations. Other centers of research interest at New York University, the University of Michigan, and the University of Washington have undertaken related work on the general principles of social accounting and the social audit process. A UCLA group has tended to serve as a bridge between social responsibility, business-society relationships, and the social audit process. Major consultant organizations such as A. D. Little, Battelle-Seattle, and Stanford Research Institute have shown interest in the social audit process, while smaller firms such as Abt Associates and Fry Consultants focus on special talents in this area.

---

[16]Adolph A. Berle, Jr., "The Corporation in a Democratic Society," *Management and Corporations 1985*, Melvin Anshen and George Leland Bach, eds. (New York: McGraw-Hill, 1960), p. 84.

[17]T. J. Gordon, H. Strudler, and D. Lustgarden, *A Forecast of the Relationship of Business and Society in the Next Five Years*, R-21, (Middletown, Conn.: Institute for the Future, April 1971), pp. 60–61.

[18]"Corporate Priorities: A Study of the New Demands on Business," a service of Daniel Yankelovich, Inc., N.Y., 1972.

[19]Clark Abt, "Managing to Save Money While Doing Good," *Innovation* no. 27 (January 1972): 38–47.

[20]Of the Fortune 500 companies, 55 percent made some quantitative disclosure of social responsibility programs in their 1976 annual reports. "Social Responsibility Disclosure; The 1977 Survey," Ernst & Ernst, 1300 Union Commerce Building, Cleveland, Ohio, 44115.

Altogether, it would appear that many academic and business leaders feel that the social audit is an idea whose time has arrived, and are actively trying to bring it to the position of a major reporting and control tool in the American business world. But where the foregoing might imply that a social audit is a standardized commodity of definable quality, nothing could be farther from the truth. In the first place, many of the strongest supporters of the idea object strongly to the use of the term *audit* to describe this process. The difficulty is that the word *audit* has at least two meanings. The more general one that relates to oversight and review of an activity is completely appropriate. The more specialized meaning that relates to the formal accounting process that is termed an audit implies a precision and certainty of results not now attainable in social accounts. However, much effort is being focused on the problem of bringing a greater accuracy to the dollar valuation of the underlying social factors. It is an appealing idea that a corporation can look at its interaction with its own environment and try to assess the impact that it is having; in fact, this concept has broad support. But there is considerable disagreement about the precision and accuracy of the social cost estimates that are now possible.

Also, there is more than one school of thought concerning the choice of the things that are most important to measure. For example, some of the thinking on the social audit is very heavily colored by the development of tools that attempt the valuation of the human assets of the firm. R. G. Barry has published balance sheets based on this kind of appraisal of its own organization,[21] and Flamholtz and others have written about the use of a rather different approach to the same kind of valuation.[22] While neither of these approaches could actually be termed a social audit, both deal with concepts important to the development of any technique that will lead to significant precision in social audits.

The Future of Social Audits

The social audit concept is spreading; in a survey published in 1974, Corson and Steiner reported that 76 percent of the firms responding to the questionnaire had engaged in some activity in this area.[23] Examples of some of the guidelines that have been published to aid interested companies in performing social audits include one for a comprehensive but nonquantitative audit from the Public Affairs Council[24] and one from the Foundation for Business Responsibilities.[25]

One of the reasons why the social audit concept is gaining acceptance is that it is beginning to demonstrate its value for some purposes to hardheaded management groups. Another reason why management acceptance is increasing is the obvious need to deal with corporate social impacts in some way, and the lack of other tools

[21]Jim Hyatt, "R. G. Barry Includes its Employees' Values on its Balance Sheet," *Wall Street Journal,* 3 April, 1970.

[22]Eric G. Flamholtz, "On the Use of the Economic Concept of Human Capital in Financial Statements," *The Accounting Review* XLII, no. 2 (January 1972): 148–160.

[23]John J. Corson and George S. Steiner, *Measuring Business's Social Performance; The Corporate Social Audit* (New York: Committee for Economic Development, 1974), p. 24.

[24]"Guidelines for an Internal Corporate Social Audit—a Working Paper," Washington D.C.: Public Affairs Council, September 1971.

[25]John Humble, *Social Responsibility Audit: A Management Tool for Survival* (London: Foundation for Business Responsibilities, 1973).

with which to do it. Within some bounds then, the social audit is proving its value; this should lead to its increased usage, particularly as social auditing techniques are improved and made more applicable.

One of the leading authorities on social audits (Professor Bauer of Harvard) has suggested that the social audit is now of sufficient value that corporations should begin to learn how to use it.[26] But he has cautioned strongly against making overambitious attempts at quantification or forming excessive expectations for the first painful audit attempts. He has suggested that many organizations should start with a *process audit* and then expand the audit procedure in successive cycles until it reaches the level that best serves the corporate interest.[27]

This process-inventory concept focuses on the corporation's ongoing processes for dealing with social problems and suggests that initial study of the process should precede the attempt to determine optimum solutions. Thus, a process audit (or *social inventory*, to use a term that some prefer) could start by listing all the social programs of a particular management together with their costs and the numbers of people who benefit. Then this list can be reviewed to see how well it is fulfilling the objectives that have formed the basis for appropriation of the money. Such an inventory presumes (correctly in most cases) that most corporate managements come to the social audit process with scattered and poorly integrated social programs. In other words, some things are being done for employees, others for communities, and still others in relationship to particular marketing, research, or even public relations projects; but often the social component of these investments is never identified, or the costs and benefits of the various programs are never compared.

Obviously, a process approach starts with a much less ambitious objective than the type of social audits that Abt Associates and the Bank of America, among others, have published. But the experience that is being reported by the workers in this field suggests that it is difficult enough to get the data well organized and a simple project reported in a meaningful way before expanding the effort. From a simple social inventory, the process can be extended to more ambitious audits, and some corporations are taking this route.

At the end of this route, however, is another area of major uncertainty in deciding how to value a corporation's efforts in social areas and how to judge the proper degree to which these efforts should be extended. For instance, Abt suggests the determination of cost-benefit tradeoffs in the perceptions of a given community so that a corporation can spend its corporate citizenship dollars in such a way as to attain maximum favorable response from that community.[28] This technique could be of prime short-term interest but offers no suggestion about the level of corporate contributions that would be most appropriate. This measurement focuses on community perceptions and demands, when the strategic level of business policy decisions must consider at least whether the long-term self-interest of the business is consistent with the long-term needs of the community. Such considerations

[26]Raymond A. Bauer, "The Corporate Social Audit: Getting on the Learning Curve," *California Management Review*, Fall 1973, pp. 5–10.

[27]Raymond A. Bauer and Dan H. Fenn, Jr., "What Is a Corporate Social Audit?" *Harvard Business Review*, January–February 1973, pp. 37–48.

[28]Clark Abt, "Managing to Save Money While Doing Good," *Innovation* 27 (January 1972): 39–47.

represent a much more important force than present community demands, even though these may focus in the same areas.

The purpose here is not to single out a particular approach for criticism; all of the approaches published so far have vocal critics. The standards are still evolving, and all of the contemporary efforts must be viewed as tentative, exploratory, and inevitably somewhat controversial.

Social audits for Abt Associates and Eastern Gas & Fuel Associates are included in the appendix of this chapter to illustrate the audit process; the comments on the value systems that have been used point up some of the basis for controversy. For instance, the Bank of America audits have been criticized for the way in which socially responsive student-loan programs were credited as a social program when they also turned out to be profitable business for the bank. While nothing says that a social program must not be profitable, many business leaders have built in this implicit assumption. Removal of that assumption leads into equally difficult areas since many of the most successful product development and marketing programs have succeeded because their concepts include a significant social benefit as a result of the purchase and use of a product or service. After all, social change is a major source of business opportunity so that it is no surprise that many products cater to this kind of development.[29]

The point of this criticism is to suggest that what is being developed as a social audit is a tool that will acquire considerable value when two more components can finally be added. The first of these components is the array of additional tools necessary to carry out the careful quantitative measurements that a true audit would require; the second is the basis for the judgment that will permit management to choose the level of social effort that balances the many pressures on the corporation most effectively.

While the fact that these two components are not yet fully available may sound like a serious indictment of the social audit concept, it is not. So long as the limitations of the resulting information are kept in proper perspective, the value of attempting a social inventory or even a full social audit is already established. While the result cannot truly be an audit or even a definitive quantification, it can serve as a useful qualitative or semiqualitative exploration of the measurement concepts employed— thus, it is a useful guide for management decision. A much more perfect decision tool would be desirable, will perhaps evolve, but is not yet available. Today's social audit concepts fill a portion of the void in a useful manner.

Summary

This chapter has reviewed the development of social cost concepts and their application to the corporate interface with society through the mechanism of the social audit. The attempt has been to describe the social audit as a logical outgrowth of the interest in social costs that developed as economists and others realized that

---

[29]George C. Sawyer, "Social Issues and Social Change: Impact on Strategic Decisions," *MSU Business Topics*, Summer 1973, pp. 15–20.

private profit was often greater than society's gain from a given transaction. However, the social audit technique still is experimental and limited by the measurement tools available.

The social audit is a useful qualitative tool at this early stage in its evolution but remains far from the point at which it can be a guide in major areas of management action. To consider not only the limitations of the social audit technique but also realize the potential for going farther, the following chapter will move on to a discussion of the limiting concept of social balance, in which no social costs are incurred.

Appendix: Social Audits and Their Concepts

Because of the degree of interest in social audits, this section presents two illustrations that suggest something of the range that has been covered by present experience with the application of the social audit concept.

Abt Associates Social Audit

Each year since 1971 Abt Associates has published a social audit of its own operations as a part of its annual report. The 1972 social audit illustrates this process well:

Abt Associates pioneered its social audit in the 1971 annual report. A social balance sheet and a social income statement was prepared which tabulated the effects the Company had on "society," defined as staff, the local community clients, and the general public. For the sake of comparability, the same format is used in this report, with updated figures to show changes in condition from last year to this. Also presented is a newly-developed format which integrates measures of social performance into the financial report. This allows the estimation of *financial return on social investment,* a concept drawn from Company efforts in the last year to advance the state-of-the-art in social accounting.

The pages that follow present the 1971 and 1972 social balance sheet and income statement, notes explaining the rationale and calculations supporting those statements, the integration of social and financial statements, comments on the results of this new presentation and explanatory notes on that presentation.

These statements must be considered separately from the company's regular financial statements. Generally accepted auditing procedures have not been developed with respect to such statements, and accordingly our independent auditors are unable to express an opinion thereon.

The social balance sheet and income statement are "society's statements" and not the Company's, in that they show the net social assets and net social benefits "owned" by society as a result of the Company's activities. The main categories of social assets are: *staff assets* made available by the company to society; *organization assets*, representing the cost which society would have to incur if it reconstituted the Company in 1972; *research assets* having social value; and taxes paid net of public services consumed.

Social liabilities or commitments include staff and organization commitments to *non-socially productive contracts* and *environmental pollution*. On the social income statement, social benefits include extraordinary benefits to staff in the last period, net of social costs imposed on staff; social benefits to the community, net of social cost; and social benefits to the general public, net of social costs imposed on the public.

Because the "net social income" from the income statement is considered to be a social dividend paid out to staff, community and general public, it does not accrue to the social net worth shown on the balance sheet. Other normal accounting flows from balance sheet to income statement, such as conversion of assets and liabilities to revenue and expense, have not yet been encompassed by these social accounting methods.

Notes to the Social Balance Sheet and Social Income Statement

Note A: Career advancement is expressed as the added earning power from salary increases for merit and/or promotion. In 1972, 97 employees (22% of total staff) were promoted, compared to 49 (18% of staff) in 1971. In 1972 67% of employees earned merit or promotion increases versus 79% in 1971.

Note B: The social cost of layoff is estimated to be one month's salary for each layoff, i.e., the mean time to next employment is one month.

Note C: Staff-contributed overtime worked but not paid is equal to approximately 33% over the required 40 work hours. This represents a social cost to staff in free time foregone.

Note D: Equality of opportunity is defined in terms of the costs to individuals of the inequality of opportunity for appropriately remunerative work and advancement, as measured by the income loss equal to the difference between what the minority individual earns and what a majority individual doing the same job with the same qualifications earns. The $26,000 social cost of inequality of opportunity was incurred entirely by women, as a result of a strongly discriminatory labor market that company policy was not completely able to overcome within national wage-price policy constraints. No inequality of opportunity cost was incurred by ethnic minorities. Minority advancement of blacks, Chicanos, Indians and Orientals promoted in 1972 was 14% compared to 13% in 1971, and 24% of women were promoted in 1972 compared to 25% promoted in 1971. This should be compared with 25% of white males promoted in 1972 and 10% in 1971, and a company average of 22% promotions in 1972, and 18% in 1971. The aggregate ethnic minority and female staff promoted in 1972 was 21% of total minority and women compared to 22% in 1971. The total minority and female staff was

Abt Associates Inc. Social Balance Sheet

Year ended December 31, 1972 with comparative figures for 1971

	1972	1971
Social assets available		
Staff		
Available within one year (Note G)	$ 4,166,125	$ 2,594,390
Available after one year (Note G)	12,566,700	6,368,511
Training investment (Note H)	1,008,548	507,405
	17,741,373	9,470,306
Less accumulated training obsolescence (Note H)	247,541	136,995
Total staff assets	17,493,832	9,333,311
Organization		
Social capital investment (Note I)	2,192,685	2,192,685
Retained earnings	515,684	219,136
Land	307,430	285,376
Buildings at cost	1,736,825	334,321
Equipment at cost	136,638	43,018
Total organization assets	4,889,262	3,074,536
Research		
Proposals (Note J)	37,898	26,878
Child care research	6,629	6,629
Social audit	18,130	12,979
Public services consumed, net of tax payments (Note E)	160,514	90,452
Total research and tax assets	223,171	136,938
Total social assets available	22,606,265	12,544,785
Social commitments, obligations and equity staff		
Committed to contracts within one year (Note K)	29,451	43,263
Committed to contracts after one year (Note K)	88,836	114,660
Committed to administration within one year (Note K)	57,538	62,598
Committed to administration after one year (Note K)	173,558	165,903
Total staff commitments	349,383	386,424
Organization		
Financing requirements (Note L)	1,463,438	415,156
Facilities & equipment committed to contracts and administration (Note K)	182,398	37,734
Total organization commitments	1,645,836	452,890
Environment		
Pollution from paper production (Note M)	5,345	1,770
Pollution from electric power production (Note N)	41,451	10,601
Pollution from automobile commuting (Note O)	20,130	10,493
Total environmental obligations	66,926	22,864
Total commitments & obligations	2,062,145	862,178
Society's equity		
Contributed by staff (Note P)	17,144,449	8,946,887
Contributed by stockholders (Note Q)	3,243,426	2,621,646
Generated by operations (Note R)	156,245	114,074
Total equity	20,544,120	11,682,607
Total commitments, obligations and equity	$22,606,265	$12,544,785

Abt Associates Inc. Social Income Statement

Year ended December 31, 1972 with comparative figures for 1971

	1972	1971
Social benefits and costs to staff:		
Social benefits to staff:		
Health insurance, life ins., sick leave	$ 193,560	$ 93,492
Career advancement (Note A)	331,872	345,886
Company school & tuition reimbursement	1,326	6,896
Vacation, holidays, recreation	304,932	207,565
Food services, child care, parking	122,305	57,722
Quality of life (space and its quality)	84,268	61,002
Total benefits to staff	1,038,263	772,563
Social costs to staff:		
Layoffs and involuntary terminations (Note B)	14,849	9,560
Overtime worked but not paid (Note C)	882,721	654,000
Inequality of opportunity (Note D)	26,000	—
Total costs to staff	923,570	663,560
Net social income to staff:	$ 114,693	$109,003
Social benefits and costs to community:		
Social benefits to community:		
Local taxes paid (Note E)	$ 71,352	$ 38,952
Environmental improvements	22,053	10,100
Local tax worth of net jobs created	39,886	20,480
Total benefits to community	133,291	69,532
Social costs to community:		
Local taxes consumed (Note E)	66,848	55,700
Net social income to community:	$ 66,443	$ 13,832
Social benefits and costs to general public:		
Social benefits to general public:		
Federal taxes paid (Note E)	$ 272,000	$165,800
State taxes paid (Note E)	61,750	55,500
Contributions to knowledge (publications, etc.)	17,700	14,100
Federal & state tax worth of net jobs created	173,674	69,800
Total benefits to public:	525,124	305,200
Social costs to general public:		
Federal services consumed (Note E)	128,880	83,000
State services consumed (Note E)	46,368	31,100
Total costs to public:	$ 175,248	$114,100
Net social income to general public:	$ 349,876	$191,100
Net social income to staff, community & public: (Note F)	$ 531,012	$313,935

66% of the entire staff (287 of 432) in 1972, compared to 55% (150 of 271) in 1971.

Note E: Taxes paid are considered a social contribution or benefit while public services paid for by taxes that are consumed by the company are considered social costs. When the company does not consume public services paid for in part by company paid taxes, a net social income contribution is produced. Federal and state public services consumed are calculated by multiplying the ratio of company revenues to total federal or state corporate revenues times the total of federal or state tax collections. The company's share of local services consumed is computed by multiplying the ratio of company population to total local population times the total local taxes, on the assumption that local services used is roughly in proportion to the number of people using local services. This share is then reduced by the percentage (29%) of the local budget devoted to services not consumed by the company (local schools). The balance sheet item "public services consumed, net of tax payments" consists of the net of total (federal, state, and local) taxes paid over total services consumed; this is carried as an asset for one year's time. The counter entry is an addition to society's equity generated by operations. This represents a change in treatment from the 1971 statement; the 1971 figures are restated to reflect the change from a liability to an equity account.

Note F: In its 1971 social audit, the company showed an addition to social income calculated as "benefits to clients." This was defined as quantifiable social benefits resulting from specific projects which exceeded the contract revenues net of social costs imposed by contracts. This was calculated at $17,765,041 in 1971. This item is omitted in 1972 because research is still underway to more rigorously quantify these benefits. The measurement problem addressed by this research is a common delay between project completion and the occurrence of social benefits. Methods are being developed to estimate benefits on a time basis consistent with the company's fiscal accounting period.

Note G: That portion of company staff engaged in social research is considered a social asset. The valuation of the asset is based on the year-end staff payroll, discounted to present value, the discount rate a function of mean staff tenure and pay raise rate. The discount rate for 1972 was .9634 for staff available within one year and 2.906 for those available after one year, based on a mean staff tenure of 4.59 years. For 1971, mean staff tenure was 5.45 years. (Note K)

Note H: Training investment is estimated at 25% of first year salary for all staff. Training obsolescence is based on a straight-line depreciation of training investment over the mean staff tenure. (See Note G)

Note I: The social capital investment is equated with the capital cost of reconstituting the organization. It is computed by weighting the capital stock account from 1965 (the year of the company's founding) to the present, by the consumer price index (1967=$1.00) expressed in current year dollars.

Note J: A portion of the research carried out by the firm is performed in connection with the preparation of proposals submitted to prospective clients. The cost of this research is estimated at $37,898 in 1972 and $38,280 in 1971. This cost is reduced by the costs associated with proposal resulting in client contracts, in which the research developed was exploited, and any remaining amount is written off at the end of one year.

Note K: The total staff payroll was used (Note G) to calculate staff assets available. Since part of the staff is engaged in administrative and contract activities not considered socially productive, these liabilities or commitments are created counter to the asset. Total year-end staff payroll in these categories is subjected to the same discounting procedure described in Note G.

Note L: The company's financing requirements are considered an opportunity cost to society. They are equated here to the mean of the financing outstanding during the year.

Note M: A substantial portion of the company's activities are expressed in tangible form through the printed word. The company used 102 tons of paper in 1972 and 26 tons of paper in 1971. The company recognizes an obligation to society based on the cost of abatement of the water pollution created by the manufacture of this paper. This cost is estimated at $35 per ton.

Note N: The company consumed 1,542,524 KWH of electric power in 1972 and 476,053 KWH in 1971. The company recognizes an obligation to society based on the cost of abatement of the air pollution created by the production of this power. This cost is estimated at $.02 per KWH.

Note O: The company generated 783,750 commuting trip miles in 1972 and 615,960 miles in 1971. The obligation to society based on the air pollution thus created is estimated at $.01 per mile.

Note P: Staff assets available less staff commitments.

Note Q: Organizational assets available less organizational commitments.

Note R: Research and tax assets less environmental obligations.

The Integration of Social and Financial Balance Sheets

The financial statements presented on the previous pages are "society's statements," showing the assets, liabilities, costs and benefits accruing to various segments of society from the company's operations.

In the socially-motivated company, decision-making requires a comparison of social investment with financial return and of financial investment with social return, as well as the usual comparison of financial investments and returns. Some of the net social investment of the company is expected to have a beneficial financial result, while some of it may affect the company's financial performance negatively, or not at all. These effects are netted out and evaluated by integrating the company's net social investment into its own financial statement.

This treatment "internalizes" social costs and benefits. The pages which follow internalize social assets net of liabilities. All of the net asset is considered "social equity" in the restated net worth. On the page following the integrated statement, this restated net worth is discounted, in recognition that only a portion of it is likely to produce a return.[30]

---

[30]Annual Report, Abt Associates, 55 Wheeler Street, Cambridge, Massachusetts 02138, pp. 12–20.

The first thing to note is that Abt has been required to keep its social balance sheet separate from the normal statements for the business. While it is easy to be critical of the insistence by the regulatory and financial community that only generally accepted accounting principles be used for formal financial reporting, the fact is that the Abt approach and the parallel approaches used by others involve a host of new concepts of valuation that permit the size of an entry to be shifted radically by making a change in the concept.

In the first place, Abt has chosen to define the balance sheet in terms of society's view of the corporation (as Abt sees it) rather than as a corporate social balance sheet that reflects the same internal point of view as the financial balance sheets. While this same choice probably would have been made by many others, a good case could also have been presented for centering the analysis on the corporation.

The balance sheet notes illustrate the series of value judgments necessary in such a social audit procedure. For example, career advancement is valued in terms of earning power. This assumption is reasonable but neglects any changes in the nonmonetary component of job status and job satisfaction. In the same way, a monetary value on the cost of a layoff is necessary; Abt uses one year's salary. Clearly, there are circumstances where the disruption of being laid off would cost more than this—where family life patterns are upset or re-employment is difficult. In other cases where equivalent jobs are readily available, layoff costs would be less.

In the same way, each of the concepts described in the other notes, including the benefits to clients and the valuation of social research or the social capital value of the company, are based on specific value definitions. Thus, equating the use of paper, electricity, and travel with degradation of the environment would be applauded by some and attacked by others. Abt's contribution is to put values on these intangibles. These values are rational and defensible but not necessarily correct. And public attention is focused on this valuation process, as a step toward the eventual definition of generally accepted public value standards for the various components of corporate social impact.

On the last page of the Abt social audit is an introduction and transition to a later section of the annual report in which the social income statement and balance sheet (society's point of view) and the conventional financial balance sheet are combined. This difficult section tends to lose credibility because it is based on so many unfamiliar social value concepts. Probably it was too far ahead of its time. Abt has not repeated it in subsequent reports.

Altogether, the Abt social audit is an interesting and useful experiment. It has value to the extent that a particular management is comfortable using the value systems and value judgments built into the audit as a basis for decisions. Another management could develop a social audit based on its own particular social value concepts that would be quite different from Abt's. Thus, in reviewing social audits from the different sources, one finds that it is important to isolate and focus on the valuation concepts underlying each audit.

Eastern Gas & Fuel Associates Social Audit

Some managements have chosen to move into the social audit field slowly so that they can gain value from a more rational organization of existing programs and collect the necessary internal corporate data. One of the best-known reports of this type is that of Eastern Gas & Fuel Associates under the direction of the late Eli Goldston.

Goldston's approach to the initiation of a social audit at Eastern Gas & Fuel could be called a *social assessment* in Bauer's nomenclature.[31] Such a social assessment is the first step in Bauer's concept of *process audit* and could evolve naturally into a more ambitious social audit in subsequent years. The 1972 social report was entitled "Toward Social Accounting" and read as follows:

To Our Shareholders:

There has been much talk in recent years of corporate social responsibility and of the need to develop some sort of social accounting to gauge how well a given firm is performing—not just as an economic unit, but as a citizen. Indeed, some have suggested that these measures of corporate performance beyond net profit should be subjected to an independent social audit.

This insert for the 1972 Annual Report of Eastern Gas and Fuel Associates has been designed as an experimental exploration of two aspects of social accounting for "self-auditing" purposes:

(1) What are some internal topics on which management can presently assemble and organize reasonably accurate and coherent data?

(2) Which issues of social accountability are of external interest, and to what extent are shareholders in particular interested, if at all?

To explore the first of these aspects we have gathered statistical information that covers four topics from among the many that are currently of concern to those studying corporate social responsibility:

Industrial safety

Minority employment

Charitable giving

Pensions

To explore the second aspect we have included, at the end of this insert, a short questionnaire which, if you will mail it back, will serve as a useful measure of shareholder concern with corporate social responsibility and the reporting of it. No generally accepted standards or methods of presentation have been developed for shareholder reporting on such topics nor is there clear evidence as to shareholder interest.

The topics for this first report were not chosen because they are necessarily the most important ones, or the ones that might make us look good, but because they are the most readily measurable, because our goals with respect to them are comparatively simple and clear, and because they lie in areas where management can rather directly influence results. In addition, managerial decisions on these topics can have a significant impact on earnings per share.

---

[31]Raymond A. Bauer and Dan H. Fenn, Jr., *The Corporate Social Audit*, Social Science Frontiers, no. 5 (New York: Russell Sage Foundation, 1972).

In the process of making this first consolidation of social data from our various operations, we found that our records were less complete and less certain than we had believed. We also found that even inadequate disclosure begins to exert a useful pressure on management to comply with new public expectations as to the conduct of large corporations. It may also be some of the best evidence that management is sincerely concerned and making an effort to meet proper expectations.

Four major recurring principles for the quantification of social responsibility have been suggested:

The first is that our priorities have been changing with some rapidity. Many of our political, economic and commercial measures of progress have become obsolescent. We need a new kind of social accounting that goes beyond GNP for the nation and goes beyond net profit for the firm.

Second, while we think of our current economic and accounting measures of GNP and net profit as very precise, when you really get into the nitty gritty of how they are put together, their certainty is delusive.

Third, many proposed imprecise measures of social accounting can be sufficiently accurate to be instructive. They are not hopelessly less accurate than GNP or net profit, and so they can be quite useful, even though they lack precision, for many purposes for which we cannot use GNP and net profit.

And finally, while our efforts to calibrate our concerns by social accounting will reflect this new sense of priorities, without personal observation in the field and a weighing of the figures that we create with moral concerns, social accounting itself becomes only a new numbers game.

As we proceed with these early attempts to develop some form of internal social accounting, we should acquire additional useful insights into this new art.

Eli Goldston, President

1. Industrial Safety

Recent legislation has demonstrated that a major current public concern, especially in the heavy industries in which Eastern is involved, is the health and safety of employees.

Our industrial accident record in recent years has not been very good. One standard measurement is the accident frequency rate (number of accidents versus hours worked), and our rate has almost doubled in the last three years, going up most dramatically in gas operations. It is clear that our safety performance has been slipping. In addition it seems that our record is poorer than that of a number of firms with whom we have compared specific records. Just where we stand in our various industries is difficult to gauge because meaningful comparative figures are not available.

Another measure of safety performance is the severity rate, which takes into account time lost as a result of accidents. Here Eastern's record has been steadier, and apparently more in line with other firms for our industries. But much room for improvement remains.

Accident Frequency Rate

(Lost time accidents per million
employee hours)

	1970	1971	1972
Coal & coke	43	61	78
Gas	14	26	30
Marine	34	41	43
EGFA Avg.	36	50	64

Accident Severity Rate

(Employee days lost per million employee
hours)*

	1970	1971	1972
Coal & coke	2,948	3,427	4,209
Gas	222	191	303
Marine	1,707	2,015	1,423
EGFA Avg.	2,225	2,516	3,033

*Excluding days charged for fatalies.

Frequency and severity rates, either for a single firm or for an industry, are rather elusive statistics. They may appear worse simply from improved reporting, or may appear better if excessive pressure to improve the record results in variable reporting practices. Comparisons are complicated by numerous variables. Our river towboat crews, for instance, live aboard the boats and so are at their workplace even when not actually working. A greater awareness by both employees and management of the importance of safety may increase the number of reported accidents. Improved benefits could encourage accident reporting. Comparisons are also difficult because of different bases of reporting. We are trying for 1973 to improve both our performance and our ability to supply managers with comparable industry statistics.

Job related fatalities, of course, are the most salient and tragic accidents. We require full reports to top management on all serious injuries and fatalities along with proposals to prevent recurrence. At Eastern we are constantly trying to develop more effective ways to impress on all our people the need to guard against the ever present hazards in their particular line of work. Here is our recent record of fatalities:

Fatalities

	1970	1971	1972
Coal & coke	8	3	4
Gas	0	0	0
Marine	1	1	2
EGFA Total	9	4	6

Critics of industry often assume that management has more ability to reduce accident frequency and severity and to eliminate fatalities than may be the case. We do not accept at all the rationalization that "accidents just happen" and we would be the last to suggest that a victim alone is at fault. But it is obvious that we need to be better persuaders and to improve training, motivation and enforcement when it is considered that in at least five of the six 1972 fatalities, the victim was an experienced employee who was clearly violating a standard safety work rule of the company at the time of his death. The need for and difficulty of broad safety indoctrination is evidenced by the fact that 11 employees were fatally injured in 1972 in accidents off the job.

The economics of safety reinforces our social/humanitarian concerns. Compensation of employees injured on the job cost Eastern at least $3,600,000 last year, or about $.20 in earnings per share.

We are continuing to increase our commitment of men and money to ongoing safety programs in all operations. One of our headquarters officers has been assigned to regular field checks of safety practices and the compilation and analysis of accident statistics. Eastern Associated Coal Corp. has further strengthened its existing safety program by engaging the highly respected safety department of a firm in another industry to help us improve our safety performance in coal operations. In Boston Gas Company, a safety campaign has commenced that focuses not only on safe work habits but also on continuing "defensive" use of equipment and procedures to avoid dangerous situations.

2. Minority Employment

An important thrust of Eastern's social concerns effort is to respond positively to the apparently clear national desire to bring an end to discrimination in employment and promotion because of race, religion or other difference from that elusive notion of "the majority."

It is difficult to generalize fairly and judiciously about Eastern's minority employment statistics. Numerically, minority employment in the company has increased in recent years, but has not quite maintained its percentage proportion. This has been particularly noticeable in coal operations, but in this instance, the increased employment has come in areas where there has been a smaller minority proportion in the local population. And it may be that the improving employment prospects for minority members either with our competitors or in fields previously closed to them have reduced the relative attractiveness of jobs with us. Boston Gas has had an excellent record of integrating its work force, but the addition of new territory with a different population mix has appeared to slow the trend.

Measuring progress in integration is further complicated by the fact that companies were forbidden to record the race of employees until quite recently. Many of our operations are so geographically scattered that it is difficult to determine in many cases if our percentages of minority employ-

Minority Employment

	1970	1971	1972
Coal & coke			
Total	5,703	6,050	6,448
Minority	526	544	517
% Minority	9.2%	9.0%	8.0%
Gas			
Total	1,466	1,500	1,611
Minority	66	96	115
% Minority	4.5%	6.4%	7.1%
Marine			
Total Employees	1,077	1,332	1,358
Minority	64	84	79
% Minority	5.9%	6.3%	5.8%
EGFA*			
Total Employees	8,349	8,995	9,526
Minority	659	727	716
% Minority	7.9%	8.3%	7.5%

*Includes Boston Office

Minority Employment Levels

	1971	1972	1972 Total in Category	1972% of Total
Officers & managers	15	12	1,229	1%
Professional & technical	19	34	648	4.9%
Clerical	58	56	895	6.1%
Skilled	364	398	5,091	7.8%
Unskilled	271	216	1,663	1.3%
	727	716	9,526	

ment are in line with the minority population in reasonably relevant areas, although this does seem to be true.

Passing over complicated matters of definition, the figures seem to indicate that Eastern has done a reasonable job but still has some distance to go in reaching a fair proportion of minorities in the work force and in levels of employment. Our effort in recruitment and advancement is to give due recognition to merit and performance while still showing concern for the need to achieve appropriate representation of minorities. There are local instances in our operations which will require continuing attention and prodding if this is to be accomplished.

3. Charitable Giving

The figures we present below on our charitable giving through The Eastern Associated Foundation are far from complete. Although most charitable gifts of $500 and over have been made by all operations through the Foundation, a good many smaller gifts are made directly from operating funds. In addition, there are expenditures that get classified as personnel expense or sales expense in Eastern that could properly be considered charitable giving. For example, we provide recreation directors for several of our mining communities and we subsidize a summer camp for the children of mine employees. Particularly in the mining areas, equipment is donated or the use of it given to various causes. In addition, company employees are sometimes loaned or assigned to assist in charitable campaign drives or social service projects.

Charitable Giving by the Eastern Associated Foundation

	1970	1971	1972
Total contributions	$185,442	$210,320	$216,429
1% of pre-tax income	336,450	240,750	225,250
$ per employee	23.77	23.11	22.78
Earnings per share	1¢	1¢	1¢

The Federal Income Tax law permits contributions to the extent of 5% of taxable income; many studies, however, have shown that the majority of large public corporations make charitable gifts of about 1% of pre-tax income. We have been using this 1% figure as a guide so far as Foundation gifts are concerned.

We have employed outside professional consultants to help us decide how (a) to respond thoughtfully to the charitable concerns of the communities with which we are related and (b) to balance the interest of numerous applicants. On the basis of their suggestions we have considered it appropriate to channel Foundation giving about one-half to health and welfare, one-fourth to higher education, and one-fourth to civic and cultural causes. Costs of educational assistance to active employees is in addition to this giving.

Per Cent of Foundation Giving by Category of Interest

	1970	1971	1972
Health and welfare	56.3%	57.1%	53.8%
Higher education	26.4	20.7	22.8
Civic and cultural	17.3	22.2	23.4
Total	100.0%	100.0%	100.0%

Charitable giving budgets are established annually by each of the operations and are reviewed along with our other business plans to be sure they are adequate and balanced. Through a matching gifts program, where the company matches an employee's gift to an educational institution, employees can themselves help determine the scale and direction of company assistance to higher education.

4. Pensions

Where at one time company retirement plans had been an accepted, almost competitive, way to attract and keep employees, current thinking turns more to their adequacy of coverage and fiscal soundness. In both of these areas it is virtually impossible to generalize about the pension arrangements for Eastern's employees.

In the matter of coverage, all of our employees are, of course, covered by Social Security, with the employee and the employer paying their equal shares. In 1972 each paid 5.2% of the first $9,000 of an employee's earnings but this has since increased to 5.85% of the first $10,800. In addition, substantially all of Eastern's employees participate in one of the 23 separate formal retirement plans to which the company and its subsidiaries are a party.

Eastern's pension arrangements involve very substantial amounts of money. Total Social Security payments by the company in 1972 amounted to about $4,300,000. The expense for the various types of pension and welfare plans supplemental to Social Security has climbed to more than $12,500,000 annually in recent years. Social Security, health and retirement costs thus add an average of almost $2,000 per employee to the average of $10,000 a year paid to an Eastern employee.

Annual Cost of Pension & Welfare Plans
($000)

	1970	1971	1972
Union welfare & pension plans	$5,814	$5,724	$ 8,904
Other formal & informal plans	2,693	2,967	3,649
	$8,507	$8,691	$12,553

(Costs charged to income in the fiscal year of the company)

Eighteen of the formal retirement plans are maintained by negotiations in collective bargaining with various labor unions. In most of these we have no control over management of the funds or the amount of the benefits. We participate in the control of others to varying degrees.

So far as we know, none of these funds has been challenged as to the competence of its management except the Health and Welfare Fund of the United Mine Workers. Contributions to this fund, based on a per tonnage contribution made by all unionized operators, including our Eastern Associated Coal Corp., have been brought under Federal court jurisdiction because of alleged mismanagement.

So far as fiscal soundness is concerned, we annually charge as an expense against income an amount which reflects the actuarial obligations of the current year. In addition, the past service obligations that existed when various funds were established or resulted from amendments, are being charged to the current year on the basis of 30-year amortization periods.

We have been funding each negotiated plan in accordance with the relevant collective bargaining agreement. In the case of Eastern's Retirement Plan for Salaried Employees, which is non-negotiated and non-contributory, funding has recently been brought up to the level for which concurrent tax deductibility is permitted. This plan is fairly well funded compared to the plans of most companies.

An accrued total liability of almost $35,000,000 is funded by assets in trust with a market value of about $27,000,000. The additional $8,000,000 must be paid to the Trustees or earned through fund investment income in excess of annual expenditures in order for the plan to be considered fully funded.

Status of EGFA Salaried Plan Funding

Fiscal Year Ending June 30, 1972
($000)

Liability for retired employees	$18,872
Liability for active & terminated employees	15,825
	$34,697
Accrued liability	$34,697
Plan assets at market value	26,671
Unfunded liability @ Market	$ 8,026

It is difficult to determine how adequately funded the various negotiated plans are since many cover other companies in addition to our own companies and, with continuing changes in benefits, actuarial assumption, and market value of assets, there will be variations which defy simple explanation.

We are regularly reviewing both our negotiated pension arrangements and our salaried plan, using an independent insurance firm as consultants when appropriate. We believe that the expense, the benefits and vesting provisions of our numerous retirement plans are reasonably in line with those of the different industries in which we operate. Since the Health and Welfare Fund of the coal industry is portable within that industry, some of the issues as to portability do not apply to our single largest employee group. There may be continuing pressure to require us and other employers to liberalize vesting and portability. These are, no doubt, desirable pension changes, but they must be recognized as being increases in actual pension cost.

The compilation of this report has helped to clarify Eastern's goals in these areas of social concern.

Our goal in industrial safety is to reverse an unfavorable trend and to significantly reduce the frequency and severity of industrial accidents.

Our goal in minority employment is to achieve full equality of opportunity for all and to adequately reflect in our work force the minority proportion in the population of the areas of our operations without sacrificing performance standards.

Our goal in charitable contributions is to maintain, possibly to increase, a level of about 1% of pre-tax income as an appropriate amount of support for various social causes.

Our goal in our retirement programs is to make certain that company benefits are adequate and that promises to employees are secured through proper funding.

Shareholder Comments

The attached questionnaire has a number of specific questions and also an opportunity for general comments. We will greatly appreciate your detaching it, filling it in and mailing it to us. We hope to be able to make a preliminary report at the shareholders' meeting on April 26, 1973 as to any significant shareholder opinion.[32]

This social report attempted to establish a dialogue between Eastern Gas & Fuel management and its stockholders and to present the results of a limited, difficult process. Eastern, a very diverse corporation, had for the first time organized itself internally to measure four areas (safety, minority employment, charitable contributions, and pension policies) in a sufficiently clear and uniform fashion to permit objective comparisons with performance elsewhere. Goldston reported that the level of stockholder interest in this type of report was not great but that most of the responses received were supportive of the effort.

The realism in the Goldston approach is in its engagement with the problem of getting a large organization in motion by defining a useful initial level of effort. Such a process can be undertaken without major disruption of corporate processes and then can be extended gradually in subsequent years.

Questions for Analysis and Discussion

1. List some of the unpaid costs of industry. How could these be made into actual costs that were charged directly to the firm that caused them? Would this be a good thing to do?

2. Analyze society's investment in a productive adult and explain where costs arise if this individual is disabled or dies prematurely.

3. Develop your own example of a case where marginal social and private net products differ, first, to the advantage of society and, then, to the disadvantage of society.

4. Can you think of any circumstances in which society would wish to make the marginal private net product larger than the marginal social net product? Explain.

---

[32]1972 Annual Report, Eastern Gas & Fuel Associates, 2900 Prudential Towers, Boston, Mass., 02199.

5. Give additional examples of social costs incurred both during the production of various products and during or related to their consumption.

6. How would you go about estimating the social cost of defacing a scenic landscape or destroying an historic landmark? (Suggestion: Do not worry about quantification; attempt to define the concepts such valuation would require.)

7. Study the valuation concepts in the Abt Associates income statement and balance sheet. Choose any three of the notes and discuss the way that the valuation concept presented there might relate to the actual social cost incurred by society.

8. Find other published social audits and compare their valuation concepts with those that Abt Associates chose to use.

9. What could be done next to build on the Eastern Gas & Fuel report presented here and to move it a few more steps in the direction of a formal social audit?

For Further Information

Abt, Clark C. *The Social Audit for Management.* New York: Amacom, 1977.

Ackerman, Robert W. "How Companies Respond to Social Demands." *Harvard Business Review*, July–August 1973, pp. 88–98.

Bauer, Raymond A. and Fenn, Dan H., Jr. *The Corporate Social Audit.* Social Science Frontiers, no. 5. New York: Russell Sage Foundation, 1972.

Blake, David H., Frederick, William C., and Meyers, Mildred S. *Social Auditing: Evaluating the Impact of Corporate Programs.* New York: Praeger, 1976.

Butcher, Bernard L. "The Program Management Approach to the Corporate Social Audit." *California Management Review*, Fall 1973, pp. 11–16.

Corson, John J., and Steiner, George A. *Measuring Business Social Performance: The Corporate Social Audit.* New York: Committee for Economic Development, 1974.

Frantzgreb, Richard B., Landau, Linda T., and Lundberg, Donald P. "The Valuation of Human Resources." *Business Horizons*, June 1974, pp. 73–80.

Frederick, William C., and Meyers, Mildred. "The Hidden Politics of Social Auditing." *Business and Society Review*, Autumn 1974, pp. 49–54.

Gadac, Louise S. and Finkelstein, Larry. "The Corporate Social Audit: An Annotated Bibliography." Washington, D.C.: Public Affairs Council, 1973.

Humble, John. *Social Responsibility Audit: A Management Tool for Survival.* London: Foundation for Business Responsibilities, 1973.

Linowes, David F. "The Accounting Profession and Social Progress." *Journal of Accounting*, July 1973, pp. 32–40.

Sadan, Simcha, and Auerback, Len B. "A Stochastic Model for Human Resource Valuation." *California Management Review*, Summer 1974, pp. 24–31.

Social Audit Limited. *Social Audit.* Published quarterly by Social Audit Ltd., 9 Poland Street, London WIV, 3 DG.

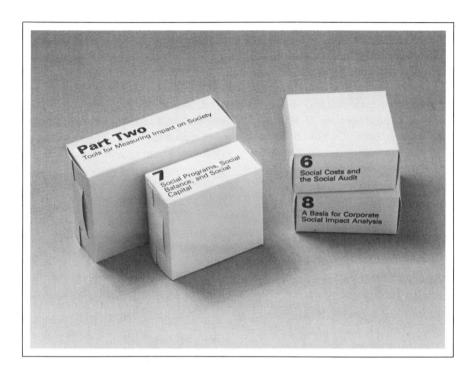

7
Social Programs, Social Balance, and Social Capital

Many corporations have seen the need for new social programs and have begun to develop something that meets the need at least partially. The organizational pattern of a few of these programs is reviewed here, as well as some of their elements.

The chapter discusses the achievements and limitations of such programs and then introduces the management concept of avoiding the creation of social costs. This consideration requires looking at the nature of the social capital against which such a social balance would be measured. The exploration of the social balance concept is handled as part of the process of defining a management approach that bypasses at least some limitations on the effective extension of corporate social audits and programs and addresses the full scope of corporate management problems and opportunities. Later the concept will be further studied and analyzed.

The concept of corporate social responsibility requires new thinking on the part of managers. Implementing a sense of corporate responsibility can be both beneficial and dangerous to a business. Hence it should be managed in the same way as other critical corporate functions are managed.[1]

VERNON M. BUEHLER AND Y. K. SHETTY

Corporate Social Programs

Many corporations have organized social or corporate responsibility programs. One of the difficulties has been the lack of clear guidelines as to how far such responsibility should extend or how much expense it should warrant versus the claims of the stockholders and other needs of the business. This difficulty has generated a frustration and created a receptivity to new measurement tools that has, in turn, been frustrated by the imperfections inherent in the tools. Thus, the corporate efforts toward defining and fulfilling a corporate responsibility have developed largely on an empirical basis.

Organization

Ackerman and others have documented the rapid spread of corporate programs;[2] a significant number of the leading corporations have gathered their responsibility-related activities into some sort of organizational framework and developed a pattern of publicly reporting these activities.

In 1973 Paluszek studied the organization of the programs of seven companies that were among the early leaders in establishing corporate programs. These cases illustrate the range of structures employed in initiating this corporate function. For example, the Bank of America appointed an executive vice president of social policy who reports to the president. On the other hand, Equitable Life Assurance Society assigned the responsibility of administering corporate programs to the senior line officers and appointed a senior vice president of corporate relations to coordinate their efforts. Whirlpool Corporation established its departments of urban and public

---

[1]Vernon M. Buehler and Y.K. Shetty, "Managing Corporate Social Responsibility," *Management Review*, August 1975, p. 4.

[2]Robert W. Ackerman, "Social Responsiveness in the Large Corporation," *Proceedings, Business Policy and Planning Division*, Academy of Management National Meeting, Boston, Mass., August 1973.

affairs under the direction of a vice president of corporate public affairs and its department of consumer services under the direction of a vice president of consumer services; both these vice presidents report to the chairperson and chief executive officer.

In the First Pennsylvania Bank, social responsibility functions were centralized in an urban affairs department under a vice president of urban affairs reporting to the bank president. Levi Strauss centralized these same functions in its community affairs department, with the director reporting to the chairperson and chief executive officer. As with Equitable, Atlantic Richfield Company put primary responsibility for social responsibility programs in its line organization by vesting responsibility for specific corporate programs in its vice president of public relations. Standard Oil Company (Indiana) moved from concentrating these programs in its urban affairs department to creating a new area of responsibility for a vice president who reports to the office of the president and is responsible for all external concerns, including those involving government, communications (public relations), and the physical and social environment.[3] These organizational structures represent events in the evolution of new corporate operating patterns that deal with new corporate social concerns. The best organizational arrangement will depend on the specific corporate circumstances. However, a pattern has emerged of establishing a new high-level function that is highly visible and is under the control of a senior executive; this pattern indicates clearly the degree of management interest in and support for the new corporate social effort.

It is difficult to generalize about corporate program organization because so many organizational forms are in use. It is possible to start from the need to have at least one high-level executive assigned to the program, to organize in a way that fits with the nature and style of the company, and to work toward the point when many of these activities become routine responsibilities that require only a minimum amount of separate organization. Beyond this, it is interesting to note the special units that different companies have developed, such as the Office of Social Research at Equitable. Such organizational forms serve to give emphasis within the organization to the start of a new corporate program.

Achievements

When corporate programs are considered, their very pervasiveness deserves first recognition; in one study 160 out of 232 major corporations had formulated specific social objectives.[4] Thus, the majority of corporate annual reports from major corporations have devoted at least a section to the corporate social program.

As an example, the Norton Company, like many other companies, has devoted sections of its social report to corporate contributions, environment, employment policies, and public service. There is also a section dealing with the corporate

---

[3]John L. Paluszek, *Organizing for Social Responsibility* (New York: The Presidents Association, a division of American Management Association, 1973), pp. 13–32.
[4]Buehler and Shetty, "Managing Corporate Social Responsibility."

rationale for the continuation of Norton's operation in South Africa. The Norton report was entitled *Response*. In content the Norton report (as in the case of most corporate reports) focuses on responding to conspicuous areas of public pressure and presenting the corporate contribution program. This is a good report on what appears to be a good program.

Aetna Life & Casualty Company, CNA Financial, Dayton Hudson Corporation, and many others publish similar reports, some of which are more extensive both in detail and presentation. The Quaker Oats Company publishes a social progress plan that presents a thorough review of the Quaker Oats programs. Whirlpool has developed and publicized its "Cool Line" program for prompt and effective response to customer complaints, and Southern New England Telephone Company retained the services of a former governor of Connecticut to conduct an in-depth analysis of the environmental impact of its service efforts.[5] There is no question that these corporate programs have merit, insofar as they represent a contribution to society, but they are hard to evaluate. On one side, they represent both a corporate effort and a skillful public relations presentation. On the other, they represent corporate compliance with equal opportunity and other legislation and the use of corporate resources for charitable and community purposes.

Norton points with pride to cash contributions to charitable causes that average over 2 percent of pretax income, as compared to a quoted corporate average of 1 percent. Dayton Hudson sets aside 5 percent of pretax income for the same purpose. If diversion of pretax income is a good yardstick, then some companies are devoting either too much or too little to this purpose. However, the equation between company and society is too complex to be resolved simply by agreeing on a particular allocation of pretax income.

With charitable activities, as in the case of compliance with laws governing employment and environment, the corporate role needs analysis; presentation of an attractive corporate program is necessary but not sufficient, since standards for corporate conduct have not been completely developed.

Current Status

Most large corporations have now taken steps toward the organization and formalization of their corporate social program; many have begun to issue corporate social reports. This trend is progressive and worthwhile.

From a past time when external corporate activities were concentrated in a contributions or community relations function, the area has broadened. A more extensive corporate involvement with society is necessary, and it has grown out of the older and narrower corporate giving concepts into many programs such as those reported here.

This growth has the potential to span the full range of corporate-society interactions from the social implications of corporate growth strategy to the social impact of a relocation, merger, or divestiture. When measured against this potential, most

---

[5]John N. Dempsey, *Impact: A Report on the Environmental Effects of the Service Efforts of Southern New England Telephone*, New Haven, Conn.: Southern New England Telephone Company, 1972.

corporate social programs have much room left for growth and progress; any serious appraisal of the prospect for this additional growth must deal with the same type of limitations on available measurement and management tools that are limiting the growth of the corporate social audit.

To some extent, these reports and programs represent an answer to the activists who attack the attitudes and actions of large corporations and, to some extent, they do not. Heilbroner has reported unethical and illegal corporate actions;[6] Nader has called out for "whistle-blowers" inside corporations to bring unsavory practices to public attention.[7] Both men are campaigning to activate public interest in extending the standards for corporate activity into new territory that has not been within the scope of most corporate responsibility programs in the past. Again, there is the need for new tools so that management can manage, and society can evaluate, such programs more effectively.

Present Limitations

The discussion here and in the previous chapter has focused on the usefulness and limitations of these social programs and social audits. The need is for some way to bypass the limitations.

The concept of a social audit or of an equivalent system of social accounting is based on the assumption that the relevant costs can be identified, first qualitatively and then quantitatively, in such a way that their values can be weighed and compared. However, social costs are difficult to measure because (1) they involve so many subjective elements, such as personal utility or the value of an historic landmark and (2) the value of certain elements changes with time as public consciousness of overall social values increases and public value systems shift. For example, public interest in having clean air to breathe has increased sharply.

Social costs are primarily considered using subjective values. Until objective measurement concepts are developed further, direct social cost measurements will be laborious and uncertain. In the meantime, other measurement concepts must be found to meet corporate management needs.

A possible way of bypassing the social cost measurement problem is to direct attention to the elimination, rather than the size, of social costs. It can be argued that the measurement of many social costs is not really important because, once these costs have been identified, the only socially acceptable solution is to eliminate them. If they are to be eliminated, their size no longer matters. For example, while techniques for estimating the social cost of a polluted stream have been devised at least in part, these costs are only relevant to corporate decisions as long as society will permit the pollution to continue. When society mandates that the pollution be eliminated, that issue must be faced. The actual size of the social cost becomes meaningless since it will not affect society's attitude or the necessary corporate response.

---

[6] Robert Heilbroner, ed. *In the Name of Profit* (Garden City, N.Y.: Doubleday, 1972).

[7] Ralph Nader, Peter J. Petkas, and Kate Blackwell, eds. *Whistle Blowing* (New York: Grossman, 1972).

Social Balance

Instead of incurring debits at the expense of society and then trying to evaluate the alternatives for correcting them in the midst of political stresses and social cost calculation problems, it would be more desirable for a corporation to operate in such a way as to avoid such debits or, at least, balance the ones that are unavoidable. This concept provides the basis for the definition of *social balance* as the equilibrium point across each business-society interface at which society is gaining at least as much as it is losing as a result of the business operation.

Clearly, a social balance is desirable; its ability to be measured and achieved will be further examined later in the book. For example, if the performance of a company's products completely fulfills the expectation created by the advertising and promotion and if the products cause no untoward side effects and no extraordinary disposal costs, then an adequate social balance exists in the product area.

In summary, the social balance concept is conceived around the avoidance of social costs; no net loss to society must result from the impact of the corporation in any sector of its activity if a social balance is to exist. A business normally contributes to society by selling goods and services whose value equals or exceeds the exchange value received for them. But a business can also drain off society's assets by conducting improper practices in other parts of its operation. The result of establishing social balance is to conserve society's assets (sometimes called *social capital*) in all areas and increase those assets in the areas where the firm makes a contribution.

Social Capital

Social cost represents a debit, a diminution of wealth, and an expense to society. As a result of a social cost, society is poorer than it would otherwise have been; the total wealth of society (the total social capital) has been reduced. As a next step then, social capital must be more clearly defined to provide a basis for discussing how to measure the gains and losses that occur on the social balance scale.

Social capital is defined here as the collective stock of wealth of a society, including the holdings of its businesses and individuals. The definition encompasses not only physical wealth but also the state of health and welfare of its people.

This concept of the collective public stock of goods has been widely developed in the writings of past and present economists. For instance, Rostow defines one of the requirements for takeoff into industrialism in a developing country as an accumulation of the necessary stock of *social overhead capital.*[8] Bowen speaks of the investment in people as an important part of the general stock of wealth: "Investment in human beings is intended to produce further returns in the form of knowledge, skills, strength, character, or morale. The returns may be reaped in the form of higher

---

[8]W.W. Rostow, *The Stages of Economic Growth* (London: Cambridge University Press, 1960), pp. 24–26.

[9]H.R. Bowen, "Charity and the Corporation," *Management Record,* February 1962, p. 31. See also Bertram M. Gross, *The State of the Nation* (London: Social Science Paperbacks, Associated Book Publishers, Ltd., 1966), pp. 20–23.

productivity, better citizenship, or greater personal welfare."[9] Again, in *Toward Social Economy,* Bowen distinguishes between material and nonmaterial capital goods as a part of the total supply of capital: "At any given moment in the history of a society, then, there are in existence human beings with attributes, propensities and skills which have been produced through past productive efforts which comprise the available non-material capital goods."[10]

Bowen did not claim to have originated these ideas; in fact, previously Adam Smith had noted that the education and training of individuals adds to the total fixed capital of society.[11] Smith also recognized the duty of the government to undertake public works that were necessary for the general good but not profitable as private businesses.[12] Here is a bridge between the intangible types of capital to which Bowen refers and the social capital of Rostow that comprises the measurable fixed investments in railways, electric systems, and other physical components of national capital. In this book social capital is intended to include Rostow's concepts and also the concepts of cultural and intellectual wealth of Bowen and Smith, that is, to include both tangible and intangible wealth.

Tangible social capital includes not only the national infrastructure (the transportation system and other public utilities and services)[13] but also natural resources and geographic assets. Thus, petroleum reserves, which represent a valuable natural resource for any modern industrial society, are more valuable in the North Sea, where they are geographically close to the industries that consume them, than the same reserves in the Near East, which are separated by many hazardous miles from potential users. The great reserves of the Alaskan North Slope are not only remote in miles but are made less accessible by the severe arctic climate. The physical stock of social capital includes all these factors in its assessment, transportation as well as resources, and the resources are assessed in proportion to their value to the society.

Intangible social capital includes the nonmaterial assets, such as the cultural and intellectual wealth to which Bowen refers and also the state of health and welfare of the population; as Smith observes, the wear and tear on the health of free workers represents an expense to the industry that must employ their services.[14]

This stock of social capital is not only determined by the cultural and intellectual assets of the nation but by the way in which these assets are employed. For instance, Veblen defined conspicuous leisure as a goal in American society; here he referred to visible idleness as demonstrating the degree of material success that is sufficient to free one from the need for gainful employment.[15] On the other hand, Weber described a strong and unbounded accumulation as a continuing measure of

---

[10]H.R. Bowen, *Toward Social Economy* (New York: Rinehart & Company, 1948), pp. 85–88.

[11]Adam Smith, *An Inquiry into the Nature and Causes of the Wealth of Nations,* vol. 1 (Homewood, Ill.: Richard D. Irwin, 1963), p. 214.

[12]Ibid., vol. 2, p. 239.

[13]In economic terms the *infrastructure* represents the basic national investment in transportation, public buildings, utilities, and public services of all types.

[14]Smith, *Wealth of Nations,* vol. 1, pp. 64–65. Consider also Gross's observations: "A healthy population is one of the greatest of all natural resources," and ". . . the level of technology in any society is a dimension of human ability." In Gross, *The State of the Nation,* pp. 49–51.

[15]Thorstein Veblen, *The Theory of the Leisure Class* (New York: Mentor Books, 1953), pp. 41–59.

Figure 7.1   Ingredients of Social Capital

Collective stock of wealth of society

Physical wealth—natural resources—geographical location—climate—minerals, rivers, forests, arable land

State of health and welfare of its people—numbers—knowledge, strength, skills—cultural and intellectual wealth—national or cultural drives—mechanical bent or tradition—entrepreneurial tradition

Accumulation of necessary stock of social overhead capital—national infrastructure—public works—roads, railroads, public utilities, airports, industrial complexes with necessary supporting services—harbors—energy supplies

---

both success and spiritual and temporal favor.[16] Currently, many young Americans are rejecting the materialism on which both Veblen and Weber built in favor of a return to simpler values.[17] A given stock of cultural and intellectual wealth will clearly result in a greater accumulation of material wealth and more rapid economic progress if employed in the ethic described by Weber than if left idle while spiritual values are sought or dissipated in the pattern described by Veblen. Figure 7.1 summarizes some views of social capital.

Social capital is the economic property of society. An individual business has no right to infringe on this social capital unless society makes a decision to subsidize that business. Thus, social costs can be also defined as uncompensated or unauthorized charges against the social capital. Such charges must be avoided or counterbalanced by a responsible firm; this obligation forms the basis for one definition of social responsibility and for the social balance concept.

Summary

As the national and corporate needs have become more obvious and more acute, many major corporations have adopted or enlarged their corporate social programs. Often these programs have grown from long-established community affairs or public relations functions by having new emphasis placed on those aspects of urban, consumer, or corporate responsibility that seem most appropriate to a particular management.

Many of these programs are excellent, both in their social purpose and in their

---

[16]Max Weber, *The Protestant Ethic and the Spirit of Capitalism* (New York: Charles Scribner, 1958), pp. 47–48.

[17]"This book is for people who would rather chop wood than work behind a desk so they can pay P.G.&E. [Pacific Gas & Electric] . . . when we depend less on industrially produced consumer goods, we can live in quiet places. Our bodies become vigorous; we discover the serenity of living with the rhythms of the earth. We cease oppressing one another." Alicia Bay Laurel, *Living on Earth* (New York: Vintage Books, Random House, 1970), introduction.

linkage with corporate communication channels that obtain appropriate publicity for these efforts. The limitation of such programs is in their frequent lack of an objective basis, which would be helpful in determining how much of the corporate resources should be funneled into social efforts. As we discussed earlier, society's demands are urgent, and good tools are not yet available for objective and defensible division of resources between social programs and other corporate purposes. Although the achievements made through empirical allocations and intuitive program design are to be applauded, they do not reduce the need for a better theoretical framework.

One constructive approach to the problem is the attempt to reach a social balance in each area of corporate impact. In other words, as the corporation has impacts on society in various areas of its operation, there is a possibility that it will somehow cause costs that it does not pay. These costs fall on the relevant portion of society and represent an invasion of the social capital, which is the collective stock of wealth of society.

Society's motivation for many of the restrictions on corporate behavior seems to have resulted from the need to redress or gain reprisal for past unauthorized social costs. This situation is responsible for much of the tension existing between corporations and society. Thus, it seems most wise for management to operate in such a way that it causes a minimum of social costs; that is, to attempt to achieve a social balance in each impact area. This chapter has provided a part of the necessary foundation for defining the basis for guidelines for the achievement of such a social balance.

The next step is to define the basis for a corporate impact analysis so that we can explore the use of the social balance concept and explain its potential for aiding corporate management in dealing with today's numerous social responsibility issues. This chapter started by providing a perspective on the many, rapidly improving corporate social programs, then suggested some of their limitations relative to a total management solution of the corporate social impact problem, and finally defined the concept of social balance between corporate operation and the total social capital as a normative style that will be tested for practicality in later chapters.

Questions for Analysis and Discussion

1. Select and analyze a current social report. (Suggestion: Review annual reports; many now contain some treatment of social programs or even a full social report.) What are its major components?

2. What do you think is the best way for a corporate social program to be organized and directed?

3. In your opinion, how large should the corporate budget for contributions and social programs be? One percent of pretax income? Five percent? Or should it be measured in some other way?

4. To what extent should a corporation publicize employment and environment programs that primarily represent compliance with the law?

5. List some of the major elements in the social capital of a community and comment on their relative importance.

For Further Information

Ackerman, Robert W. "Social Responsiveness in the Large Corporation." *Proceedings, Business Policy and Planning Division*, Academy of Management National Meeting, Boston, Mass., August 1973.

Lund, Leonard. *Corporate Organization for Environmental Policymaking*. New York: The Conference Board, 1974.

Paluszek, John L. *Organizing for Corporate Social Responsibility*. New York: The Presidents Association, a Division of American Management Association, 1973.

Westman, Walter E. "How Much are Nature's Services Worth?" *Science*, 2 September 1977, pp. 960–964.

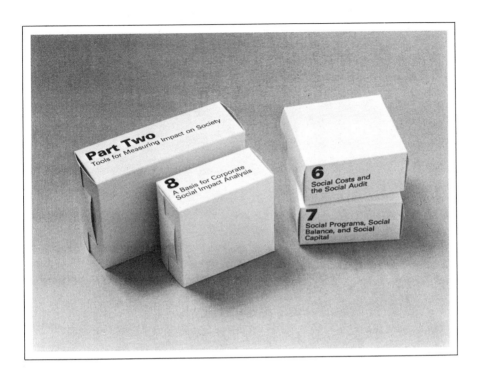

8
A Basis for Corporate Social Impact Analysis

In response to the need for an objective procedure for managing corporate social impact, the concept of social balance was introduced in the previous chapter. This concept requires that there be no negative corporate impacts in any area as a result of the firm's operation. The need addressed here is to construct a bridge between that concept and an analytical framework within which corporate social impact in different areas can be measured. In this way we will be able to test the practicality of attempting to achieve a social balance. After alternatives are considered, the chapter defines and explains such an analytical framework in preparation for the area-by-area review of corporate social impact in the later chapters of the book.

Not until businessmen recognize that they are administrators of power systems can they face realistically how to discharge morally the power they wield.[1]

SYLVIA K. SELEKMAN AND BENJAMIN M. SELEKMAN

Social Balance and Corporate Impact Analysis

The social responsibility concept is, among other things, the embodiment of a variety of ideas about the causes and cures of the growing stress between corporation and society. The reality of this stress, which has grown rapidly in the recent past, is indisputable, as is the fact that the stress has led to the increasing development of major programs in corporations and in the academic institutions that study them. Chapter 6 reviewed the social audit programs with passing reference to major related efforts at the development of social accounting techniques. Chapter 7 dealt at some length with social capital, the social balance concept, and a sampling of current corporate social programs.

Key questions concerning the nature and extent of social responsibility have not been answered completely; to some extent the asking of these questions is still somewhat premature. First, it would seem necessary for us to look more deeply at the nature of the stress between corporation and society before we try to define responsibility for the appropriate curative action. Parts Three and Four of this book will be devoted to such an examination.

Without trying to establish and defend a final definition of the necessary relationship between the corporation and society, a tentative definition of the relationship will be chosen for the purpose of facilitating the flow of the analysis in Parts Three and Four. Two elements are of primary importance to this relationship.

1. *Increasingly, corporations will be held responsible for the impact of controllable actions.* Reference was made earlier to the growing tendency to hold corporations accountable for all impacts of their actions on the surrounding society. This tendency is sufficiently strong and significant to foreshadow serious pressures on corporate managements in the future.

2. *Individual areas of corporate activity must be considered separately.* Each of us, and each element in society, tends to show greatest concern for individual problems and interests rather than for those that involve the general welfare. Hence, activists

---

[1]Sylvia K. Selekman and Benjamin M. Selekman, *Power and Morality in a Business Society* (New York: McGraw-Hill, 1956), p. ix.

who were angry about the production of napalm gave no attention to any of the constructive programs the Dow Chemical Company had developed in other areas of its business—nor could they have been expected to. Each sector of society will tend to judge corporations independently based on observation of what is happening in that sector, and corporate managements must expect their actions to be reviewed on this basis.

As a means of studying corporate impacts on the many different sectors of society, the social balance concept provides a convenient focus and will be applied. The concept of a social balance was introduced in Chapter 7 to describe a pattern of operation in which a firm arranges its business in such a way as to avoid incurring social costs or at least to avoid social costs that are not properly and promptly compensated.[2] By restating this definition to include the concept of social capital that was introduced in the last chapter, we can simplify the social balance definition to a requirement that social capital not be depleted by a business in any of its operations. The social balance concept is intended to be applied to the activities of each individual firm and is defined to aid us in judging whether a firm's contributions in one area compensate for any drains that are made on the capital of society in the same area.

Initially, the social balance concept of operation represents only a theoretical approach. This theory provides both a useful point of departure for a review of the problems that corporations face in the many different areas of their contact with society and a way of testing how far the solutions to the problems in each area have progressed. Thus, the next step will be to select an analytical framework that can facilitate such a review.

Alternative Analytical Viewpoints

Such an analysis of the balance between a business and society in the various sectors of business operations is necessarily based on a system for classifying business activities into sectors; the nature of this classification tends to focus the emphasis in the subsequent analysis. Classifications have been constructed from many viewpoints, including those of the business, the individual community, and society as a whole. The question is to determine which classification viewpoint is more useful here.

The Business Point of View

A frequent division of the external relationships of a business is constructed for the use of the executives who manage these relationships. Perhaps one of the best-known developments of this classification is the stakeholder's analysis prepared by Stewart and others and embodied in past long-range planning seminars of the Stanford Research Institute. This analysis takes the viewpoint of the chief executive

---

[2]Social balance is used here as a microeconomic concept. For a discussion of social balance as a macroeconomic concept, see the appendix at the end of this chapter that is entitled "Galbraith's Social Balance."

and deals with the question of who among those the business activity touches have a stake in the well-being of the business. "The stakeholders of a firm are: its owners; its customers; its employees; both leaders and followers; its nonowner financial sources, including creditors, lenders, brokers and underwriters; its suppliers; and to some degree, the society of which it is a part."[3]

This analytical approach is important and constructive for the primary purpose of teaching business leaders to recognize their proper role over their entire range of responsibilities. The limitation of this analysis is that, for the present purpose, the point of view of the business leader is not the most important.

The real leaders of the business community have felt that they were doing their job well and responsibly, but the public has sometimes disagreed sharply. Andrew Carnegie, for instance, expressed his business philosophy very cogently, and his writings are important in explaining the thinking of that business era. Yet at the time of the Homestead strike, the public formed its judgment on the basis of the way his company broke the strike rather than on the basis of Carnegie's written words. McCloskey tells of Carnegie's surprise at the degree of contradiction that people found between his actions and his words.[4]

Although a business leader's point of view is valuable, it does not necessarily represent the opinion of society. Business operates by the sufferance of society; in the ultimate analysis a business must be judged from the point of view of that society rather than in its own light.

The Community Point of View

"In my judgment it is the social responsibility of management: first to work to improve local community conditions;. . . ."[5] In one of the early works on the social responsibility of business, Ruttenberg emphasized several aspects of relationships with employees as being secondary in importance to the company's obligation to improve local community conditions.

The community's point of view is valid and important in evaluating the performance of a business, but in many ways business has outgrown the local community. Some firms are national and international giants, and the competitive environment of all firms is conditioned by influences that reach beyond the local community.

> The large corporation takes its place along with the church and the armed services as an organization that transcends the local territory and cuts across political boundaries, at times even those of the nation and state.[6]

---

[3]Robert F. Stewart, et al., *The Strategic Plan*, Long Range Planning Service, report no. 168 (Menlo Park, Calif.: Stanford Research Institute, 1963), p. 6.

[4]Robert Green McCloskey, *American Conservatism in the Age of Enterprise 1865–1910* (New York: Harper & Row, Torch Book Edition, 1964), pp. 127–167.

[5]Stuart Chase, Stanley H. Ruttenberg, Edwin G. Nourse, and William B. Given, Jr., *The Social Responsibility of Management* (New York: New York University Press, 1950), p. 28.

[6]Norton Long, "The Corporation, Its Satellites, and the Local Community," in Edward S. Mason, ed., *The Corporation in Modern Society* (Cambridge, Mass.: Harvard University Press, 1961), p. 202.

Society's Point of View

The preceding analysis concluded that the corporate impact and the degree of social balance achieved by the actions of a given corporation are judged most appropriately from society's point of view. The local community view can be too narrow, although its interests are a legitimate part of the total. Since corporate activities often transcend national and community boundaries, the question arises as to what portion of society is actually the proper judge of the actions of an international corporation.

Basic to the existence of the modern industrial system, however, are the laws that permit the formation of corporations and define corporate rights and duties. Even in a very small country, the corporation's right to operate is controlled locally and must be justified locally; the social balance concepts under discussion are proposed as a means of arriving at this justification. A U.S. corporation lives within a reasonably uniform national environment but must recognize important elements in state and local laws and sometimes justify its actions on a local level.

Therefore, the analytical viewpoint used here will be derived from the political units that define the rules governing corporate behavior.[7] This viewpoint will be developed by analyzing the operational impact of business on its balance with society as a whole and with each of the major groups that make up the society around that business.

A Framework for Corporate Impact Analysis

In examining the firm from the point of view of society, we should first consider its inputs and outputs. Resources go in, and products (goods and services) and waste come out. Next, we can observe that a firm has distinct impacts on its immediate neighborhood but also on the entire framework of society. This perspective permits a more comprehensive flow sheet as illustrated in Figure 8.1.

Some of the physical and human resources that a firm uses are consumed and some are not; this important distinction will recur later. In particular, the distinction between the use of resources and their consumption or depletion raises important issues, which are identified with the people and with the physical stock of goods the firm employs. Furthermore, the use of resources is not in any way a neutral process; the firm is at once a provider of jobs, a mainstay of the local economy, and a consumer of local natural wealth.

In developing this analytical framework, an attempt will be made to classify the firm's impacts on society according to whether they concern (1) major output streams flowing out from the business to society, (2) major inputs to the business from the surrounding society, (3) neighborhood effects on the portions of society in the proximity of the firm, and (4) society-wide effects of that particular firm.

---

[7]Thus, the viewpoint may differ for different types of problems according to whether regulations have been established by federal, state, or local laws or by regional agencies.

Figure 8.1.　The Firm as Viewed by Society

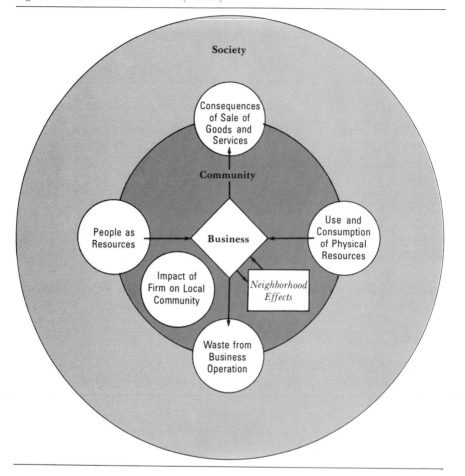

Output of Goods and Services

The major and obvious output stream is the flow of goods and services whose sale and economic value simultaneously justify the existence of the firm and provide the flow of credits and payments that permit it to obtain the resources necessary for its continuation. This flow of goods and services interrelates with the lifestyles of its customers, if they are individuals, or with the progress of their businesses, if the customers are other industrial firms.

Use of Physical and Human Resources

This category includes the raw materials and various other physical resources that are used or consumed and the human resources that are contributed by employees and any others who devote their energies to carrying out the business. In both cases it becomes important to consider not only the effect of varying kinds of business and varying sorts of policies on the different resources but also the direct or indirect social impacts that result from these policies.

Neighborhood and Community Impact

In addition to its products, a firm generates some waste or production byproducts that may be beneficial, neutral, or highly deleterious, depending on the degree to which they are adapted to the needs of the environment prior to their discharge. Also, the operation of the firm has many direct or indirect impacts on the local community or communities, including its contribution to the shaping of the local culture.

Societywide Effects

Business resource policies, such as where to invest and how to provide for the future of the business, have particular social impacts and consequences. In its operation and implementation of these resource policies, a firm is both a producer and a consumer of technology. The balance between production and consumption and the overall impact of technology generation are of considerable interest and concern to society. In addition, business has an active and passive involvement in public issues and also a network of involvements with government, its regulatory agencies, and other major sources of supporting or countervailing power throughout the society. This involvement leads into a consideration of the basis for the power and authority of business management and of the effect of political boundaries on the firm as it operates in many communities, states, or nations.

Summary

The analytical framework that has been presented will be used in Parts Three and Four to examine the business-society interaction on an area-by-area basis. The viewpoint of society was selected for this analysis as being the most useful and relevant of the alternatives. The approach used will be a microanalysis that is based on firm-by-firm considerations. This examination will then provide the basis for consideration in Part Five of the degree to which the social balance or social equilibrium theory presented earlier can provide an effective tool and a practical basis for management action.

Appendix: Galbraith's Social Balance

Social balance has just been discussed as a microeconomic concept, in contrast to Galbraith's macroeconomic concept. In a chapter on "The Theory of Social Balance" in his book, *The Affluent Society*, Galbraith analyzes the necessary macroeconomic relationship between the nation's investment in private and in public goods. He explains his balance concept in this way:

> The final problem of the productive society is what it produces. This manifests itself in an implacable tendency to provide an opulent supply of some things and a meagerness of others. This disparity carries to the point where it is a cause of social discomfort and social unhealth. The line which divides our area of wealth from our area of poverty is roughly that which divides privately produced and marketed goods and services from publicly rendered services. Our wealth in the first is not only in startling contrast with the meagerness of the latter, but our wealth in privately produced goods is, to a marked degree, the cause of crisis in the supply of public services. But we have failed to see the importance, indeed the urgent need of maintaining a balance between the two.[8]

Thus, Galbraith has dealt with the total balance in the national allocation of efforts between production of private goods and public services rather than with the allocation of efforts of an individual firm that we have stressed. In particular, our analysis deals with the way that an individual firm establishes an equilibrium with the society on which it depends and the way that it shifts its allocations to ameliorate or balance its impacts in areas where it is causing social costs.

Questions for Analysis and Discussion

1. Discuss the extent to which you agree or disagree with the following statement: "Corporations will be increasingly responsible for the impact of controllable actions."

2. "Individual areas of corporate activity must be considered separately." If you were adversely affected by a corporate action, would you ignore the injury if you knew that the corporation had done good things for others? Discuss.

3. Can you think of any examples of instances where a corporation's efforts to relate to the surrounding society have been hampered by imperfections in its own viewpoint?

4. How do you feel about the practicality of a corporation establishing a social balance with each community and legal jurisdiction in which it operates?

5. List the stakeholders of a firm and discuss their relative importance and influence.

6. Do you agree that business must conform to community standards? Discuss.

7. Select a firm to study, examine its operations, and then list some of the outputs, inputs, neighborhood effects, and effects that it has on the community as a whole.

---

[8]John Kenneth Galbraith, *The Affluent Society* (Boston: Houghton Mifflin, 1958), p. 251.

For Further Information

Jacoby, Neil H. *Corporate Power and Social Responsibility.* New York: Macmillan, 1973.

Manne, Henry G., and Wallich, Henry C. *The Modern Corporation and Social Responsibility.* Washington D.C.: American Enterprise Institute for Public Policy Research, 1972.

Mason, Edward S. ed. *The Corporation in Modern Society.* Cambridge, Mass.: Harvard University Press, 1961.

Votaw, Dow, and Sethi, S. Prakash. *The Corporate Dilemma.* Englewood Cliffs, N. J.: Prentice-Hall, 1973.

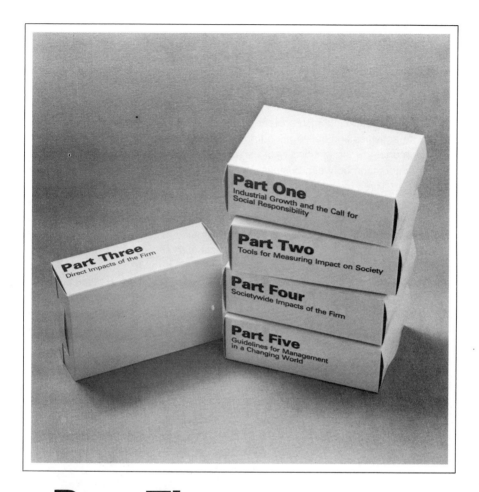

Part Three
Direct Impacts
of the Firm

The origins of the social responsibility movement and the resulting social pressure on corporate management were discussed in Part One. Part Two turned to the pattern of corporate response to this pressure as evidenced by various sorts of programs. While new procedures such as social accounting and social audits are constructive and useful, they have not entirely alleviated the problem through either their relief of society's pressure or their contribution to increased mastery of managing the business-society interface. Better tools are needed for this management task, and Part Two closed with the selection of an analytical framework for a more detailed analysis of the business-society relationship.

Our consideration of the concept of social capital as the total resources of society and of the history of incursions on this wealth that have been incidental to various corporate operations led us to a more basic definition of the need: Corporations must control their negative impacts on society to gain relief from the public pressure against corporate actions. Social balance, or the absence of negative corporate social impact, was suggested as a desirable state in which society would derive maximum benefit from corporate activities and have minimum incentive to check corporate freedom. To demonstrate the practicality of establishing such a balance, the various areas of interaction between business and society must be individually considered.

Part Three examines some of the direct impacts of a firm's operation on its surrounding community by taking an analytical look at the various direct linkages between the corporation and society. It discusses the impact of a firm's products, of its consumption and employment of resources, and of its effects on neighborhoods. Chapter 9 deals with society's view of the firm's sale of goods and services to its customers. Chapter 10 explores the impact created as the corporation both uses and consumes physical resources. Chapter 11 examines the consequences of using people as resources to accomplish the work of the firm. Chapter 12 considers the impact of wastes discharged by the business operation. And Chapter 13 discusses the impact of the corporate presence and operations on the local community. Together these chapters are intended to integrate the social impacts of various elements of the routine operation of the firm.

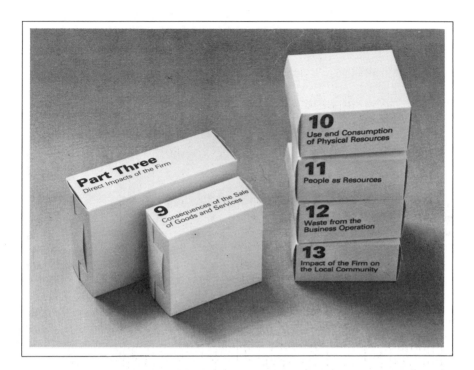

9
Consequences of the Sale of Goods and Services

The existence of a given business firm is justified by its economic role in obtaining and selling goods and services. In addition to this economic role, the sale of goods and services often has a major social impact. Areas of concern include the requirement for fair representation in advertising and promotion and the need for fair treatment in the continuing relationship between vendor and customer that follows the initial sale. This circumstance can involve an implicit commitment to continue supplying goods that the vendor may or may not be able to fulfill. Similarly, the requirements for product safety can introduce considerations that extend well beyond the intended purpose of or market for the product. Thus, product liability hazards are receiving considerable attention from some current manufacturers in the same way that social and cultural impacts of new products and services may become major areas of concern in the future.

*The ultimate rationale for the existence of business firms, both large and small,
lies in their service to consumers. One might suppose, . . . that management
would for that reason cultivate their customers and avoid any practice that might
offend those on whom it depends for its existence.*[1]

NEIL W. CHAMBERLAIN

When Henry Ford began to channel the energies of the Ford Motor Company into the
manufacture and marketing of the Model T, a turning point was reached in the
evolution of the motor car. For the first time, practical transportation that was faster
and more convenient than the horse and buggy became available at prices that were
low enough to appeal to the public at large. The public bought Ford cars in quantity
and seemed to be well satisfied with the value received.

As the company prospered and the number of cars in use expanded, the driving
public began to demand better roads. Then Ford found it necessary to establish a
dealership network for not only marketing but also parts supply and product services.
Gasoline stations and numerous other subsidiary businesses sprang up to serve the
needs of the driving public. The United States transformed itself into a society that
became increasingly dependent on the present and future availability of the automobile.

Automobile accidents became both possible and more frequent occurrences.
Parking tickets and traffic tickets were invented; control of speeding, automobile
theft, and other irresponsible automotive use became a social problem. The
increased personal mobility began to change the social structure and the relationships within the family. Discarded automobiles accumulated in ravines, in dumps,
and then on city streets. Some scientists began to express concern that the
accumulation of lead from automobile exhaust would eventually impair the fertility of
land adjacent to major highways.

Henry Ford was just one of many motor car maufacturers, of course, but one who
played a central role in the transition of the automobile from a toy for the well-to-do to
the principal vehicle for personal transportation in the United States. This transition
occurred only because Ford and other American entrepreneurs invested energy,
imagination, and capital in bringing a very imperfect invention, the horseless carriage,
to the point of utility that created a mass market. The same process was beginning in
other countries, and if these men had not taken the lead, others probably would have
emerged in their place. However, American entrepreneurs did lead and, by their
leadership, hastened a process that caused a significant social transformation. The

---

[1]Neil W. Chamberlain, *The Limits of Corporate Responsibility* (New York: Basic Books, 1973),
p. 11.

issue here is the extent to which Henry Ford, his peers, and his successors can or should be held responsible for the consequences of creating and satisfying the demand for personal transportation. This issue is primary in the specific case of the auto industry and in the general case of defining a prototype for the relationship between business leaders, their firms, and the society that buys, uses, and is changed by the influence of their products.

In its essential elements, a business is an economic entity that generates its income by selling goods and services to customers in the surrounding society. The principal dimensions of this relationship are

1. the fairness of the exchange prices as the goods and services are sold,

2. the extent to which these goods and services actually fulfill the expectations that the purchasers possessed at the time of the exchange,

3. the availability of necessary service, training, or other after-sale support by the vendor,

4. the degree to which the routine sale of the goods or services creates a dependence of the customers on their continued availability,

The Firm as Viewed by Society

5. the risk of injury from or through the use of the goods or services,

6. the social and cultural impact of purchase and use of the goods and services, and

7. the environmental consequences of the use of the goods and services.

Each of these seven dimensions requires separate discussion.

Fair Exchange Value

The most fundamental question is whether the customer receives adequate value to justify the exchange when goods and services are purchased. Because of the fundamental nature of the transaction, the act of purchase should guarantee that the customer does receive adequate value, subject to qualifications for misrepresentation or bad aftereffects.

A business exists as the result of an opportunity to sell goods and services at a profit; this requires that society be willing to pay more for these goods and services than the corporation must expend to produce them. The basic premise of an exchange economy is that society will value such products according to their relative merit in the marketplace. Purchasers will yield an exchange value that is of less utility to them than the goods if market prices permit but will not pay more than the price that is equivalent to their utility. The fact that an exchange occurs proves that value exists in the goods that are purchased. Thus, the total impact of the goods and services sold by a given corporation tends to favor society and the purchasers. This is generally true even though actual markets are neither ideal nor perfectly free. While consumers may sometimes be forced to pay more than would be justified in the classical equilibrium, the utility of the goods still represents a price ceiling, even though relative prices and utilities may be distorted.

Illegal exchanges in cases where the promotion of the product is deceptive or where the product causes injury are obvious exceptions. For instance, the collective judgment of society is that sale of addictive narcotics should be forbidden even though dealers can obtain a high exchange value. The right of society to make such laws is clear; the corporation, as a creation of the law, must operate lawfully or risk major legislative and judicial reprisals. Thus, illegal actions are almost always unwise since they are outside the permissible limits of behavior.

As discussed earlier, the market transaction proves that the purchaser perceives that the purchase has a value that is equal to, or greater than, the money necessary to buy it. The next question involves the extent to which the actual and experienced value of the purchase compares with the value perceived in advance. This correlation depends on the quality and performance of the good or service and the degree to which it was fairly represented. The issue of the accuracy of the advertising and promotion will be considered first; then the issue of product quality will be broached.

Prepurchase Expectations

While society recognizes that a business must advertise and promote its products in order to sell them, the legal boundaries of the "exaggeration and puffery" that are permissible are being narrowed more and more to require that merchandise be fairly represented; in other words, no unsubstantiated claims may be made and proper warning of any hazards attendant on use of the merchandise must be given. More frequently, it is being specifically required by various state and federal agencies that all claims made in advertising be accurate and substantially documented. The Federal Trade Commission has taken the lead in a number of areas, with the Food and Drug Administration and other agencies enforcing controls on promotion in the specific product areas where they have jurisdiction.

This regulatory process becomes real to the business world when it is enforced in the courts. For example, in the prosecution of one real estate firm the Federal Trade Commission obtained a settlement requiring the refund of almost $17 million to various customers, the statement of a clearer description of uncertainties in the development plans, the provision of a ten-day interval for purchasers to withdraw from their contracts, and strict limitations on the promise of future installation of roads, sewers, and other improvements. In addition, the firm was required to complete water, sewer, and other commitments in one large development, including the donation of 1,100 acres as a park.[2]

Here a developer was restrained from misrepresenting future improvements in the development area and was ordered both to allow buyers protection against excessive sales pressure by giving them reconsideration and withdrawal rights and to deliver on past promises to buyers. These are restraints of practices reported frequently as abuses in past real estate transactions. This case involves a federal enforcement pattern that is aimed at curbing flagrant practices of large developers.

Another frequent complaint concerns the misrepresentation of manufacturer's warranties on new products. One congressional committee charged that most manufacturers had escaped their obligations to consumers by offering product warranties with important limitations and ambiguous language.[3]

The clear direction of the federal emphasis and the motivation underlying the efforts of various state and city agencies and many consumer groups is toward requiring truth in advertising claims. There is also a demand for disclosure of sufficient information about the product or service to alert the potential buyer as to hazards or operating costs and even to facilitate the making of price comparisons by consumers. The trend is toward unit pricing in supermarkets, posting of prescription drug prices in pharmacies, and describing the relative energy efficiency of such products as air conditioners.

After-Sale Support: Parts and Service

After the purchase of a product, the consumer will expect necessary parts and services to be available at reasonable cost if the product needs repair. This has not always been true in the past but is quickly becoming a part of the necessary relationship a manufacturer must establish to maintain a role in a marketplace.

Most manufacturers of products that require special knowledge, equipment, or parts for their repair find it necessary to create or arrange for a supply of parts and

---

[2]"Florida Developer to Refund $17 million to Buyers," *New York Times*, 14 September, 1974.
[3]"House Panel Finds Catches in 50 out of 51 Warranties," *New York Times*, 19 September, 1974.

services to the purchaser. This provision of service is sometimes difficult because service costs have risen steadily and service quality is hard to maintain, to the point that the after-sale costs become a major issue in planning both marketing programs and product design.

The Timex line of watches is built around the concept of a product that is sufficiently durable to be guaranteed for an adequate life and sufficiently low in price to be discarded at the end of that life rather than be repaired—the product is a disposable watch. This eliminates the after-sale servicing problem. Other firms have found it necessary to face the after-sale service problem directly. Because of the importance of the supporting service for their products, GE, RCA, and others have established extensive service networks and have continued to promote serviceability of their products as a part of the product image.

The purchase of a car, watch, or other capital item or the routine use of a disposable product or service creates a relationship between buyer and seller. An accommodation to the habitual purchasing and operating pattern of the buyer develops that is based on the availability and performance of the seller's product or service. An expectation is also likely to develop for almost indefinite availability of the product or service and for the necessary seller support. Ivory soap or a familiar industrial machine is expected to be available when wanted, and the customer feels entitled to be angry if the wish to purchase the product cannot be accommodated. The seller will normally attempt to encourage this product dependence, thereby creating a steady market for repurchase of a specific item up to the point that the line gets old or supply of the item is discontinued. Even then, such implied guarantees are often easy to fulfill. For example, a manufacturer wishing to discontinue a line of machinery that has been on the market for many years often makes a mutually beneficial arrangement with a supply house that will continue to stock spare parts throughout the useful life of the remaining machines. A chemical manufacturer finding it desirable to discontinue a given product grade or formulation will often announce the action one or two years in advance to allow users time to plan the necessary change in their processes.

In terms of corporate impact requirements, both common sense and good business judgment govern major areas; for instance, most businesses try not to be totally dependent on a single supplier or customer, and wise purchasers routinely seek commitments on future availability of parts and service for critical machines. In the same way, wise management neither shifts purchasing relationships capriciously or without cause nor leaves customers without spare parts and service within the normal life of their machines.

Continued Availability of a Product

When electric power was first widely introduced, some utilities set up direct-current distribution lines and then later changed to alternating current, when it proved to be more favorable economically. Many of the first alternating-current systems were designed for a frequency of 25 cycles per second rather than the 60 cycles per second that is now standard in most parts of the United States. As this evolution took place, the tendency was for utilities to build new facilities with the best technology;

that is, direct-current plants and 25-cycle plants were not expanded, and almost all new installations were for 60-cycle power. The utilities and the older customers rapidly drifted into an increasingly awkward situation as both the dc plants and equipment and the 25-cycle plants and equipment became older. Even though the utilities were constrained by their franchise and public utility status to recognize the need to continue service to their existing customers, this obligation became burdensome.

Thus, a conversion time was set in one region after another, and customers were forced to change to a new electric service that required replacement or modification of most electrical equipment and sometimes much of the wiring. In some cases the utilities contributed substantially to the cost of this replacement. For instance, the Ontario Hydro (a government-owned electric utility) had distributed 25-cycle power from Niagara Falls and other older plants. When it began a step-by-step reduction in the distribution of 25-cycle power, it converted the homes and appliances on the fringe of the 25-cycle area to use of 60-cycle power at little or no cost to the homeowner. In other areas, the discontinuance of dc power caused much more serious problems since the customers were largely industries who received less public assistance in the transition and found it necessary in some cases to redesign facilities as well as replace very old dc machinery with expensive new ac counterparts.

These changes in electric distribution represent a direct and clear-cut example of an important and widespread problem—that of a manufacturer's dealings with customers who have become dependent on the continuing availability of a product. In this case the electric utilities were required to continue less efficient generating plants and distribution systems for a long period of time, and the electrical appliance manufacturers were required to continue to provide 25-cycle home appliances for many years after the 25-cycle concept had been abandoned as being obsolete and inefficient. The manufacturer needed to consider these customer commitments in planning the ongoing program and aid customers in the transition when changeover time finally came.

Part of this accommodation is simple self-interest, of course; the appliance manufacturers sold 25-cycle appliances rather than lose the trade of the people who were unable to buy and use the 60-cycle appliances on which industry wished to standardize. In other cases a good-will component enters the equation; thus a manufacturer of razors will continue to stock and sell blades for older models of razors not only up until the point where the profit level becomes unattractive but also even beyond this point if customer ties and the risk of a customer-opinion backlash in the marketplace seem to justify some subsidy of this product line. Where a customer group becomes accustomed to the continuing availability of a product and logically assumes that the future will be like the past, the rupture of such an implicit commitment can lead to social costs. Manufacturers are quite correct in remaining sensitive to the implications of such costs.

In general, management prerogatives permit a company to alter its product line at will. This power to change its products involves accepting the responsibility for the consequences and meeting the social balance requirement for appropriately handling adjustments to avoid social costs insofar as possible. In many cases this cushioning of the impact of the adjustment process is already an automatic ingredient in the response of the sales and marketing departments to the way in which a change should be handled.

A social balance analysis can make the process more explicit and can serve to justify this cushioning of impact on customers and to help establish boundaries on it. Thus, the acknowledgment of ties to a customer group need not lead to undue or lengthy subsidy of their adjustment. Additionally, such an analysis can contribute to the definition of the adjustment problem for a manufacturer who intends to discontinue service to a particular customer group and wishes to spend no more on the transition than the minimum necessary to prevent undue customer and public reaction to the social costs involved in the change.

Product Safety

In the past the rules of the marketplace carried the assumption that a buyer could be expected to be wise enough and prudent enough to insist on safe and reliable products. Since the growth of mass production and mass distribution of new and complex products, this system has been judged by the public not to provide adequate protection for consumers. Legislative and regulatory safeguards have been added repeatedly. These safeguards were initiated in the more obvious areas, such as the surveillance over safety of vaccines and other medicinal products, and have continued to be extended.

Contemporary examples of product safety controls include setting guidelines for toy safety and limiting the flammability of children's sleepwear. The Toxic Chemicals Act sets new controls on chemical materials. Another regulation controls the design of match folders. The generalization is that products are either required or expected to be safe.

In addition to regulatory controls and pressure from consumer groups, the manufacturer has an increasing product liability exposure where injury results directly or indirectly from product use. Product liability follows from demonstration of injury, and much of the new regulation is aimed at prevention of injury.

Safety Hazards

The complexity of anticipating all the possible consequences of a new product or service is still beyond contemporary scientific methodology, even though the field is evolving rapidly. As an example, consider the thalidomide disaster. Here a product was introduced to the European market and had received wide acceptance for its intended purpose as a relaxant and tranquilizer. In most respects the product was extremely good and safe; however, it was found to cause terrible birth defects when taken by pregnant women. The product became available on the market because this type of drug side effect had not occurred frequently enough to have gained attention. Routine tests for the prediction of such side effects had not been developed; neither medical scientists nor government regulatory authorities in Europe or the United

States had anticipated the problem.[4] Of course they were wrong, and one by-product of the disaster was the institution of a thorough screening for this type of side effect from all drug products proposed for market.

Perhaps wiser scientists could have foreseen and avoided this problem, but more subtle and even less predictable problems of the same type have emerged. For example, the discovery that the daughters of mothers who were given certain hormones have a high incidence of cancer after they reach puberty illustrates a much more indirect and long-term effect but unquestionably a serious one. Today's world has reached the stage at which unexpected, long-term effects of products and practices of the 1940s and 1950s are now being discovered, and regulatory philosophy evolves with each new occurrence.

For the next several years, however, it seems likely that public discomfort over product safety will continue as new discoveries reveal undesirable consequences from products now in use. Unfortunately, present knowledge does not yet permit any pattern of testing that guarantees product safety in many areas because the complex interrelationship between human biochemistry and biology and specific products over the long run is not well understood. Present testing techniques can only establish the probability that the recognized types of product problems will not be triggered anew. New and unfamiliar types of product problems cannot yet be anticipated with any certainty.

Total suspension of new product introductions has been suggested by some, but this does not represent a feasible solution. Even though it is based on imperfect standards, the continuation of new product introductions is necessary not only because our society is moving ahead and has new needs but also because it has become dependent on products that are proving to be unsafe or ecologically bad and, consequently, must be withdrawn or replaced.

Product safety will be difficult to assure in advance until more is learned about how to predict future effects. Meanwhile, better mechanisms are needed, and can be designed and required, to provide rapid response to unexpected problems as they appear. New problems should be recognized quickly. Increased pressure is being placed on manufacturers to recognize and deal truthfully with the hazards created by their products.

For example, a member of the Federal Trade Commission has severely criticized the manufacturers of polyurethane and other insulating foams for not recognizing and acknowledging the fire hazards inherent in the use of this material.

> Industry advertisements directed to both the intermediate processors of these materials, and to end users, proclaim the architectural achievements which have been made possible by these foams during the past "Decade of Progress." "New Foam Homes" ads appearing in *American Home* describe them "as sturdy as concrete, as sculpturally free as the homeowner and architect dare to be."

---

[4]While the U.S. regulatory system was not geared to anticipate this type of side reaction, one scientist was alarmed enough by preliminary reports of birth defects in Europe to delay U.S. approval of the drug.

Industry ads also emphasize the economies of these products to homeowners insofar as foam insulation cuts labor time drastically, saves money, and "slashes heating and cooling bills." Foam is also increasingly advertised for its superior uses for wall accessories, drawers, and for decorating furniture because of its "high impact resistance, high gloss and high styling."

But these products have one additional characteristic in common which is nowhere mentioned by the industry in any of their promotional materials. These products under certain conditions can be explosively flammable. They can react violently during a fire, giving off an extraordinary intensity of flames, heat and dense, toxic smoke. While these materials will not ignite casually, once they do catch fire they can burn with a speed and intensity which renders them capable of destroying a large structure within a matter of minutes.

In Kahoka, Missouri in 1969, a fire broke out in the basement of a private home in which the interior walls had been coated for insulation purposes with one of these foam components and left in an exposed condition. The foam insulating material had been labelled by the manufacturer as "non-burning and self-extinguishing." The fire resulted in the death of two small children and the total destruction of the house.

In November 1970, 145 teenagers were killed in St. Laurent-du-Pont, France by a fire which broke out in a dance hall whose walls had been lavishly sprayed with foam in order to give the appearance of a "white grotto or cave."

On August 5, 1970, a major fire occurred in a modern 50-story skyscraper in New York City which was only partially occupied at the time causing two deaths, 30 injuries and $10 million property damage. The investigation showed that a major factor in the fire was polystyrene insulation whose surface was left internally exposed in hidden areas such as ceiling spaces. Of equal importance was the presence of foamed plastics in the building's interior furnishings.

Thus the fire hazard potential in these products is by no means theoretical. It is real—and lethal. Yet there is still very little—indeed virtually no—effort being made publicly, so far as I know, to promote a widespread understanding of the general flammability hazards which lurk in these products or of the specific steps which must be taken in their construction or use to eliminate or minimize their special flammability characteristics.

Indeed, despite the fires which have involved these products, industry continues to promote them as self-extinguishing. The ASTM standard which provides the justification for this claim remains in effect and unmodified and industry, so far as I know, has made no effort to promote the development of a new set of standards or codes which can be used as guidelines for the proper use of these products.

These cautions and ambiguous statements about responsibility for product safety and the particular hazards presented by cellular foam products [are] in sharp contrast with the findings and conclusions of the Missouri Judge who presided over the damage suit brought by the Childress family for the deaths of their children and the destruction of their home as a result of one of these foam fires. That judge, after listening to the testimony of the circumstances of that fire, had no lingering doubts either as to the inherent flammability hazards of these products or as to industry's irresponsibility in relying on the patently inadequate ASTM flammability standards in their marketing of these products. In his words:

> The evidence conclusively established the unconscionable irresponsibility of defendant in marketing for home use an explosively flammable product as "non-burning and self-extinguishing," on the basis of a test, not explained to the buyers that any layman would be bound to regard as better calculated to conceal than reveal the deadly properties of the substance. And the result was what *anyone* should have foreseen; the house burned "with explosive intensity," and the children with it. What excuse can there be for such callous indifference to responsibility so grave?

. . . the Commission announced that it had directed its staff "to investigate the possible existence of fire hazards associated with the marketing and use of certain plastic products in the construction and furnishing of buildings and homes." The Commission staff was also directed to look into the question of "whether the flammability standards used by the plastics industry with regard to such products may be misleading insofar as end use fire environment is concerned."

But does the fact that government can and ultimately must act in order to promote the public safety relieve the business community from any concomitant responsibility for the safety of products which they develop and put on the market? I think the answer is clearly in the negative.

I am convinced that industry must assume the primary initial responsibility for the protection of the public from product hazards. It seems clear, in the instant case, for example, that only the manufacturers of these products are in the position of fully knowing their peculiar flammability propensities and of knowing these well in advance of their appearance in the market. No new product emerges in the market without careful premarket testing for performance, likely uses and market acceptance. Where, as here, the products are technologically new and require new techniques of manufacture or installation, manufacturers are well aware that they must take a leading role in developing the required degree of expertise about these new products among all of the potential users and promoters of the product.[5]

As a result of the efforts of the FTC and others, these foam fire hazards are now more widely recognized. The question posed in the previous passage is why the hazards were not recognized initially by the manufacturers rather than later, and somewhat reluctantly, after a series of serious fires. However, the pattern is familiar; well-established testing standards, the ASTM standards in this case, did not show

---

[5]Mary Gardiner Jones, (Commissioner, Federal Trade Commission), "Corporate Social Reform: The Regulator's View," speech, 1973.

the true dimensions of the problem, and no one seems to have considered the real applicability of the standards before the products were marketed.

The clear message from the FTC commissioner is that industry is expected to be responsible for anticipating these product hazards now and in the future. The public must be protected against unsafe products, by the government, if necessary, but preferably by more intelligence and foresight in selecting the products to be sent to market.

Product Liability

Product safety problems have become a necessary concern of corporate management in part because of the growing burden of product liability where injuries to consumers or others result from the products or services. The legal obligation of the manufacturer to stand behind its products and to assume any liability that can be clearly related to their use is now established. Among the hidden costs that may accompany the use of a product are the long-term effects on the user. While precedents are now quite evident for enforcing damage claims for injuries caused by faulty product performance or negligent product design, the long-term, indirect effects represent an area of less certainty. The pattern is obviously toward enforcing the manufacturer's responsibility, and the current issues concern how this responsibility can be established in the cases involving more long-term, indirect injury, such as the issues over lead poisoning and cigarette smoking, which will be reviewed next.

At this point the financial exposure represented by product liability is sufficiently large that product liability insurance is a growing business cost, and several insurance companies have withdrawn from this market.[6] Improved product safety is not only socially desirable but also a practical business necessity.

A familiar example of a product that may cause long-term injury is interior paint containing lead. While there is now speculation that some ancient Romans might have suffered lead poisoning from drinking water carried through lead pipes, this possibility was recognized only recently. Similarly, although lead pigments have been widely used in interior and exterior decoration for centuries, it is now well established that they are hazardous, particularly on surfaces that can be chewed by children (painting of cribs with lead-based paint is now prohibited) or in older houses where the erosion of the painted surface exposes the inhabitants to paint dust and flakes.

Because current practice has shifted away from the use of lead-based paint for interiors and because the problem is most acute in older housing, the issue has tended to concentrate in slums and renovation projects. There are data to indicate a surprisingly high incidence of chronic lead poisoning among ghetto dwellers, particularly the children. Thus, this hazard presents another major obstacle that the public programs for improving the lot of the disadvantaged must overcome. The resulting decision by Congress to require the removal of lead-based paint from federally financed housing projects is estimated to cost $70 million now and $35

---

[6]"Generous Juries Cost You a Bundle," *Chemical Week,* 24 November, 1976, p. 21.

million annually in the future.[7] The decision has a sound public health rationale but is invoking another social cost as a result of the delay and extra expense thus imposed on the public housing programs. In this case society has established a tradeoff. By imposing on needed housing programs a cost that will either delay the programs or reduce the number of dwelling units that available funds can provide, society will have safer housing but less of it. The implied judgment is that elimination of the lead hazard is sufficiently beneficial to society to justify the delay.

In this case the paint manufacturers were governed by the original requirement that their interior paints be reformulated without lead, but they did not become substantially involved in the issue of whether any product liability could be inferred for painting that was done in the past and might have contributed to poisoning. However, consider a parallel issue headlined more recently as: "Eating of Glossy Color Pages is Found Perilous to Children."[8] This *New York Times* story tells about the work at the Connecticut State Experiment Station showing that glossy magazines and newspapers can be significant sources of lead poisoning in children because of the lead content of some of the inks used in the printing process. Four square inches of a glossy page were found to contain a toxic dose that would lead to serious poisoning if consumed every day. The investigation had started because of the need to locate the source of the lead that had caused two cases of poisoning, which could not otherwise be explained.

Eating comics or colored magazine pages is apparently a very dangerous habit for a child. Other scientists are equally concerned about the hazards of making too many spitballs.

A moderately effective spitball could be made from 25 square centimeters of almost all the papers tested. Such a missile would weigh about 140 mg. (anhydrous). And if made from colored paper, especially green, red, or yellow, it could easily contain more than 100 micrograms of lead which could be leached out with saliva or ingested in shredded paper. If only part of the lead entered the system in that way, the manufacture of just a few spitballs could mean a lead intake of more than 300 micrograms, which has been proposed as the maximum daily intake from all sources for children. This would be on top of an assumed daily unavoidable intake of 100 to 200 micrograms from sources like food, water, and air.[9]

The obvious issue is whether either the ink manufacturer or the magazine publisher is liable if a child is poisoned by eating comics or an adolescent is poisoned by making spitballs out of colored magazine paper. For various magazine and newspaper publishers, as well as manufacturers of pigments and inks, this issue is frustrating but not ridiculous. While no one has imposed on the print media the requirement that their publications be edible, everyone acknowledges the fact that

---

[7]"Removal of Poisonous Lead Paint May Deter Plans on Housing," *New York Times*, 2 March, 1974.

[8]*New York Times*, 25 November, 1973.

[9]"Printed Media May be Hazardous to Children," *Chemical and Engineering News*, 25 March, 1974, p. 64.

children sometimes eat paper. The legal testing of the issue has not yet taken place, but the concepts of product liability and responsibility have been broadened beyond the directly intended use of the product. Thus, the extension to established peripheral uses of the product, such as the chewing of comics by children, is a conceivable result if our society wants to continue to broaden the responsibility for product-related disabilities in the future. This area of manufacturers' liability needs to become a public issue since the economic burden of extended product liability can be significant and will be passed on as an increase in the average cost of the products. In any case, some restriction of the lead content of printing pigments may result from this concern, and all producers of print media have reason to examine their own practices and postures.

In the case of cigarettes, the assertion that smoking quantities of some cigarettes under some conditions is not beneficial to the health of the user is gaining factual support. Some of the tars that have been isolated are capable of causing cancer in animals, and the carbon monoxide content of the smoke is potentially harmful. In the present public climate of requiring products to prove their right to be on the market, some further restriction on the sale or use of cigarettes seems likely in the long run, although the popular and political forces favoring the continued unrestricted use of cigarettes are very formidable.

Although there is increasing acceptance of the fact that some injury to health is possible from heavy use of cigarettes (hence the congressional requirement for a warning to be printed on cigarette labels), the banning of all cigarettes for all uses is less clear-cut, particularly since the better filters clearly reduce the amounts of some dangerous ingredients. The cigarette industry has not openly recognized the desirability of placing some restrictions on some cigarettes, such as the unfiltered ones, to give the public the benefit of the doubt on a serious safety issue. By failing to acknowledge the safety issue, the cigarette industry has increased the risk that cigarettes might be banned for all purposes in the heat of the moment if public sentiment finally stirs the political heat necessary to prevail. The industry posture seems to have been to defend all cigarettes against all attacks, in spite of the mounting evidence. A totally defensive policy seems hard to justify unless tobacco company managements really believe that no meaningful difference in safety exists between different forms of cigarettes. However, in that case, why does the industry expend effort and advertising in the promotion of filters?

It would seem that a cigarette company management that is seeking to balance its social impact in the product sector might wish either to develop a realistic program for establishing the safety of cigarettes if it is truly unconvinced about the possibility of danger or else aid in sponsoring suitable restrictions on any potentially dangerous types of cigarettes. The Tobacco Institute and some members of the industry would undoubtedly argue that this is exactly what the industry has done; certainly, the industry program has been skillfully managed. The underlying premise of this program seems to be the absence of any real health hazard; therefore, the long-term soundness of the program may depend on the soundness of the premise.

A well-established legal doctrine applies to all cases where consumers can show injury or loss as a result of products or services that are faulty, have undesirable side effects, or are associated with potential danger that can be related in some way to the manufacturer's negligence. The boundaries of interpretation of this doctrine have not been strictly defined, and product liability insurance costs are now rising as dramatically as malpractice insurance costs for doctors have risen.

Self-interested manufacturers will seek to minimize product liability exposure where practical. When it is possible to do this, the best procedure is to market only truly safe products and services, since this approach minimizes both insurance and legal costs. Thus, product liability exposure has reached the point where it motivates full corrective action without any further prompting by the corporate conscience or by its appointed keepers.

Social and Cultural Impact

The automobile has changed American society and American culture, as have many other products of the Industrial Revolution. In the past there has been little concern about such impacts except after the fact and little public inclination to link them directly to the provider of the product or services. The attitude of the public has begun to change, and in Chapter 15 the attempt to predict such impacts by means of technology assessment techniques will be examined. Here it is important to identify this component of the impact on lifestyles and culture that is created by the introduction of new goods and services and to define its approximate dimensions.

The evolution and introduction of goods and services embodying new technology can have far-reaching impacts, as is apparent in the case of the automobile, electric light, radio, television, airplane, and many other inventions; the domain of technology assessment is a public-sector initiative that is aimed at understanding or potentially even controlling this process. For the individual manufacturer, the focus is directed more toward the responsibility equation. If it lies within the power of a firm to create and market a new product or service, society will tend to attribute to that firm more and more responsibility for the consequences of the development as impacts are made on individuals or on society as a whole. The long-term evolution of this doctrine has not yet defined the rate and scope of its application but is moving in the direction of enforcing this responsibility.

Now a corporation should concern itself with the specific social and cultural impacts of its goods and services on its customers and other individuals, while remaining aware of and sensitive to the broader impacts that may emerge in the clear, but as yet undefined, area of demand from society. Examples of this sort of corporate impact that extend beyond the intended area include the development of disposable syringes as an advance in the convenient and safe handling of certain biological and pharmaceutical products. These syringes then required careful control both in their distribution and destruction after use because of the potential for their use in the injection of narcotics and other illegal drugs.

Manufacturers of snowmobiles have been challenged to produce an intrinsically safe and reliable product, but they have not been asked to deal with the risk that an unwary owner will drive out on the unsafe ice of a pond or stream and drown. The concern over adverse environmental impacts has caused restriction of where owners may use their snowmobiles but has not affected their manufacture or sale.

Control over the right to purchase and use handguns is a sharp issue in society at present, but they are likely to continue to be manufactured for the classes of use that society agrees to permit. The exception is the effort to ban very cheap handguns ("Saturday night specials") from the market entirely, since they are not of a quality that has any appeal to or value for legitimate gun owners but rather represent a class of product that fosters the worst type of aggressive use.

In general, it appears that society has increased its awareness of the social impact of new products but is rarely motivated to ban a product or restrict its manufacture strictly for this reason. However, society is quite prepared to restrict its use where customers or others are likely to be injured or illegal activity is likely to be encouraged. Society is only now beginning to consider how to deal with the broader and more comprehensive new product impacts that extend beyond this point.

Environmental Consequences

One closely related area of social and cultural impact in which society is quite willing to impose new rules is the area of impact on the environment. Two major types of issues have been raised. One concerns the social consequences and costs of product disposal that is illustrated by the case of disposal containers. The other concerns the cumulative, long-term damage to the total environment that is illustrated by the case of aerosol products possibly jeopardizing the ozone layer.

Product Disposal

For a long time, roasted nuts have been packaged in glass and tins, when a long shelf life is desired, or in cellophane bags, when a more economical, quick-turnover product is involved. Recently, manufacturers of aluminum have competed for some of these traditional markets; a deep aluminum can with a tear-off top makes a very appealing package that is much easier to open than the traditional steel can with a key. In making the decision about which containers to use, the nut manufacturer considers a series of alternative disposal costs based on the characteristics of each different type of container. The freedom to decide on a product container carries with it a responsibility for the results of the choice. Currently, the issue is focused on nonreturnable containers.

It would seem that the driving issue concerns litter, although energy and use of national resources have been a continuing part of the discussion. The first point is that litter results because individual consumers behave irresponsibly and, in some cases, illegally by dumping trash, including cans and bottles, in parks and along roadsides. At one point in time, the issue would have been defined entirely in terms of controlling this improper individual behavior. Today, however, society is challenging the manufacturers, whose decisions to use nonreturnable containers are seen as encouraging illegal littering by citizens. Returnable containers also find their way into litter but in smaller quantities. The difference is attributed to the economic incentive of the deposit; hence a ban on nonreturnable containers is seen as reducing illegal littering by citizens. This line of argument is consistent with the pattern of holding manufacturers responsible for the consequences of their decisions (in this case for their choice of a nonreturnable container) even though the act of littering, which is central to the issue, is an act of individual citizens.

Laws mandating a return to reusable containers by imposing a deposit fee were passed in Oregon and Vermont in 1973 and since then have been passed in South Dakota and California. In four more states the issue was put to the voters in the 1976 election, and it passed in Michigan and Maine. Discussion of possible federal legislation has begun. *Environment* reported that the Oregon and Vermont laws raised beverage prices.[10] More subtle, but equally important, issues concern the shift of demand from industry to industry and between regional and national firms that occurs when such a law is put into effect. Disposable containers are made by can manufacturers and are filled at a suitably located regional plant. Returnable containers are generally glass and require a more durable case or carton to facilitate their return; they must be collected and moved back to a bottling plant for washing, inspection, and refilling. Often this process involves different firms and equipment than are used for nonreturnable containers.

An important issue that is not clear-cut has been raised about energy requirements and use of natural resources. In fact, if returnable containers are returned and disposable containers are discarded, then disposable containers represent a significantly greater consumption of both energy and resources because the aluminum, steel, or glass that is produced is then thrown away. At present, however, some disposable containers are recycled and some returnable containers are lost to litter, breakage, or rejection for cracks and defects. And the energy requirements for the collection, cleaning, and reprocessing of returnable containers are not negligible. Even so, the disposable containers appear to represent a greater use of energy, although the data are not definitive.

Society's long-term direction is toward extensive recovery and reuse of both metals and glass from solid waste, as will be discussed in Chapter 11. While the program for separate recycling of aluminum containers has been quite successful, it has reached only a fraction of the total container supply. More containers could be recovered from solid waste. Hence, advocates of nonreturnable containers can argue that society will eventually recover the containers through solid waste processing, and, thus, the energy differential against nonreturnable containers will largely disappear. In the meantime, they would oppose the use of resources for setting up bottle-collection routes and washing plants that will also consume resources and use energy. This argument is convincing to the extent that a solution of national solid waste problems will become a reality.

Controversy over the energy balance between disposable and returnable container systems seems likely to continue for years, with the litter issue being well defined. Present evidence favors either requiring a deposit on the container at the time of purchase or offering a bounty on its return as a means of reducing litter significantly.

One other feature of the issue over nonreturnable containers has involved the risk of injury from the pull-tab on an aluminum can. The Oregon container law banned tear-off fasteners because of reports of injury to swimmers and wildlife. The swallowing of pull-tabs has also been reported. While these hazards may not be great, they have caused an issue with the manufacturer responsible for making the design decision that created them as the aluminum can products were evolving

---

[10]Julian McCaull, "Back to Glass," *Environment*, January-February 1974, pp. 6–11.

toward market. Now, in an attempt to respond to this issue from consumers, at least two types of cans have been marketed in which the pull-tab remains attached.

The returnable container issue represents a front line in the current battle among consumerists, environmentalists, and the affected industries. While the case is not clear-cut and many of the facts are subject to various interpretations, the recent tide of battle is against the container industry in spite of the economic impacts. The public seems to want more action toward reducing litter; a ban on nonreturnable containers appears to be the most clearly defined action that is presently available.

The nonreturnable container issue is only one of a growing class of issues that has developed over the social cost for disposal of used-up or worn-out products. Up to this point, society has absorbed the bulk of the product disposal costs, thus subsidizing any decision the manufacturers chose to make. The urgency of environmental problems is now bringing an end to this public willingness to underwrite the costs of pollution and disposal. As public pressure grows, manufacturers are being strongly reminded of their ultimate responsibility for the consequences of their product decisions.

For example, abandoned automobiles constitute a significant environmental problem, which became acute in the early 1970s. The salvage value of the materials contained in the automobile body fell sharply; only more recently did these salvaged materials again begin to find a ready market.

A car manufacturer is directly responsible for the fact that the car exists. No provision is made in the sales price or sales contract to cover final disposal of the car body. Abandoned cars represent a significant, additional environmental burden, which would not exist if the car had never been manufactured and sold. Car manufacturers cannot successfully divorce themselves from what happens to cars that are no longer used. Auto graveyards and abandoned autos have become an unwelcome social cost. Several suggestions have been made for a bond or a tax of some sort to be imposed by the government; Maryland imposed a $1 fee on title transfers to aid in disposing of abandoned cars,[11] and Senator Proxmire once proposed a disposal fee of one cent per pound on manufactured articles.[12] Thus, a fee of thirty-five dollars would be charged against the manufacturer of a thirty-five-hundred-pound automobile. Fortunately, the rise in scrap metal prices reduced the immediate pressure for such legislation.

In 1970 GM announced the development of a process for reusing scrap sheet metal from auto bodies without remelting it.[13] If this process could be applied successfully, it would not only save money for GM but also greatly reduce the supply of prime scrap metal of this particular grade. The demand for scrap, and hence the price, is determined primarily by the ratio of scrap that gives the greatest efficiency in various melting operations. This new GM process could withdraw a large prime scrap supply, thus shift a significant demand, and make the salvaging of used cars more attractive. Therefore, the decision by GM to invest in the development of a process

---

[11]Agis Salpulgas, "Abandoned Cars: A Headache for Cities," New York Times, 12 October, 1970.

[12]"Penny a Pound Fee to Pay for Disposal," Industry Week, 18 May, 1970.

[13]Wall Street Journal, 2 March, 1970.

for salvaging body scrap could help reduce the social cost caused by abandoned cars if it should become acute again.

In some parts of the country, recovery of scrap metal from abandoned cars had continued to be economical and profitable. In other areas this did not seem to be the case. Consequently, auto manufacturers have had much to gain; if a reasonable amount of mechanical development or aid to local entrepreneurs can encourage the salvaging of auto bodies then another segment of the abandoned car problem can be solved.

By looking at the whole structure of the problem, manufacturers have the opportunity to develop an efficient or even profitable solution. Their responsibility, however, is to make the problem disappear, and the public appears to be eager for the fulfillment of that responsibility, even if the initial attempts toward solution are inefficient and result in an increase in the price of cars.

The product disposal issue is based on a public desire that used-up products disappear painlessly rather than accumulate as litter and garbage. Wherever manufacturers find that they are adding directly or indirectly to the unpleasant reality of litter and garbage, they can expect public clamor.

Damage to the Environment

In issues such as the one involving containers, every manufacturer's decision takes part in the shaping of the controversy and eventually influences the formation of public policy. An even more difficult issue concerns the effect of the fluorocarbon products on the ozone layer of the upper atmosphere. Some hazard exists since these chemicals can catalyze the degradation of ozone, and if the ozone concentration is reduced, the sun's rays will cause an increase in the incidence of skin cancer.

Many scientists believe that fluorocarbons, which are now produced at a worldwide rate of 800,000 tons per year, drift into the upper atmosphere and decompose to destroy the ozone layer that shields the Earth from most of the ultraviolet radiation from the sun. A 5-percent reduction in ozone concentration has been predicted to cause 8,000 additional skin cancer cases in the United States each year. Even without firm evidence that the ozone layer is being depleted, many consider the risks to be too great to allow continued release of fluorocarbons into the atmosphere.[14]

The ozone layer is affected by many human processes. For example, depletion of the ozone layer has also been predicted as a result of the exhaust emissions from SST aircraft because of the release of nitrogen oxides into the upper levels of the atmosphere. Nuclear explosions have a similar effect. One team calculated that the atmospheric nuclear testing in 1961–1962 caused a 4-percent reduction in ozone concentration, but the Department of Defense did not accept this conclusion.[15]

Here is a case where an aerosol product using fluorocarbons (many do, but not all) has a social cost of disposal because of its unknown contribution to a more than theoretical hazard to the ozone layer. However, the dynamics of the ozone layer are

---

[14]"Aerosols in Sky Pose Down-to-Earth Threat," *Chemical Week*, 18 September, 1974, p. 59.
[15]"Pentagon Replies to Peril on Ozone," *New York Times*, 17 October, 1974.

so extremely complex that it will be many years before the factors controlling the balance between ozone formation and depletion are fully understood.[16] Fluorocarbons represent only part of the problem, since it is almost certain that other human processes besides SSTs, nuclear blasts, and spray bombs will turn out to affect the ozone layer.

The fluorocarbon controversy has brought an awareness of a serious negative corporate impact from the continued marketing of aerosol products. For some manufacturers (S. C. Johnson is an example), the result was a prompt decision to stop using fluorocarbons in its products. But their press release pointed out that this decision was not difficult or costly for Johnson's Wax because feasible alternatives are available. Now the FDA and the Consumer Product Safety Commission have restricted the use of fluorocarbons in spray cans. For some other classes of aerosols, alternative propellants are not now known, and, consequently, entire product lines may need to be changed significantly. Many other industrial processes use fluorocarbons, but in smaller amounts.

Present information does not seem to provide objective evidence as to whether the long-term ecological need is to eliminate the use of fluorocarbons or merely control the amount that is used. The data would suggest that some amounts of fluorocarbons could be tolerated but that larger amounts should not be permitted; while the acceptable levels have not yet been determined, they will probably be derived within a few years as a result of current research.

When the effects of fluorocarbons on the ozone layer are fully understood, they will only serve to define the real issues. First, this is a worldwide phenomenon and affects the ozone layer over more than one country. Therefore, how will control of agents like fluorocarbons be established on a global basis? Second, fluorocarbons are not the only problem. SSTs, nuclear blasts, fertilizers, combustion, and other sources of nitrogen oxides are now known to affect ozone concentration, and it will not be surprising to find still other substances that affect it. When the global tolerances for ozone destruction have been determined, they will somehow have to be taken into account. Specific limitations will probably have to be placed on all the processes that affect the ozone concentration negatively.

Why not just ban fluorocarbons? Perhaps this will be seriously considered, but there are real costs. For example, fluorocarbons are used in most small refrigeration and air conditioning systems and in many industrial systems. Other refrigerant chemicals are known, but have been replaced by fluorocarbons because of safety considerations. The fluorocarbons in a refrigerator or air conditioner eventually escape into the atmosphere when the unit is discarded. In the event of a leak that develops in an operating system, the fluorocarbons that escape into the home are relatively safe. Fluorocarbons have been used to replace sulfur dioxide, which is quite poisonous and caused more than a few deaths.

The fluorocarbon problem is an extremely complex public policy issue that is only partially understood at present. S. C. Johnson is to be commended for a good

---

[16]Charles E. Kolb, "The Depletion of Stratospheric Ozone." *Technology Review*, October–November 1975, pp. 38–47. This article reviews present knowledge of the dynamics of ozone depletion by various agents.

management decision. The company found that it could dissociate itself from the problem entirely, and not at great cost, by changing its products so that they do not use fluorocarbons. For other manufacturers whose costs of changeover are higher, the conversion process will be difficult. However, society sees itself as being injured by this corporate impact, and the long-term pressure will mandate the elimination of many uses of fluorocarbons.

The manufacturers of refrigerators and air conditioners have a different, difficult problem. Industry has become quite wary of using such alternative refrigerants as sulfur dioxide--in one case very real social costs were generated when a family was poisoned by the fumes. However, the technical data are still incomplete, and more knowledge may help in defining feasible alternatives. For example, atmospheric data now show distinct differences in the ability of specific fluorocarbon compounds to reach the upper levels of the atmosphere. When these differences are understood, perhaps a shift to the use of less noxious varieties of fluorocarbons will be made, even if some cost in product performance is involved.

Meanwhile, the daily flow of events continues, regardless of the lack of availability of hard scientific evidence. The public has reacted to the environmental concerns, and sales of aerosol products have fallen substantially. Unfortunately, the public does not seem to have become sensitive to whether or not the aerosols contain fluorocarbons; aerosol products both with and without fluorocarbons seem to be equally affected.

Late in 1976 the Food and Drug Administration, the Environmental Protection Agency, and the Consumer Product Safety Commission each started its own regulatory action aimed at banning the use of fluorocarbons as aerosol propellants. The FDA began to require that a warning of possible environmental hazards appear on the product label, and the three agencies set up a joint task force to coordinate the process that will eventually lead to the total phase-out of fluorocarbon propellants. Earlier, Oregon, often an innovator in environmental matters, had decided to move ahead on its own. A law was passed in 1975 banning all aerosols containing fluorocarbons that was to become effective as of March 1, 1977. The day after the law went into effect, *Chemical Week* reported laboratory evidence from the National Bureau of Standards concerning the destruction of fluorocarbons by previously unsuspected mechanisms in the lower atmosphere: "This finding may 'open up a whole new area of research previously unexplored,' notes NBS, and is the first evidence that recent government regulatory action against fluorocarbons may be premature."[17] Whether or not this evidence leads to a re-evaluation of fluorocarbon hazards, it is an indication of the way that the controversy seems likely to persist.

New industrial products, such as aerosol sprays, are introduced to the public after some consideration of health, safety, and environmental hazards. Public pressure is bringing continued upgrading of requirements and standards, but many long-term, indirect effects, such as the impact of aerosols on the ozone layer, will probably not be predictable at the time of product approval, although the review processes may become far more sophisticated. Thus, the corporations that sell goods and services

---

[17]"Chlorofluorocarbons May be Destroyed in the Lower Atmosphere," *Chemical Week*, 2 March, 1977, p. 29.

will be faced with an increasing variety of complex issues, such as the impact of fluorocarbons on the ozone layer, until detailed information about the full impact of modern technology on society and world ecology becomes available.

As an example of the complexity of these issues, consider the problems of the designers now laboring to make solar heating and air conditioning truly practical not only to save energy but also to reduce the pollution caused by combustion processes. Should they use fluorocarbons, which are now the best refrigerants available, in the spirit of an urgent, useful development? Or should they eliminate the fluorocarbon series even at the risk of delaying the development of practical package units of this type? An intelligent answer cannot be provided on the basis of the limited information currently available, but this type of issue will arise with increasing frequency in the future.

The fluorocarbon controversy illustrates an ecological problem that must be resolved at the national level. On the other hand, public concern over litter has brought pressure for legislation on the state level since the problem must take into account the regional variations. Another consequence of the growing public awareness of environmental problems is the creation and definition of the new Consumer Product Safety Commission, which, according to its commissioner, R. David Pittie, was designed by Congress to have an activist role with substantial independence from the executive branch and extensive public participation in the setting of standards.[18] While the performance of this agency remains to be proven, its interest is clearly consonant with current public sentiments and the long-term trend of events.

Consumer Pressures

Recognizing the growing pressure, some manufacturers are trying hard to handle product problems before they become public issues and, in some cases, before marketing the products. Whirlpool's "Cool Line" program mentioned earlier is an example of an organized effort to provide service or other remedial action before the consumer is antagonized or forced to seek outside help in the settlement of grievances. Another example is Dow Chemical's development and publicizing of its product stewardship concept, which originated in 1970 and requires extensive toxicological studies of products and controls on manufacturing and distribution that are aimed at anticipating or quickly solving product environmental problems.[19] Although these controls are becoming increasingly necessary now, Dow used the idea of product stewardship to mobilize its internal efforts in advance of the requirement.

We can generalize here and say that consumers are expecting and demanding both interest in and assistance from manufacturers when they have problems. The cost of building and maintaining a market franchise has been increased by the necessary increase in consumer service cost. In addition, manufacturers have developed a

---

[18]R. David Pittie, "Consumer Product Safety Commission Takes Activist Role in Safety Standards," *Professional Engineer*, May 1975, pp. 36–37.

[19]"Product Stewardship: Responsibility Never Ends," *Chemical Week*, 3 October, 1973, pp. 45–46.

strong self-interest in learning about and solving unexpected new problems before they emerge as public issues.

Summary

Customers have given value for the product they buy and expect that product (or service) to deliver this value without undue hazards or side effects. If the product, as represented, delivers this value (including parts, service, and continued availability where applicable), no problem exists. The social balance concept requires that customers actually receive the value that is represented by the product or service when it is offered for sale. Goods and services must not only be tailored to meet specific market needs but also be safe for public use; they must be free of unanticipated hazards and detriments, or else manufacturers will find that they are more and more pressed to absorb and compensate for the social costs that are generated by product disposal or various other side effects of the sale of their particular goods and services.

In analyzing the social impact of this sale of goods or services, we identified seven dimensions of this potential impact, which are summarized in Figure 9.1:

1. The fairness of the exchange price
2. The extent to which the purchase fulfills the prepurchase expectations of the buyer
3. The availability of necessary after-sale support
4. The dependence of the customers on continued availability of the good or service
5. The risk of injury from the use of the good or service
6. The social and cultural impact of the purchase and use
7. The environmental consequences of the use of the good or service

This chapter has reviewed the impact of the sale of goods and services on society. Beyond the need for manufacturers to represent their products fairly, provide adequate after-sale support, and ensure product safety, more emphasis must be placed on consideration of the social and cultural impacts. Environmental impacts deserve the most immediate attention, whether they represent the social cost of product disposal or a long-term degradation of air, water, or soil. The burden on the

Figure 9.1 Considerations in Sale of Goods and Services

Fair exchange value	Product safety and product liability
Truth in advertising and promotion	Social and cultural impact
After the sale:	Environmental consequences
Performance	Response to consumer pressures
Parts and service	
Continued supply	

These are areas where suppliers can expect continued, searching questioning from customers, regulators, and the public.

provider of goods and services is to trade fairly and not create either long- or short-term adverse corporate impact.

Guidelines for Managing Corporate Social Impact

The intent of suggesting guidelines for balancing corporate social impact is to define a normative pattern that corporate management could strive to attain. In Part Five these guidelines will be summarized and considered for practicality under competitive pressures and other forms of stress.

In the sale of goods and services, social balance will tend to be maintained if the following guidelines are applied:

Merchandise quality   On the whole, goods and services fulfill the expectations of the purchasers.

Service   Reasonable requirements for after-sale and continued support of routine use patterns are met.

Safety   Goods and services are free of danger and unexpected side effects in normal use, attempt to ensure the safety of predictable types of product misuse, and do not cause unacceptable environmental aftereffects from the goods and services or their packaging.

Impact of new products   When goods and services that change lifestyles and cultural patterns are introduced and promoted, an effort is made to minimize disruption and resentment and, thus, to avoid future challenges from society concerning the right to introduce such goods or services.

Applying the Guidelines

Merchandise quality   Automobiles are extensively promoted on television and radio, in magazines and newspapers, by direct mail, and through personal efforts of legions of sales representatives. The romance and illusion invoked in the process of promoting a car sale create a framework of customer expectations. As is the case with any product or service, the car must fulfill these expectations to a reasonable degree if the company is to continue to sell its products. For a product with a conspicuous national reputation, the social balance requirement for fulfilling customer expectations tends to work directly in the marketplace. To reinforce this process and reach less conspicuous product and service areas, society continues to devise consumer-fraud, truth-in-advertising, and other consumer-protection statutes that a responsible business should anticipate and avoid by not creating expectations that the product or service cannot fulfill.

Service   Successful automobile companies have emphasized the parts and service aspects of car care, and failure to achieve adequate parts and service support has been linked to the failure of several European car manufacturers to establish themselves in the U.S. market after good initial sales. Thus, this social balance requirement also seems to be validated by market forces.

Safety   Ralph Nader came to public prominence by mounting a documented attack against certain automobiles as being dangerous beyond reason or acceptability, and specific safety legislation has resulted. The side effects of even so valuable a drug as penicillin have caused restrictions so that the drug is not given to people who would have dangerous reactions to it. Vaccines packaged in disposable syringes have also required a degree of additional control to ensure that the used syringes are not diverted to illegal use. In addition, sales of some consumer products, such as beverages in nonreturnable bottles, have been restricted because of the concern for the resulting litter in parks and by roadsides. Similarly, much of the objection to the establishment of additional fast-food outlets in certain neighborhoods has been based on concern for the litter that results from the discarding of bags and other packaging materials. The requirement is that the manufacturer anticipate and minimize dangers, side effects, and other undesirable consequences of the use of products and services. While this is sometimes difficult, there is no question that the public will look to the seller or manufacturer to remedy any problems that arise.

Impact of new products   The fast-food outlets have achieved success in responding to a change in social patterns and lifestyles. However, in serving the trend, they have become the forefront of its extension; locally, they represent both the creators of the change and target of the antagonism of those opposing this change. Thus, in gaining local approvals required for new fast-food units, the companies have found themselves portrayed as the source of litter and undesirable traffic and have been challenged to provide controls over both areas of concern.

Disposable beverage containers have brought similar public objections, and early in the controversy Reynolds Metals Company took a major role in an effective aluminum container recycling campaign. The objective was to get at the source of both ecology and energy objections to disposable aluminum containers by establishing the habit of reuse to the point that the reason for public objections would disappear. An imaginative, effective campaign has continued to siphon increasing volumes of aluminum into recycling channels, but nonetheless the banning of disposable containers has continued to spread from state to state. Unfortunately, the litter problem involves glass and tin as well as aluminum, and the fractional part of the container market that becomes litter, while small, is the most difficult to divert back into recycling. The recycling program probably has reduced public pressure somewhat, but its limited success illustrates both the approach and the difficulty of countering a problem as basic as litter.

The cases of both the fast-food and disposable container manufacturers illustrate the difficult burden of cushioning the impact of the social change that creates the opportunity for them to offer their services and products. The cases also illustrate the risk of having the public impose restrictions on their right to do business if they do not succeed in balancing their social impact on society to an acceptable degree.

Questions for Analysis and Discussion

1. Discuss the limitations of market mechanisms in guaranteeing parity between the price that consumers pay for products and the value that they receive. Do you agree that the utility of the purchasing power a consumer surrenders must be less than the perceived valuation of the purchased product?

2. Find examples of advertising that appear to be borderline in terms of the way the promotional theme fits with current public standards of acceptability.

3. To what extent should a manufacturer be required to maintain inventories of spare parts for equipment and devices sold in the past? For how long a period of time should these inventories be maintained?

4. What should be the extent of the manufacturer's liability for illness or injury caused by uses of a product that extend beyond those for which it was specifically designed and promoted? Illustrate with examples.

5. Should a magazine or comic book publisher be required to use inks and other materials that have been approved for human consumption?

6. Find examples of other products whose disposal incurs social costs. How might these costs best be related to the specific products? Is this a good idea?

7. Investigate the local arrangements for recycling such waste products as paper, glass, and aluminum. Does the policy make salvage and reuse attractive? Is a significant volume of waste materials being recycled?

8. What would be the local impact of banning nonreturnable containers? Which businesses would be hurt? Which would benefit?

For Further Information

Editors of *Ramparts*. *In the Marketplace: Consumerism in America*. San Francisco: Canfield Press, 1972.

Heilbroner, Richard. *In the Name of Profit*. Garden City, N.Y.: Doubleday, 1972.

Ross, Donald K. *A Public Citizen's Action Manual*. New York: Grossman, 1973.

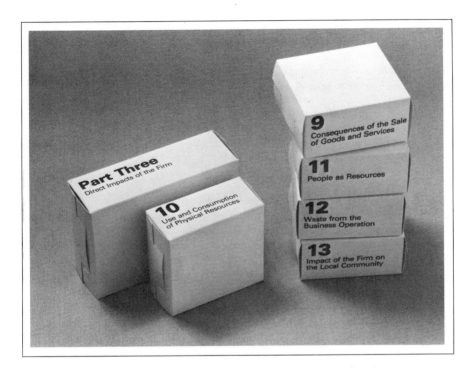

10
Use and Consumption of Physical Resources

The welfare of the business enterprise is closely related to the resources it uses and consumes, and this process may have a major impact on society. Here the concern is with the social impact of this use and consumption and the requirements for a social balance. Our analysis will deal with scarce resources, resources from current production, and surplus resources. Society's interest, particularly in the right to use scarce resources, has risen rapidly because the physical resource base is such a key part of social capital and is recognized clearly as being exhaustible in some critical areas.

The earth's thin film of living matter is sustained by grand-scale cycles of energy and chemical elements. All of these cycles are presently affected by the activities of man.[1]

THE LAST WHOLE EARTH CATALOG

The raw materials and supplies used by a business in the course of its operation are drawn from the country's stock of resources, either directly or after intermediate manufacturing and processing operations. The fact that business has given value in exchange for raw materials is evidence that they are worth at least that much to the business in the profit-making operation it pursues, or else such transactions would not have continued to take place. Many of these resources are limited in quantity or availability, however, so that their unrestricted consumption may deplete the country's resource pool.

In its use and consumption of physical resources, a business has reason for concern over its impact because the exchange transaction guarantees that the business is getting full value but does not guarantee that resource suppliers or society members are being compensated in proportion to the full value the resources represent to society. In the past society has often chosen to make resources available to business on advantageous terms amounting to a subsidy, and now the public concern is being directed toward whether some corporations are receiving subsidies that were neither intended by society nor justified by the consequences of the resource use.

The impact of raw material use and consumption on society and the effect of market forces on the values paid differ with the nature of society's supply of that material. Such materials may represent (1) a scarce resource limited in quantity, such as topsoil mined from a field or water flowing in a river, (2) a resource from current production, such as tomatoes or tobacco, or (3) surplus products of a weak segment of the economy, exemplified by industrial use of surplus grain in past years. The implications of the use of these different types of materials will be examined through a series of specific examples.

Scarce Resources

Resources are scarce for different reasons. They may represent unique historical or geographical features, exhaustible materials limited in total quantity, or products from slow processes requiring long periods for their regeneration.

---

[1]*The Last Whole Earth Catalog* (New York: Portola Institute/Random House, 1971), p. 8.

Geographical Features

Scenic beauty is counted as a scarce resource. Thus, quarrying scenic areas involves, primarily, the value of the geographical feature and, usually only secondarily, the finite nature of the rock supply in a given area. The crushed stone that is necessary for making concrete and is used in the heaviest construction work commonly comes from quarries. As the New York metropolitan area began its dynamic growth, rock for its buildings was quarried from the New Jersey Palisades. Although this rock was being taken from cliffs owned by the company operating the quarry, the collective judgment of the surrounding society was that the defacement of the Palisades was detrimental to the lower Hudson valley and the cost to society was above and beyond the payment that the quarry companies had made for the property they were mining. As a result, existing quarries were purchased and new ones were prevented from

The Firm as Viewed by Society

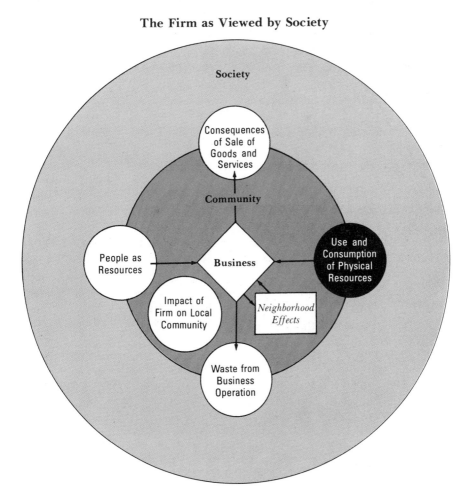

opening.[2] Those supplying building stone for New York City found it necessary to move further up river and find mining areas of less fundamental scenic value.

This restriction of quarry operation exemplifies the overall social authority that has been embodied in zoning laws, landmark preservation requirements, and similar legislation. These laws are based on the concept that the overall good of society must sometimes supersede the rights of individuals to use their own property. Although this concept has provoked much opposition, its legality appears to be accepted and its application is spreading.

Exhaustible Resources

In the years when Minnesota's Mesabi Range contained the largest known reserve of high-grade iron ore in the world and was the principal source of iron ore for the United States, its depletion represented a cost to the public beyond the land purchase and mining costs that were incurred by the mining companies. This reserve was seen as a unique resource whose exhaustion could disrupt U.S. industry. Fortunately, the development of processes for using taconite, a low-grade iron ore, has eased the threat of exhaustion of U.S. resources, and worldwide exploration programs have uncovered ample high-grade iron ore deposits.

In such a case a business can be expected to recognize that it is depleting a critical natural resource (Mesabi iron), but the specific responsibility of that business—or the effect of its operations on the overall social capital—is much less clear. Society is the arbiter, but in the case of the Mesabi range, society's evaluation of these obligations has changed several times.

1. When the iron was discovered, its rapid large-scale exploitation clearly served the national interest. Huge volumes of ore justified the construction of special railroads and loading docks and the installation of a fleet of special ore-carrying ships on the Great Lakes. Tremendous ore reserves and specialized, low-cost transportation meant low-cost iron and steel. The resulting strength of the U.S. steel industry was an important ingredient in the growth of the railroads, the nation, and our modern industrial economy. The challenge to each company was to mine and smelt as fast as possible, and the public applauded each new production record.

2. At the end of World War II when exhaustion of the Mesabi Range seemed near, the potential collapse of the steel industry threatened industrial disaster. Prophets of gloom saw a major shift in world industry as a result of the exhaustion of the richest U.S. ore deposits. Iron ore became precious and not to be wasted. Severing it from the ground seemed almost a sin.

3. In the 1950s the development of taconite processing averted a U.S. industrial disaster, and discovery of large iron ore deposits in Labrador, South America, and elsewhere in the world solved the overall ore supply problem. Now the emphasis is back on production of steel at minimum cost. The quantity produced is no longer

---

[2]Palisades Interstate Park Commission, *60 Years of Park Cooperation—New York—New Jersey: A History 1900–1960* (Bear Mountain, N.Y.: Palisades Interstate Park Commission, 1960), pp. 17–20.

important since the public has lost its awe of vast tonnages. Effective competition with the Japanese and German steel companies has become the focal point.

This shift in the public point of view occurred over the space of thirty years; the first signs of concern about the exhaustion of the ore surfaced at the end of the 1930s and faded away in the early 1960s as large-scale taconite production became routine. Such changes in public attitude indicate the need for a more fundamental rationale than current public opinion on which to base long-term planning of resource use, since some managers and some facilities have experienced a double reversal in public pressures in the course of their working lives.

Slowly Replenished Materials

Forest products are crops of a special type that are different from most field crops primarily due to the long growth cycle. Rapid early development of the U.S. forest industries contributed greatly to national growth, but little thought was given to the transition from the heavy harvests of virgin forests to a sustained yield that could be obtained on a continuing basis. The painful transition from "slash and burn" to the beginning of constructive forest management is well known. Accompanying it was the transition from lumber companies with a superior ability to harvest virgin stands to forest management companies that have slowly shifted to tree farming to maximize the yield of their forests.

Through this evolution the lumber companies have been under continuing attack. Initially, individual companies could hardly have turned their efforts to sustained-yield forest management when industry economics were based on plentiful virgin stands; however, a minimum effort toward conservation and fire protection could have greatly reduced the damage and increased the lumber supply and profits in the next generation. It has been suggested that both the national interest and industry self-interest would have been well served by a slightly more long-range view. Had the lumber industry provided the genesis of forest conservation practices rather than adhering to a policy of determined opposition, both it and the public might have fared better. If we look at this case from the perspective of the present, we can see that industry management did not truly succeed in maximizing profits through its failure to act in its own self-interest.

The Use of Scarce Resources

When Ricardo explained the economic role of rent, he based his analysis mainly on the differential fertility of land.[3] Those fortunate enough to claim ownership of a fertile, well-watered valley had an advantage over the holders of more barren properties. As demand raised prices to bring marginal land into cultivation, the holders of the best land might recover a very handsome rental income.

The same analysis extends to other valuable resources—to oil wells and iron

---

[3]David Ricardo, *Principles of Political Economy and Taxation* (London: Bell & Sons, 1922), pp. 44–61.

mines, where the fortunate owner may sometimes receive substantial profits as a reward for the discovery of the resources. Since society has the established right to control the development of such resources, the privilege of unrestricted develop-ment and unrestricted profit becomes a passive subsidy of the business. The precedent for interfering with this subsidy is growing; many U.S. mining areas have imposed severance taxes on the ore, as a means of sharing in the profits (for example, the Minnesota tax on iron ore). South American and Middle Eastern countries have demanded a direct share in mining and oil profits, as well as an ever-increasing control over the price of the oil and over who may buy it.

In terms of a corporate impact analysis, a particular manufacturer who is using scarce resources should realize this fact and recognize that the right of unrestricted operation represents a subsidy. From this recognition, self-interest should suggest sound resource development and conservation policies. Otherwise, conservation groups or national planners will agitate for another extension of public control, and recent history suggests that they will succeed if industry practices are not beyond reproach.

Several steel manufacturers foresaw the need for new sources of ore and also for taconite recovery processes. Their efforts had much to do with the solution of the ore supply problem by developing the use of taconite. Pickands & Mather and others had active programs in Minnesota for many years; a small commercial taconite process-ing plant was operated briefly prior to 1924.[4] This development and exploration work was clearly in the self-interest of the business. In addition, it protected society against the exhaustion of a critical resource and business against potential interfer-ence in the management of its holdings of iron ore reserves.

In the same way, a lumber company might have foreseen the need for land management and fire protection to assure regrowth of forests. While such programs would have required areawide public sector action, an industry-sponsored request for state conservation legislation would have protected the long-term position of the industry and the public.

Public Concerns

Since the public is more aware of the actual or potential limits to the supply of natural resources, industries are subjected more frequently to public audit and review when new projects are proposed. New developments are not always welcome and, even when they are, the public is prepared to support activist groups that search the details of each proposal for any possible design weaknesses.

For example, Walt Disney Enterprises proposed a major resort development on public land in the Mineral King Valley and obtained the necessary concession from the Forest Service in 1965. As development plans were defined, opposition developed. The proposed access road was to cross a corner of the Sequoia National Forest. In addition to some cutting of sequoias, damage to the drainage in that section of the grove was feared, as well as incidental environmental damage from the heavy traffic and winter road maintenance. The very logic of such a large

---

4"Iron Ore Dilemma," *Fortune* 32, no. 6, (December 1945): 137, 257–260.

development involving the Mineral King Valley was challenged, out of concern that the ecology of the region would not support the resulting tourist load and that the wilderness area would be lost. Conservation groups protested. The Sierra Club, which led in this fight, has managed through a series of court actions to block the development in the intervening years.

For a corporation that had maintained a very good public image since the creation of Mickey Mouse, the controversy represented a dramatic reversal of public attitude. While the past aura of Disney dealings must have helped with the speedy approval of the early phases of the project, the plan did have flaws. Thus, the credibility of the Disney Enterprises proposal was questioned, and concerned citizens insisted on being heard.

Two questions could be raised as to the merits of the Disney Enterprises proposal to predigest nature at Mineral King, California for the benefit of society.

First, Disney has not projected the financial return to be gained by the development of Mineral King. If, "in 1968 . . . the corporation had one of its finest fiscal years," one can assume that the long range plans made by Disney Enterprises are astutely developed to insure maximum monetary gain solely for its own benefit. "In 1960, Walt Disney inquired whether the Forest Service might not again be putting the land out to bid." The conservation of natural resources therefore is of secondary importance to Disney Enterprises.

Second, if the Mineral King project is for society, one must ask what other endeavors of social responsibility has this company participated in? How many scholarships have they awarded to students who are potential ecologists with whom the natural resources of this society can be entrusted? What is their record in the free distribution of their products for use in needy children's programs throughout the country? Where are the accolades therefore that Disney Enterprises has received for its contributions to society, given freely and without monetary gain?

Before we are duped into believing that there are merits in the demolition of our natural resources, I feel that Disney Enterprises should give an accounting of the financial gain to be derived from the project, since Mineral King is public domain. Also, the character of Disney Enterprises in the area of social responsibility should publicly be made known before it is entrusted with responsibility for the natural resources of our nation.[5]

The lesson is that citizens' groups are increasingly alert to and suspicious of all new developments and that groups such as the Sierra Club are very effective in blocking or at least delaying dubious projects. Thus, if Disney Enterprises ever does succeed in getting an approval, it will be for a development plan smaller in scope and with less jeopardy to the environment than the original proposal. The Sierra Club has already

---

[5]Margo M. Sawyer, Letter to the Editor, *New York Times,* 21 September 1969, in response to "The Battle of Mineral King," *New York Times Magazine,* 17 August 1969, pp. 24 ff. Copyright © 1969 by The New York Times Company. Reprinted by permission.

succeeded to the extent of gaining a ten-year delay and removing some of the most controversial features of the project, if it has not blocked the project completely.

For other corporations that are planning projects with significant public impact, the message is that projects should be conceived and audited with great care to ensure that their impact is anticipated and balanced clearly enough so that approval is possible without substantial delay. And, where important natural features such as Mineral King Valley are at risk, fundamental issues may be raised over the wisdom of any development, regardless of the degree of forward planning.

Use Without Consumption

Some resources are not consumed as they are used. Examples would include the land itself or water that is pumped from a river to be used for cooling. These resources are limited in quantity. Since they are scarce resources, their use stirs social interest. Resources that are returned immediately, such as water, have come under social control as to the level of purity or temperature at which they may be returned. Land that is to be mined is also increasingly controlled to be certain that the surface is left in usable condition afterwards. Land that is put to use for longer periods, such as land on which buildings and parking lots are constructed, is less often subject to restrictions as to what will happen at the end of the use, even though society's interest is the same. However, it is now no longer rare for certain types of long-term leases to require restoration of the land to its initial condition after the lease has expired.

Society's concern for scarce resources that are used but not consumed is basically the same as for any other scarce resource. Nonetheless, the manifestations of this concern do differ from case to case, depending on the nature of the resource and the degree of current social interest in the specific area.

Resources from Current Production

When Kentucky Fried Chicken or any other large user of chickens contracts to obtain its supply of broilers, millions of eggs are produced and hatched. Over their seven- to eight-week lifetime, the chickens consume feed from current national stocks of grains and nutrients. Since these markets (including the broiler market) involve few scarce resources and are highly competitive, the users of chicken have received little or no subsidy for the resources used, but have contributed constructively to food supply and agricultural employment. Thus, when this kind of resource consumption is handled so that it does not disrupt market mechanisms, the purchasing corporation has little reason for concern over the impact of this portion of its activities. If future world food shortages develop as predicted, however, all usage of foodstuffs may come under closer social review.

Surpluses and By-products

In the years of chronic crop surpluses, new industrial uses were sought for farm products. A major search was made by the U.S. Department of Agriculture and others for new cash crops for marginal land and land idled by planting restrictions. The guar bean had been introduced from India in 1903 as a source of a special type of flour but had found little favor. USDA laboratories explored new uses for guar products. As a result, General Mills became interested in guar as a source of gum for industrial and food products. A development program was undertaken, guar planta- tions were established, a guar bean processing plant was set up in 1943, and a market development program started for the gum that resulted.[6]

Over a number of years guar gum found an established place, and a minor new cash crop for U.S. farmers was added. General Mills, in addition to the profits it gained, could properly claim credit for making a contribution to the economic health of a small segment of U.S. agriculture.[7] In the course of its profit-focused business development, the company had contributed to increased employment of underem- ployed farm resources.

Another resource that is beginning to receive public attention is the clumsy and formidable solid waste stream generated by our cities. Not only is garbage a substantial pollution and disposal problem but also a reservoir of precious, previously used natural resources. Several studies have revealed the recovery potential for these materials. Projections of future resource needs show impending shortages; for example, the paper supply may be limited by a shortage of wood pulp unless recycled fiber recovered after use becomes an important additional source.[8]

While recovery alternatives are discussed further in Chapter 12, municipal solid waste streams in this context provide an additional example of a surplus material of great social interest. Subsidy of raw material recycling processes has been sug- gested and may evolve in a manner comparable to the public sector activities to encourage utilization of surplus agricultural products in the 1930s and 1940s. For a firm active in utilization of such resources, the corporate impact is in the nature of a contribution to, as well as a subsidy from, the surrounding society.

Summary

A business firm that uses scarce resources and obeys relevant legal and ethical standards while doing so cannot be expected to set or enforce national resource policies. However, its own self-interest could require it to recognize any depletion of the social capital represented by this usage and to propose and attempt to implement the sort of regulation it would prefer to live under. If it does not, the social processes predictably will bring a sharp correction at some future time. Such conservation proposals cannot be defined as a social responsibility except in a sense secondary to the interests of the business. They are more correctly defined as the recognition of an implicit, but valuable, subsidy from society and a proper and self-interested

---

[6]James Gray, *Business Without Boundaries, The Story of General Mills* (Minneapolis, Minn.: University of Minnesota Press, 1954), pp. 249–250.

[7]"Guar gum and its derivatives are also expected to earn continued growth." *General Mills 1971 Annual Report*, p. 11.

[8]Arthur D. Little, *The Future of Secondary Fiber in the U.S. Pulp and Paper Industry* (Cambridge, Mass.: Arthur D. Little, August 1975).

response to the risk that this subsidy will be withdrawn if waste or unwise plans for development of the resources comes to public attention.

This chapter has reviewed the use and consumption of physical resources, including those that are scarce in nature and those that derive from current consumption or surplus, and has defined some of the reasons for society's increasing interest, as summarized in Figure 10.1. Although corporate resource use is sometimes subsidized and sometimes restrained, it must always correspond closely to total social interests if adverse corporate impacts are to be minimized.

Guideline for Managing Corporate Social Impact

In the use and consumption of physical resources, social balance will tend to be maintained if the following guideline is applied:

Conservation A firm whose operation is using or consuming scarce resources develops an understanding of the role of these resources in the total social capital, both in actuality and in popular belief, and manages its operations with a sensitivity that minimizes the chance that its right to use these resources will be restricted or withdrawn.

Applying the Guideline

Both the development of oil resources in the Mideast and copper from the mountains of Chile proceeded freely through the hands of private companies at first. Then success awoke a local sense of national depletion. Great wealth was being generated for others from a limited resource. A major national asset was being exhausted without review of the consequences. The eventual result was political intervention and national redirection of the development process.

A similar issue is defined in the United States every time that a lumber company cuts a stand of virgin redwood or sequoia trees. These trees represent a limited natural resource that is unique and irreplaceable because thousands of years were required for their initial growth; good forest management now calls for smaller harvests. Each harvest of a virgin stand reduces the

Figure 10.1 Physical Resources Versus Business Needs

Consumption of scarce resources:
    Limits on supply
    Protection of environment
	Consumption of resources from current
	    production

Consumption of surpluses and by-products	Right to use resources that are not consumed
	Right to consume resources

In its use and consumption of resources, the business firm has a major impact on society. And society's limits on what the firm can do are major constraints for the business.

quantity preserved in perpetuity as a part of the national heritage of history and beauty.

No national policy has been set on how much of the national stock of forest or mineral wealth should be set aside in this way. Decisions by timber companies to harvest trees on their own property serve to reopen the issue over the need to establish a national heritage conservation policy, and in each case the company involved becomes the focus of intense attack by environment and conservation groups.

The redwood issue is a conspicuous example of a generic problem. All businesses use some physical resources, and the public is becoming more and more aware of the limited nature of the physical resources of the nation and of the world. The social balance requirement is to use these resources wisely in a manner that is likely to meet with public approval as attention moves to that area and a specific policy is formulated.

This requirement sometimes imposes a heavy burden. A company owning virgin forest may find that it is not free to use the timber and that the restrictions prevent the sale of the land at a fair price, unless a government or conservation group has funds and wishes to buy. Several times controversy over the use of such a resource has frozen or devalued otherwise sound corporate investments. One of the reasons for a clear definition of social balance requirements is to enable managements to anticipate such issues more often before they actually arise.

Questions for Analysis and Discussion

1. In your opinion, how should the use of essential raw materials be regulated?

2. Find a current example of the controversy over the use of limited and precious natural resources. Briefly summarize the problem.

3. What are other examples of society's subsidy of the utilization of surplus materials?

4. One theory of regulating land use involves a system of permissions and prohibitions—zoning. Another approach is to tax land uses in proportion to the desire of the community to discourage them—permitting any use for which the owner is willing to pay the required tax. What are the advantages and disadvantages of each method? Which do you favor?

5. Where scarce resources are being mined, some countries have imposed a severance tax to gain revenue and control the development rate of resource use. Others have taxed company profits to share in the wealth produced, and still other countries have nationalized their mines. As a public policy alternative, what are the merits and demerits of each of the three choices? Which do you prefer and why?

6. When should a company enter into long-term contracts to assure its supply of slowly replenished resources? When is this unwise?

7. Resources that are surplus at one point in time (such as corn and wheat) can become scarce later. How does a company recognize this in its forward planning and shift its policies accordingly?

For Further Information

Brown, Harrison. *The Challenge of Man's Future.* New York: Viking Press, 1954.

Meadows, Donella H., Meadows, Dennis L., Randers, Jorgen, and Behrens, William W., III. *The Limits to Growth.* New York: Universe Books, 1972.

Stacks, John F. *Stripping: The Surface Mining of America.* San Francisco: Sierra Club, 1972.

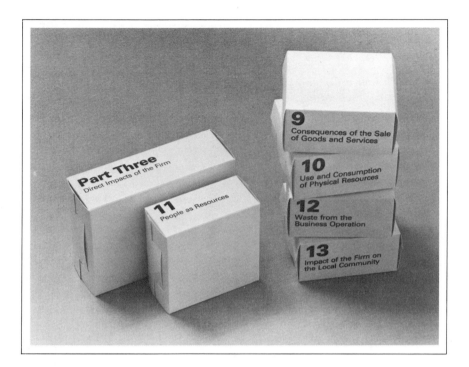

11
People as Resources

Individual people make up the management, the work force, the fabric of the organization, and the critical resource that governs and directs the use of all other resources. As the organization uses people, it consumes their working lives at the rate of at least .01 percent per day and is expected to offer a variety of programs and benefits in return.

In the management of corporate social impacts, the various aspects of the employment relationship are of great importance in the understanding and management of the impact on the people who form and perpetuate the organization. The current reawakening to old hazards, the discovery of new hazards in the workplace, and other factors to be considered here emphasize both the stresses of change and the urgent need for it. Next, a review of some of the major components of the relationship between employer and employee provides the basis for defining guidelines and constraints that lead to a minimizing of adverse corporate social impact as business employs people as resources, without consuming them at an excessive rate or causing them injury.

*For the first time a German firm was spelling out its duties to its men . . . a
health service, a relief fund . . . a pension scheme, hospitals and homes for the
aged . . . life insurance . . . the largest, most stable company town in
history . . . low cost housing colonies . . . a bread factory, a wine store, a butcher
plant . . . a charity fund for families left destitute—soup kitchens and public
works projects . . . available to the unemployed . . . a chain of non-profit retail
outlets open to all employees and their families. . . .*[1]

WILLIAM MANCHESTER

*The innovative efforts in industrial welfare of Alfred Krupp . . . were among
the first steps toward industrial social responsibility.*[2]

EUGENE C. MCCREARY

Early in the development of the industrial system, far-sighted employers began to
recognize the need of the employment relationship to provide not only day wages but
also the entire lifetime needs of worker and family. Robert Owen was an early
English leader who attempted to recognize the rights and the dignity of the individual
worker but Krupp provides a better prototype for the nineteenth-century evolution of
industrial employment practices. Far ahead of his time in recognizing the importance
of planning for the workers' material needs, he saw no need to consider individuality,
freedom of choice, or freedom of expression. Totally authoritarian, he ordered
dismissal of any worker suspected of political activity. Dismissal meant expulsion
from the company town, Cologne, and subsequent blacklisting by all German
industry. There was no appeal.

> No other industrialist . . . esteemed the personal freedom of his workers so
> little and their material well being so highly as did Alfred Krupp.[3] He began
> to speak freely of chaining his workers to the factory.[4]

As the employment relationship between individual and company has developed,
its intrinsic requirements have been recognized, although slowly and painfully. The

---

[1] Krupp evolved its health plans and related benefits over the years from 1840 to 1872, when
they were formally codified in the General Regulations. Life insurance was added in 1877.
William Manchester, *The Arms of Krupp* (Boston: Little, Brown, 1968), p. 152.

[2] Eugene C. McCreary, "Social Welfare and Business: The Krupp Welfare Program 1860–
1912," *Business History Review* 42, no. 1 (Spring 1968): 24–25.

[3] Wolf Schneider as quoted in McCreary, "The Krupp Welfare Program," p. 24.

[4] Ibid., p. 41.

employer seeks effective labor at minimum short- and long-term cost. The employee seeks satisfying, rewarding, and secure short- and long-term employment. From an initial approach that was based on buying physical labor day by day, the industrial system has evolved. Changes have been brought about by the complexities of family and lifetime relationships, the cumulative impact of bad working conditions and toxic chemicals, the special need for educated workers, the demand for meaningful work, and the city, state, and federal regulations aimed at curbing abuses and making fair practices more uniform.

Today industry is strained by institutional change, as companies continue to discard employment practices that were once considered to be satisfactory and seek to come to grips with the employer-employee requirements for a lasting economical and productive relationship. After we have recognized and analyzed some of the major areas of past bad practices, which are still coming to light and are hard to remove from the system, we will define some of the issues and suggest some of the bases for evolving a sounder system for the future.

The Firm as Viewed by Society

People as Consumable Resources

As a business operates, it employs people, buys from people, sells to people, and is managed by people. The business exists in a network of both individual and collective relationships among people. Its existence is sustained by the labors of the people it employs as workers and managers. The business represents one piece of the fabric of the society to which it contributes.

The firm draws people in with the offer of opportunity that employment represents and uses their time and energy in exchange for salaries and wages. The people who become employees are resources employed by the business. The talents and energies of its people are an important component of the social capital of the community, as discussed in Chapter 7. Thus, through its employment practices, the firm obtains the use of a portion of this social capital that might otherwise have been applied to other work or, in some cases, left idle.

As a firm employs people, it uses and consumes scarce resources. A day of employment represents the use of a small fraction of a working life. Where society in general and a given family in particular have invested for many years in the growth and education of a child, this investment can result in a productive adult life of perhaps 10,000 days of work (45 years × 223 days/year). Therefore, each workday represents about .01 percent of the potential return to the individual and society from the social investment that has been made in a productive adult.

Beyond the use of the fraction of an average lifetime that a day of employment represents, some types of work consume human resources by significantly shortening the worker's remaining life, and thereby reducing the productive potential of the work force. This decrease in human productivity creates social costs beyond the direct loss of potential productive time. Elements in this cost would also include medical and maintenance expenses for ill and disabled workers, along with some valuation of the pain and trauma to the affected individual and the immediate family.

In evaluating the employees of a firm as resources consumed or employed in the business, the key elements are the needs and expectations of both the individuals who enter employment and the firm that employs them. In both cases the needs and expectations must be measured in the context of the value system of the surrounding society. It would appear that within the contemporary value system our society strongly endorses the workers' entitlement to fair compensation for work. Society is now also moving toward the firm endorsement of a requirement that work not only be meaningful and fulfilling but also not cause short- or long-term injuries to the worker.

In the early 1800s a company would often contract with a foreman for the work to be done, and each day the foreman would hire enough labor to complete the required task. Day-to-day and month-to-month survival were the driving force for work performance. Little or no thought was given to the long-term cumulative effects of the work or to compensation for illness or injury. The design of working conditions was casual, was based on the immediate needs of working efficiency, and involved no awareness of the long-term effects of working under marginal or unsatisfactory conditions. These conditions provide the historical base for the evolution of a system that is now being redirected toward more productive and socially acceptable employment practices.

Exposure to Dangerous Materials

Today the concepts of avoidance of injury and compensation where injury occurs are becoming well established. As increasing numbers of familiar industrial materials prove harmful, and even deadly, previously unrecognized worker exposure problems are continually revealed.

Thus, the *Wall Street Journal* reported the experience of a union leader who attended a seminar in Washington on hazards in the workplace and then returned to his job at a small rubber products plant in Connecticut to learn that two female workers had been hospitalized with aplastic anemia. From the seminar he remembered that benzene solutions, which were used in the plant, can cause aplastic anemia. He called for the union's industrial hygienist who, after flying in and inspecting the plant, confirmed his fears. A part of the resulting health-improvement plan negotiated with management required the elimination of the benzene solution and a full study of the plant conditions.[5]

Only in the 1970s have such long-standing medical problems begun to be widely recognized, as union and management representatives have perceived the extent to which familiar chemicals can cause serious disease or injury. In another case a commercial ink solvent turned out to be the culprit. One hundred thirty workers in a plant making vinyl-coated fabrics were stricken with a nerve disease causing weakness and loss of coordination, with crippling in severe cases. Ohio officials banned the use of methyl butyl ketone, a solvent used in applying decorative patterns, and plant officials improved ventilation and moved the lunch area away from the work area.[6]

Familiar construction materials have also proven to be dangerous. Asbestos is the most dramatic example because of the number of people who have been exposed to it in the past. Although asbestos has been widely used as insulating material for several generations, the hazards of asbestos have only recently been recognized. Excessive inhalation of the dust causes asbestosis, a respiratory disease known for many years. More recently, it has been discovered that even moderate exposure to asbestos dust can cause cancer, often twenty-five to forty-five years later. In one study 210 members of asbestos workers' families were examined and 40 percent were found to have lung abnormalities of the type common to asbestos workers, probably as a result of their exposure to fibers carried home on the workers' clothes.[7] As might be expected, other past uses of asbestos have also cast a shadow on the present and future, as happened when World War II shipyard and construction workers in the United States and Britain began to develop cancer.[8] The widespread

---

[5]Walter Mossberg, "More Unions Devote Efforts to Eliminating Hazards in the Workplace," *Wall Street Journal,* 13 August 1974.

[6]"A Solvent that Crippled Workers," *Business Week,* 23 February 1974, p. 100.

[7]"The Contagion of Asbestos," *New York Times,* 22 September 1974.

[8]"A Grim Cancer Legacy from World War II," *Business Week,* 20 September 1975, p. 31.

industrial use of asbestos raises a frightening specter when considered in the light of these problems of the former shipyard workers.

Now familiar plastics have also come under scrutiny. Specifically, vinyl chloride, the chemical used to make the vinyl plastics, appears to have caused cancer in many workers. Where either an employer or the original producer of the chemicals is at fault or can be shown to be responsible for creating the condition in question, employees may be able to collect substantial damages for the injury to their health. Even a very low exposure to this material may be injurious. One of the lawsuits claims injury from the fumes resulting from the electric cutting and sealing processes in a supermarket's meat-wrapping operation.[9]

This suit over possible injury from vinyl chloride fumes stands as one of a major new class of actions. Exposure to toxic fumes and materials represents a significant cause of work-related illness, disability, and death. The new standards that are needed are being instituted, so that all recognized hazards can be controlled. However, as discussed in Chapter 9, the complexity of human biochemistry is such that it is not yet possible to predict with certainty whether or not a particular chemical or material will cause long-term injury. At the present time, it is only possible to say that a given material has not shown injury potential in tests that would have detected past problems. Thus, many of the acute health problems in the workplace today are long-term consequences of exposures that occurred many years ago, at a time when scientists did not recognize the potential threat to human life from industrial materials.

Noise

Another measure of the healthiness of working conditions is the amount of noise in the workplace. Noise in factories is commonplace and in the past was linked closely with industrial progress. Now the cumulative effects of noise on the worker's health are receiving attention. Beyond the fact that noise can cause tension and irritation, it can also cause deafness.

Historically, society accepted deafness as a consequence of certain occupations and neither found fault nor questioned the cause. It seemed normal that the hunchback of Notre Dame had almost totally lost his hearing after years of exposure to the clamor of the bell he rang. Cannoneers, boilermakers, and others have long suffered occupational deafness, which has been accepted as a natural consequence of their occupations until recently. A study of occupational deafness among black-smiths was published in 1830. More recently, operation of farm tractors and work in weaving and other textile mills have been linked to serious long-term hearing loss among workers. Within the last few years, an employer's liability for gradual hearing loss due to long-term exposure to noisy conditions was established and upheld on appeal in the states of New York and Wisconsin. A member of the Wisconsin Industrial Commission predicted that occupational hearing loss claims totaling $1

---

[9]"Goodyear, Borden Sued for $284 Million Over Polyvinyl Chloride Meat Wraps," *Wall Street Journal*, 21 August 1974.

billion would be filed in the United States as a result of these precedents,[10] and a member of Congress quoted an EPA study citing a $12 billion claim potential.[11]

The issue over industrial noise is important in several ways. First, it represents a major class of workplace problems that has been ignored for a long time. Second, it requires a significant change from past institutional practices, which were based on simply ignoring noise. The change is difficult because standards based on the total elimination of long-term injury to hearing will involve changes in most factories and many offices. Consistent standards to protect children and housewives would necessitate changes in many homes.

The modern world is a noisy world that produces long-term hearing damage. This world can be made more quiet, but the costs of doing so are large, particularly with respect to effecting changes in existing factories. Protecting the worker with ear plugs or ear muffs is more economical and can be effective against some noise conditions if the ear protection is conscientiously worn. Control of noise at the source is more sure but, again, is exceedingly expensive. Society is in the process of initiating and negotiating acceptable standards, and the potential damage claims by injured workers will add to industry's incentive for finding a way to comply.

Substandard Living and Working Conditions

Just as noise control represents a new idea that must change industrial practices almost as old as the industrial system, other old employment patterns persist, especially in marginal industries and depressed areas. "In Harlan County, Kentucky, are some of our country's richest natural resources—and some of its poorest people." This was the subtitle chosen by former U.S. Senator Fred Harris for "Burning Up People to Make Electricity," a report on his participation in the Citizens Public Inquiry into the causes of a long and bitter strike at the Brookside mine in Harlan County, Kentucky. Excerpts from this report are as follows:

"This whole country is like a layer cake," Si Kahn says, "a layer cake of shale, coal, and sandstone. Drift mines back into the mountains follow the seam of coal wherever it goes." Duke Power Company of North Carolina, he says, is the sixth largest utility company in the world. It has assets worth $2.5 billion. Its profits in 1973 were $90 million, up 14 percent from the year before. Duke went into the coal business directly in 1970 when it organized Eastover Mining Company as a wholly owned subsidiary and, through it, bought several mines in eastern Kentucky, including the one at Brookside. Kahn says that the miners were encouraged by Eastover's management, headed by Norman Yarborough, to join a small "company union," the Southern Labor Union. There was no standard contract for the miners. Each contract varied

---

[10]Theodore Berland, *The Fight For Quiet* (Englewood Cliffs, N.J.: Prentice-Hall, 1970), pp. 28–34, 256–257.

[11]"Putting the Damper on Decibels," *Environmental Science and Technology*, November 1975, pp. 1016–1018.

from mine to mine. Pay ranged from $17 to $32 a day, the average being $25. There was no functioning safety committee. Medical and retirement benefits were minimal and unreliable.

In June of 1973, in a National Labor Relations Board election, the miners at Brookside voted 113 to 55 to affiliate with the United Mine Workers. But negotiations for a contract with Eastover soon broke down, and on July 30 the miners at Brookside began the strike that now, as we arrive, is in its eighth month.

The committee has invited owners as well as workers to participate in the hearings, but the impression we get is that management will not appear. Dan Pollitt reads a letter from Carl Horn, Jr., president of Duke Power Company, respectfully declining our invitation. Norman Yarborough, head of Eastover Mining Company, is not coming either. Horn's letter questions the fair-mindedness of the inquiry members. We agree that most of us lean toward the miners, but we think we can be fair in trying to learn the facts. The letter states that Eastover has now raised the wages in their other mines to the UMW scale and is paying the miners for time spent with the mine moving to and from the face of the coal. They have done this only since the Brookside strike.

In the year of "the energy crisis," Coal is King again at $30 a ton. But what of the people of Harlan County? I look at the government statistics once more. There are nearly 40,000 people in the county, a drop of 36 percent since 1960. The median family income is $4600 a year. Only 23 percent of those in the county over the age of twenty-five have completed high school. Forty percent of the county's dwellings lack some or all of plumbing, water, or toilet facilities. Thirty percent of the families lack automobiles. More than twenty-four babies out of a thousand die before they are one year old, and the expenditure per child in the public schools is one-half the national average. The unemployment rate in the county is 7 percent; that doesn't count those who have long since given up looking for the scarce or nonexistent jobs.

. . . mostly the scenery is depressingly bleak. Garbage along the roadside. Overturned car bodies everywhere. Our drive takes us upstream along the yellow-brown Clear Fork River. Toilet paper clings to the bushes and tree limbs five or six feet up from the rushing stream. Toilets are built out over the river, and the water has obviously been much higher in the recent past. Jacqueline Brophy asks why public services have broken down. Why haven't the car bodies been removed from the highway and the streets? Why is garbage left on the roadway? Why are people allowed to dump raw sewage in the streams? Typical of counties with low income, counties where the mine companies own everything and pay low taxes, our UMW driver says.

We first hear from a number of the striking miners about safety conditions in the Brookside mine. They relate federal mine-safety figures which show that in 1971 the accident rate in the Brookside mine was three times the national average, and in 1972 was twice the national average. They file with us copies of specific federal safety violation reports, and they say that nothing was ever done to correct these violations. Three of the federal reports state that there was no safety committee at Brookside, as required by law. J. D. Skidmore says that, back in the mines, the phones are always out of order, there is no transportation out until the end of the shift, and it's a one-hour walk to daylight. The roof is approximately forty-eight inches high in the mine. "Try walking out of there, carrying a man with a broken back," one of the miners says. "Roof falls are a constant hazard, but the bosses just keep on rushin'."

Darrell Deaton, president of the Brookside UMW local, says he was caught in a belt line last year because he had to work alone, without a helper. A shoulder blade and five of his ribs were broken. He'd worked seventy-eight hours straight the preceding week. It was two o'clock on a Monday morning when the accident occurred, and he'd been in the mine more than twelve hours. It took forty-five minutes for someone to come and help get him out, Deaton says.

The miners say that they often have to stand knee-deep in water while handling 440-volt electrical cables. There's water in the mine because the pumps often won't work. When fuses blow, they are not immediately replaced; the cable is spliced or "hot-wired" around the fuse. Breaks in the cable, they say, are often just wrapped with masking tape and exposed again to the water. When a miner complains, Jerry Johnson says, the foreman says, "If you don't like it, you can always get your bucket," meaning pick up your lunch bucket and get out.

Bill Doan says that he was hurt in a rockfall at 7:15 one morning and that he didn't get out of the mine until nine o'clock. Other times, he says, "Roof was workin', rock was a-hangin', and it sounded like thunder. The bosses wouldn't go in, but I've had them make me go in and pin it because it wasn't done right the first time. If you wouldn't do it, they'd just say, 'Get your bucket.' I don't like workin' in them kind of conditions." James Sizemore says that frequently float dust, which is dangerously explosive, would get too heavy in the mine, and he would complain, but that the foreman would just say, "We gotta run coal."

What about federal inspection? The miners say that, somehow, management always knows when the government inspectors are coming. Don Dalton, UMW Safety Director for Region Six, explains this. On one excuse or another, such as not having the personnel readily available to accompany the inspector into the mine, the company can delay the inspection. And, even so, it usually takes forty-five minutes to an hour for the inspector to get from the mine entrance to the face of the coal. Word precedes him. "Boss walks up and says, 'We've got to make this mine look good now, boys; the inspector's comin',' " Jerry Johnson says. Louis Stacy says that he has several times been running a defective roof-bolting machine when word came that the inspector was on his way. "I've had the foreman to tell me to set timbers or something until the inspector got gone. The men's life depended on my job, but I knowed if I protested I'd a got fired."

Bill McQueen says that when the shuttle's lights and brakes were not working and the inspector was coming, the foreman would say, "Park it." Bill

Doan says that the roof bolts often didn't have enough torque on them, sometimes causing roof falls as high as thirty-five feet above the regular ceiling, and that once he complained about this to the visiting inspector in the presence of his foreman. He was transferred to a worse section, he says. "They sent me to 'Waterhole No. 3.' You come out of there lookin' like a hog that's been rootin' in the mud." Darrell Deaton says there is a direct telephone line to Washington for safety complaints, "but if you identify yourself, you're gonna be out of a job."

Sudie Crusenberg, a plain woman in a cotton dress, gives us some idea of what life is like for a coal-mining family. "I've seen some hurt and some killed. Seen 'em carried out on a stretcher," she says. "My daddy's a retired coal miner, and he's got the black lung. My brother died at the age of forty. I've got five living children and four dead. My man was mashed up in the mines. He can't never walk again." She's been picketing with the other women.

The women furnish the panel with a copy of a report from the Harlan County Health Department, dated October 12, 1973, which states that the drinking water in the Eastover mining camp, where approximately thirty of the striking Brookside families live, is "highly contaminated" with fecal bacteria. They say no action has been taken on this report. Only three of the families in the camp have indoor toilets. In one of these, the septic tank has been out of order for several months. Many of the houses have no running water, and these families have to carry all their water from a common outdoor spigot. Freda Armes says, "I take a cloth and strain the water to cook with. Sometimes, they'll be a black scum on the rag." Some of the women say they haven't had a drink of water since moving to the Brookside camp. No wonder R C Cola has so many signs everywhere.

The members of the Inquiry panel leave the Community Center to visit the coal camp at Brookside—rows of dilapidated frame houses, identical except for their weathering gray, green, red, and beige paint. The three houses with baths rent for $24 a month, plus $14 a month for electricity. Those with running water rent for around $20 a month, plus electricity. Nannie Rainey takes us into her four-room house where she and her husband and five children live. There is no water in the house. She pays $10 a month for rent and $10 a month for electricity. She doesn't know where she will go when the camp is closed. There are very few vacant houses in the county. The kind of house she would like, if she could find one, would rent for about $50 a month, but she and her husband cannot pay that much.

The prospects for settlement do not look good unless Duke begins to feel public pressure. Talking to Aaronson, I am reminded of an old tin sign I saw tacked on a tree along the highway as I left Harlan. It read: RE-ELECT GAW, JAILER. It seems to me that for a great many people in Harlan County—for poor people and a lot of coal miners—the whole county is a jail. They're trapped. It is not all Duke's fault by any means. We're all involved. And we're burning up people to make electricity.[12]

---

[12]Fred Harris, "Burning Up People to Make Electricity," *Atlantic Monthly,* 15 July 1974, pp. 29–36. Copyright © 1974, by The Atlantic Monthly Company, Boston, Mass. Reprinted with permission.

The Brookside mine story is a horror story, which is told with authority and also an admitted bias, by ex-Senator Harris. The key here is not this specific strike but is the agony caused by overdue social change in a county so poor that over one-third of its population has left since 1960. The issue involves the inherent danger of work in an industry whose existence has been threatened repeatedly. The dramatic shrinkage of coal markets as railroads and home heating went to petroleum products after World War II hurt the coal industry badly, with regrowth due to demand for cheap fuel for electric central stations. Then the era of cheap oil challenged this market, largely displacing coal except in the inland areas that were remote from supertanker delivery. Now coal is more profitable again, and perhaps through the combined efforts of the utilities, their customers, and the rest of society the evolution of Harlan County and other similar areas to more modern and humane living and working conditions can be accomplished.

Because different industries and sections of the country have not progressed at a uniform rate, the standards and practices for employment of human resources are uneven. In some areas the corporate social impact of employment practices is positive, as is evidenced by the health of the area and the support it receives; in other cases it is highly negative, as would appear in this report from Harlan County, and is complicated by conditions that demand correction.

Disease

Where the issue at the Brookside mine is specific and local, the coal industry faces a number of national issues over working conditions. One is over black lung disease, or pneumoconiosis, a common condition among coal miners that results as inhaled dust accumulates in the lungs, forming lesions and inhibiting transfer of oxygen to the blood. Eventually, it makes strenuous work impossible, causing coughing, shortness of breath, and in advanced cases, death. In 1969 Congress passed a federal black lung benefit program to compensate miners disabled by the disease or families of miners killed by it. In 1975 payments of $72 million per month were going to 370,000 miners or their families.[13]

To some extent, each of the older industries had developed its own pattern of disabilities. Comparable to black lung in the coal industry, fine dust in the textile industry leads to a condition called brown lung disease, or byssinosis, which had affected 23 percent of one group of cotton processing workers.[14] In industries processing arsenic or related metals that contain traces of arsenic, exposure to the vapors appears to be producing a significant incidence of lung cancer and lymphatic cancer.[15] Beryllium workers and uranium miners appear to have similar exposure problems. Dust from sand or silicone materials has long been known to cause silicosis. Dust and fumes are unhealthy in any case and appear to lead to serious disease when various chemicals and minerals are involved.

Many industries have an urgent need to control dust and fume exposures, and new

---

[13]Bob Arnold, "Government Attack on 'Black Lung' Ills Has Mixed Results," *Wall Street Journal,* 27 August 1975.

[14]"Attack on 'Brown Lung'," *Chemical Week,* 16 December 1970, p. 18.

[15]David Burnham, "High Levels of Cancer Found in Arsenic Workers," *New York Times,* 30 August 1974.

standards have been developed and are being improved. Meanwhile, the foregoing review suggests something of the backlog of past injuries already discovered or still coming to light.

Discrimination

In the same way that dust fumes and noise were formerly considered as constituting a normal part of the workplace, business firms carried local social customs and sanctions into the work environment. The parts of the industrial system that were created in an era of bias, class distinction, and male supremacy reflected these patterns in the conduct of the business enterprise. Many traditional business practices have been based on a sharp separation between workers and managers, racial segregation, and clearly divided and institutionalized roles for men and women.

As the United States has shifted to a more educated society and has tried to move toward greater equality of opportunity, business and other large organizations have felt the thrust of this change. They have been constrained to proceed with the social equalization process at a somewhat higher rate than the rest of society because of the open and conspicuous role they occupy in society. Racial discrimination was the first area to receive attention. Earlier, prejudice against the Irish, the southern European immigrants, and others had tended to fade with their integration into the culture, leaving discrimination against blacks, orientals, American Indians, and Spanish minorities in various parts of the country as principal targets. Then the social emphasis on equality of opportunity was broadened to include women, who had formerly been relegated to a secondary status by the legal and cultural patterns of western society. Thus, the United States undertook to remove the legal barriers, attack each and every cultural barrier, and then require positive industrial programs that would in truth establish equality of opportunity for all races and both sexes in the industrial world for the first time.

The concept of equal opportunity is obviously sound; it releases for social use all the talent, energy, and imagination that was formerly locked away by the pattern of discrimination. However, such a pattern does not change easily; it is deeply ingrained in all members of society, particularly with regard to those elements that concern and define the roles of each sex. Beyond the legal and intellectual acceptance that change is necessary, required, and must be carried out, there is a pattern of reaction and conditioning that is very difficult to overcome. If the effect of the change is to be positive, more is involved than just decreasing the level of discrimination in putting people into jobs. Indeed, profound changes in the behavior and attitudes of those in both majority and minority positions are essential.

Integration of minorities is occurring with less difficulty than the integration of women, in part because the minorities are able to adjust more smoothly since less cultural change is required. The change in the traditional role of the sexes is far deeper, and the women have as much difficulty as the men in establishing roles that foster full development of equality.

The view of discrimination as a disease is based on the degree to which it has continued to warp and distort behavior and also restrict full development of potential available human resources. Good management calls for steady pressure toward full use of all available resources, including human resources, so that the well-managed corporation will progress toward integration and equality of opportunity. But, in each society in each part of the world, a host of local practices, customs, proscriptions, and prejudices are embedded in the culture and resist change. In the United States the forces of change have been given the force of law. In some other societies the forces for change are less active. Rooted as it is in the local society, the corporation must respect the fact that heritage, including prejudices, must obey the social laws, and should, out of self-interest, represent a steady force for change in the direction of greater equality of opportunity.

Industry must use people as resources in order to operate. Each individual has a limited working life, and, therefore, the use of a portion of a limited resource should be compensated beyond the daily wage. The pattern of compensation needs to provide for not only the duration of the working life but also beyond. The need is to use human efforts more productively day by day and to compensate consumption of this limited resource more fairly.

However, in the present and from the past, the system is heavily burdened with practices that cause discrimination, disability, disease, and premature death, all of which shorten the working life and represent reckless and unwarranted consumption of human resources that is morally unjustified, despite the offer of compensation either before or after the fact. This situation was not created out of stupidity or avarice as much as out of ignorance.

From today's perspective it is now clear that long-term injury is likely whenever workers are systematically exposed to dust, fumes, or noise; the specifics of the injury potential vary greatly from case to case. Since dust, fumes, and noise were formerly considered as being normal components of the workplace, massive requirements for their elimination will impose a major lag in institutional development, with worker injury liabilities continuing to accumulate until this transition is completed.

Effective Use of Human Resources

From the preceding discussion, it is clear that workers have often been ill used or injured in the past. The emerging pattern requires that working conditions be such that no short- or long-term injury to the worker will result from the employment. This social balance requirement will be enforced by public anger and legal liabilities for worker injury. But freedom from injury is only one component in the complex of employment relationships that govern the effective use of people's labor. Some other components will be discussed in the following sections.

Continuity

The act of hiring brings an employee into the work force and creates a new relationship. Employment is on a day-by-day, week-by-week, or occasionally month-by-month commitment. While any position is normally not contracted on a long-term basis, many business operations depend on the development of long-term relationships as much as employees do. Most organizations rely heavily on a core of skill and knowledge that is carried forward from day to day and year to year by the work group.

When a job is offered to an employee and when that employee accepts the job, the day's labor that results has an opportunity cost, which is represented by the fact that the employer presumably could have hired someone else and the employee presumably could have accepted some other job. This same situation holds on the second day, in the second year, or in the twentieth year, except that other opportunities usually become less accessible with time. Thus, the accumulating opportunity cost to the faithful employee is in the increasing remoteness of equivalent alternatives. The employer-employee relationship grows and the commitment for its continuance is implicit.

Implicit commitments are not always fulfilled. Nothing in the law prevents a corporation, which has employed employees for twenty years, from terminating their employment at any moment in time. However, when long-service employees are discharged, the very fact that a single employment relationship has kept them out of contact with the job market may make it more difficult for them to find other jobs. For the employers the loss of knowledge and experience built up over many years often makes satisfactory replacement difficult.

Some human relationships develop to the point of recognition by the law as time passes, for example, acknowledgment of legal status for squatters' rights and common-law marriages. So far the employer-employee bonds are only beginning to be recognized, even though a somewhat parallel logic could be applied.

In terms of responsibilities and costs, there has been growing recognition that a corporation must take into account the cumulative opportunity cost for the employee group by ensuring continued employment. The accumulating investment of an employee in that employment is often recognized by seniority rights, length of vacation, preferred parking places, rights under insurance plans, and many other valuable but usually nontransferable benefits that accrue to the senior employee. Disability and retirement plans provide some cushion against the day when employment might cease, rights under labor contracts make employment more secure, and unemployment insurance (sometimes reinforced with severance pay) recognizes the adjustment in a necessary interruption or termination of employment.

Career Paths

In the construction and staffing of an organization, career paths are designated, either by accident or design. Then, as the organization functions and employees are promoted, replaced, or retired, these career paths are made real by the kind of horizontal and vertical movement of employees within the organizational structure. Good management calls for a pattern in which the desired mixture of necessary talent can be found inside the organization. The creation of such a talent pool requires a structuring of career paths and an encouragement of ambitious candidates so that appropriate talents will have been developed by appropriate people by the time they are needed. In this process management will try to avoid excessive loss of good people who lose patience and look elsewhere for the opportunity to use and be rewarded for developing their abilities.

A company that does a good job of developing the talents of its employees and then challenges them to use those talents makes a very favorable impact on the surrounding society. Thus, a capable management avoids social costs and social impact problems in the course of doing its management job well.

Job Design and Employee Rights

The step beyond career development is the concern with the nature of the present job and with employee rights and treatment. This area encompasses not only the demand for meaningful work discussed in Chapter 4 but also the dignity of the employee on and off the job.

Since the greatest productivity occurs when a job is interesting and motivating enough to provide work incentives that reinforce monetary and other rewards, widespread redesign of traditional jobs has been recognized as a necessity and is in progress. Concurrently, standards of dress and off-the-job conduct are being relaxed as the greater permissiveness of today's society reaches the workplace.

At the same time, employees are developing a more open relationship with their employers—at least in many firms. In any case an employee is protected by federal law from discharge or reprisal for union activity, and the OSHA law provides similar protection in another area, that of complaints for unsafe or unwholesome working conditions. Still beyond this boundary is whistle-blowing, the concept that was discussed in Chapter 5 under which an employee is expected by some to report an employer's legal and ethical violations.

Mobility

The growing trend toward job mobility in the United States shows that an increasing number of individuals are willing to sacrifice a part of accumulated employee benefits in exchange for the freedom to change jobs. When these benefits are sacrificed, however, they fail to serve their long-term purpose. Even though the failure may not be directly attributable to the business firm, the end result is a group of employees without desired protection, whether it be medical insurance coverage or reserves against retirement needs. And corresponding to the group of individuals who have changed jobs and sacrificed benefits as a result is a significant group who would prefer to make a job change but are deterred by the size of the sacrifice.

For example, consider a chemistry student who is short of funds and uncertain about academic goals. The student gets a two-year technical degree, leaves college, and finds employment as a technical assistant in an analytical laboratory. The job goes well, involving an advance to a higher grade of technical assistant and then to technician. However, at the end of five years, the technician has become restless and bored by routine analytical work. Nothing else is available in that firm that is tailored to the span of the technician's qualifications. Five years of accumulated seniority has value; by now the technician has a spouse, children, a home with a mortgage, and a growing need for regular income.

Time passes; in another five years the assayer has become deeply entrenched in this particular rut and is quite disenchanted with it. Yet expanding family needs make it increasingly difficult to sacrifice the benefits that have been accumulated and go elsewhere. At this point, our technician is thirty, with thirty-five more working years until retirement and poor prospects for surviving in a job that has become detestable. This individual either will become a discipline problem as the level of restlessness increases or else will begin to lose the ability to think rationally about the routine manual job being performed. Thus, the outlook for decades more in the same job is one in which both employee and employer will increase their investment in the employment relationship every year but will receive less benefit from its continuance.

Drucker has said that, with the longer average working life in today's society, the employer must provide more opportunities for workers to change jobs or even change careers in the course of their span of active work.[16] Although this applies particularly to the technically skilled employees (the "knowledge workers"), the entire work force has occasional need for the option to move to other forms of employment without undue fear or sacrifice.

> Lifetime employment is no longer desirable, even in Japan. For while it protects a man as long as his company or industry is doing at least reasonably well, it makes it virtually impossible for him to move elsewhere should his company or industry fail. But the underlying principle is sound; it is the responsibility of the employer to provide job security.[17]

The present employee security system in the United States is based on social security benefits that are supplemented by individual pension and welfare plans to bring the total payments to a more satisfactory level. To the extent that employees do not have supplementary benefits or lose them due to job transfers, the present system is inadequate. The concern of individual employers in this regard is that further action may be needed relative to their own employees and to those who leave their employ. Business self-interest calls for recognition of the social cost where benefits are insufficient (or are lost on job changes) and for active support of the most economical solution to the problem.[18]

Educational Assistance

The need to change from one assignment to another has been at least partly recognized through educational assistance programs, which have been further spread by competitive employment pressures. In a company with an adequate program that is located within convenient distance of a college or university, the disgruntled assayer in our previous example could have obtained a bachelor's and master's degree in chemistry in evening study and perhaps might have transferred into a chemical development department that was able to pay a better salary and

---

[16]Peter F. Drucker, *The Age of Discontinuity* (New York: Harper & Row, 1969), pp. 291–296. Also Peter F. Drucker, "Worker and Work in the Metropolis," *Daedalus* 97, no. 4 (Fall 1968): 1243–1262.

[17]Drucker, *Age of Discontinuity*, p. 305.

[18]A broadly transferable fringe-benefit package could afford one solution; extensions of the social security system could provide another.

make more constructive use of the increased level of expertise. Thus, by creating opportunity and by giving some subsidy to self-improvement, the employer provides a valuable safety valve for frustration as well as a means for members of the organization to increase their value to the company.

High-turnover jobs can sometimes be turned into an asset as a result of educational assistance programs. One chemical laboratory needing chemically trained people for routine work was able to attract high-quality students short of funds by offering supplemental education programs; these students did not need to give up their educational goals entirely. Even though they would often leave again after a year or two, their work was greatly superior to that of those otherwise obtainable for such routine work. Although the laboratory continued to have a high rate of turnover, it was able to upgrade its work force substantially at minimal cost on the basis of the educational assistance programs.

Another result of educational assistance programs and other training methods is the qualification of an employee for opportunities that the present employer cannot offer. Thus, it is not rare for an individual to receive additional training at least partly at an employer's expense and then obtain a better job elsewhere. On the surface, this would appear to be a direct loss to the employer who has sponsored the additional education. However, as discussed previously, it is in the interest of both employer and employee, as well as society as a whole, that an employee not be left to fester in a job that has been outgrown. In such a case it is advisable to help the employee to advance and move on, even if this means that the present employer loses the employee's services.

In many cases this apparent loss is truly a two-way street; the same firm that is losing an employee it has trained beyond its present job requirements may be hiring someone in another area of specialization who also must change employers to fully utilize training. A general tendency to help employees improve their qualifications works to effect an improvement in the average caliber of the work force; almost everyone benefits from this achievement. Also, as an employer's career develop- ment programs become well established and effective, employee ambitions will more often be channeled into areas where the investment can be recovered by progress within the company.

Employment Opportunity Cost

A social cost and a frustrated employee result when a man or woman is held too long in a job. The more desirable alternative for all parties is to encourage employees who have truly outgrown a given assignment to move freely to another. The loss from the transfer of an experienced worker may be real, but the only opportunity for minimizing this loss or turning it into a gain may come from helping that employee to move in a mutually beneficial direction. Where vested interests in fringe benefits become a barrier that prevents otherwise desirable transfers, the terms of the benefit package may need to be altered. The individuals who must move to continue their development and cannot move because of the sacrifice in benefits are not free; the expensive benefits become an impediment and lose their intended value.

The corporate side of the opportunity cost is the loss that is suffered if employees are not well motivated, if investments in training and growth are nullified by the number of resignations and departures, or if turnover jeopardizes the smoothness of the operating pattern. The idealized objective is a pattern of employee development and growth over the course of a working career in which each individual can find sufficient challenge to be fully motivated and contribute according to personal ability. Where circumstances make this objective less than completely achievable the resultant loss in motivation and output is the employer's opportunity cost.

Failure to Act

As discussed earlier, an employer who accepts the services of an employee over many years allows the development of a dependence and, thus, accumulates some obligation to mitigate the resulting hardships if it should be necessary to terminate this employment. Perhaps the most painful example of these hardships is the case of an individual who performs a job poorly but whose poor performance is tolerated over a long period of time. By failing to deal with the problem promptly, a corporation can increase its obligations to both the employee and society.

For example, an individual graduates from high school, is hired as a clerk, and shortly thereafter becomes a marginal bookkeeper. Over years of steady and diligent service the position is maintained. As a result of management's inattention to staff performance and also of the bookkeeper's increasing knowledge of the business, employment is continued, even though the demands of the work increase. After twenty years, this individual is still marginal, narrowly specialized, and firmly set in a work pattern.

The company suffers reverses. Budgets must be cut, efficiency raised, and money saved. The mediocre bookkeeper comes to management's attention and is discharged for incompetence. With little versatility, no other work experience, and minimal ability, the individual struggles unsuccessfully to find other employment. Some part of the unemployment cost (both in dollars and in humiliation) must be attributed to the former employer.

Even if this individual had been incompetent from the beginning, by continuing to employ the bookkeeper year after year, the corporation publicly endorsed a measure of value and implied to the employee that the standard of performance was satisfactory. A condition that was not created by the corporation and that might have been remedied by a more selective hiring policy or an early discharge was allowed to become a vested interest through passage of time. The corporation cannot avoid sharing the responsibility for costs that follow when such a person seeks more productive employment.

Layoff and Termination

In the course of operating any large organization, unpleasant decisions must be made. Business fluctuations may raise the issue of excess labor. Poor performance or other problems may define the need to discharge an employee. Layoff and termination represent two different mechanisms for severing the employment relationship. Both have social costs, can represent an adverse corporate impact on the surrounding society, and are sometimes necessary.

Good management uses expensive human resources with care and judgment. This policy leads to stabilization of employment patterns because of the disruption and cost involved in laying off, rehiring, and retraining employees. The policy also contributes to a constructive work environment, in which most employees succeed and discharge for cause is rarely necessary. But when discharge is truly necessary after due consideration, management must act even though a social cost might result. Failure to take necessary action can damage current operations and create other commitments and costs, as the previous section suggests.

To create social costs through firing is to create an adverse corporate social impact, which requires restoration of balance if a sound relationship with society is to be maintained. Sometimes this balance can be achieved easily and sometimes it cannot. When a misfit employee is fired or asked to leave, the corporation can occasionally guide his or her relocation into a different and more suitable position, and the final result of the discharge may even be beneficial. Unfortunately, such cases are rare. Usually, a discharge becomes a step in a sequence that can lead to less suitable employment or even to public support and other social costs posed by an unemployable.

The consequences when an alcoholic, a drug addict, or other problem employee is terminated will be a real social cost. Although the corporation may not be able to moderate or balance these costs, it should, at least, recognize its role in precipitating them and should attempt to offset them in some way through other positive programs if it is to achieve a balance with society.

Layoff costs are less severe, but nonetheless real. Of course, they vary with the particular industry and individual circumstances. A different kind of employer-employee relationship develops when layoffs are frequent, and the difference is not beneficial to the employer. Where management can find a means of stabilizing employment and minimizing layoffs without sacrificing productivity, the results have been beneficial. However, where this is not possible, at least the adverse corporate social impact of the layoffs should be recognized. The suggestion of such a broad proscription against layoffs requires, first, the ability to recognize characteristic differences in normal employment patterns in different industries. The two determinants of this industry or company characteristic are the employment pattern that is created and the nature of the commitment to the employees that is implied.

For example, a contract packaging house with only a small permanent labor force had developed a pool of local labor interested in working for a few days or a few weeks when a contract came in. This group did not expect permanent employment, vacations, or pension benefits. The nature of the temporary work pattern almost eliminated negative corporate impact from layoff. And yet, some of these employees began to budget around the expectation of a certain average amount of income from that part-time work and would have had their lives disrupted to some degree if it ceased altogether.

Construction workers, dock workers, and auto workers are among those long known for intermittent work patterns. Construction often stops in snowy, stormy winter weather or in heavy rain. Dock workers traditionally have been employed only on a job-to-job basis. Automobile plants have a pattern of shutdown for model change and for inventory adjustment. But in recent years the pressure at each negotiation has been toward guarantees of work or, at least, income. The auto workers have negotiated such guarantees, as have some groups of dock workers. Industries with a pattern of variable employment can still generate social costs by layoffs. The union pressure for various sorts of work stabilization or income guarantees is a result of the adverse impact of greater than normal layoffs, because layoffs that exceed the pattern on which employees base their spending plans have an adverse social impact.

Loss of Benefits

Among the costs of termination is often the loss of accumulated pension and other benefits, which is undesirable. Even though the employer may feel that the right to benefits has been forfeited, the result can be a charge against society, which includes other related social costs, for supporting the worker and family after they are too old to work. Because of the way that employee benefits originated, they are usually related to continued employment by the same firm. However, many retirement plans allow an employee who becomes ill or changes jobs after a certain age or length of service to retain some portion of the accrued benefits, and federal law requires protection of this sort. Some firms recognize a portion of service elsewhere in computing vacations, and a transfer of retirement benefits sometimes becomes a part of the negotiation in hiring a senior employee from another firm. But, in general, fringe-benefit packages are designed to cement job ties and discourage job changes and, thus, may cause social costs when an employee must leave, or should have left and does not.

Evolution of a Managerial Class

Unskilled workers are hired directly into jobs, and skilled workers have had a traditional apprenticeship and training pattern. Early in the development of the industrial system the managers emerged from the ranks, first as foremen, and then in a higher capacity. However, members of the more specialized skilled labor groups, such as accountants and lawyers, have also risen into top management. As the knowledge requirements have risen, more engineers and specialists of various types have joined the organization, to the point that it is not rare to find a firm using the first line supervisory position as an initial assignment for technical and management trainees, rather than as a role to which members of lower ranks are promoted.

Some organizations have gone further, by bringing top management trainees into middle management ranks, based on selection of top M.B.A. graduates or other advanced employees who are given a "fast track" indoctrination that is intended to guarantee an upper middle management assignment if they stay in the organization. The effect of these training programs is to shift the hiring from the old "entry at the bottom" pattern to a new pattern where there are several entry levels, each of which tends to provide a restriction, if not a ceiling, on the opportunities of those entering at lower levels. These levels reduce opportunity and, therefore, motivation and block promotion opportunities necessary to establish career paths and maintain a healthy turnover in the lower parts of the organization.

While the training needs of the organization and the needs for qualified replacements must truly be served, both equality of opportunity and the dynamics necessary for maintenance of a healthy organization demand that promotion opportunities for each level of the organization be maintained to the greatest extent possible. Here is where educational assistance and related programs have their most important role—in making the means to job progress available to those with sufficient ambition and ability to qualify themselves for work at a higher level in the organization.

These restrictions on upward mobility have tended to separate the managerial class from various other lower strata. Beyond various moral and political reasons for insisting on equality of opportunity, a corporation has a strong self-interest in maximizing the productivity of its human resources. Equality of opportunity means a larger pool of talent competing to contribute to the growth and prosperity of the firm as a route to their own advancement. Since the corporation clearly benefits, why keep part of the employees from joining this competition?

This does not mean that requirements should be lowered; rather they should be clearly defined and an environment created where the ambitious invest in further education and training, with company assistance as appropriate. Then the employees should have a reasonable hope of reward if they can meet necessary standards. Earlier discussion has dealt with the frustration and negative impacts if no opportunities are available to an employee group. Here the emphasis is on the positive aspect, with clear rewards going to the corporation if paths of upward mobility are kept open. To forgo these rewards suggests weak management, if not mismanagement, because then the organization is allowed to stratify, frustrate the ambitions of most of its employees, and evolve toward having its own managerial class.

Human Resources Management

The sum of the efforts and personalities of the employees is what constitutes the firm, since a business corporation is only a legal fiction in the ultimate analysis. Thus, the collective will and direction of the firm has a profound long-term effect on the individual employees. The effect of the employees on the firm is a composite of what all the employees actually do (including the evolution of the individual moving along a career path) and what they do not do (that is, the opportunity cost of alternative employment not pursued, mobility not permitted, or potential for promotion and growth not realized). The corporation must understand these effects and deal with them wisely, if it is to establish a satisfactory social balance with the employees who stay in or move through its work force.

The essence of the human resource management problem is the need to obtain productive, goal-oriented work from people, individually or in teams. Daily, these people will be exchanging .01 percent, more or less, of their productive working lives to serve the needs of the firm. In return, they will insist on receiving both meaningful work and fair compensation. This relationship is demonstrated schematically in Figure 11.1.

This compensation must include fringe benefits related to current personal and family needs and necessary provision for the needs during the period of time after retirement. If the working conditions lead to injury or other shortening of that productive life, a social cost results. Society has demonstrated that it will reaffirm with penalties the obligation of the firm to compensate any such social cost whose source can be traced. Thus, more frequently the full costs of employment are now

Figure 11.1   The Employment Equation for a Day

What the worker gives:	What the employer gives:
Productive output from 0.01% of a working life	Wages, including fringe benefits 0.01% of necessary provisions for a full life, including retirement
An option on more working days in the future	An option on further employment in the future

The balance between worker and employer contributions must be fair, so that the employer can operate a productive enterprise and that the needs of the employees and their families can be satisfied. Otherwise stress and troubles will disrupt the fabric of the relationship.

being brought back to the employer, where formally many of the costs beyond the day's compensation were left to the worker, the worker's family, and society as a whole.

As the explicit cost of employing human resources rises to its full and true costs, including social costs, the employer is increasingly challenged to obtain full productivity from these resources. Also, the firm's investment in human resources becomes more long-term in nature, as pension costs, termination costs, and long-term effects of working conditions are tied more closely to each day of employment. The employer has to recognize the extension of the time frame encompassing these activities and to manage accordingly.

Since the necessary investment in an individual employee is normally best recovered over a long span of employment, a clear and increasing congruence of employer and employee interests develops in (1) the meaningful and motivating nature of the work, (2) the effective career paths for individual growth and development, and (3) the organizational development pattern that encourages real and productive internal teamwork in pursuit of business goals. Many familiar human behavior types of organization and management concepts suddenly come into focus as important management tools for obtaining maximum long-term productivity from an expensive investment in human resources.

Summary

As the firm operates, it employs people as resources, as summarized in Figure 11.2. However, the firm must be careful not to consume these resources as it operates beyond the degree to which the passing of each day consumes a fraction of each working life. Otherwise, the firm must face the risk of social cost and social reprisal for any injury or abuse.

Figure 11.2 People as Resources for the Business

People employed or consumed	Use of people to do work
Injury from familiar materials	Continuity
Injury from the workplace	Meaningful work
Careless management	Career paths
Discrimination	Opportunity
Human resource management	Security

The most essential business resource are people. This resource area gives maximum return to good management, but inept or incompetent management sacrifices the potential and creates adverse corporate social impacts on employees and the community.

This daily use (and thus consumption) of human resources is inevitable but not necessarily bad, although the power to use the day invokes a responsibility for the consequences. To the extent that a day of work represents about .01 percent of a working life, the resource represented by each individual is consumed consistently. To the extent that such a day is spent in meaningful work under wholesome conditions, with fair compensation and benefits, the use of that day itself can be productive and rewarding to each worker. Out of such work is drawn the strength and dedication that makes organizations outstanding and carries them to great levels of accomplishment.

Such strength and dedication in the organization rarely comes about by chance; it must be built up over time through prudent management of the relationship between the organization and its employees. This process requires management of the organization's impact on individuals, in terms of providing career paths, continuity, security, opportunity, and a mutuality of interests so that each person can give energy and enthusiasm to a specific work task and to the organization without sacrificing self-interest or human ties.

Unfortunately, conditions in many organizations are far from ideal. As stresses, conflicts, injuries, and confusion decrease the effectiveness and increase the regulatory and liability exposures of such organizations, the adverse social impacts thereby created also stir the antagonism of the surrounding society. In this area of use or abuse of people as resources, the avoidance of negative impacts and the attainment of social balance are more necessary and more rewarding than in almost any other area. The potential benefits are not only outside, in the interface with society, but also inside, in the effectiveness of the organization and the productivity of its people. Good management can no longer permit the diversion and waste that is caused by the stress and frustration of human resource misuse.

To a large extent then, the requirement for management of corporate impact on the people of the organization and for making substantial progress toward a social balance in this area is another statement of the quality of performance that is expected from capable, profit-oriented management.

This chapter started with an emphasis on the new awareness of dangerous chemicals and work conditions and bad employment practices, all of which serve to illustrate the firm roots of the system in past practices that must be changed. To minimize adverse social impact, corporations should, in the course of this change, develop a sensitivity to the relationships and dependencies that they create and build a strong plan of using employee abilities to the fullest possible extent. This sort of operating pattern would appear to serve the self-interest of the business well and simultaneously create a satisfactory social balance.

Guidelines for Managing Corporate Social Impact

In the use of people as resources, social balance will tend to be maintained if the following guidelines are applied:

Value given and received   Each member of the organization receives fair compensation (including adequate provision for dependents and for old age benefits), works under conditions that will not impair health now or in the future, and in return is expected to deliver full productive energy during the time allocated to the job.

Opportunity   Meaningful tasks, challenging career paths, and equality of opportunity to pursue these tasks and paths are maintained with minimum possible disruption.

Applying the Guidelines

In planning its employment, a company should attempt to create conditions such that members of the organization participate in rewarding activity and receive fair compensation of a more conventional sort. This establishes an environment where the productivity of the individuals and the organization can be maximized, both in physical output and in innovative and intellectual processes. Personal career opportunities also grow easily in such a climate, and the balance achieved eliminates most of the frictions and inefficiencies otherwise characteristic of most organizations. The barriers between different parts of an organization, the stress and distrust between management, unions, and other employee groups, and the misdirection of effort to fit personal ambitions of individual managers all have a direct cost in loss of the organization's efficiency and also a social cost resulting from the frustration of and reduced opportunity for the organization's members. Effective management of expensive human resources is equally desirable not only for creating and maintaining the social balance necessary to manage corporate social impact but also for increasing the profitability of the business.

Questions for Analysis and Discussion

1. How do you feel about the concept of people both as resources employed by a business and as resources consumed by a business?

2. Find current examples of business practices that appear to be causing injury or reducing the productive life of the employees.

3. If most wage earners and salaried workers began to think of each day's work as .01 percent of a working life, what changes in attitude might result? How would this new attitude affect the workers' pressure for pensions and other fringe benefits?

4. Develop your own example of how the principle of implied continuity leads employees to expect and depend on corporate actions that may not occur.

5. Develop your own example of loss due to the opportunity cost of staying in a particular employer-employee relationship.

6. Look for examples of employee development programs. Who seems to benefit most, the corporation or the employee? How would the benefit versus the cost of the program be judged?

7. Choose an organization with which you are familiar and trace typical career paths in one or two areas. Do these career paths lead to the full advancement potential of the employee, or are they dead-end positions?

8. Does the employer or the employee benefit most from educational assistance programs?

9. Find an example of a program that draws disadvantaged or handicapped people into the work force. Does the corporation appear to be gaining by this effort? In what way?

For Further Information

Government, Business and Society: The Changing Contract. Glastonbury, Conn.: The Futures Group, 1976.

Jenkins, David. *Job Power.* Garden City, N.Y.: Doubleday, 1973.

Lincoln, James F. *A New Approach to Industrial Economics.* New York: Devin-Adair, 1961.

Marrow, Alred J. *The Failure of Success.* New York: Amacom, 1972.

McGregor, Douglas. *The Human Side of Enterprise.* New York: McGraw-Hill, 1960.

Torbert, William R. *Being for the Most Part Puppets.* Cambridge, Mass.: Shenkman, 1973.

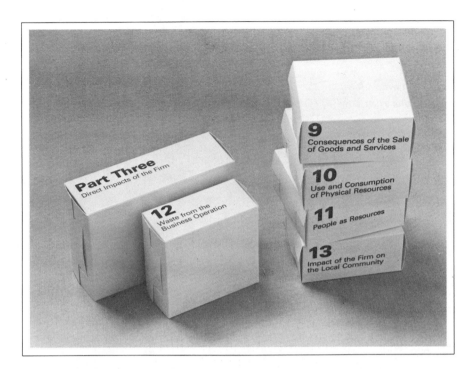

12
Waste from the Business Operation

An outstanding characteristic of modern industry has been its production of waste. The social impact of waste discharges has become an important management problem requiring remedy, which is made more difficult because of the complexities of modern wastes. This chapter will consider present and future requirements, after discussing liquid wastes, discharges into the air, solid wastes, noise, nuclear wastes, and several special waste problems. These types of wastes will be placed in the context of their environmental impact, where they may be seen to represent simple treatment load, toxic materials, wastes capable of poisoning or unbalancing major natural systems, or a combination of these three types. This analysis should aid in defining the pattern by which the corporate social impact of waste materials can be better anticipated and balanced in the future.

The old norm allocating the cost of pollution to society was so well established
that no one even tried to compute the social cost. Each producer had to keep
polluting or suffer a competitive disadvantage.[1]

JOHN MACDONALD

The right to a decent environment is a natural right of man.[2]

RENE DUBOS

Emergence of the Industrial Waste Issue

The outcry over industrial waste has become an effective, urgent public issue only
recently. Conservationists and idealists have been concerned with this issue for a
long time and have finally received broad support within the past few years.
Nonetheless, the vestiges of the old attitudes toward industrial waste are as
common as the old plants not yet converted to modern standards.

The day-to-day operation of a business corporation affects the environment around
it in several ways. Materials are taken in and are discharged. Each of these acts has
some impact on the surrounding society. Currently, a most acute concern is with the
waste streams; a social cost is incurred if the wastes discharged into the water and
air are not sufficiently purified to ensure that no measurable detriment to the
environment results.

This issue, which was formerly a loosely defined moral obligation, has not only
become a major public issue but also a legal obligation that is increasingly specific
and hazardous for a business to disregard. The power of the U.S. Army Engineers to
refuse to permit discharge of pollutants into navigable waters or their tributaries
under the 1899 Rivers and Harbors Act was rediscovered,[3] and the public was invited
to share the fines generated by its strict enforcement.[4] The potential impact of this
new use of the old law was so great that U.S. Steel decided to test its constitutional-
ity, but Congress passed the Clean Waters Act to establish timetables and clarify in
advance any legal issues. Thus, while the clean water and air standards are being

---

[1]John MacDonald, "How Social Responsibility Fits the Game of Business," *Fortune* 82, no.
12 (December 1970): 133.

[2]Rene Dubos, "The Future Natural Environment," speech before the Yankelovich Monitor
Environmental Conference, Waldorf-Astoria, New York City, 1 November 1973.

[3]*New York Times,* 10 February 1970, and 24 December 1970.

[4]Joe Wing, "The Good Earth Crusade," syndicated column in *Rockland County Journal News,*
(Nyack, N.Y.), 30 September 1971.

tightened, the right of conservation groups to recover actual and punitive damages from polluters is becoming well established.[5]

Both the need to avoid adverse corporate impact on the environment and the legal obligation not to pollute are simultaneously exerting similar pressures on corporate behavior. Over the long run, self-interest demands that business comply, but short-term pressures are increasing rapidly as well. Some older plants have shut down entirely because legal compliance was too expensive, and a major shift of national resources is occurring as corporations budget billions of dollars for pollution control. From the viewpoint of corporate impact analysis, few issues remain conceptually unresolved, although the practical, national task of making difficult tradeoffs and enforcing implementation of effective pollution control will take more than a few years.

The Firm as Viewed by Society

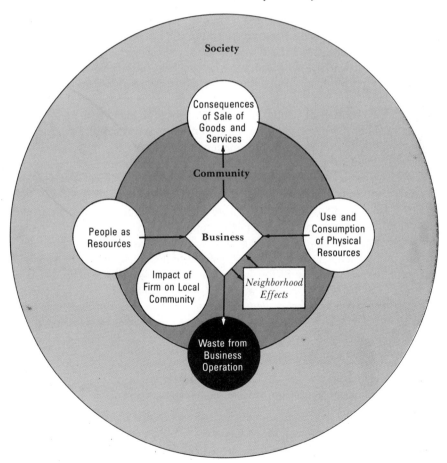

[5]John V. Conti, "Cleaning Up in Court: Conservationists Press Suits to Assert Right to Clean Environment," *Wall Street Journal,* 26 March 1971.

Many corporations have not yet adjusted to this new climate of opinion, in which pollution and its control have rapidly gained attention as important public issues. The sudden emergence of these issues has resulted at least partially from the fact that the inherent capacity of natural systems to absorb pollution has finally been overtaxed in a decisive manner.

> Even twenty years ago the industrial and municipal effluent being discharged into public waters was in most cases too little to pollute. Nature has a built in system to break up and clear away pollution. But today it is a different story. Many of our rivers and lakes have passed the level of tolerance and even the oceans are in danger. Today's polluters cannot avoid the issue of environmental responsibility. The additional cost to protect the environment must now and forever be included in the cost of any item.[6]

Although many individual firms have benefited from this natural capacity to absorb pollutants, it is one form of nature's bounty that has never been made uniformly available. A wise or fortunate choice of site has made possible a significant, although unrecognized, subsidy to the chemical plant or paper mill that has been able to dump untreated wastes without penalty. Thus, whereas the penicillin plant cited in Chapter 2 enjoyed a subsidy through its opportunity for unrestricted dumping into the Wabash River, the same subsidy was not available to the Pfizer plant because of the limited waste-carrying capacity of Honey Creek. Then, as society expressed general concern about the water quality of this river basin, regional standards were imposed that tended to equalize the standards by restricting the pollution.

The same sort of subsidy can exist where no damage is being done to water quality, when there is access to the natural waste-treating capacity of a lake or river. The ability to take advantage of such an opportunity depends on the total environmental balance. A discharge that has never caused any problems over a period of years can suddenly become unacceptable when the addition of other discharges into the same stream causes the natural system to be overtaxed. A critical threshold is passed as the natural system collapses. Fish die or the stream becomes septic. At this point the past subsidy of free treatment has expired, and a treatment plant becomes essential where no such facility was needed before.

In the estimation of present and potential corporate social impact, it is quite important for a firm to recognize any dependence it may have on unrestricted access to natural systems for purifying its waste streams and to plan for the possibility that this subsidy might someday be withdrawn.

Impact of Industrial Wastes on Environmental Resources

The ability of natural processes to purify and eliminate waste material is an important natural resource. Where an amazing variety of waste materials can be degraded and converted into an input for a naturally useful biological process, other wastes are

---

[6]Walter J. Hickel, "The Making of a Conservationist," *Saturday Review*, 2 October 1971, p. 66.

more toxic or more difficult to treat. They tend to overload and destroy the natural biological treatment system. Thus, the right of using nature's bounty for waste treatment carries with it a responsibility not to overload and destroy the system. Because of the past abuses of this responsibility, there is a greater tendency for the standards for protecting the natural environmental systems to be set in the public sector and be administered by a public agency.

The nature of the industrial waste problem and therefore, the nature of the pollution that it represents determine both the principal alternatives for the corporation that is generating the waste and the social cost of its discharge into the environment. The principal types of waste streams are liquid wastes, solid wastes, discharges into the air, noise, and heat. In addition, special problems with nuclear wastes and ocean dumping require separate discussion.

In terms of their impact on the environment, these categories of waste can represent one or more of four different types of treatment load. They can impose (1) a simple biological or chemical load on the natural systems, (2) a solid or toxic load that will permanently take possession of the dumping ground, (3) local toxicity on the biology of the environment, or (4) systemic poisons capable of contaminating or unbalancing entire natural systems. An apple core exemplifies a simple biological load and a broken bottle, a dumping load. Salt and sulfuric acid are examples of wastes with local toxicity, and mercury and fluorocarbons represent wastes capable of upsetting important natural systems. The problem presented by a given waste material is determined partly by whether it is a liquid, gas, or solid and importantly by the classification of its discharge as one of these four types of environmental impact.

The purpose of discussing these types of waste streams and waste impact is to define the most cost-effective route to a social balance, since society has clearly signaled its desire to end social costs due to pollution. The obvious public interest has already led to a series of specific enforcement programs encompassing most of the types of waste streams that have thus far come to public attention. Therefore, all waste discharges should be reviewed with the expectation that society will sooner or later refuse to accept any further adverse social impact from the specific discharge.

Liquid Wastes

In the case of liquid waste discharges, the problem is to establish standards for the local lakes and streams by taking into account the characteristics of the waste that requires treatment and to install appropriate treatment facilities to prevent any environmental overload prior to discharge.

This is not the same as requiring a zero discharge standard for all wastes, because a true zero discharge standard may be neither necessary nor desirable. For instance, in the continuing controversy over pollution of Russia's Lake Baikal, the world's largest fresh water lake, one scientist protested that if a zero discharge standard were actually enforced on all of the incoming water streams, the natural biological systems of the lake would be disrupted for lack of nutrients.[7] On the other hand,

---

[7]Theodore Shabod, "Russian Revises View on Lake Use," *New York Times,* 20 May 1973.

many of the natural waters in the United States have been so grossly overloaded with pollution that the pressure toward zero discharge standards can continue for many years before there is any danger of overcompensation.

Some liquid wastes, such as those that contain toxic materials or those that precipitate solids on dilution and degradation, require preliminary treatment before discharge. Otherwise, they cause environmental damage regardless of the state of readiness of the natural waterway. These and other liquid wastes must be evaluated to determine which of the four types of treatment load they represent.

Progress With Compliance

The Water Pollution Control Act of 1972 mandated that all discharges into U.S. waters be treated with the "best practicable" methods by 1977 and by the "best available" treatment technology by 1983. Although there is concern that many municipalities and some industries are lagging behind this timetable, the pressure of the law has set previously static industries in motion, and many corporations are reporting dramatic progress.

One success story is from the Fibreboard Corporation paper mill at Sumner, Washington, where a new waste water system recycles 1,600 pounds per day of solids that were formerly discharged into the Stuck River. In addition to the material savings, the $300,000 system saved $155,000 in equipment costs, plus another $2,000 per year that would have otherwise been necessary to finance the dewatering and disposal of the solids. The system also cut plant water usage from 940,000 to 450,000 gallons per day.[8] The net impact of the project has meant improved fiber recovery, which represents improved use of forest resources, and has also cut water consumption, saved money, and reduced the waste discharge burden on the Stuck River. Thus, Fibreboard is getting some additional return on the investment initially required. Fibreboard's achievement is commendable, and the new Great Lakes Paper Mill at Thunder Bay, Ontario, has proposed to go even further. It is to recycle all liquid waste streams and discharge no effluent at all.[9]

The new pollution control requirements affect the nation's agriculture because fields and feedlots yield discharges into the nation's rivers. For example, pesticide run-off from the fields can become a human health hazard. In one action the Environmental Protection Agency (EPA) forbade the use of the pesticides aldrin and dieldrin on corn and citrus crops in spite of the importance of these materials in reducing insect damage. These substances are very long-lasting materials that find their way into water supplies and animal feeds. They have been found to cause cancer in laboratory animals.[10] Of course, this example is just one in the series of concerns that has developed over residues and run-offs from various chemicals and fertilizers used on the nation's fields and farms.

The run-off of animal wastes from feedlots is an almost equally objectionable form

---

[8]"Recycling Helps Paper Mills Clean Up Their Image," *Chemical Week*, 1 May 1974, pp. 33–34.

[9]"Two Kraft Mills Will Waste Not," *Chemical Week*, 5 November 1975, pp. 60, 64.

[10]"Of Mice and Men: Alarm over Plastics," *Time*, 14 October 1974, p. 64.

of stream pollution. When it rains, the run-off from a fifty-acre feedlot has been calculated to be equal to the raw sewage from a city of sixty thousand people. Several feedlots have installed systems to retain the run-off water and use it later to fertilize surrounding acreage.[11]

Thus, any industrial activity, whether corporate manufacturing or farming, is receiving pressure to conform to the new clean waters requirements.

System Poisoning

Unfortunately, some of the pollution problems are more fundamental in nature and more difficult for an individual industry to adjust to and eliminate. Where mercury pollution problems caused major changes in industrial practice and the phasing out or substantial modification of traditional mercury-cell electrolytic processes, other industrial materials are posing equally formidable problems. An illustration is provided by the furor over polychlorinated biphenyl (PCB) contamination of rivers and fish that began to come to a climax when the New York State Department of Environmental Conservation ordered GE to stop dumping PCBs into the Hudson River from two plants in the Troy area. The order specified a $2 million performance bond to be forfeited if the deadline could not be met. The concern focused on the possibility of irreversible ecological and economic damage to the river and its commercial fisheries.[12]

After a number of years of scientific worry over growing evidence of PCB toxicity, Ogden Reid, Environmental Commissioner of New York State, precipitated the confrontation that has since led to plans for total phase-out of PCB manufacture and use. Formerly, PCBs had seemed as safe as they are effective and had been very widely used.

In an analysis of the problem as it appeared in 1973, *Environment* magazine reviewed the extensive use of PCBs in polystyrene cups, bread wrappers, frozen-food bags, plastic liners for baby bottles, and other products in contact with food. Because of problems with PCBs leaching into some food products, strict federal standards were set.

PCBs had found wide use since their introduction in 1930, and had seemed to be quite safe. In 1966 high concentrations were discovered in the flesh of fish from the Baltic Sea, and this led to a series of investigations aided by rapid improvement in analytical methods that began to reveal the full dimensions of the problem. PCBs were found to have an almost amazing ability to move through biological systems and contaminate the human food chain.

From 1930 to 1970 the United States produced about one billion pounds of PCBs, of which an estimated three-fourths has entered the environment. Major quantities have also been produced in Europe, Russia, and Japan. With rising production and usage, contamination of human food has been found repeatedly. In 1970 the

---

[11]Ralph E. Winter, "Antipollution Laws Force Livestock Men to Devise Ways to Collect, Use Manure," *Wall Street Journal,* 5 March 1974.

[12]"G.E. Ordered by State to Stop Dumping Toxic Waste," *New York Times,* 8 September 1975.

Campbell Soup Company in New Jersey found that chickens had been contaminated by PCBs in bread wrappers that had been ground into their feed with stale bread; 140,000 chickens had to be destroyed. In 1971 a major poultry producer in North Carolina traced a decrease in egg hatchability to PCBs in the feed, which were, in turn, traced to a leak in a heating system in a fish-meal pasteurization plant. Major losses of feed, eggs, and poultry occurred as contaminated materials had to be destroyed. In Baltimore PCB contamination of milk was traced to contamination with spent transformer fluid. In Georgia, Florida, and Ohio, PCBs from a sealant used on silo walls were found to cause similar contamination of milk from cows who ate the silage.

In Japan a massive outbreak of a skin disease was traced to rice oil contaminated with PCBs from the heating system in the oil plant. Over one thousand people were afflicted, and the poisoning was serious in many cases.

In 1971 Monsanto Company, the sole U.S. PCB producer, agreed to stop selling these compounds for any application likely to leak into the environment. In other words, the substance could only be used in closed systems from which the PCBs were theoretically recoverable. Concurrently, the Food and Drug Administration issued new regulations limiting or prohibiting PCB usages that could lead to contamination of human and animal food or food processing.[13]

The PCB issue slowly emerged in a pattern similar to other major environmental contamination controversies. After decades of large-scale production and use, adverse impact data began to turn up—the detection of PCBs in Baltic Sea fish, the poisonings in Japan, and the contamination of U.S. chickens and milk. Scientific concern, amplified by the new data, brought about the elimination of PCBs from 40 percent of their former uses. Only those essential electrical uses continued that were not thought to contribute to environmental contamination.

Thus, the PCB problem appeared to be solved, but only until new data showed that the true dimensions of the problem had been underestimated. Toxicity in laboratory animals was found to occur at much lower PCB levels than had previously been suspected. Monkeys fed PCBs had many miscarriages and the surviving infants were sickly. Adults fed 2.5 parts per million of PCBs lost their hair and suffered a general metabolic disturbance. This consequence becomes more meaningful when it is known that contaminated fish often have more than 5 parts per million of PCBs in their flesh. Laboratory rats developed liver cancer on a diet containing PCBs. Widespread contamination of fish with PBCs was found, and mink fed contaminated fish from the Great Lakes failed to reproduce.[14]

As evidence of the toxicity of PCBs continued to accumulate, the confrontation between GE and the state of New York proceeded in the courts. GE had at first stood on its rights, since it had valid permits for all of the waste it had discharged. Then it began to spend $12 million to reduce discharge from its two plants in the Troy area, meanwhile arguing with the state over the realism of the proposed zero discharge

---

[13]Kevin P. Shea, "PCB: The Worldwide Pollutant That Nobody Noticed," *Environment,* November 1973, pp. 25–28.

[14]Jeffrey A. Tannenbaum, "Persistent PCB's: Industrial Pollutants May Be Worse Threat Than DDT to Ecology," *Wall Street Journal,* 10 October 1975.

standard. As the dimensions of the problem continued to develop, GE prepared to phase out PCB usage altogether.

In 1972 and 1973 when the nonessential uses of PCBs were curtailed, no alternative products for electrical equipment manufacture were available that would not have caused major impairment of product performance. By 1975 Dow Chemical and McGraw-Edison announced that a new Dow material would be adopted by McGraw-Edison as a substitute for PCB in its transformers. In a four-year joint development program, the substitute material (monochlorodiphenyl oxide) had proved safe, effective, less toxic, and biodegradable. However, it was somewhat more expensive. Other manufacturers have similar substitutes under development.[15]

Monsanto announced its plans to cease manufacturing PCBs and withdraw completely from the market on or before the end of October 1977.[16] With no new manufacture of PCBs in the United States, one component of the problem is decisively controlled.

Meanwhile, GE and New York State debated the problem of attempting to restore the upper Hudson to a safe condition. One expert recommended a $20 million program of dredging up eighteen inches of bottom mud from the entire upper Hudson and incinerating it at high temperature to destroy the PCBs.[17] Even though this program could achieve its objective, others felt that it might cause fresh problems downstream because some of the toxic mud would be washed away during the dredging. Eventually GE agreed to a judgment under which it and the state of New York would each contribute $3 million for PCB removal and GE would devote an additional $1 million to research on how best to carry out this PCB removal.[18]

This $4 million judgment against GE is important for at least two reasons. First, it emphasizes that PCB removal is a very large problem that scientists must develop techniques for solving in a practical and effective way. Because PCBs are so totally resistant to normal biological degradation processes, no natural process thus far discovered has provided a solution. The worry is that the contaminated mud of the upper Hudson could provide an almost infinite source of PCB contamination for the entire Hudson Valley. Second, the judgment against GE is important because the dumping that caused the damage was approved repeatedly by state and federal authorities. In the past it was normal to consider that once the dumping was socially accepted, the consequences became society's problem. Now New York State has reached beyond this boundary and GE has agreed to shoulder a share of the responsibility for the consequences of its state-approved actions. Similar judgments in other pollution cases seem likely to flow from this precedent.

Meanwhile, the PCB contamination continues to show new and frightening dimensions. The Hudson River has been closed to commercial fishing since the

---

[15]"PCB Substitute Is Safe for Environment," *Chemical Engineering,* 8 December 1975, p. 7.
[16]"Monsanto to Quit PCB Business Next Year," *Chemical and Engineering News,* 11 October 1976, p. 6.
[17]"State Puts Cost of PCB Cleanup in the Hudson at $20 Million," *New York Times,* 26 April 1976.
[18]"General Electric Will Pay $3 Million in PCB Dumping," *Chemical Marketing Reporter,* 13 September 1976, p. 3.

acuteness of the PCB pollution became apparent, and there are no present prospects for its reopening. Restriction of fishing in rivers near Rome, Georgia, as a result of PCB levels in the fish triggered a $500 million class action lawsuit against Monsanto and GE.[19] Michigan health authorities cautioned the public not to eat salmon or trout more than once a week due to PCB levels.[20] A number of shipments of fish have been seized because of high PCB content, including fish from the Great Lakes and carp from the Mississippi River. High PCB levels have been reported in shellfish from many fresh and salt water sites and reproduction failures are suspected in some fish that would parallel those demonstrated in mink. And all evidence suggests that the contamination is continuing to spread, particularly because of the large proportion of Atlantic Coast fish that spawn in the Hudson and other contaminated waters.

An EPA survey showed that just over one-half of 1,000 human subjects tested had traces of PCB in their tissues.[21] Meanwhile, PCBs have been established as carcinogens. Mobil Corporation reported that seven out of a group of ninety-two workers exposed to PCBs have developed cancer. Monsanto reports a high incidence of lung cancer among its exposed workers. An EPA study showed traces of PCBs in mothers' milk in ten states. Dangerous quantities of PCBs have been found in areas as remote as South Africa.[22]

At this point scientists do not yet know the true long-term implications of the PCB contamination levels thus far created. The U.S. production of PCBs is being suspended, as was done earlier in Japan. However, the marine biological systems are worldwide and might well necessitate worldwide elimination of PCB manufacture. The possibility of adopting controls on such a grand scale is another unknown, although the reasons for the controls are quite clear.

Another feature of the PCB case and others like it was the difficulty in gaining recognition of the problem. When a familiar and seemingly safe material shows unexpected toxicity, the first reaction is often to disregard the data. The press reported that Ogden Reid was dismayed to discover that members of his environmental control staff had been upset for years by the serious implications of the PCB toxicity data they had been collecting but had been unable to get their reports up the executive chain of command or to the public. Then when Reid confronted GE, the urgency did not at first seem sufficient to his superiors to justify a government-industry public issue of this sort in a difficult year. Some felt that this confrontation was the reason for Reid's replacement as environmental commissioner, even though his case against the PCBs was later proven to be sound in law and in the urgency of its execution.

Unfortunately, the problem with the PCBs is not unique. The mercury pollution crisis that preceded it was in some ways similar but was an issue that was more easily controlled after it was recognized. Two current problems that have not yet unfolded to their full scope involve the PBBs, brominated compounds that found their way into animal feed in Michigan, and Kepone, a toxic pesticide responsible for

---

[19]"PCB Action Widens," *Chemical Week,* 29 September 1976, p. 18.
[20]"Of PCB ppms from GE and a SNAFU from EPA and DEC," *Audubon,* November 1975, p. 127.
[21]"PCB's: Problems for All Parties," *Chemical Week,* 3 December 1975, p. 40.
[22]"The Evidence Mounts against PCB's," *Business Week,* 13 September 1976, p. 39.

causing a pattern of personal injury, toxicity to wildlife, and river mud contamination in a story resembling that of the PCBs. The Kepone problem differs in that Allied Chemical Corporation handled it in such a way as to expose itself to record fines and is now the defendant in a series of suits claiming several billions of dollars in damages. Still other system-level pollution problems similar to the ones we have discussed will undoubtedly emerge. It is hoped that each new system-level pollution problem will be recognized more quickly and controlled with less environmental damage than those that have preceded it.

Criteria for Waste Impact

The PCB problem is important both in itself and as a prototype for other environmental problems. As with DDT and earlier problems, the PCB case shows how an agent can reach large-scale worldwide use without any hint of its serious, long-term impact. In addition, it shows that screening of pollution problems has several dimensions that have often been neglected in the past and are even now difficult to anticipate accurately.

Traditionally, waste treatment has been considered primarily in terms of the immediate treatment load, often expressed as biological oxygen demand. It is correct that this is the first impact to be screened, since most of the serious problems with the nation's lakes and rivers have been caused by biological overload. In this respect, the PCBs show no problem; they are essentially inert and therefore represent almost no treatment load at all.

Another impact criterion for waste is that of toxic residues. Copper sulfate controls algae in ponds, but eventually enough copper can accumulate after routine use to poison the mud at the bottom of the pond. Some scientists have suggested that the measured accumulation of lead in soils bordering major highways is such that the eventual poisoning of these soils by lead from automobile exhausts is predictable. In these examples copper and lead are accumulating toxic residues, as are PCBs. The PCBs are a type of toxic residue easy to miss, however, since they do not seem to kill the organisms with which they come into direct contact in most biological systems. Instead, they accumulate in the shellfish and marine life, perhaps impairing reproduction, and serve, in turn, to poison the higher levels of the food chain. Rather than killing directly and immediately, they are passed along from one organism to the next, until an entire natural system is poisoned.

The PCBs have shown their potential for poisoning or unbalancing major biological systems. Mercury, DDT, and PCBs all have this property. This type of poisoning was largely unsuspected until the environmental pathways of such pollutants were studied. The complexity of the natural food-chain and metabolic systems impairs our ability to predict the effect of PCBs. Scientists have really just begun to consider how to screen new chemicals to avoid such impacts on natural systems in the future.

Another impact of the furor over PCBs has been experienced in the political arena, where the unfolding of this drama demonstrated both the complexity of the problem and its potential consequences. Concern both within the EPA and in Congress that the agency and other regulatory authorities lacked the authority to ban PCBs fueled the demand that eventually led to the recently enacted Toxic Chemicals Act. Thus, although manufacture of PCBs was already being stopped by voluntary action, this issue has helped to establish a new and more comprehensive set of regulations over chemical products.

Most domestic wastes and many other common liquid wastes primarily represent a biological load. Biological waste overload has been associated with a high level of pollution and damage to rivers and lakes in the past, but treatment methods are known and can be applied.

Some waste streams carry either solids or ingredients that precipitate as solids during dilution or treatment. This introduces an additional waste problem. The original issue between various environmental groups and Reserve Mining was whether it was proper to allow a corner of Lake Superior to be filled with mine tailings from the massive water discharges of the taconite washing plant. The Army Engineers had judged that the surface and shores would not be significantly affected during the anticipated life of the mill. But the deep lake is a natural resource with a finite geological life. Should Reserve Mining be allowed to shorten this life, even minimally? This specific issue aroused sharper conflict over asbestos, but the general theme continues to recur: When is it socially acceptable to dedicate portions of the environment to the disposal of wastes? In other words, when should dumps be permitted and at what environmental cost? This issue concerning the right to create a refuse heap is encountered in the deposit of solids from a liquid waste stream and in the disposal of garbage and other solid wastes.

Beyond the impact of their biological load and solid waste content, some liquid wastes, such as those from cyanide plating baths, are toxic. The consequence of their discharge is to kill part or all of the biological systems that they contact, until their toxic effect is destroyed or diluted below its destructive threshold. Treatment of such wastes before discharge is necessary to minimize this toxic impact.

More difficult are the system-level impacts of waste ingredients beyond any immediate toxicity. Mercury and PCBs accumulate and concentrate in the food chain, and otherwise beneficial phosphate and nitrogen compounds fertilize algae growths that biologically unbalance lakes and rivers. A list of known system-level pollutants is building rapidly, and each new problem suggests guidelines and criteria for application to other wastes, but a sound basis for predicting the absence of system-level impacts from new waste materials will not be available for some time.

Thus, as liquid wastes are evaluated for their environmental impact, the biological load problems are usually definable and treatable, the deposit of solids and toxic materials is largely prohibited, and the known system-level pollutants are increasingly restricted within the limits of allowable concentrations. Existing industrial installations are in the throes of adjusting to present discharge standards, while the standards continue to change, particularly as system-level impacts, carcinogenic properties, or other long-term effects of specific waste ingredients are recognized.

Dumping into the Ocean

One consequence of the public pressure on dumping of liquid wastes is for corporations to look for other means of disposal. Many small firms now aid in these disposal-reclamation tasks but, must, in turn, find reasonable outlets. In one case

Union Carbide Corporation was not well served by such a vendor whose trucker illegally stored some barrels above ground and buried others. The result was a class action suit on behalf of 150 property owners whose wells were condemned by the New Jersey Department of Environmental Protection because of the resulting contamination. The amount of toluene found in this water was as much as 30 parts per million.[23] Of course, Union Carbide assumed responsibility for this waste and became the major defendant against the claims for pollution of the local ground water.

Another alternative in the past was to carry noxious wastes out to sea for ocean dumping. There is great concern that the oceans are becoming seriously polluted. The pressure is to stop ocean dumping. An NL Industries plant had dumped two bargeloads of acid wastes in the sea 14 miles offshore daily for about ten years, until environmentalists began to challenge the process, which gave a yellowish cast to the surrounding waters.[24]

Among others, duPont faced a similar challenge of its right to continue dumping up to 230 tons per day of inorganic salts and organic waste from three of the company's manufacturing units. The wastes had been shipped 1500 miles by duPont by way of the Kanawha, Ohio, and Mississippi rivers to Westwego, Louisiana, for transfer into oceangoing vessels for disposal at sea.[25] In a subsequent development, the EPA ordered duPont to stop dumping these chemicals 230 miles off the coast of Florida in the Gulf of Mexico, even though no specific damage to the environment from this dumping has been demonstrated.[26]

Another disposal alternative is incineration at sea. The incinerator ship *Vulcanus* can handle 20 tons of waste per hour and burned 4200 metric tons of waste in one test run.[27] This procedure removes the fumes from the combustion as far as possible from land, but is primarily a stopgap measure, pending construction of more permanent disposal facilities.

In at least one case, the result of the protests against deep-sea disposal seems to have worked to the advantage of the corporation as well as the ecology. *Field and Stream* tells how American Cyanamid Company, which had insisted that ocean dumping of 6000 tons of acid wastes per day was the only viable alternative that would permit continued operation of its Savannah plant, discovered that a recycling plant would also be profitable, recover useful by-products, and employ seventy more people.[28] The benefit to the corporation as a result of the additional investment required by the environmental agencies was significant.

Inland disposal patterns have been followed by seashore industries and communities that have dumped their wastes into the sea. Here, too, the natural capacity to treat and purify simple wastes is truly impressive. However, nature's bounty has

---

[23]"Fouled Water Spawns Suit," *Chemical Week,* 30 October 1974, p. 14.

[24]David Bird, "Ecologists Seek End of Dumping at Sea," *New York Times,* 24 March 1975.

[25]"Close Gulf to Wastes?" *Chemical Week,* 10 April 1974, p. 19.

[26]Gladwin Hill, "DuPont Must End Dumping in Gulf," *New York Times,* 4 October 1974.

[27]"Incinerator Ship Scores Apparent Success," *Chemical and Engineering News,* 18 November 1974, pp. 43–44.

[28]George Riegler, "The Great Acid Dump—A postscript," *Field and Stream,* April 1973, pp. 12, 16.

frequently been exhausted, resulting in foul waters, polluted beaches, and other consequences of pollution. The Clean Waters Act and various local regulations are tightening controls to prevent biological overload or discharge of toxic wastes more effectively.

One means of complying with the controls on dumping difficult materials on land and in inland waters has been to barge these wastes out to sea. The Army Engineers established a dumping area off the mouth of New York harbor, and New York and other cities have dumped sewage sludge and other waste to the point that the dumping area is now stagnant and the sludge shows signs of migrating, perhaps to the Long Island beaches. In the examples cited earlier, duPont and American Cyanamid sought to use similar ocean sites for dumping chemical wastes.

When the waste impact criteria are applied to ocean dumping, the problem of biological load is the simplest and easiest to solve. Most of the harbor and city shoreline pollution has been from biological overload, which is now being reduced by new standards the corporations and municipalities must meet.

Toxic wastes, solid wastes, and wastes that poison natural systems are critical in their adverse impact. Solid waste dumping involves establishing a permanent dumping area, and society is increasingly restive about continuing to fill in and extend such dumps. Ocean dumping can only be considered as a temporary expedient that must seek periodic reaffirmation of social approval for its continuance and is likely to be prohibited at some point in the future. In any case toxic materials that leave the dump area and system-level contaminants for natural systems have a most serious social impact, and such discharges are best minimized where possible.

Solid Wastes

Some solid wastes are relatively easy to treat. Thus, manure and various vegetable materials can be applied to the land in a way that is beneficial to its cultivation. However, conventional garbage and other more difficult forms of solid waste present a serious treatment problem. In the literal sense, there is no capacity for the environment to absorb dumped municipal garbage without detriment. Although the best sanitary land fill programs can help with the problem of waste disposal, piles of waste continue to accumulate somewhere.

Land Fill

Properly managed, a sanitary land fill operation disposes of solid waste by confining the biological load to the dump site. It can also provide satisfactory disposal of certain toxic materials that are confined by the fill process in the same way. The process consumes land, however, and makes no recovery of materials or energy from the waste.

At present, the most interesting approach to the solid waste problem involves separating various components from the garbage for recycling. In theory, paper, glass, and metals could be recovered, leaving a waste that would, in fact, be a source of clean and sanitary fill that could be deposited in areas where the remaining fill volume is socially desirable. Of course, since the technology of these recovery and recycling programs is still being developed, many solid waste streams are being dumped without being satisfactorily treated simply because no demonstrated capability for better treatment yet exists.

Garbage disposal is urgent because of lack of space, potential environmental impact of dump fires, degradation of the surrounding area, and drainage from dumps into streams. One approach is to build with garbage, and Du Page County, Illinois, built a 120-foot high toboggan and recreation area called Mount Trashmore. A marshy area was excavated and used as land fill for local garbage, and the clay from the excavation was used to seal and cover the wastes so that the recreation area could be built.[29]

Other concepts that have been suggested include the use of garbage for construction of a land fill island off of the mouth of New York harbor and compaction of garbage into bricks suitable for some types of construction.

Value Recovery

Another interesting possibility is the recovery of the rather high mineral content from urban wastes; some writers have referred to this resource as urban ore. If, as has been suggested, it should prove economical to process the urban ore for recovery of metals, then a host of other disposal problems and social costs of disposal would be resolved. A pervasive theme in the literature on solid waste is that garbage is an important new source of scarce industrial materials. The EPA has estimated that each year U.S. garbage contains $1 billion in recoverable metals and another $1 billion in energy.[30]

One of the first major attempts to realize some of the fuel value of garbage was to be in St. Louis, where the Union Electric Company announced a $70 million plant to process the entire solid waste stream from the city, generating electricity by burning the combustible portion.[31] The utility expected to recover and sell about 150 pounds of steel and 10 to 20 pounds of other metals per ton of garbage processed, in addition to receiving the dumping fees previously paid by haulers to land fill or incinerator operators. On this basis, the project seemed economically attractive for private capital.[32]

In spite of a promising start, the Union Electric project encountered local zoning opposition and cost estimates increased. Then the project was cancelled. Several similar projects have also been delayed,[33] but the St. Louis cancellation has been the most significant because the prototype unit operating there had been a resource recovery showcase.[34] The basic concept of this type of recovery appears to be sound

[29]"Building with Garbage," *Getting Down to Earth—An Environmental Handbook* (San Francisco: Bank of America, Bank Investments Securities Division, 1973), p. 24.
[30]Gene Smith, "Garbage, the Cinderella Fuel," *New York Times* 24 February 1974.
[31]Marjorie Mandel, "Trash," *Science News,* 30 March 1974, pp. 212–214.
[32]"St. Louis Will Start Running on Garbage," *Business Week,* 18 March 1974, p. 30.
[33]"A Trash Deal Union Carbide Lost," *Business Week,* 21 March 1977, p. 447.
[34]"A St. Louis Trash Plan Goes Down the Drain," *Business Week,* 28 February 1977, pp. 30–31.

and other projects have gone forward, but progress toward full-scale application has been much slower than was previously expected.

Recycling

The conversion of garbage into a practical fuel does not develop its full potential value. One new process developed by the Biocel Corporation aims at almost total recovery of the paper fiber and other valuable materials contained in the garbage.

> The refuse is shredded, dried and air classified to segregate ferrous metals, nonferrous metals, glass and a light fraction consisting of paper, wood, fabrics, plastics and degradable wastes.
>
> The light fraction, which contains more than 90% paper, is processed in the pulping section.
>
> After dewatering, the plastics and other contaminants are screened out. The sonic device continues to clean and loosen the paper fibers, and de-inking is done with the addition of calcium hypochlorite.
>
> The materials that have been separated from the light fraction are used as fillers in the fertilizer, which consists of phosphates, paper coatings, ink, food wastes, potassium sulfate and an aggregate of ceramics, stone, leather, wood and thermosetting plastics. Aggregate is about 10-15% of the fertilizer by weight.
>
> A typical yield for a 1,000-tons/day facility would be 250 tons of pulp, 125 tons of fertilizer, 2.5 tons of aluminum, 30 tons of ferrous metals, 10 tons of other metals (lead, copper, tin, zinc) and 35 tons of glass.[35]

Clearly, if such a process can be made to operate successfully, it represents a better resource use than burning or pyrolysis. In addition, the appeal of developing major recycling streams from garbage is in its potential for reducing the energy and resource demands of industrial processes.

The strong national thrust is toward partial or full recovery of recycleable materials and/or energy from garbage, but the technology is not yet well enough established to give clear evidence of the types of processes that will prove to be most economical.

Impact of Solid Wastes

First, it is important to recognize that the decision about which waste materials represent a social cost is a somewhat arbitrary product of social processes. Abandoned cars and aluminum cans are conspicuous new additions to the waste stream; society easily identifies the costs they create. Broken glass and waste paper are in some ways equally offensive, although more familiar; so far their disposal costs

---

[35]"He Processes Trash for Profits," *Chemical Week*, 4 June 1975, p. 36–37.

have been accepted as a part of modern living, and no serious attempts have been made to transfer the costs back to the product and its manufacturer.

For each corporation seeking to manage the corporate impact of its solid wastes, the problem is on several levels. On the simplest level, corporate participation in a municipal solid waste district represents one more user of the service; many offices and light industries are in this role. As taxpayers, the businesses support the local municipal system, or perhaps there are specific collection fees. In any event, they are members of the system that create no special impact.

Most larger industries are forced into a more conspicuous role by the quantities of waste or the special types of waste that their operations generate. On this level, the first consideration is to the environmental impact and the second is to the consumption of physical space if a dump site is created. Manure and some cannery wastes have been beneficially recycled to the land. Toxic materials and materials that have an impact on natural systems must be removed, detoxified, or confined, with any remaining solid wastes dumped in a manner acceptable to society.

The old norm for industrial practice has left the countryside dotted with waste heaps next to old mines and certain types of processing plants. A sugar beet processing plant, for example, traditionally has built up a mound of gray white waste solids from the spent beets. Many chemical plants have companion heaps or lagoons in which calcium salts and other process wastes accumulated in the past. Of course, these private dumps are of a special type; they become a part of the environment, they consume acreage, and they pre-empt land from other use just as a municipal garbage dump does.

As the nation begins to deal more positively with its municipal garbage problems, similar policies on disposal programs and land use are likely to be defined for its industries. These policies will probably be enforced more quickly and decisively for industries than for cities because industrial waste is conspicuous and the political and financial implications of effecting industrial compliance are less complex. Where possible, the corporate social impact of solid waste streams should be moderated and balanced by new process design or innovations in treatment or recycling, before an impatient society gets to the rule-making stage.

Discharges into the Air

The traditional approach to venting smoke and fumes has been to dilute them sufficiently to prevent objectionable odors and effects. This approach is still sound if modern standards are fully utilized. But in addition to the need for causing visible discharges and bad odors to be diluted beyond the point of detection, scientists have now learned of the importance of checking for nitrogen oxides and many other kinds of toxic by-products. Again, as with the lakes and rivers, the problem is to avoid overloading the natural purifying capacity of the atmosphere; the solution involves the removal and treatment of specific fume ingredients prior to discharge. One concept is to require catalytic converters to eliminate nitrogen oxides and carbon monoxide from automobile exhausts. Another is to require scrubbing systems to remove sulfur dioxide from furnace flue gases.

Compliance

Public and regulatory pressure on air pollution has also produced its quota of success stories as various industries have addressed their problems directly and vigorously. An example from the paper industry was the Mead Corporation project to build an odor-free kraft paper mill in Escanaba, Michigan. The *Wall Street Journal* reported the distress in the local community as the new mill had start-up problems, causing serious odors and blanketing the community with white snow-like flakes of fallout. Mead paid for damages, including car-washing costs, and struggled with the equipment until the odor problems were brought under control. Where Mead apparently had started in good faith to build a plant that would reduce the odor problems associated with the kraft process, Escanaba insisted on totally eliminating odor, and the company had some difficulty in complying.[36]

Another success story is the conversion of Union Carbide from a gross and refractory polluter at its Alloy, West Virginia, plant, which had been called the world's smokiest factory, into a corporate citizen seriously addressing its pollution problems and well on the way to full compliance with state requirements. According to the *Business Week* account, Carbide first installed precipitators on its coal-fired power plant; a special design was necessary to get the 99.4 percent collection efficiency on the ash from the low-sulfur coal. Then the metallic emissions from the smelting furnaces were removed by cooling the hot gases sufficiently to permit filtration of the dust with bag collectors. All of this cost $35 million and added $3 million per year or about 16 percent to Carbide's costs.

> "It has made it tougher for us to compete," says Case [manager of the Alloy plant], noting that ferroalloy plants in other states are only now beginning to be controlled. Fortunately for Carbide, ferroalloys have been in short supply, and the company has not lost any customers. And by tackling the job before many of its competitors, Carbide has avoided the even higher costs now facing others. "If we had to do it today," says Case, "it would cost $50-million."
>
> After Carbide controls its last furnace early next year, only one serious problem will remain: capturing the "fugitive fumes" that escape when workers tap the metal from the furnaces every two hours or so. Says Case: "We know how to take care of 80% of those fumes by next year, and we'll figure out how to do the rest, too."
>
> That "can-do" approach contrasts with Carbide's attitude in 1970. Then, recalls Beard [executive director of the West Virginia Air Pollution Control Commission], Carbide "had a sorry record of broken promises." But backed by national concern over environmental quality, Beard's agency got Carbide to sign a strict abatement schedule. "You have to respect them," says Beard. "Their attitude has changed 180 degrees."[37]

---

[36]Everett Groseclose, "How a Paper Company Became Friendly Again With Town It Polluted," *Wall Street Journal,* 29 June, 1973.

[37]Excerpted from "Union Carbide's Big Cleanup Job," *Business Week,* 9 November 1974, p. 184.

Union Carbide had reacted with great reluctance at first. As more attention was focused on the situation at the Alloy plant by federal and state authorities, Ralph Nader, and various citizens' groups, Carbide began to take notice. When West Virginia issued its rule (now known as Regulation VII) on 1 July 1970, the direction seemed clear. When it did decide to act, Carbide moved in a direct way, which has brought favorable comment from its former critics.[38]

A noteworthy part of this account is the $35 million capital investment required, plus the increase in operating costs—a competitive burden in a cost-competitive industry. Now Union Carbide may have an advantage because its competitors, by being tardier in compliance, must pay higher equipment and construction costs due to inflation.

Shutdown

U.S. Steel has had to face similar problems between the burden of converting old open-hearth furnaces to meet emission standards and the need to compete in a market where it may already have a competitive disadvantage due to the relative age and technology of its production processes. In the case of its Gary Works, a confrontation led to shutdown and unemployment when the company failed to meet the court-ordered timetable.[39]

Pollution can be stopped by closing mills, but this is not the desired direction. Serious issues have arisen concerning how the United States wishes to partition its efforts between economic growth and increase in living standards, on the one hand, and reduction of pollution, on the other. Present legislation is aimed at a compromise, with a major diversion of capital funds into new pollution-control equipment within a time period and a range of limits that should permit the attainment of some economic progress. As these policies are implemented, however, they will cause premature closing of many old plants that no longer justify the investment necessary to make them conform. Newer and more viable installations may also be jeopardized, depending on how the regulations are administered.

In the case of the Weyerhaeuser mill at Everett, Washington, the company closed it rather than invest $12 million in curing what was considered to be a rather minor water pollution problem in a way that might well have created a much more serious air pollution problem. An executive of Weyerhaeuser addressed the issue in a speech as follows:

> We have closed mills before; jobs have been eliminated for many reasons from time to time. But Everett sulphite is different! It is profitable, not yet obsolete from a production standpoint and its specialty grades of pulp remain in demand. It contributed more than $1 million to the company's profit last year. The mill will be closed because of environmental treatment requirements . . . the first major Weyerhaeuser mill ever to be so affected.
>
> The mill was built in 1936 on what had been the location of Weyerhaeuser's

---

[38]Gerd Wilcke, "Cleaning Up Union Carbide," *New York Times,* 28 May 1972.
[39]"Shutdown in Gary," *Time,* 20 January 1975, p. 48.

first manufacturing plant—a sawmill which was purchased at the turn of the century. It is located on tidewater, at the foot of Rucker Hill. The stacks barely extend above the rim of the hill—and Rucker Hill is a prime Everett residential area.

The nuisance-type air pollution problems, as you can imagine, have continually haunted managers of the mill. Most problems have been reduced over the years, but not eliminated. Today it has the tightest control of sulphur dioxide emissions of any pulp mill in the world. The major continuing problem is caused by the burning of solid waste in the power boilers resulting in a visible plume because of the high moisture content and a stubborn cinder problem.

. . . In the late 1940s, concern was voiced by sports and commercial fishermen that the biological oxygen demand of the wood sugars in the mill's waste discharges might be damaging to marine life in Port Gardner Bay. Studies at the time indicated that a real or at least a potential problem for fish did exist in portions of the bay. So, in 1951, in conjunction with an adjacent paper company, we installed a 3,000-foot long outfall and dispersion line, out into Puget Sound to a depth of 300 feet. This outfall in combination with in-plant controls has protected the fish life of the bay.

Since installation of the outfall, we have conducted regular testing of the receiving waters in combination with biological studies. These studies have shown conclusively that Port Gardner Bay's biological quality has not been adversely affected by the mill since 1951 in any significant way. The quality of the continuing sports and commercial fishery in the bay and its tributaries continues to attest to the accuracy of these conclusions.

In 1956, the mill received its first waste discharge permit. The permit set fiber discharge limits, required automatic flow recordings and sampling, and required continued operation of the outfall system already installed. In 1962, another permit was issued requiring the removal of fine material from hydraulic barker effluents.

[New requirements followed a survey in 1962. One—] which would have required incineration of wastes—was opposed by the company on the grounds that: (1) it would not significantly improve the beneficial uses of Port Gardner Bay; (2) it would cause an additional air pollution problem; and (3) the high capital costs might result in making the mill uneconomic.

. . . the decision was made in 1969 to accept a permit offered by the state which gave us the additional option of trying to develop through accelerated research a new pulping process which would provide the equivalent to the treatment they required without the related air problem.

The permit required that the company announce by March 31, 1972, its intention to do one of three things: (1) rebuild the mill either at Everett or elsewhere using a new pulping process; (2) rebuild or remodel the existing mill to provide for incineration of wastes; or (3) close the mill by May 31, 1973.

It became apparent late last year that the $2.5 million research project promised no results that could be implemented during the time frame of the permit. This research is, however, still under way and we remain confident that a new pulping process will be developed.

That left us with two options: rebuild the mill at the Everett site at an estimated cost of $52 million without increasing capacity or product versatility, or spend $10 to $12 million for a recovery process which would provide no significant improvements in biological water quality, but which because of its effect on air quality, would make the mill much more of a nuisance to the residents of Rucker Hill.

We remain convinced that continued testing of the waters of Port Gardner Bay will justify our contention that the closure will have little impact on the biological quality of the water.

From the total standpoint of our corporate business, the loss of the Everett mill is not overwhelmingly significant. Following its premature closure, our other operations can take up the slack and continue to service Everett's customers.

But the implications for our company and the nation are ominous. It has clearly defined the following issues related to environmental regulation:

(1) A rationale evolved which assumes no difference in the biological and physical characteristics of different receiving waters—it required treatment for treatment's sake.

(2) It paid no attention to the total environmental needs and priorities. It attacked the least of the environmental problems in isolation and thereby threatened to intensify the community's real problems of air pollution and solid waste disposal.

(3) It paid no attention to economic considerations. This will result in the loss of jobs for 330 employees, a $3.7 million annual community payroll, and a significant portion of the community's tax base . . . in a region already suffering economic depression.

(4) It will result in a premature mill closure without improving the environment.[40]

The Weyerhaeuser statement poses real issues for national consideration. Whatever happened at the Everett mill, the risk of some enforcement officials insisting on "treatment for treatment's sake" is very great, considering the momentum of enforcement processes and the great public skepticism about corporate credibility in this and other areas. Because of the necessity to maintain the economic base underlying the U.S. standard of living, no random disorientation of industrial productive processes must be permitted. On the other hand, the national need to reduce pollution is so urgent that cleanup enforcement processes must not be diverted from their long-term objectives.

The requirement that the local environment be protected is clear, although the application pattern is still developing. At present, it appears that the corporate source of any noticeable local discharge into the air will generate an increasing amount of

---

[40]John S. Larsen, "Mill a Victim of Pollution Control Policy," *NAM Reports,* 19 June 1972, pp. 6–8.

public pressure. Thus, all visible smoke is bad, all odors are being tracked to the source, and even simple plumes of water vapor are repeatedly challenged by citizens who assume that they represent a noxious discharge. On a regional basis, reduction of sulfur and nitrogen oxides and other fume components is being required. Predictably, other system-level wastes will also begin coming to attention as fluorocarbons and PCBs from incinerators are tracked to their source.

Noise

A new area of public concern is with noise pollution, although the neighborhoods around airports, quarries, and various heavy industries have suffered with noise problems for many years. The spreading public concern represents another threshold effect, where the fraction of the population that has been directly affected by noise problems has risen to the point where general concern has been attracted to a significant public issue.

Reinforcing the concern about noise pollution is the steadily accumulating amount of scientific data that show not only hearing loss but also various other detrimental effects on the emotional and physical well-being of people exposed to excessive levels of noise, particularly for chronic exposure extending over many years. As scientists have studied the effects of noise and crowding on animals, there have been repeated indications of noise as a major causative agent in the complex that checks the growth of crowded populations and warps individual development.

The impact of the noise pollution problem is divided between a firm's employees and the public. The employee problem is one of safe and adequate working conditions, as considered in Chapter 11. The impact of noise pollution on the public is a very straightforward social balance problem that is not easy to solve. Physical or emotional damage to the public from noise is obviously a social cost that a business firm must strive to avoid, but the boundaries of the acceptable noise impact levels are far from clear. Modern society has many sources of noise, including industry, children's play, and rock concerts. Thus, a key problem in analyzing corporate impact and handling community relations is to intelligently define standards for noise acceptability so that a management will have rational guidelines to direct its actions.

Nuclear Waste

One consequence of the development of nuclear power and assorted applications of isotopes and radiation processes is the issue over environmental pollution from nuclear wastes.

The nuclear age is barely a generation old, but the U.S. has already produced radioactive wastes that will remain highly toxic for up to 250,000 years. The very thought of an environmental threat persisting for so long defies comprehension. Neanderthal man, after all, first appeared only 75,000 years ago. "We nuclear people have made a Faustian bargain with society," physicist Alvin Weinberg wrote in 1972. "On the one hand, we offer . . . an inexhaustible source of energy. But the price that we demand for this magical energy is both a vigilance and a longevity of our social institutions that we are quite unaccustomed to . . ."

. . . Radioactive wastes are created when spent nuclear fuel is removed from commercial or military reactors. The material is dissolved in acid, and the reusable fission products are reclaimed. What remains is a brew of liquid wastes—including strontium 90, cesium 137, and plutonium 239—that are among the most toxic and long-lived substances known.

Both strontium and cesium take 600 years to decay to harmless levels, and in the process they emit radiation that can cause cancer. Plutonium, deemed hazardous for at least 250,000 years, emits little radiation, but even tiny amounts can be lethal if inhaled, ingested in food, or absorbed into the body through skin lesions.[41]

The essence of the problem is that safe standards for radiation exposure or for long-term storage of waste materials have not yet been developed. Today's estimates are far better and far more stringent than those first adopted by the Atomic Energy Commission. In the intervening years enough has been learned to make the problem more real and more fearsome. Many cities feel that even more rigid limits on radiation exposure and on handling of nuclear wastes are needed.

This debate will continue for the foreseeable future, with more definitive standards evolving as exposure and storage information continue to accumulate.

Thermal Pollution

Another major consequence of large industrial processes is the generation of tremendous amounts of waste heat—in particular, from large electric generating stations—whether nuclear or conventional fuel is used. Experience in a number of rivers and bays has demonstrated that the entire ecology of the local waters can be changed by infusion of the tremendous volumes of warm water discharged by the cooling equipment in a large central station. The problem of the disposal of this heat has become an important design consideration when the environmental impact of a new plant is examined. In fact, a serious proposal has been made for a series of nuclear-fueled electric generating plants off the coast of New Jersey.

Offshore Power Systems—a partnership set up in 1972 by Westinghouse Electric Corp. and Tenneco, Inc.—plans to build 16 floating power plants in a shipyard-like factory in Jacksonville, Fla. OPS will then tow them to ocean sites, where they will be moored just within the 3-mi. limit. The reactors will be protected by a massive breakwater reef designed to withstand 300-mph winds, 50-ft. waves, and impacts from supertankers.

So far, OPS has sold four 1,150 Mw reactors, priced at $375-million each, to Public Service Electric & Gas Co. in New Jersey, which will moor the first two near Atlantic City by 1980. . . . The Jacksonville Electric Authority has signed a letter of intent for two others, fattening the OPS order book to $2.2-billion.

---

[41]Excerpted from "The Deadly Dilemma of Nuclear Wastes," *Business Week,* 3 March 1975, p. 70.

. . . Both OPS and PSE&G claim that offshore plants offer many environmental advantages—and some environmentalists agree. For one thing, the thermal pollution that has killed so many fish on inland rivers is a minor problem at sea, where the vast quantities of ocean water will quickly quench hot water discharged from the reactor. For another, ocean siting eliminates the need to put nuclear plants on scenic land along rivers and lakes. The PSE&G complex, for example, will need only 100 acres of ocean. On land, it would take 500 acres, if the utility could find a site. Finally, ocean siting provides a 3-mi. buffer between the plant and the nearest community—more than at some existing plants.[42]

The reality of the thermal pollution problem is brought home by the consequences of a plant shutdown. Thus, a Jersey Central Power and Light plant shut down for routine work, and almost immediately several hundred dead fish were found floating in the ocean water nearby. The fish had become dependent on the warm water discharged from the plant cooling system and died when the water began to cool toward a more normal winter ocean temperature.[43]

The issue over thermal pollution illustrates the way that a corporation can, through its operation, change the local environmental conditions. Such issues continue to arise. For example, any industry using large quantities of cooling water becomes immediately involved in the problems of separating water from fish and wildlife. Thus, the Hudson River Fisherman's Association won an agreement that the Bowline Point plant of Orange and Rockland Utilities would reduce water intake during the striped bass spawning season. In addition, the company agreed to pay $50,000 in support of environmental studies of the plant's impact.[44]

The problem for the corporation in such cases is to try to find a simple and straightforward way to operate without either killing fish and other wildlife or letting the day-to-day operation revolve around avoidance of environmental damage rather than economic performance. Yet the corporation is no longer in a position to ride roughshod over ecological considerations and must allow these considerations to govern the operation if no practical overall protection of the ecology can be established.

Enforcement

A variety of different enforcement mechanisms is developing that range from the early invitation to citizens' groups to share in the fines when unauthorized pollution is exposed to official and unofficial enforcement action.

In some areas environmental agencies have established their own surveillance systems. Pennsylvania's Bureau of Water Quality Management has what the *Wall*

---

[42]"A Step Forward for Floating Nuclear Plants," *Business Week,* 9 February 1974, pp. 57–58. By 1977 the installation dates for the two Atlantic City stations had been restated as 1984 and 1986: "A Second Chance for Floating Reactors," *Business Week,* 25 April 1977, pp. 31–32.
[43]"A Plant Shutdown May Cause Fishkill," *Bergen Record* (Oradell, N.J.), 13 January 1974.
[44]"O&R Agrees to Help Fish," *Rockland County Journal News* (Nyack, N.Y.), 11 January 1975.

Street Journal called "environmental cops," formally environmental protection specialists, who can patrol the waterways and sample suspicious discharges from industrial plants.[45] A much more aggressive and much less official type of enforcement is the vigilante approach of the Fox of Kane County.

And who is "The Fox"?

He's sort of an antipollution "Zorro" who has been harassing various companies, evading the police, and making himself a minor legend around Aurora, in Kane County. . . . whenever he blocks a company's drainage system, tries to seal off its chimney, puts a dead skunk on the porch of an executive or dumps dead fish in a lobby, he leaves a note telling why, and always signs it "The Fox."

"I'll give you an example. There's this stream, Mill Creek, and it used to have good bluegill fishing. Then this soap manufacturing plant dumped soap curds and other waste in it until it was lifeless.

"The plant has a 42-inch drain, so I plugged it up with bales of straw, rocks, logs and things. I guess I did that about five times. So every time they'd have problems and have to get in there and clean it out. I'd always leave them notes, saying things like 'Why not put your engineers on this problem and eliminate your pollution?' Why, when we tried to stop up the chimney of an aluminum processing company—I had help on that one—we had to get up on their roof the first time to measure the chimney, and a second time to install the chimney cap. Actually, it didn't work too well, but they got the message.

"The soap company has reacted properly. They are making an effort to improve and it shows in the creek. But the aluminum plant—they're stubborn. You should see the filth that comes out of their chimney and drain. So that's why I had to go to their parent company and throw those fish around. It was a nauseating thing to do, I guess, but why shouldn't they get a sample of what they are doing to nature?"[46]

Underlying the dialogue between corporation and society is a combination of legal formality, agency bureaucracy, and deep public feeling about both the urgency of cleanup and the impropriety, and even foulness, of corporations that continue to void the excrement from their processes on society. The Fox of Kane County had the appeal of a Robin Hood—corking up drains, capping a smokestack, dumping a container of sewage in the middle of the offending corporate headquarters. This behavior is illegal but is hard to prosecute in the courts. Certainly, steady progress toward corporate compliance is more sensible than the kind of recalcitrance and outrage that causes environmental vigilantes like the Fox to play tag with a corporate giant while society laughs.

---

[45]Eric Morgenthaler, "Pollution Patrol: An Environmental Cop Helps Keep Waters Near Pittsburgh Clean," *Wall Street Journal,* 7 August 1975.

[46]Sam Love and David Obst, eds., *Ecotage* (New York: Pocket Books, 1972), pp. 143–147, 176. Copyright © 1972 by Sam Love and David Obst. Reprinted by permission of Simon & Schuster, Inc.

Summary

In the process of assessing and dealing with the impact of industrial waste discharges, the corporation is one component in a dynamic and changing debate. As new problems come to light, new scientific evidence of the effect of wastes on the environment is uncovered, and new social pressures result.

The different types of wastes as summarized in Figure 12.1 represent different problems as to local environmental load but the same problem in any contribution of radiation or systemic pollutants to the environment. The natural environment has a substantial capacity to absorb the biological waste load without harm, and there is every reason to make use of this natural bounty so long as it is protected from overload or toxic materials. Standards need to evolve for the other varieties of solid wastes that require the creation of permanent dump sites. Although society has started assigning a proper priority to this use of a limited resource, dumps constitute a sufficiently central feature of industrial life that their complete elimination is difficult. Air pollution standards are already evolving rapidly as the urgency of finding solutions increases but are slowed by specific major control costs. All these standards interact, as the Weyerhaeuser example so aptly illustrated. To eliminate a water pollution question, Weyerhaeuser was ordered to incinerate the waste and create air pollution. Instead, the plant shut down.

By working constructively to mold requirements to comply with real environmental needs at the lowest economic cost, the business community can greatly aid itself and society as a whole. Society should not accept bad compromises, and industry is hurt by poorly defined requirements and regulations.

When a corporate social impact test is applied to waste discharges, the stated requirement is that no uncompensated cost to the society should result. If all the waste streams are truly processed to the point where they are socially satisfactory for discharge, then no social cost can exist. However, the more normal situation now is one in which a social cost does exist and where current discharges are not satisfactory in the long run due to technological and various other limitations. In this case business should recognize the need for making steady progress in the evolution toward a satisfactory social balance at a rate that is sufficiently fast to meet

Figure 12.1   Waste from the Business Operation

Types of problem	Treatment issue
Liquid waste	Biological load
Solid waste	Dumping load
Discharges into the air	Toxic materials
Noise	System-level poisons
Nuclear waste	
Thermal pollution	Social interface
	With local ecology
	With enforcement
	processes

A business is known by the impact of its wastes.

increasing legal requirements and to maintain a safe lead-time in advance of the mounting social pressure on polluters.

This chapter has dealt with the principal types of waste from the corporate operation, including liquid waste, solid waste, discharges into the air, noise, and thermal waste, in addition to special problems with nuclear waste and ocean dumping. These types of waste can have an impact on the environment as biological loads, as solids dumping loads, as toxic loads, and as system-level poisons to the food chain or other major biological systems. For the most part, the treatment technology exists for solving the problems that have been recognized, except in the case of some system-level poisons for which the horizons of scientific knowledge have not been extended far enough to permit clear predictions of the action or its avoidance. Individual corporations have a role in helping to shape rational social standards for the adjustment process as past pollution practices are undone and reversed and also a role in bringing individual discharges into a social balance with society ahead of legal action or public wrath.

Guidelines for Managing Corporate Social Impact

In the management of waste from the business operation, social balance will tend to be maintained if the following guidelines are applied:

Pollution   Wastes discharged from the business operation do not cause any measurable detriment to the environment.

Building dumps   Wastes going to land fill or ocean dumps, or otherwise making permanent use of surface area, have social consent for this dedication of land or ocean resources; nevertheless, such discharges are best minimized or avoided in anticipation of increased dumping costs and restrictions.

Resource waste   Energy and resource content of waste streams are minimized by recovery or recycling, which functions as an operating economy, as a means of reducing environmental burdens, and in anticipation of further social pressure toward careful resource use.

Applying the Guidelines

Most factories and other installations discharge some wastes. To avoid adverse social impact, the various waste streams must be controlled or treated to the point that they do not reduce the quality of the environment. This does not preclude judicious and proper use of the natural capacity of the environment to treat some simple wastes, so long as the net effect is not to overtax or degrade the air, water, or other natural systems. Solid waste dumping should be minimized where possible, and all disposal should be kept within dumping areas and conditions specifically approved by society. All waste streams should be appropriately classified or treated to recycle recoverable materials and reclaim waste energy to an extent that is acceptable to the local society as not being wasteful of resources or energy.

Questions for Analysis and Discussion

1. A waste stream can have bad effects as a pollutant or good effects as a source of necessary materials; for example, some brines are difficult wastes to purify yet are quite valuable as a source of chemicals in a company equipped to process the brine. Try to find other examples. How can such values be salvaged more frequently?

2. Recycling of paper, glass, and cans contributes to solving solid waste problems. What are the limitations of such recovery? To what extent could these limitations be removed by constructive programs?

3. Noise pollution becomes irritating and annoying to the public even at levels below those of proven health hazards. How can we set fair standards that achieve a balance between these public attitudes and the industrial burden?

4. Find an example of a company that depends on its free access to natural systems that purify its wastes.

5. Find an example of an industry that has been forced to close or curtail operations by restrictions on air or water pollution. Do you think that society gained or lost by the closing?

For Further Information

American Chemical Society. *Cleaning Our Environment; the Chemical Basis for Action*. Washington D.C.: American Chemical Society, 1969.

Berland, Theodore. *The Fight for Quiet*. Englewood Cliffs, N.J.: Prentice-Hall, 1970.

Goldman, Marshall I. *Ecology and Economics; Controlling Pollution in the '70's*. Englewood Cliffs, N.J.: Prentice-Hall, 1972.

Helfrich, Harold W., Jr. *The Environmental Crisis*. New Haven, Conn.: Yale University Press, 1970.

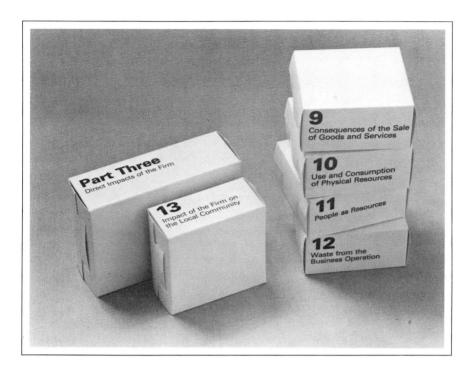

Part Three — Direct Impacts of the Firm

9 Consequences of the Sale of Goods and Services

10 Use and Consumption of Physical Resources

11 People as Resources

12 Waste from the Business Operation

13 Impact of the Firm on the Local Community

13
Impact of the Firm on the Local Community

Both a mutual interdependence and a mutual interest in each other's successful and effective operation grow between corporation and community. As a major supporter of community services, the corporation has a proper interest in the adequacy and economy of the services, including an interest in a fair share of their support. Definition of this fair share concept leads to a further consideration of the fraction of the community that is neither part of nor directly supported by members of the work force and to a closer look at the relationship with other firms and other community institutions. The objective, of course, is to develop a framework in which the firm can pursue its economic self-interest without having an adverse impact on the community. Such a relationship is very much in the interest of the corporation and the community.

Responsibility for the quality of life is to the self-interest of business . . . a
healthy business and a sick society are not compatible. Healthy businesses require
a healthy, or at least a functioning society.[1]

PETER F. DRUCKER

Inevitably, the actions of the firm have impacts on employees, community groups, unions, service organizations, banks, local institutions, local governments, and political parties. Whether or not management tries to control these impacts, the local community still represents one of the most important corporate social impact areas.

In this chapter the interdependence between corporation and community and the trauma that results when a corporation leaves a community will be explored to develop the nature of the relationship. Next, from the nature of the relationship of the business to the community, the analysis will turn to the degree of corporate responsibility to the community, the fair share concept of support of the community and its fringes, and the interaction with the educational system and the neighborhoods around the business. The chapter then concludes by presenting a series of examples of different types of corporation and community interrelationships and discussing the influence of business hiring practices on the community.

Interdependence with the Local Community

The interrelationship between a corporation and its employees also affects the local community. For instance, if people work for a business throughout their productive lives, retire, and then must seek public assistance because their retirement income is not adequate, then the remainder of the real needs of these people (both those that are met by the community and those that remain unsatisfied) demonstrate that the business has not contributed its fair share to the maintenance of the community. In the same way, the community feels the impact of hirings, firings, layoffs, strikes.

Perhaps the most dramatic impact on a community is the total loss of a basic industry, which has occurred in a number of New England towns where major textile

---

[1]Peter F. Drucker, "U.S. Society Holds Business Responsible for Upgrading, Maintaining Quality of Life," *New York University Alumni News* 13, no. 3 (December 1968): 1.

companies once supported the community. Now the companies either are out of business or have moved to the South. The entire Northeast suffered economically because of the loss of many of its principal employers and has recovered only slowly as new industries have been attracted. When a business leaves a town, it creates a difficult problem, which can cause strong public reactions. In a number of more recent cases, industrial firms with a greater sense of their own responsibility have made an effort to cushion the shock of the withdrawal of an industry that is fundamental to the economics of a local community.

When General Foods consolidated Jell-O division plants into a new plant in Dover, Delaware, it closed down plants in four towns, two of which were small and heavily dependent on the General Foods plant. In these two towns (LeRoy, New York, and Orange, Massachusetts), General Foods aided in an industrial survey of the area and the formation of an industrial development commission to find new industry. In all

The Firm as Viewed by Society

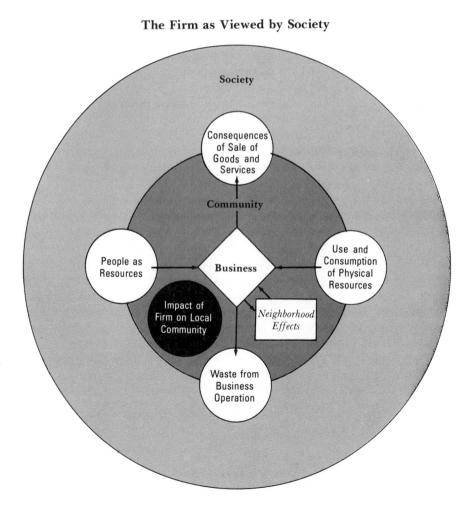

cases the employees were offered a transfer or a generous termination allowance and effective assistance in finding new employment.[2]

Similarly, duPont was faced with the necessity of closing a plant that was the principal support of a small southern community. Rather than leave two thousand people unemployed, blight the community, and lose a healthy relationship with a loyal work force, a process for manufacturing a new product was installed, and the work force was retrained with the help of the local school system. Overall, the successful transition took five years and a major effort from corporation and community.[3]

The equity in cases like this lies with the fact that in a long-standing employer-employee or employer-community relationship, indefinite continuance of the relationship is implied, as discussed in Chapter 11. When termination of the relationship becomes necessary, hardships that can be properly classified as social costs result. Businesses like General Foods and duPont have voluntarily recognized the obligation to cushion the layoffs, even in communities where the business will no longer be active. A business that fails to prepare for its departure appropriately only invites greater public regulation to prevent irresponsible business activity in the future.

Many communities trace their growth and prosperity to the success of one or several local industries, and the decline of a town frequently follows soon after decline of its industries. On the other hand, a prosperous industry in a declining town is not common; where some industries could benefit from a readily available labor supply, the tax costs that result from community malaise tend to be high, and professional and scientific staff can be hard to attract to a declining town.[4]

The fortunes of a community and its industries are that they tend to succeed together or fall together. Thus, a definite interdependency exists between the community welfare and the well-being of its businesses: acute self-interest leads industry and community to a genuine concern for each other's welfare.

One of the corollaries of the business-community interdependence is a mutual need for the relationship to continue into the future. Thus, employees expect their jobs to continue, customers plan to repurchase familiar brands (or to obtain needed parts and services), suppliers look for repeat orders, and governments anticipate continuing to receive revenues. Although spontaneous and often unplanned, an implicit commitment develops that the future will be a smooth continuation of the present. Many of the social costs a business can cause result from changes that violate these implicit commitments. And one of the areas where these commitments best express joint business-community interests is in planning of community services.

---

[2]W. James Schmidt, "Public Relations in Plant Relocation," *Public Relations Journal,* November 1966, pp. 51–54. See also Edmund S. Whitman and W. James Schmidt, *Plant Relocation: A Case History of a Move* (New York: American Management Association, 1966).

[3]John A. Laberee, "The Social Responsibility of Business," *Fort Worth Business Review* 12 (December 1963): 8–9.

[4]The Chairman of the Board of Consolidated Edison Company of New York has said: "If the cities deteriorate, so will the business investment in the cities. If the cities flourish, so will business." Charles F. Luce, "1001 Good Mistakes in Training Hard-Core Jobless," *Employment Service Review,* December 1968, p. 6.

Use and Support of Community Services

The first element in the relationship between a business and the services of the community is a proper recognition of the overwhelming interest of a business in both the adequacy and cost of such services. Together, a business and its employees make a significant contribution to the tax revenue in a local area. And while the employees' hard-earned dollars are their own concern, the company interest remains because the company's wages must purchase an adequate level of living. If excessive taxes or other community charges are being levied on the employees, the company will come under increasing pressure to raise wages or otherwise compensate for the high living costs. Likewise, if community services are poor, the employee needing these services will suffer—either by paying a second time for a service that is already funded by taxes but is inadequate or by doing without the service for lack of funds. Then this employee will be looking for ways of forcing the company to increase wages to make up the gap.

Davis and Blomstrom cite the curing of malaria in Birmingham as an example of this type of corporate self-interest in adequacy of community services:

> In the first decade of this century, Birmingham, Alabama was menaced by serious health problems. Malaria, typhoid fever, and other diseases were prevalent because of unsanitary community conditions. This city was the site of a United States Steel Subsidiary, Tennessee Coal and Iron Company, whose productivity was lowered by illness. Tennessee Coal and Iron organized a health department and hired a prominent specialist in the offending diseases from the Panama Canal Zone. In its first year of operation the health department spent $750,000 for draining swamps and improving sanitary facilities. This amount was thirty times the total health budget of the entire state of Alabama.[5]

In effect, U.S. Steel was able to change the community by eliminating a serious malaria problem. U.S. Steel did this to improve its Birmingham operation, since the health of the business quite literally related to the health of the community.

Or consider the benefits to Olin Mathieson from participating in the replanning of a school bond issue. In Hannibal, Ohio, a $3.5 million, twenty-two-year school bond issue was proposed; Olin objected. Its newspaper ads showed that interest charges would push the total cost to the taxpayers to $6 million. The voters rejected the bond issue and later approved a pay-as-you-go program costing $1.9 million. The savings to the taxpayers were over $4 million. Olin, whose holdings accounted for 90 percent of the ratable property in the district, realized a $3.6 million saving as a result of its concern for the wise use of local school funds, in addition to any savings in taxes realized by its employees.[6] This exceptionally clear-cut example does serve to

---

[5]Keith Davis and Robert L. Blomstrom, *Business, Society, and Environment,* 2d ed. (New York: McGraw-Hill, 1971), p. 277.

[6]George Melloan, "Playing Politics," *Wall Street Journal,* 17 February 1964.

emphasize that community expenditures for local services are directly reflected in the tax load that the corporation and its employees must carry.

Consider the case of a local hospital board that finds the addition of a new hospital wing necessary to provide adequate service to the community. It plans an expansion. In the resulting fund-raising effort, company and employee contributions are solicited and company assistance is requested in managing the fund raising. Then what is the proper choice between attending to the business of the corporation and diverting time and funds to aid in obtaining additional community services?

The first assumption is that the additional hospital beds are necessary. Here the business corporation as a member of the community has several interests. Directly and indirectly, the business will be not only a significant contributor to the cost of the hospital but also a significant supporter of its operation through its medical plan. Therefore, that business has a direct interest in whether or not money is being wasted; it becomes desirable for the individual corporation or for the business community as a whole through group action to participate in the hospital planning to assure itself that the expense is both necessary and well conceived. The other side of the corporate interest in the hospital is that adequate hospital services are an important feature of the community from the standpoint of company and employee welfare. Inadequate hospital service could become a significant detriment to employee recruiting and could have a negative impact on the employee group as a whole. Thus, the business should encourage the provision of adequate hospital facilities in its own interest and that of its employees.

To assure itself that adequate community facilities are being provided, a business must become interested in some aspects of the welfare of its employees and their families, while respecting their rights and desires for privacy. The justification for the corporate interest is in the long-term effect of the community atmosphere and the adequacy of its services on the productivity of the employees, the desirability of the employment, and the value of the medical and other fringe-benefit plans the company helps to supply. This reason for interest is sound but does not justify any invasion of personal privacy or interference in the employees' pattern of living.

A Fair Share of the Community

Should this responsibility be extended beyond the employees and their families? For instance, should it be extended to the whole community? Requiring a business to assume responsibility for an entire community could be dangerous and unreasonable if one business was placed in the position of having to redress damage done by another. The entire concept of a private enterprise as a profit-making entity requires limiting the costs for which it can be held responsible. It is strongly argued here that no cost should be charged to a firm unless it can be related to the results of that firm's operations. A business should bear its full costs, including social costs. However, if it is required to go further than this, it tends to lose its focus and its nature as a profit-seeking entity and therefore become unmanageable. The problem, therefore, is in establishing the limit on the areas of cost attributable to a specific firm.

As an aid in defining the boundaries of business responsibility to the community, consider a company that has entered a remote area and built a plant and a town for its employees.

The One-Company Town

The Aluminum Company of Canada (Aluminium) built a huge new smelter at Kitimat in the wilderness of British Columbia, thus creating a major industrial installation in a wilderness area remote from civilization. In doing so, the company built the beginnings of a town. Because of the obvious needs of the employees who operate the smelter, Kitimat has homes, schools, and other community services. This company recognized the practical need for creating an intact community to attract the necessary employees. The complete town was created by Aluminium, but the concept of Kitimat was that the town would grow and become private. People would buy land from the company on favorable terms, other businesses could be established, and the town would not become totally dependent on the one employer.[7]

The population of such a town is limited to employees and families only at the beginning. As years pass, employees become ill, disabled, or reach retirement age; they leave the work force. They are no longer members of the employee group but are still members of the community. A functioning society begins to have its share of unemployables, foundling children, and other social charges. Some of the small firms that have joined the community to provide necessary services go out of business and leave their former employees without medical and pension protection. People who may have their own independent means find the community and settle there because they like it. One way or another, the total group of people in the community who are not associated with the businesses become larger than the total roster of the employees of all businesses plus their immediate families.

Any balanced community contains a significant number of people who are not in the work force and are not directly supported by anyone who is; the question here is the extent to which any business should be concerned with the needs of such people. Of course in a primary way, western democratic society encourages people to provide for themselves in the best way possible; they should have the opportunity of working out the type of life they want. However, society is increasingly recognizing the obligation of the community as a whole to provide at least minimum needs for those who cannot provide for themselves.

As a one-company town (such as the one just discussed) begins to mature, the initial responsibility of the business to assure that adequate community services are provided has expanded perceptibly. Through the addition of community members not directly dependent on the employed work force, the community group has slowly grown. Thus, the business would find itself bearing a share of responsibility for helping to see that the local hospital is adequate not only for its employees and their families but also for those on the welfare roles, retired stockbrokers, and any other

---

[7]"Aluminium Ltd. Unlimited Aluminum," *Fortune* 49, no. 5 (June 1954): 105 ff.

community members. In a one-company town it is difficult to envision legitimate company concern about the adequacy of community services that does not involve the entire community.

Other Employers

As other businesses become active and the community ceases to be a one-employer town, these businesses can be expected to assume their proportion of responsibility. Thus, in a typical community with many employers, responsibility for the adequacy of community services would be shared among them. This share of the corporate responsibility to the community can be defined as the sum of two elements: (1) a responsibility for ensuring that community services are adequate for the needs of its employee group, retirees, and their immediate families (those immediately dependent on the employees for support) and (2) a proportionate share of the needs of those in the community who are neither in the community's work force nor directly dependent on its members. The latter is not a responsibility for a donation but for sharing fairly in the community processes (including the cost) that lead to the provision of adequate community services.[8]

This share is proposed as the most logical level of corporate responsibility to the community as a whole. Thus, if the community needs six hundred more hospital beds and a major employer finds that its share of the community is 10 percent, then that business could be asked to address itself to the question of whether the sum of the contributions of the group that it represents will pay for 10 percent (sixty beds), and if not, how the corporation can best aid the community in finding more money or obtaining the expansion at a lower cost. Much of this money may come from a public fund drive. The business has a direct interest in the fund raising, since it can reduce its direct liability by assisting the community to obtain the necessary funds elsewhere.

Business has many ways of discharging its responsibility for its share of the community. Some may best be met by exerting the corporate influence toward effective and efficient community programs. In the case of unemployables, a recognized but difficult cure for the problem is to make them employable and bring them into the productive work force. Members of this group, which is a burden on the tax and welfare system, can sometimes be absorbed into the payroll at little or no cost to the business system if business managers use their ingenuity in capturing all suitable hiring opportunities. When hiring programs for the marginal and low-skilled

---

[8]This parallels an early statement of policy from a former president of Rayonier, Inc.: "In recognition of the company's responsibilities to its many employees, it embraces the financial responsibilities of the community for roads, schools, services, etc. We are completely willing to pay our fair share of the tax burden . . . we also recognize that within each community some genuine needs exist, beyond the scope covered by taxation. To meet such needs, each operating manager on the basis of his own judgment submits a recommended budget which is usually approved through corporate procedure. Such budgets may range from relatively low to extremely generous, depending upon, again, the real needs of the community as the manager sees them." Russell F. Erickson, "The Corporate Image as a Guide to Community Relations," in James M. Hund, ed., *Social Responsibility in Business: A Conference* (Atlanta: Emory University, 1962), pp. 84–85.

laborers must be created simply because of the social need, the cost can be high. Yet, as suggested later in this chapter, a corporation may sometimes be able without sacrifice of efficiency to tailor its hiring programs to include a portion of this group.

The self-interest of the corporation can be defined as a rather concise allotment of management responsibility and fiscal support for various community projects. To contribute more than this fair share, employers need special justification to assure the stockholders that their money is not being dissipated. To contribute less means that the business is not paying its proper share of the social cost of its operation, since the cost of the community services made necessary by its share of the community appear to be part of the true costs of doing business over the long run.

The Fringe of the Fair Share

In defining a share of the community as the area of proper concern for the business, a proportionate share of the "fringe" of the normal community was also included. This fringe group consists of those who are neither part of the work force nor dependent on one of its members and those who are adequately supported by a pension or other payment from one of the town's employers. The group consists of the unemployed, unemployables, public charges of all types, the balance of the retired, and those of independent means. As defined here, the extent of the business interest in this group is a concern for the adequacy of the available community services, including welfare and other social services.

Business could continue to assume, as it has in the past, that this fringe group was of concern only to social and welfare agencies. This posture allowed some parts of the business community to disclaim all interest in ghetto problems, families on welfare, high school dropouts, and any others not meeting established business hiring standards. However, this broad disinterest in the fringe group is inappropriate for at least three reasons.

1. The interdependence of business and community extends to a kind of symbiosis, in which both components must be healthy for either to prosper over the long run. In recent years it has become clearer that some of the fringe group need help, in some cases, less because of individual merit than for the health of the whole. Otherwise, patterns of poverty and disadvantage perpetuate themselves from generation to generation. Business self-interest in a healthy community calls for an effort to deal constructively with this fringe group.

2. Business is a major taxpayer, as is its employee group. Welfare and social service expenses are rising rapidly. Self-interest in minimizing tax burdens demands some attack on the source of the problems.

3. Business responsibility for its full social costs has been strongly argued here. Yet business can hardly judge its full impact on the community, particularly in individual cases. Consider cases in which the wife of an ex-employee becomes an alcoholic, the rehabilitation of an ex-convict is disrupted by a job refusal, the necessary discharge of an employee has a destructive impact on the course of the subsequent life of the former employee. In such cases the degree of responsibility that business bears may be variable, uncertain, and subjective, but, nonetheless,

could be real. Business managers must use objective and profit-oriented standards for making decisions, even though unintended or indirect impacts on the community may generate social costs either directly or as second- or third-order consequences of these decisions. To balance such costs, some effort focused on society's fringe is appropriate and proper.

The concept of a fair share of the community is suggested here as a rational, measurable, and workable guideline for business involvement with this fringe group. In a normal community if all businesses dealt effectively with their proportionate share, several major social problems would cease to exist for the most part. Of course, some businesses will lack resources or fail for other reasons—and the resulting gap can well be closed by the community social services; no individual business could fairly be required to repair the shortcomings of another.

Cities and Suburbs

It is easiest to apply this fair share analysis to an isolated community, but in the real world more and more business firms are located in cities or in the suburbs of cities and, in addition, may have many plant and office sites in different parts of the country. Although the same basic logic of analysis is also appropriate, it is more difficult to apply.

In the first place, a company with many plants and facilities must deal separately with its need to be a part of the community in each area where it is active. In small towns its role may be one of leadership, and its activities may be crucial to the success of the effort. In a large city a much greater level of effort may have minimum visible impact, and yet the social balance requirement for contribution remains.

In cities or suburbs where the employee population comes from many parts of the greater metropolitan area, a corporation will, by the tests proposed here, find itself with an obligation to every community where its employees and their dependents make up more than a negligible fraction of the total population. This approach is primarily the one used by many large suburban corporations to gauge their social involvement.

The Limits of the Fringe

In the process of defining a business responsibility for a share of the community, a necessary qualification exists for separating normal community problems from unusual situations exceeding business resources. Where a business operates in a community racked by layoffs or a considerable influx of marginally employable people from other areas, the fringe group may become very large and impose a significant burden. Some limit on the size of this responsibility to the fringe group seems fair where the circumstances are unusual. The limit proposed is the boundary between normal and crisis social problem levels. In a balanced community where the major businesses have active programs focused on their share of this fringe population, a reserve capacity exists for handling new arrivals, pulling them into the work force, and re-establishing the normal balance.

In areas such as Appalachia, major urban ghettos, or regions suffering economic reverses, the problems have exceeded the normal level and overtax normal community and business resources. Then governmental intervention and assistance become a necessity. These major social problems have reached a crisis level and are the clear province of government, although business assistance may render the program more effective and less expensive.

Business and the Educational System

Another important area of business impact on the community is in its interaction with the educational system. Here the business firm has at least three roles: (1) as a supporter of the educational system through its taxes and contributions, and those of its employee group, (2) as a provider of education through the training of its employees, and (3) as an agent of change in education through its influence as an employer and setter of standards for those who have received this education. The quality of such education is critical to the future of the community and perhaps to the business as well.[9] The cost of providing education is something of which most parents are keenly aware and the overall social investment that such training represents has been documented by Becker and others.[10]

Since education is an investment in individuals, its value is partly reflected in the wage rates that they receive. These wage rates reflect current levels of supply and demand in the labor market and may or may not compensate for the total investment in this education. From the standpoint of the individual, this fact is not important so long as the differential in wage rates does compensate for that portion of the cost of education represented by the personal investment in money and time, which is usually the case. Most studies show that personal investments in additional education provide a good return on the average.[11]

Public Schools

From the standpoint of society, education is subsidized as a major social investment. The balance of the cost beyond the direct personal contribution of the individual is raised by taxes and donations. Therefore, one may look at a given business firm and the educational requirements that its hirings represent and ask whether that firm is giving its fair share of support to the educational system.

The firm supports education not only directly by its taxes and contributions, but

---

[9]"The Bell system sees the quality of public education as critical: Each year more than 95% of our new employees comes to us from public high school. So we are quite dependent upon the quality of effective public education for the quality of people who provide our service." John D. deButts, "Responsibility—a Two-Way Street," *Business Today*, Autumn 1968, p. 27.

[10]Gary S. Becker, *Human Capital* (New York: Columbia Press, National Bureau of Economic Research, 1964). See also Vernon R. Alden, "Just How Much is a Degree Worth," *New York Times*, 10 January 1972.

[11]W. Lee Hansen and Burton A. Weisbrod, *Benefits, Costs and Finance of Public Higher Education* (Chicago: Markham, 1969), pp. 17–54. Becker, *Human Capital*, pp. 153–159. Stephen B. Withey, ed., *A Degree and What Else?* (New York: McGraw-Hill, 1971), pp. 58–80. Andrew Speckke, "Is Going to College Worth the Investment?" *The Futurist*, December 1976, pp. 297–304.

indirectly through the taxes and contributions of the entire employee group. This support is manifested in several ways: (1) through active personal and financial support of the educational system by the firm and its employee group; (2) by the influence of the managers and other employees in assuring that educational expenditures are well conceived and represent efficient use of the community's resources; (3) by supplemental contributions, scholarships, donations, and endowments by the firm or its employee group; and (4) through educational activities carried out or supported by the business in the course of its routine operation. The use of society's educational investment by a given business depends on the nature of its needs; a firm that hires only unskilled laborers will represent quite a different demand on the system than a firm that hires large numbers of Ph.D.'s.

One of the tenets of U.S. society is that basic primary and secondary education will be provided to all. School attendance up to the age of sixteen is compulsory in most areas, and society strongly encourages education at public expense at least through high school. Thus, a business firm that has done its share in supporting the needs of the community in which it operates will, in effect, receive a subsidy in the form of its ability to hire additional high school graduates educated at public expense. This subsidy is built into our present social system, and the direction of change is toward increasing this subsidy by offering more forms of public-supported supplemental education (for example, adult education and vocational training) and by increasing public support of higher education.

Various private primary and secondary schools also exist through the country. These schools came into existence originally to permit a specially focused curriculum or a special type of education and have traditionally been maintained at the expense of the parents and the sponsoring institutions. These schools represent a part of the total educational system; pressure for public support has grown, and for some peripheral expenses, such as transportation and books, public funding is no longer rare.

Where the public primary and secondary educational system is inadequate, business has a responsibility to lend its support to the creation of an adequate system. A business firm should share in the support of private schools only to the extent that an expanded private system might truly represent the most economical use of community resources, and even then only in some way analogous to the tax support of public schools. However, individual members of the organization often may choose to support private schools as a part of their personal value systems, which is clearly their right.

Higher Education

The tax support of a state or other public university system is an embodiment of social norms established by the society of which the business managers and the rest of the employee group are a part. This tax support represents a limited extension of society's subsidy of the investment in education. The limits, as set by society, range from free open-admission plans (such as the ones that operated for several years in New York City) to a significant tuition level in states (such as New Jersey) where the available facilities may accommodate only a portion of the qualified local applicants. A business firm has a legitimate concern for the needs of its share of the community, including their right of access to that level of support for higher education that society has chosen to provide.

In addition to its basic tax contribution, a business may have specific interests that cause it to contribute to higher education through scholarships and research grants. The business may need an evaluation of an experimental herbicide, an appraisal of trends in animal nutrition, investigation of a chemical synthesis, or simply a point of contact with the best academic minds. Or a business may decide to establish scholarships or fellowships that will increase the opportunity for hiring outstanding young scientists as they graduate. All these things will encourage a flow of money from a business in support of education, particularly to graduate schools, in areas where the self-interest of the business justifies the expense.

To a large extent, such expenses will be in proportion to the major technology and skills needs of the business. The technically oriented business with large needs for research and scientific skills will almost automatically have extensive ties to the academic community. A business that has little concern with research or technical details will need fewer people with graduate qualifications and is likely to have few routine contacts with the professional or technical academic centers of the country.

Also, it may be a part of the proper concern of a business to encourage and help provide broader support of certain specific aspects of the educational system. An electronics firm may foresee the need for more graduates in a particular engineering specialty, for instance; more scholarships and educational loans on better terms may be needed. Business leaders may be able to influence the course of events and promote greater social support for such areas of future needs. This involvement can follow from self-interest in the same way that a program of scholarships for children of employees may represent an attractive fringe benefit that also serves to enhance the company's reputation with scientific job candidates.

Different corporations also invest in a wide variety of training and educational programs specifically designed to increase the skills of their employees. These programs vary to include everything from fully paid attendance at special university programs (Harvard Business School training), educational and training seminars (American Management Association), and tuition assistance for college work, to the offering of vocational programs (computer programming) and full college degree programs (General Motors Institute). Each of these programs represents a decision that investment of corporate funds is justified by the return, as compared with the alternatives. Where very special training is needed (sales training with specific products) or very scarce skills are required (highly specialized graduate scientific specialties), direct investment of corporate funds may be the wisest and best way to assure a supply of the needed knowledge.

The area of education is one where the business can establish an adequate social balance if (1) the business and its employees collectively support their fair share of the needs acknowledged by society through taxes and contributions as necessary, and (2) the leaders of the business and of the employee group exert their constructive interest toward assuring that proper needs receive social support and that public programs are defined for efficient use of society's resources. Beyond this, the firm's specific self-interest, when fully explored, will normally lead to adequate contributions toward graduate education, scholarships, and special programs.

Balance with the Local Community

A business is a part of a local community as well as one of the major influences on its nature in many cases. It is in this role as a neighbor that the good (and bad) impacts of business activities are most intensely felt. Societies and communities develop a pattern and a tolerance for the extent to which neighbors can infringe on each other's rights through such things as noise and odors, and industrial plants fall under the same type of regulation.

Thus, a business obligation to and impact on its neighbors is a more immediate and personalized expression of established obligations to control noise, odor, and pollution. Not only does a business influence the local community by the inherent nature of the business but also by its standards of conduct and by the kinds of people and types of traffic that flow through the community as a result of the business activity.

> When IBM discovered that Lexington, Kentucky realtors were not aiding in finding housing for blacks transferred to that plant, IBM adopted—and publicized—a policy of dealing only with realtors who observed no racial discrimination; that was sufficient to open the local housing market to all IBM employees.[12]

IBM had a very substantial leverage on the local realtors and decided to use it in the interest of its employees. The key elements for business management in establishing a social balance with the local community are: (1) the recognition of the many ways in which the business creates impacts on the community, both directly and through its employee group, and (2) the recognition of the basic business-community interdependence. Within this framework, a responsible business should encourage programs adequate for the needs of its fair share of the community and establish its own tentative standards in areas where community standards are as yet undeveloped. In this case IBM chose to define an employee need that also influenced a change in community standards.

A Symbiotic Community

Corporations have built communities and have also destroyed them, but the basic relationship is and must be symbiotic. A strange example is the relationship between a leading copper company and its home community.

> Like all company towns, Butte, Mont., leans heavily on its chief economic benefactor, the Anaconda Co., the nation's third largest copper producer. Anaconda employs one-third of Butte's work force, pays 58% of the property taxes in Silver Bow County, and pumps millions of dollars into local business. But as vital as Anaconda is to Butte, many of the city's 23,000 residents deeply resent "The Company" and are troubled by its mining activities. For

---

[12]Jeanne R. Lowe, "Race, Jobs and Cities: What Business Can Do," *Saturday Review,* 11 January 1969, p. 91.

Anaconda's open pit copper mine is literally eating away portions of the city.

Opened in 1955, the Berkeley pit is now a mile wide, more than a mile long, and deep enough to swallow the Empire State Building. More than 1,000 homes have been razed for the pit's expansion, and the whole operation, including buildings and dumps, covers nearly 20% of Butte. Many of the city's residents fear the pit will someday engulf the city's core, and that fear has contributed to urban decay.[13]

According to *Business Week,* Butte has struggled with a long period of decline since its days as a boom town of 100,000. Over the last decade, this problem has been heightened by uncertainty over Anaconda's plans for the central business district. The mayor reports that the banks refuse long-term loans there, no major new retailers have opened in the past five years, and there has been almost no new building in the past twenty years.

Since 1961 Anaconda has had the right under state law to condemn surface lands needed for extension of its open pit operations. Anaconda has used this power only twice and normally pays more than fair market value for the property it purchases. But the company's power to take the property gives an advantage in the negotiations, and the uncertainty over Anaconda's plans for the business district have contributed to its decline, including the decline of property values there.

An alternative would be relocation of the business district to a section called the Flats, and in 1972 Anaconda offered to move its offices to this area as a part of any new development plan. *Business Week* reports the development of public anger because Anaconda has been so tight-lipped about whether it would ever extend the pit into the business district in the years since 1955 when the Berkeley pit was opened. The local suspicion is that Anaconda's interest in getting the business district relocated represents a step toward acquiring the old central area advantageously. Yet no municipal redevelopment plan could succeed without Anaconda's participation because of the profound impact of its decisions on the town.

When the community is directly confronted with the power of the corporation, as Butte is with Anaconda's power to enlarge its mine in any desired direction, the company must move with great skill and tact to avoid creating profound adverse social impacts by its actual and anticipated actions. Important elements here include the expected effect of the company's actions on the town. Thus, the old business district is blighted in part by the possibility that Anaconda will mine there. Whatever the company's actual plans, the uncertainty surrounding them casts its pall over the area. Anaconda's potential impact is so great it must mediate its impact to avoid serious social costs to those areas that it may, in fact, never mine. Anaconda is apparently now attempting to work more closely with Butte and has offered $11 million in cash and property toward relocation of the business district in exchange for the old business district property that would be vacated.[14]

---

[13]Excerpted from "An Open Pit Dilemma for Butte, Montana," *Business Week,* 1 December 1973, pp. 92, 94.

[14]"Anaconda Aids Butte," *Chemical Marketing Reporter,* 12 July 1976, p. 7.

A Dependent Community

In the mining area of Hutchinson, West Virginia, the development plans of the coal companies appear, according to one newspaper account, to be squeezing out the people of the community.

> Thirty-two families face eviction from their ramshackle homes here to make room for a $15-million coal processing plant—a facility planned to help meet the nation's rediscovered need for coal as a result of the energy crisis.
>
> It is a classic landlord-tenant clash, but what points up the old eviction drama here is that, for the aged widows of miners, the young welfare parents and the cheerful, dirty-faced children, there is literally almost no place else in Logan County for them to go.
>
> In recent times there would have been a glut of other shabby but sheltering coal camp "company houses" for Hutchinson's refugees to move to at nominal rents. Mine mechanization had sharply reduced the half-million-man work force that once filled the hollows, leaving hundreds of gritty, abandoned ghost towns.
>
> But the coal companies, to reduce their taxes, tore down many rows of look-alike miners' houses as they became vacant, and most of the others have been sold off.
>
> As in most of the mountainous central Appalachian coal fields—a region whose timbered, steeply sloping terrain reduces the habitable, flat acreage along creek and river bottoms to only 5 per cent of the total area—there is a long-term housing crisis here.
>
> The coal industry is booming and congratulating itself now more than ever for its foresight in buying up at yesterday's prices almost three-quarters of the 291,725-acre total area of Logan County. There is even less disposition now than in the past to sell land for housing that may interfere with mining. Says Teemer Rivenbark, a Logan County home builder: "You can't find a house lot here to buy for love or money."
>
> For the 108 people facing eviction in Hutchinson—a tumbledown, junk-filled, 60-year-old coal camp owned by the Dingess-Rum Coal Company—it is an irony that their landlord and nine other corporations own 220,494 of Logan County's 291,725 acres and apparently will release none of their coal-land holdings even to house the manpower that must mine it.[15]

Naturally, the coal companies want the free use of their property within proper legal bounds. That is what Dingess-Rum is seeking, and it has shown at least some flexibility in imposing deadlines and dealing with some hardships. The apparent problem is that people being displaced have no place to go.

The reasons for the hardship are historically intertwined with the geographic limitations of the region and the past practices of the coal industry. The coal industry

---

[15]Ben A. Franklin, "Mine Families Lose Homes as Coal Prospers Anew," *New York Times,* 17 October 1975. Copyright © 1975 by The New York Times Company. Reprinted by permission.

established a pattern in which it built company towns and became a major supplier of housing for its workers. Now the remnants of the community, not only active miners but also other coal industry people who came and grew old there, are dependent on the company housing. No other housing is available according to the report, and these people lack either access to vacant land or resources with which to build.

This appears to be a case where the industry has allowed a dependency to develop and now must deal with the consequences. Today's managers, who do not necessarily even represent the same companies that allowed this situation to develop, must deal with a situation in which substantial social costs may result as the community is forced to move from the company housing. This extremely difficult management problem in some ways transcends the clear legal right of the company to proceed with the evictions.

Keeping a Business Out

A company may find that a community does not want to expose itself to the potential local impact of the business. Several fast-food chains have encountered local resistance to their proposals for new locations. In New York City about 250 residents of the Sunset Park area launched a campaign to prevent a Burger King restaurant from opening in their neighborhood.[16] McDonald's has faced several similar confrontations in its search for Manhattan locations.[17]

Society makes the rules that govern corporations. Thus, where rules are already made, Burger King and McDonald's must seek society's acceptance of their plans and cannot proceed without it. While the objection to the fast-food outlets seems to center on the traffic and litter that could result, many other types of corporations encounter opposition for other reasons, as was illustrated in the Maine Clean Fuels' refinery case discussed in Chapter 2. Xerox Corporation is only one of many to find that a proposed location for its corporate headquarters generated substantial opposition—in this case from the citizens of Greenwich, Connecticut.[18] Since the company planned an attractive facility that was designed to minimize environmental impact, and even traffic impact, the discussion concerned the simple issue of whether the corporate headquarters type of development and addition to the tax base was consistent with the desires of the Greenwich community. A great many members of that community indicated clear, strong opposition.

Shutting the Company Down

An even more difficult decision for a local community involves deciding how to deal with serious impacts from a principal employer, for example, the impact of arsenic from the ASARCO smelter on the Ruston, Washington, community. Ruston children are absorbing four to seven times as much arsenic as found in children elsewhere.

---

[16]"Burger King Meets Beef in Sunset Park," *New York News,* 31 October 1974.

[17]"McDonald's—Another Flap," *New York Post,* 21 January 1975.

[18]Anthony Bailey, "A Classy Company Troubles a Classy Town: Worried About Being Xeroxed," *New York Times Magazine,* 18 November 1973, pp. 42ff.

Some scientists feel that the effect could be an increased incidence of cancer late in life. ASARCO had already spent $20 million to reduce the pollution levels causing the community exposure but said that it could not justify the $70 million additional investment necessary to meet the new air quality standards fully. Closing the smelter would eliminate 1,000 jobs, a $12 million annual payroll, and the only U.S. source of arsenic for industrial and other uses.

Although higher concentrations of arsenic have been associated with cancer, the company has insisted that there is no evidence of a health hazard from the exposure levels occurring in Ruston. Meanwhile, the people of the community continue to grow and eat their own vegetables in spite of state warnings of the hazard due to the levels of arsenic and other metals that they contain.[19] Here the community and society as a whole must decide whether ASARCO can continue to operate. In the light of new medical evidence, society has imposed new standards that ASARCO may not be able to meet. The alternative could be to effect a shutdown which would result in a healthier environment, a national shortage of arsenic, and a need for the people of Ruston to find new jobs.

Bringing Business In

The need for industry and jobs to keep a community healthy often causes a troubled community to seek for new industry and to offer incentives for location there. In Auburn, New York, community resources have been mobilized to attract new industry.

A 150,000-ton-a-year steel mill is being built here on a 196-acre site for a Japanese trading company, and when it goes into production next year it will provide 250 badly needed new jobs for Auburn.

The plant is a direct result of the work of the Auburn Industrial Development Authority. This five-year-old job-generating agency is Auburn's hope for economic survival in the same way that a similar agency, being set up for New York City this summer, may become New York's hope for rebuilding its shrinking manufacturing industries, now 400,000 jobs smaller than they were in 1950.

"Our problem is jobs," said Mayor Paul W. Lattimore, who has pushed the work of the development authority since it was founded. "We have 3,000 boys and girls in our high school," he said, "and we graduate 900 of them a year after spending maybe $15,000 apiece to educate them. But we can't keep them here, even the ones who don't go away to college, because we don't have enough jobs. That's bad for them and it's bad for us, because we don't get any return on our investment in them."

Auburn, with a population of 35,000, has a work force of 10,000. More than half of those employed work elsewhere, most of them in nearby Syracuse. For more than two decades, Auburn and predominantly rural

---

[19]Herbert G. Lawson, "Dilemma in Tacoma; Smelter's Emissions Threaten Populace But So Does Possible Loss of 1000 Jobs," *Wall Street Journal,* 16 July 1975.

Cayuga County, of which it is the seat, have been a depressed area, with an unemployment rate 40 to 50 per cent higher than the state average.

The troubles began in 1948, when the International Harvester Company, the city's principal employer, closed its farm machinery plant and left 2,000 people without jobs. Then the Firth Carpet Company went out of business, putting 700 people out of work.

Other companies followed. Some were unable to keep up with technological change and just disappeared. Others, hampered by antiquated plants, moved to take advantage of cheaper labor, lower taxes and other incentives offered elsewhere.

"It took a long time for us to come back from those blows," Mr. Lattimore said, "and we are still feeling the effects of them today."

What brought Ataka and Auburn together was a $35,000 study financed by the development authority that proved the feasibility of a small steel mill in this part of the state. The area has what such a plant needs—electric power, water, road and rail access, surplus labor and a good supply of scrap metal to feed the mill's 50-ton furnace.

Auburn, through its development authority, also was able to offer cheap financing.

In the case of the Auburn mill, the authority is issuing bonds worth $22-million. That was the projected cost when the project was planned two years ago. Design changes and inflation have increased the cost to $35-million.

Matsuo Tominaga, executive vice president of Ataka America, said the agreement provided "good mutual advantages" to Auburn and to his company. For Ataka, he said, it provides an opportunity to retain American markets for steel reinforcing bars used in building construction that the company was losing because of the rising costs of shipping such bars from Japan.[20]

Auburn's industrial development program has been successful thus far—Ataka is a major new employer and apparently a welcome addition.

Company Investment in the Community

The corporation side of the equation with the community can also be active. For example, Ford Motor Company's long-standing relationship with Detroit and the role developed by the company led Henry Ford II to take initiative in 1972 in a plan for redeveloping a key downtown area.

In a few years, the results of doing things "Detroit style" will be evident in Renaissance Center, a $500 million development of offices, a hotel, shops,

---

[20]Michael Stern, "Hard-Pressed Upstate Town Induces Japanese to Build a Steel Mill," *New York Times,* 12 September 1974. Copyright © 1974 by The New York Times Company. Reprinted by permission.

apartments and condominiums and places of entertainment covering 33 acres of what is now industrial wasteland on the Detroit riverfront at the base of the city's central business district.

We broke ground in May for the first phase of construction, a $235 million complex which will include a 70-story hotel of 1500 rooms and four 39-story office towers. This first phase is scheduled to be completed by 1976.

In size, it is a third again as large as New York's Rockefeller Center and four times as large as the much discussed Peachtree Center in Atlanta. As the most recent of the major urban renewal projects, it will set a new pattern of design innovation drawing on the talents and the experience gained in other cities by architect-developer John Portman.

And what visiting city planners find most remarkable of all, it is being financed completely by private investment through the Renaissance Center Partnership. The partnership, which consists of 49 companies that have invested $37,550,000 in equity capital for the first construction phase, is described by the U.S. Chamber of Commerce as the largest investment group ever assembled in the United States for a major redevelopment project.

Like most major undertakings, Renaissance Center started as the idea of one man—in this case Henry Ford II, chairman of the Ford Motor Company. But the project required broad acceptance and support, and Mr. Ford was quick to point this out. In announcing his proposal to the Detroit City Council less than two years ago, Mr. Ford explained, "The size of the development is such that no single company can handle it by itself. We want and will need the participation of other companies to bring the plan to reality."

"This revitalization is a task for the business community here," Mr. Ford said at the outset. "There are more than enough resources, human and financial, to undertake a job of this kind. What we have been lacking is a solid first step to get something started."

The project began with not one, but two solid first steps—a feasibility study which indicated that such a project could work, and the architectural design of a center that would fill the city's needs.

The feasibility study revealed the need for one million square feet of additional office space per year in the downtown area, despite an office building boom in the suburbs. Renaissance Center's 14 office towers will contain five million square feet of office space, more than has been built in the city in the past ten years. Over half of the 2.3 million square feet of office space included in the first construction phase has already been reserved by prospective tenants.

The study indicated that while Detroit's convention business is thriving it would be even better if the city had additional modern hotel facilities to complement Cobo Hall, one of the country's finest exhibition centers. Western International Hotels will manage the 1500-room Renaissance Center Hotel which, at 70 stories, will be the tallest building in Michigan.

Finally, the feasibility study showed that shops, restaurants and places of entertainment would attract Detroit-area residents and serve as a catalyst for further redevelopment in the downtown area.

With the feasibility study and the architect's drawings in hand, Mr. Ford began calling on his counterparts in other major corporations that had reason to be concerned with the future of Detroit. His objective was to assemble the $35 million in equity capital needed to secure mortgages on the first $235 million phase of construction.

"Renaissance Center is simply too big for a typical real estate developer to tackle," Mr. Ford told potential investors. "So that leaves us, the corporations. It is time for us to step up to a problem that no one else has been able to solve and to demonstrate that this can be done, and, most important, that it can be done at a profit."

Today, 49 companies, two-thirds of them included in the top 500 industrial companies in the United States, are members of the partnership, with individual investments ranging upward from $250,000. Their total investment now stands at $37,550,000, well beyond the original equity target.

In assembling the partnership, we invited only companies with strong Detroit orientation on the theory that these firms would be most likely to carry their support of Renaissance Center beyond financial investments and into other uses of the facilities. About half of the investors are headquartered in Detroit and the remainder have major plants in or around the city.

While the Renaissance Center Partnership was organized to develop only the first 14-acre $235 million phase of the project, member companies in the partnership will be given first opportunity to invest in the two remaining phases which will be undertaken in the decade.

The catalytic effect we expect Renaissance Center to have on the revitalization of the central business district has already begun to be felt, even before the buildings begin to rise on the riverfront. Shortly after ground was broken for the center, Michigan Bell Telephone announced plans to erect a $12-million building adjacent to the site to house the telephone equipment which will be needed to serve the complex.

In addition, the University of Detroit announced that it will spend some $5 million to renovate several buildings on its law campus near the Renaissance Center site. Before the riverfront development was announced the university had mentioned plans to close that portion of its campus.[21]

Primarily by investing his leadership, Henry Ford II defined and sold a $500 million development concept that was built and began to open in 1977. The community impact can be dramatic as the project succeeds, and the $6 million Ford Motor Company investment should yield a handsome return. A fundamental element in plans of this sort is making available the opportunity for strong leadership to take a major initiative and define a self-fulfilling prophecy in which the development succeeds, returns profits to investors, developers, and the community, and then forms the centerpiece for other related developments, such as the proposed renovation of the University of Detroit Law campus. Hence we see the leverage of a major corporate position in a community producing a positive transformation as dramatic as the negative transformation posed by the threat of the nearby mine to downtown Butte in the previous example.

[21]Wayne S. Doran, "Industry Rebuilds Detroit," *NAM Reports,* 15 October 1973, pp. 6–8.

Corporate Responsibility to the Community

In the course of the development of its business, PepsiCo acquired the Rheingold breweries and then proposed to shut them down. This move generated an intense local controversy since PepsiCo was in good financial health but chose not to invest its profits in rebuilding a business that had been declining, even though the closing would cause significant local hardship.

> By the time PepsiCo entered the picture, beer was still yielding about 70% of Rheingold Corp.'s sales, but perhaps only 30% of net income. The percentages were almost the reverse for Rheingold's soft drink ventures, including its large Pepsi-Cola bottling operations in California, Florida, Mexico, and Puerto Rico.
>
> Industry observers who have watched Rheingold beer's decline spread the blame equitably among management and the unions. The former get low marks for letting the endangered Brooklyn brewery grow old yet still dominate the company's beer business. It houses most of Rheingold's brewing capacity, 2.5-million bbl. a year, compared with 1.5-million bbl. at Orange and 500,000 bbl. at New Bedford. At the same time, they note, the unions continued to press wages and benefits well above industry levels in Brooklyn, despite increasing evidence that breweries were fleeing the high-cost New York area.
>
> The consequence, industry sources say, is that a brewer such as Schlitz, one of several to cease operations recently in the metropolitan area, can brew and bottle a case of beer in a modern plant in South Carolina and deliver it to a tavern in Brooklyn at lower cost and higher profit than Rheingold can within its home borough.[22]

An interim agreement delayed the closing, and fifteen hundred employees were out of work while attempts to save the business continued.[23] City Council President Paul O'Dwyer and others joined the efforts to save the brewery. O'Dwyer announced that the unions had offered substantial concessions to potential buyers.[24]

On February 27, 1974, officials of the Teamsters Union announced that Chock Full O'Nuts Corporation had agreed with the employees on a basis for the takeover of the Rheingold brewery. This included concessions from the unions to increase productivity. This agreement was confirmed by William Black, chairman of the coffee and restaurant company. PepsiCo officials said that during the previous year they had offered the brewery to U.S., Japanese, and European concerns on the same basis: purchase for $1 on condition that the buyer assume $10 million in short-term debt while PepsiCo kept approximately $20 million in long-term obligations.[25]

---

[22]Excerpted from "PepsiCo Spurns the Beer it Bought," *Business Week,* 26 January 1974, pp. 25–26.

[23]Martin McLoughlin and William Heffeman, "4 Day Delay Given in Final Shutdown of Rheingold Plant," *New York News,* 5 February 1974.

[24]William Heffeman, "Brew Talks Not Mere Near Beer," *New York News,* 13 February 1974.

[25]"Chock Full O'Nuts Corp. Moves Toward Purchase of PepsiCo Brewing Unit," *Wall Street Journal,* 27 February 1974.

Many people felt that PepsiCo had defaulted on its responsibility to the Rheingold employees when it planned the shutdown. Yet PepsiCo did not create the situation and had tried repeatedly to find someone like Chock Full O'Nuts to take over the brewery. Over several years Chock Full O'Nuts tried to bring the Rheingold operations back to a reasonable profit level but did not succeed. To stem continuing losses, the Brooklyn plant was shut down and the operating base shifted to the Orange, New Jersey, plant. Finally, in October 1977 Chock Full O'Nuts gave up, selling Rheingold to Schmidts of Philadelphia, which laid off the remaining brewery employees.

PepsiCo had bought an ailing business, kept the healthy soft drink operations, and sold the sick beer business. Chock Full O'Nuts did not succeed in its efforts to restore the soundness of the business. The origin of the problem was back at the point where the Rheingold business became unprofitable, compared to other breweries, and the workers and community were the losers as the business was liquidated. Of the several companies involved, it is easiest to fault the original management for not maintaining the profitability of the business. It is less clear whether PepsiCo, which separated the sound and unsound parts of the business, could have been asked to do more.

The Fringe of the Community

Many corporations have experimented with programs for incorporating the hard-core unemployed, handicapped, ex-convicts, and other disadvantaged members of the community within the work force. Kemper Insurance reports considerable success in its employment of ex-addicts:

> "A few years ago, management shunned the former alcoholic," says James S. Kemper, Jr., President of Kemper Insurance. "Today, enlightened hiring practices have proven the worth of the rehabilitated alcoholic. Hopefully, industry will realize that drug addiction is in the same category of emotional illness and can be successfully treated." . . .
>
> "It may take several more years for the business community to accept rehabilitated addicts," Kemper concedes. But he is convinced that ultimately it will. He rates his own company's program as a distinct success because of its experience with seven former addicts, six of whom are still on the payroll
>
> . . . As an insurance company, Kemper has a vested interest in reducing crime, and that is related to addiction. James Kemper says that the problem transcends any single organization's concern. "Alcoholism was completely stigmatic 10 years ago," recalls Kemper whose company pioneered its treatment as a behavioral illness. "It may take a few years until several more major national companies go on the line for drug abuse for it to become a respectable concern." he says.[26]

---

[26]Excerpted from "How Kemper Aids Ex-Addicts," *Business Week,* 26 February 1972, pp. 42–43.

The successful Kemper program involved a small number of ex-addicts, and the effort required to implement the program suggests something of its total costs to the company. In addition, public funds were being used for treatment of the addicts up to the point of employment.

Clearly, this program served Kemper's interests by shifting a few individuals into productive work, but it seems unlikely that the payoffs definable by Kemper's own direct self-interest could have been sufficient to balance the costs of the program. However, the additional leadership investment in a new type of re-employment program seems meritorious beyond any direct return, even if we consider the program's public relations value. By this type of leadership investment, however, Kemper might hope to help pilot a program that could be self-sustaining and that could aid in the social rehabilitation process necessary to shift a significant group from involvement in criminal activities and providing a major drain on public funds to full and productive membership in society.

Business Hiring Practices

Every time that business eliminates a vacancy in its work force by the act of hiring, the business and community change. The community benefits by the placing of an individual; the business adds to its work force. Either directly or as a result of a chain of replacements, the community's pool of unemployed changes composition; it is diminished by one Ph.D. or unskilled laborer, one white or black, or one male or female, depending on who has been hired. And the newly hired person represents a community investment in education and services; business is now employing that investment.

The way that business selects these new employees can have a profound effect on the community. As an example, consider the effect of requiring a high school diploma in an entrance-level job. Assume that a business has a work force in which new hourly employees are hired as utility workers or janitors—with promotion into higher levels as opportunities within the work force arise. Because many of the jobs to which these workers could eventually be promoted require a good basic education, the policy of that business has been to hire only high school graduates. Overall hiring experience indicates that within two years of hiring 25 percent of the high school graduates have actually moved into jobs where the education is beneficial and 50 percent have left the company.

An analysis of work requirements and causes of turnover suggests that if only 60 percent of the new employees were high school graduates, an adequate promotional pool would exist, as illustrated in Figure 13.1. Good high school graduates would be easier to hire if smaller numbers were needed and there were better prospects for their promotion. The turnover of newly hired graduates would be reduced as well. Many of the community's marginally employable members would be satisfactory in the actual janitorial jobs, for which reading skills are not required.

By hiring 40 percent of its employees from the group without high school diplomas and attempting to draw semiliterates and illiterates into this element of the work force where possible, a company could improve its hiring position. (This would be done through a relaxation in educational requirements calculated to produce the

Figure 13.1 An Idealized Entry-Level Hiring Plan

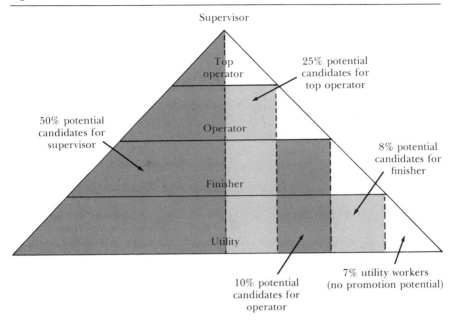

The theoretical mix of ability among newly hired utility workers is just sufficient to provide the necessary pool of talent. There will be an adequate range of choice among qualified candidates for each opening as promotion opportunities occur, but no excess of talent that will cause frustration because opportunities are too slow in coming. (Real-world situations are rarely stable enough over time to permit more than an approximation of this approach.)

desired balance, rather than direct use of quotas.) Simultaneously, the company could improve the morale in the lower ranks and draw marginal workers into productive employment; hence society would benefit. The business would also benefit; the lower turnover among the better qualified workers and the reduction in welfare and other community costs raised by taxes as a result of having more marginal workers employed would outweigh the possible higher costs of hiring marginal workers.[27]

Each business hiring decision is presumably aimed at filling a vacancy in the work force in a manner consistent with the overall productivity of the business. However,

[27]The Chairman of the Committee for Economic Development has said: "Another factor to consider is what it costs not to do the job. The cost is corporate, employee, and shareholder taxes to pay for the efforts of public agencies." William C. Stolk, "Beyond Profitability," *Conference Board Record* 5, no. 12 (December 1968): 53. The President of McGraw-Hill has put it even more dramatically: ". . . slums could siphon off your profits. Slums are a luxury few cities can afford, and much of what they cost is paid by taxes on business." Joseph H. Allen, *Business and the Urban Crisis*, McGraw-Hill Special Reports (New York: McGraw-Hill, 1968), p. 3.

secondary motives such as promotability are important considerations in making the choice. By emphasizing different factors, the business can significantly shift its balance with society, particularly as it changes its dependence on the educational system and its interaction with the welfare system. Obviously, efficient operation of the business must be paramount in hiring practices. But the sort of internal options just discussed often give business management the opportunity to consider its relationship to the community and to select that balance in its hiring that will be most favorable to the concerns of both business and the community.

Summary

The processes and relationships between corporation and community are so complex that many more examples would be required to explore them completely. However, the examples presented do aid in pointing up the basic principles of the interdependence, community of interest, and implied continuity of the established business-community relationship. The principal impact areas of corporation on community are summarized in Figure 13.2.

The fundamental element in the corporation-community relationship is interdependence, since each depends to a significant extent on the other to perform its role effectively. For best performance, both corporation and community should be healthy. If the corporation falters or fails, the workers and the community may be able to find other employment and other employers, but not without effort and pain. If the community fails to function effectively, business must assume the extra burdens and costs of aiding employees in obtaining necessary services, of paying more in compensation for the lack of services, or of relocating the firm to another community.

Within the scope of this interdependence with the community, the business has a deep interest in the adequacy and cost of community services because it is a large buyer, directly and indirectly, of such services. This interest also extends to assuming responsibility for providing an adequacy of these services not only for its own employees but also for a fair share of the community, including the community's fringe up to the normal limits of the welfare and social overhead burden. Primary and

Figure 13.2   Impact of the Firm on the Local Community

Interdependence with the community	The educational system
Use and support of services	Effects on neighborhoods
Fair share of the community 　　The fringe of the community 　　Limits to the fringe	Industrial development 　　Bringing a company in 　　Being kept out
Influence of business hiring practices	

Corporation and community must live together and support each other— better in peace and prosperity than in conflict.

secondary public education is another important community service area where the firm has similar interests and responsibilities. Other levels and kinds of education are normally supported only to the extent that this serves the direct self-interest of the firm.

In addition to its impact on and relationship with the community as a whole, the firm has a more immediate and intimate relationship with the neighborhood in which it is located. Here is where the physical presence of the firm is felt—noise and odors (if there are any), buildings and roads, and traffic and activity patterns characteristic of the business. Good or bad, the characteristics of the firm help determine the character of the neighborhood, and this is a significant social impact for better or worse.

The Anaconda versus Butte example illustrates one facet of the love-hate relationship of a dependent town and a powerful, but still dependent, company, and it also exposes the depth of the existing, but less visible, relationship between other firms and other towns. In the coal company versus housing example, the company, within its rights, is caught in a pattern of supplying housing that its industry created in the past. The company is less free to change this policy than it would like to be because the coal companies have bought so much land that the members of the former company town have no place to relocate.

Other dimensions of the corporation-community relationship involve the power to keep certain types of business out, for example, when the community restricted fast-food units. Or a community may induce an industry to enter, as in the case of the Japanese steel firm. On the corporation side, strategic leadership investment can stimulate renovation and redevelopment, even on the scale of the Ford effort to catalyze the rebuilding of downtown Detroit. The exact extent of corporate responsibility to community is hard to generalize, but the PepsiCo shutdown of the uneconomical Rheingold plant would have had heavy social costs, which were deferred for several years by the transfer of the brewery to Chock Full O'Nuts. Corporate programs aimed at the fringe of the community were illustrated by the Kemper program for ex-addicts, although there are many other programs addressed to the needs of various fringe groups.

The chapter closes by suggesting the firm's need to pattern its hiring practices to embrace individuals with a wide range of ability and potential. This need, which grows legitimately out of the internal needs of the business, also offers considerable leverage for recruiting marginally employable members of the fringe group at little or no cost and much benefit to the firm.

Hopefully, continued discussion of the corporation-community relationship will aid in development of clearer public standards, so that managements of such companies as PepsiCo or Dingess-Rum will have a clearer picture of what they must do beyond meeting today's legal obligations in order to maintain social balance. Clearly, however, today's society has moved beyond the point where it will quietly countenance a plant closing where the employees lose employment and benefits or the old and disabled are evicted, even if the present laws and the rights of the corporate property holder permit such an action.

This chapter has explored the underlying relationship between corporation and community, emphasizing their interdependency, the need for corporate concern for a fair share of the community including its fringe, and the responsibility to help provide for education and other community services. Corporations have requirements, obligations, and power to act. Through skillful use of this power, large projects can be accomplished in the community with little diversion of corporate resources and good return to corporation and community. Given a sound business and a capable management, corporate social impact on the community can be well balanced in most cases and can work to the benefit of the corporation as well.

Guidelines for Managing Corporate Social Impact

In the management of impact on the local community, social balance will tend to be maintained if the following guidelines are applied:

Dependence   A firm recognizes the degree to which it is dependent on and served by the health of its surrounding community and encourages this health wherever and however possible.

Fair share   A firm operates in such a way that it and its employees support their fair share of the costs of community services, including those used by the business and needed by both the employees and the fringe of the community.

Neighborhood effects   A firm recognizes its own effect on the nature and character of the neighborhood around the operation and minimizes adverse effects insofar as possible.

Applying the Guidelines

To a corporation that analyzes the details of its own impact on the community, adverse impacts will be easy to identify, and the money that flows directly from the corporation and indirectly through its payrolls for taxes and community services will define the areas of immediate self-interest. Programs to minimize the adverse impacts of the corporate operations should result from such impacts, and from the money flows should come a priority of interest in the efficiency of the community processes and concerns for the fringe groups within the community. The corporate need is for a healthy community, and it acts in its own self-interest in this regard, preferably through programs that use the leverage of its position to catalyze community processes at minimum additional cost.

Questions for Analysis and Discussion

1. How do you feel about the degree of interdependence between a healthy business and a healthy community? Can you cite examples in support of your opinion?

2. Do you feel that local businesses support more or less than their share of community services? Why?

3. Discuss the fair share concept as you see it applying in your area. How well does it apply?

4. To what extent would you make businesses responsible for the adequacy of services for the fringe group in the community? Discuss your reasoning.

5. Do you see local businesses as having a good impact on the educational system? A bad impact? Discuss.

6. In the West Virginia coal company versus housing example, what possible solutions to the problem of Dingess-Rum exist?

7. Find other examples of a major corporate investment, such as Ford's Detroit project, that have caused other investments and eventual redevelopment of the area.

8. How should a major corporation handle the process of a major operational shutdown?

For Further Information

Becker, Gary S. *Human Capital.* New York: Columbia University Press, 1964.

Eells, Richard. *The Corporation and the Arts.* New York: Macmillan, 1967.

Moore, Wilbert E. *The Conduct of the Corporation.* New York: Random House, 1962.

Reiss, Alvin H. *Culture and Company.* New York: Twayne, 1972.

Sethi, S. Prakash, ed. *The Unstable Ground: Corporate Social Policy in a Dynamic Society.* Los Angeles: Melville, 1974.

Wheatley, Edward W. *Values in Conflict,* Miami: Banyan Books, 1976.

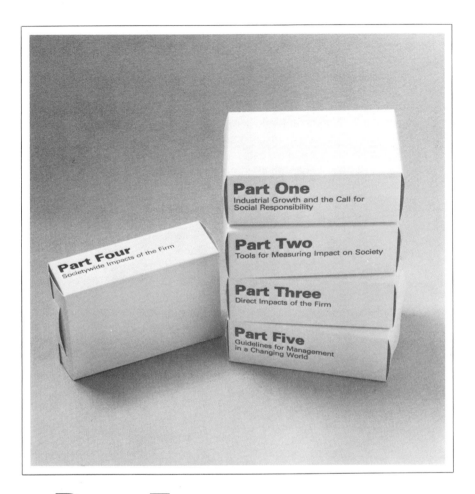

Part Four
Societywide Impacts of the Firm

Part Three looked at areas—consequences of the sale of goods and services, the use of physical and human resources, operational wastes, and community impact—in which the consequences of management decisions most directly affect individuals and groups of people. In each area the analysis concluded with suggested operating guidelines conceived around the long-term need to achieve a social balance in order to assure the society's acceptance of continued operations. This attempt, to define the ideal operating state in the areas of direct corporate impact, is continued in Part Four for societywide impact areas. Part Five will then evaluate these

257

guidelines, suggesting an operating pattern that can minimize adverse corporate social impact while allowing corporations to successfully handle the other realities of their environment.

By its nature a modern industrial corporation is a complex system of increasingly numerous and complex interdependent elements. The corporate impact areas considered in Part Four are those where the societywide effects are likely to be at least as important as any direct effect of the corporate action. Such a determination cannot be unalterable as circumstances may broaden or shrink the impact area. For example, as a coal mine is worked out or an oil field is abandoned, this exhaustion of scarce resources is a matter of immediate local concern. But as energy resources such as coal or oil grow scarce, interest becomes more urgent at the national level.

Part Four deals first with the impact of the corporation on society. Chapter 14 examines the social impact of resource allocation decisions as a business operates. Chapter 15 discusses the implications of the generation of new technology and the flow of new products. Chapter 16 explores the inevitable involvement of the corporation in public issues. Chapter 17 considers the operating constraints on a corporation as it both conforms to and molds society's requirements. Chapter 18 deals with the relationship of the corporation to society's governance processes, and Chapter 19 discusses defining and maintaining proper corporate allegiances and loyalties in the face of the conflicting claims of various social forces and jurisdictions. While many of these six impact areas have local importance, the breadth of the issues involved encourages their consideration on a societywide scale.

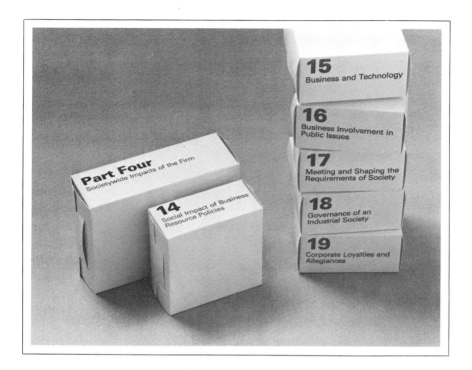

Part Four
Societywide Impacts of the Firm

14
Social Impact of Business
Resource Policies

15
Business and Technology

16
Business Involvement in
Public Issues

17
Meeting and Shaping the
Requirements of Society

18
Governance of an
Industrial Society

19
Corporate Loyalties and
Allegiances

14
Social Impact of Business Resource Policies

Because society is so dependent on the industrial system for goods and services and because the production of these goods and services is derived from business firms' investment and use of their resources, it follows that the corporate policies for the investment and use of their resources can have a profound impact on society. Some of the decision areas involve the choices that determine whether or not a corporation maintains and increases the productive stock of resources on which its business is based. Other decisions involve the use of its profit flow and the manner in which it handles reallocation and transfer of assets from one geographical area or portion of the business to another. Each of these and other types of resource decisions has its own set of consequences for both the firm and society. With the power of the corporation to make such decisions goes the responsibility for the consequences, and society is moving toward an increasing expectation that the social impact of most corporate resource policies will be nondeleterious and that unavoidable adverse impacts will be balanced in some way.

A business enterprise can exist only in an expanding economy, or at least in one which considers change both natural and acceptable. And business is the specific organ of growth, expansion and change.[1]

PETER F. DRUCKER

Because a business firm manages a portion of the productive resources of a society, its actions and decisions as it increases, dissipates, or shifts those resources have very deep impacts on the surrounding society. The wisdom with which the corporation utilizes, maintains, and replenishes those resources determines the degree to which its role in the community can be continued and expanded. The corporate approach to directing its profit flows and the corporate pattern of allocating, reallocating and shifting resources in imposing layoffs and transfers on its work force define a social impact. The purpose here is to examine these impacts and consider the possibilities for achieving a social balance that will avoid or offset them.

Maintenance of Business Capital and Opportunity

A familiar story among small or family-owned businesses is of attaining early success, making good profits, and then living off the profits for a period of time. The cycle ends with an economic reversal or an environmental change that brings a cold reappraisal. Suddenly, facilities are found to be obsolete, operation becomes marginal, and funds for replacement are unavailable. The business has dissipated its resources and lacks sufficient profit flow to attract new capital. The doors close and those dependent on the business are cast adrift.

This grim and stylized example is neither rare nor impossible. A business that dies in this way has failed to discharge its responsibilities to those dependent on it who had accepted the implicit commitment to continued operation. At the moment of corporate death, the business managers have few options remaining, yet social costs have been incurred for which no compensation is made.

> New England has suffered since 1920 because the owners of many huge and once profitable factories had made no provision for the upkeep of real estate or machinery. The fact that many New England owners failed to provide

---

[1]Peter F. Drucker, *Management: Tasks, Responsibilities, Practices* (New York: Harper & Row, 1974), p. 65.

anything for replacement of machinery when it would be worn out or obsolete was a major reason for the collapse of many textile plants. And the major sufferers were the workers who had devoted their lives as low-paid workers in those plants and had earned large profits for the employers. The communities which had been built around these plants were left with a relief burden and no industry.[2]

The first requirement for an individual firm seeking a proper social balance in this area is wise management of its own assets and sufficient consideration of industry-wide problems to share in planning for public protection where necessary. However, it is also necessary for a firm to find some source of growth on which it can rely to

The Firm as Viewed by Society

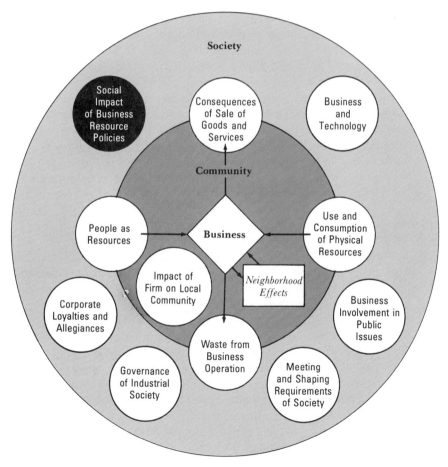

[2]Robert J. Watt, "Social Responsibilities of Business: A Labor View," *Annals of the American Academy of Political and Social Science* no. 208 (July 1939): 83.

provide steady employment in times of adversity and healthy career paths for its employees over time. Naturally, such growth should be and normally will be advantageous to its stockholders. Certainly, a healthy relationship with the surrounding society and particularly with the employees and the local community flows most easily from a steadily growing firm.

In one way or another business growth usually requires additional capital. Thus, the requirement for maintenance of business capital should be projected into the future. Depreciation and depletion allowances are conceived around the protection of past investments, but replacement costs may be higher, particularly since modernization and improvements are necessary and desirable in most cases.

Since a narrowly conceived business venture tends to have a life cycle just as products do, businesses that maintain steady long-term growth tend to do so through introducing new series of products and new activities that broaden the base of the firm's activity. This expansion also requires new capital investment. Therefore, the firm should operate not only to conserve its initial capital but also to plan for the flow of additional capital necessary to fund future maintenance of its opportunities and those of the people dependent on it. IBM is frequently cited as an example of this sort of planning.

> IBM is a capital-goods producer. Its products are used almost exclusively by business. By definition—employment in such an enterprise is extremely sensitive to economic fluctuations. At IBM's main competitors, employment was cut back sharply during the depression years. IBM management decided, however, that it was its job to maintain employment. There was obviously only one way to do this; to develop new markets. And IBM was so successful in finding and developing these markets that employment was actually fully maintained right through the thirties.[3]

Drucker quotes one IBM executive:

> We grew because we had committed ourselves to the maintenance of employment. This forced us to find new users and new uses for existing products. It forced us to find unsatisfied wants in the market and to develop new products to satisfy them. . . . I am convinced that we would not today be one of the world's leading producers and exporters of office machinery but for our commitment to maintain employment during the depression years.[4]

The purpose is not to suggest that all firms must imitate IBM but to point out that in its relationships with society there is precedent for a firm's looking ahead, defining requirements for stability, meeting them, and benefiting very greatly thereby. While the solution may be unique to each firm, the problem is general; in maintaining its balance with society, a firm should look to the requirements for maintaining its capital and its level of opportunity in both the present and the foreseeable future.

---

[3]Peter F. Drucker, *The Practice of Management*(New York: Harper & Brothers, 1954), p. 260.
[4]Ibid., p. 261.

Community Capital

A business's own capital investment is of interest to the community because it makes up a portion of the total productive capacity from which the livelihood of the community is drawn. At the same time, the business uses a share of the community capital, which provides much of the transportation and services that a modern industry requires. For this the business should pay, through its taxes or otherwise, in some proportion to its actual usage, unless the community wishes to subsidize a particular activity. Thus, community planning of new roads and waste treatment plants is frequently linked to the needs of the business and its tax support of the community, if not to the specific project.

If the community fails to provide or extend the necessary services, self-interest requires business to proceed on its own. When Upjohn Company relocated its plant from downtown Kalamazoo to the town outskirts 6^1/$_2$ miles away, one of the first requirements was for effective mass transit for the employees. The local bus companies were reluctant to extend their lines so Upjohn established its own service, which it operated until the City of Kalamazoo Travel Authority agreed to take over the routes, subject to Upjohn guarantees of sufficient numbers of riders.

Consider the case where several businesses operate in the same community and purchase their utilities from it. One business discovers, on reviewing its operation, that it is contributing a major share of the load of the municipal waste treatment plant and paying only the same sewer tax rate as other businesses that produce little waste. This company is placing a cost burden on the community. In effect, it is receiving a subsidy through waste treatment services rendered below cost. In the long run the business should be expected to compensate the community more fully for the waste it is creating, unless the community has made a deliberate decision to grant this subsidy. Efforts to achieve an appropriate balance between business and the community should also take place in the case of purchased utilities, use of roads, and use of public facilities of any type where the capital investments of the community are used at least partially for the business.

In the course of a 1970 appraisal of a property in a Missouri city, it was pointed out by the seller that new processing operations could be installed without concern for waste treatment cost since the plant was connected to the municipal system. This system levied its costs as a tax on all property and at that time made no attempt to recognize differences in discharge load from an individual property. Thus, the opportunity to discharge additional waste without incurring additional charges amounted to an implicit subsidy of industrial expansion within the boundaries of that sanitary district.

The relocation of the American Cyanamid corporate headquarters to Wayne, New Jersey, provides an interesting example of balancing corporate investment with community services. A modern office building with extensive grounds and attractive landscaping was proposed and built. Although Cyanamid management had expected this facility to be a welcome addition to any suburban community, the first public proposal for a site in Alpine, New Jersey, drew serious local opposition. The company withdrew, stating its desire to go where it would be welcome. Wayne provided such a welcome, and the teacher whose letters first called the area to Cyanamid attention briefly became a local celebrity. Now several years after completion of the relocation the town has found the local service requirements of such a facility to be significant. The town has benefited from the tax revenue and the prestige of having these headquarters located in Wayne as forecasted, but the net effect is no longer unanimously considered as being beneficial to the community.

Since the operation of a business is, in part, dependent on the availability of roads and public services of various types, these community assets (sometimes referred to as the capital infrastructure of the community) represent a portion of the total capital required for the operation of the business. Thus, when a corporation plans its economic base to provide for maintenance and replenishment of the business capital, provisions must be made for the maintenance and replenishment of the portion of community assets that are also required for the business operation. To maintain these assets, the corporation will contribute by paying appropriate taxes and the public sector will allocate funds through appropriate channels.

Use of Profits

One of the results of the operation of a business is a flow of profits from the business. Where a business is highly profitable, this flow can be substantial, and the way that the profits are handled has an impact on society that should be considered as an element in the overall social balance. The handling of such profits, which will already have been taxed at the going rate, is somewhat controversial. Yet the profit level has become a public issue repeatedly, often because of the handling of the profit flow. Thus, many countries that permit and encourage investment by foreign firms restrict or prohibit repatriation of the profits, and many income tax laws are written to encourage reinvesting profits in the business rather than paying them out to stockholders.

Where a business is sound and is not injuring society by its operation, profits retained in the business represent a desirable additional investment from the standpoint of society. Bullis lists such investment as a part of the social responsibility of business.[5] Certainly, reinvestment of profits is a convenient means of financing the growth necessary to maintain a given level of opportunity.

A firm must have ties with its stockholders because they are the owners and have a claim on the equity that includes the right to choose or replace the management. Even though a more passive role is considered to be normal at present, the occasional proxy fight or takeover bid serves to keep management aware of latent stockholder power. Past abuse of the rights of small or gullible stockholders has led to extensive regulatory involvement, so that compliance with the law now largely constrains a corporation to deal equitably with its stockholders.

Profits paid out to the stockholders are income to the recipients; this income has an impact that depends on where the stockholders may be and how the money is spent. Volkswagen has been criticized because the profits from U.S. sales (to the extent that they are not retained for expansion of the U.S. business) flow out of the

---

[5]Harry A. Bullis, *Manifesto for Americans* (New York: McGraw-Hill, 1961), pp. 116–117.

United States and back to the German owners. Although the various stockholders of a U.S. automobile company may spend their money in different ways, most of their expenditures flow into the U.S. economy in one way or another. The flow of corporate profits across national borders is a matter of public policy, which an individual corporate management has little chance to influence or control. Although Volkswagen can point to the much heavier influx of U.S. corporate profits from foreign investments of U.S. companies, it must remain aware that its own profit flow raises a sensitive issue.

Of course, the expenditure pattern of individual stockholders, even in the United States, may be more or less beneficial to society depending on whether the money is donated to build libraries and art galleries, invested in other businesses, or paid out for travel and personal services. A corporation is hardly in a position to tell its owners where to live or attempt to influence the way that they spend their money. However, it can make some decisions about reinvestment and payout to provide for future growth, ensure that the overall social impact of the use of its profits will be satisfactory, and moderate social pressure against the size of its returns.[6]

For instance, it has been argued that one of the best justifications for a high rate of profits in pharmaceutical companies is an aggressive research program aimed at finding means of reducing the cost and improving the quality of medical care in all areas. While the fruits of such research might well turn out to represent new profit opportunities, the continuing flow of benefits to society as discoveries occur can tend to make the profit rate of the firm more socially acceptable. This is a slightly modified version of one of Schumpeter's concepts. Where he argued that profits go to the innovator of new products,[7] here the firm seeks the role and profit justification of socially beneficial innovation over the long run. Economically, this concept is sound; it remains to be determined whether it will prove to be at least partially acceptable to a critical society.

A firm also benefits from the prestige and publicity when part of its present or past profits are used in the public interest. Examples include the grants made by the Ford Foundation and the community facilities and services in Hershey, Pennsylvania, which have been provided by the chocolate company. A newer example is the Roche Institute of Molecular Biology, which was established by Hoffmann-LaRoche Inc. for independent research at the most fundamental levels of human medicine.[8] By investing many millions of dollars in physical facilities and in the annual operating budget necessary to maintain a top-caliber scientific staff, Roche is likely to catalyze basic discoveries toward which it and other pharmaceutical companies can direct their research efforts in hopes of finding salable products. In the meantime, however, the institute will advance fundamental research in human biology and medicine by an investment of current business profits toward the furthering of the general good.

---

[6]Here the tax laws favor the corporation, which can deduct many types of donations as business expenses, effectively permitting about twice the contribution level possible if the profits were taxed and then the donations were made by the stockholder from the corporate dividend flow.

[7]Joseph A. Schumpeter, *The Theory of Economic Development,* trans. Redvers Opie (New York: Galaxy Books, Oxford University Press, 1961), pp. 128–156.

[8]"An Unusual Research Institute," *Medical Times,* February 1972, p. 271.

In managing the use of its profits, a corporation makes one of two decisions: (1) to hold and employ the money in the business or (2) to pay it out to the stockholders. The normal pattern favors making some sort of division, except in the case of corporations with high growth and large capital requirements where dividends may be suspended entirely. In arriving at this division between profit reinvestment and payout, each part of the use of profits has a social impact that is best considered in advance.

In summary, society will ask more and more about the fate of the profits from any conspicuously successful business as time passes. While no clear-cut standards are yet available for establishing the division of these profits, it seems very desirable for a business to be able to demonstrate an adequate balance between the use of these profits and the needs of society.

Asset Reallocation

A corporation has the power to reallocate resources and redistribute expenditures. Olivetti-Underwood shifted typewriter manufacturing outside the United States, textile manufacturers moved to the South, and electronic assembly has tended to shift to the Far East. These examples illustrate corporate use of this power and profit responsibility in reallocating their resources and budgets as necessary. The power to withdraw resources invokes a responsibility for the consequences to the deprived areas. This impact is primarily at the level of the workers and the communities, as can be seen from the following illustrations.

Abandoned Communities

What follows is an excerpt from the story of a town that became obsolete and was confronted with the pain and social cost of its abandonment by the railroad. The town was a victim of a shift to new technology; as the railroad system moved to diesel engines, the savings included reduced maintenance. The town, which had been a maintenance point, was no longer needed. The social issues include the impact of new technology, but the railroad management had little real choice since it needed the improved operating economy of the diesel to have any hope of attaining profit. Balancing the social impact of such a shift is difficult at best but is a requirement for a social balance. This example illustrates one of the most challenging types of circumstances that can face a management seeking to balance its social costs.

> Caliente was built in a break in an eighty-mile canyon traversing the desert. Its reason for existence was to service the steam locomotive. There are few resources in the area to support it on any other basis, and such as they are they would contribute more to the growth and maintenance of other little settlements in the vicinity than to that of Caliente. So long as the steam locomotive was in use, Caliente was a necessity. With the adoption of the diesel it became obsolescent.
>
> This stark fact was not, however, part of the expectations of the residents of Caliente. Based upon the "certainty" of the railroad's need for Caliente, men built their homes there, frequently of concrete and brick, at the cost, in many

cases, of their life savings. The water system was laid in cast iron which will last for centuries. Business men erected substantial buildings which could be paid for only by profits gained through many years of business. Four churches evidence the faith of Caliente people in the future of their community. A twenty-seven bed hospital serves the town. Those who built it thought that their investment was as well warranted as the fact of birth, sickness, accident and death. They believed in education. Their school buildings represent the investment of savings guaranteed by bonds and future taxes. There is a combined park and play field which, together with a recently modernized theatre, has been serving recreational needs. All these physical structures are material evidence of the expectations, morally and legally sanctioned and financially funded, of the people of Caliente. This is a normal and rational aspect of the culture of all "solid" and "sound" communities.

Similarly normal are the social organizations. These include Rotary, Chamber of Commerce, Masons, Odd Fellows, American Legion and the Veterans of Foreign Wars. There are the usual unions, churches, and myriad little clubs to which the women belong. In short, here is the average American community with normal social life, subscribing to normal American codes.

Yet suddenly their life pattern was destroyed by the announcement that the railroad was moving its division point, and with it destroying the economic basis of Caliente's existence.

Division points on a railroad are established by the frequency with which the rolling stock must be serviced and the operating crews changed. At the turn of the century when this particular road was built, the engines produced wet steam at low temperatures. The steel in the boilers was of comparatively low tensile strength and could not withstand the high temperatures and pressures required for the efficient use of coal and water. At intervals of roughly a hundred miles the engine had to be disconnected from the train for service. At these points the cars also were inspected and if they were found to be defective they were either removed from the train or repaired while it was standing and the new engine being coupled on. Thus the location of Caliente, as far as the railroad was concerned, was a function of boiler temperature and pressure and the resultant service requirements of the locomotive.

Following World War II, the high tensile steels developed to create superior artillery and armor were used for locomotives. As a consequence it was possible to utilize steam at higher temperatures and pressure. Speed, power, and efficiency were increased and the distance between service intervals was increased.

The "ideal distance" between freight divisions became approximately 150 to 200 miles whereas it had formerly been 100 to 150. Wherever possible, freight divisions were increased in length to that formerly used by passenger trains, and passenger divisions were lengthened from two old freight divisions to three. Thus towns located at 100 miles from a terminal became obsolescent, those at 200 became freight points only, and those at three hundred miles became passenger division points.

The increase in speed permitted the train crews to make the greater distance in the time previously required for the lesser trip, and roughly a third of the train and engine crews, car inspectors, boilermakers and machinists and other service men were dropped. The towns thus abandoned were crossed off the social record of the nation in the adjustment to these technological changes in the use of the steam locomotive. Caliente, located midway between terminals about six hundred miles apart, survived. In fact it gained, since the less frequent stops caused an increase in the service required of the maintenance crews at those points where it took place. However, the introduction of the change to diesel engines projected a very different future.

In its demands for service the diesel engine differs almost completely from a steam locomotive. It requires infrequent, highly skilled service, carried on within very close limits, in contrast to the frequent, crude adjustments required by the steam locomotive. Diesels operate at about 35 per cent efficiency, in contrast to the approximately 4 per cent efficiency of the steam locomotives in use after World War II in the United States. Hence diesels require much less frequent stops for fuel and water. These facts reduce their operating costs sufficiently to compensate for their much higher initial cost.

In spite of these reductions in operating costs the introduction of diesels ordinarily would have taken a good deal of time. The change-over would have been slowed by the high capital costs of retooling the locomotive works, the long period required to recapture the costs of existing steam locomotives, and the effective resistance of the workers. World War II altered each of these factors. The locomotive works were required to make the change in order to provide marine engines, and the costs of the change were assumed by the government. Steam engines were used up by the tremendous demand placed upon the railroads by war traffic. The costs were recaptured by shipping charges. Labor shortages were such that labor resistance was less formidable and much less acceptable to the public than it would have been in peace time. Hence the shift to diesels was greatly facilitated by the war. In consequence, every third and sometimes every second division point suddenly became technologically obsolescent.

Caliente, like all other towns in similar plight, is supposed to accept its fate in the name of "progress." The general public, as shippers and consumers of shipped goods, reaps the harvest in better, faster service and eventually perhaps in lower charges. A few of the workers in Caliente will also share the gains, as they move to other division points, through higher wages. They will share in the higher pay, though whether this will be adequate to compensate for the costs of moving no one can say. Certain it is that their pay will not be adjusted to compensate for their specific losses. They will gain only as their seniority gives them the opportunity to work. These are those who gain. What are the losses, and who bears them?

The railroad company can figure its losses at Caliente fairly accurately. It owns 39 private dwellings, a modern clubhouse with 116 single rooms, and a twelve-room hotel with dining-room and lunch-counter facilities. These now become useless, as does much of the fixed physical equipment used for servicing trains. Some of the machinery can be used elsewhere. Some part of the roundhouse can be used to store unused locomotives and standby equipment. The rest will be torn down to save taxes. All of these costs can be entered as capital losses on the statement which the company draws up for its stockholders and for the government. Presumably they will be recovered by the use of the more efficient engines.

What are the losses that may not be entered on the company books? The total tax assessment in Caliente was $9,946.80 for the year 1948, of which $6,103.39 represented taxes assessed on the railroad. Thus the railroad valuation was about three-fifths that of the town. This does not take into account tax-free property belonging to the churches, the schools, the hospital, or the municipality itself which included all the public utilities. Some ideas of the losses sustained by the railroad in comparison with the losses of others can be surmised by reflecting on these figures for real estate alone. The story is an old one and often repeated in the economic history of America. It represents the "loss" side of a profit and loss system of adjusting to technological change. Perhaps for sociological purposes we need an answer to the question "just who pays?"

Probably the greatest losses are suffered by the older "non-operating" employees. Seniority among these men extends only within the local shop and craft. A man with twenty-five years' seniority at Caliente has no claim on the job of a similar craftsman at another point who has only twenty-five days' seniority. Moreover, some of the skills formerly valuable are no longer needed. The boilermaker, for example, knows that jobs for his kind are disappearing and he must enter the ranks of the unskilled. The protection and status offered by the union while he was employed have become meaningless now that he is no longer needed. The cost of this is high both in loss of income and in personal demoralization.

Operating employees also pay. Their seniority extends over a division, which in this case includes three division points. The older members can move from Caliente and claim another job at another point, but in many cases they move leaving a good portion of their life savings behind. The younger men must abandon their stake in railroad employment. The loss may mean a new apprenticeship in another occupation, at a time in life when apprenticeship wages are not adequate to meet the obligations of mature men with families. A steam engine hauled 2,000 tons up the hill out of Caliente with the aid of two helpers. The four-unit diesel in command of one crew handles a train of 5,000 tons alone. Thus, to handle the same amount of tonnage required only about a fourth the man-power it formerly took. Three out of four men must start out anew at something else.

The local merchants pay. The boarded windows, half-empty shelves, and abandoned store buildings bear mute evidence of these costs. The older merchants stay, and pay; the younger ones, and those with no stake in the community will move; but the value of their property will in both cases largely be gone.

The bondholders will pay. They can't foreclose on a dead town. If the town were wiped out altogether, that which would remain for salvage would be too little to satisfy their claims. Should the town continue there is little hope that taxes adequate to carry the overhead of bonds and day-to-day expenses could be secured by taxing the diminished number of property owners or employed persons.

The church will pay. The smaller congregations cannot support services as in the past. As the church men leave, the buildings will be abandoned.

Homeowners will pay. A hundred and thirty-five men owned homes in Caliente. They must accept the available means of support or rent to those who do. In either case the income available will be far less than that on which the houses were built. The least desirable homes will stand unoccupied, their value completely lost. The others must be revalued at a figure far below that at which they were formerly held.

In a word, those pay who are, by traditional American standards, *most moral.* Those who have raised children see friendships broken and neighborhoods disintegrated. The childless more freely shake the dust of Caliente from their feet. Those who built their personalities into the structure of the community watch their work destroyed. Those too wise or too selfish to have entangled themselves in community affairs suffer no such qualms. The chain store can pull down its sign, move its equipment and charge the costs off against more profitable and better located units, and against taxes. The local owner has no such alternatives. In short, "good citizens" who assumed family and community responsibility are the greatest losers. Nomads suffer least.[9]

At the end of World War II and in the midst of considerable social change, the disruptions caused by the shift to diesel locomotives received little public attention. In the intervening years social consciousness has increased. Today the real social costs inherent in the abandonment of Caliente and other similar towns would be much more likely to require some redress.

Where the railroad shift to diesels occurred long ago, a similar shift in the production of pineapples currently appears to be in progress. The *Wall Street Journal* reported the announcement by Dole and Del Monte that because of heavy losses pineapple production on the island of Molokai would be suspended, idling 17,000 acres and causing a projected 75 percent unemployment rate on that island. Both companies are shifting pineapple production to locations in the Far East and Africa, such as the Philippines and Thailand, where labor and other costs are lower. This action has brought a local outcry about the power of a multinational company to abandon one area in favor of another.

These cutbacks represent the continuation of a pattern. The year before Stokely-Van Camp closed its plantation and cannery on Kauai. Dole halved its acreage on Oahu. Altogether six companies have closed since 1950, leaving only Dole, Del Monte, and an independent company, Maui Land & Pineapple Company. Maui Land is a public company and must publish its earnings, which show that it is, at least,

---

[9]W. F. Cottrell, "Death by Dieselization: A Case Study in Reaction to Technological Change," *American Sociological Review,* June 1951, pp. 358–365.

making a profit from its pineapple operations, in contrast to the statements from the other companies.[10]

The degree to which the canning companies are forced to move is unclear. Certainly, they feel economic pressures, and a shift to cheaper production will help—but only at the expense of creating socioeconomic disruption in Hawaii. The report of political turmoil is understandable in the light of the social cost of lost employment. Whatever the economic facts, Dole and Del Monte seem to be risking political reprisals of one kind or another.

Layoffs and Transfers

A company that must cut work forces or relocate operations can have a major local impact. An example would be the seizure in 1975 of the Fairchild Camera & Instrument Corporation plant at Shiprock, New Mexico, by a group of workers. This electronic components plant has represented a major achievement through its success in giving employment to Navaho Indians. But the employment had been reduced from what was previously about 1,000 workers a year to about 650, mainly by attrition. The layoff of an additional 150 workers triggered the seizure. The very factors that had made the installation such a widely heralded achievement, including the poverty of the area and the absence of other employment, made the work force reduction unusually painful. Fairchild, with corporationwide profit stringencies, was unable at that time to maintain the implicit commitment to provide continued employment in its Shiprock plant.[11]

On the other hand, IBM prides itself on its program for retraining and reassigning employees to avoid layoffs. In thirty-five years the company reported that it has never laid off a worker for economic reasons. Between 1970 and 1975 5,000 employees were retrained and relocated. The benefits to IBM include a greater flexibility in making assignments that comes from being able to offer greater security.[12]

When AT&T planned its headquarters relocation recently, it offered substantial incentives to its employees to relocate with it. This dimension of the maintenance of opportunity is also motivated by the corporate need to keep the skills of the group and its employee investment intact. AT&T designed a package of benefits aimed at easing almost every aspect of the relocation from downtown New York to suburban Basking Ridge, New Jersey. Included in the package were moving costs, aid in buying a new home and selling the old one, and advice from consultants retained to help employees understand the local housing market.[13]

In the case of Fairchild Camera, the need to cut back has hurt a community and a program of which Fairchild has been justly proud. IBM has managed better through its broad program to prevent layoffs through reassignment and retraining. Note,

---

[10]Herbert G. Lawson, "The Pineapple Industry in Hawaii Sours; Dole, Del Monte Assailed for Cutbacks," *Wall Street Journal,* 11 April 1974.

[11]"Navajos Seize Plant of Fairchild Camera at Shiprock, N. Mex.," *Wall Street Journal,* 25 February 1975.

[12]"How IBM Avoids Layoffs through Retraining," *Business Week,* 10 November 1975, pp. 110, 112.

[13]Joan Marks, "When Ma Bell Moves, She is Gentle," *New York Times,* 15 September 1974.

however, that this alternative is only possible because IBM's size and overall growth provide a substantial base for the retraining and absorption of relatively large numbers of workers.

Beyond retraining is the hardship caused when work is moved from site to site. AT&T is attempting to compensate for many of the specific cost elements in this dislocation as it shifts headquarters personnel from Manhattan to suburban New Jersey. This compensation is expensive, but it is fair and also necessary in order to induce most of the staff to move with the company. American Can followed a similar pattern in its move to Connecticut, as described in Chapter 2.

Renewal

The Ames Company is an example of a company that has maintained continuity and some growth in spite of ups and downs over its two-hundred-year history. Ames grew from a small New England shovel producer to a nationally distributed manufacturer that has the world's largest shovel factory. Founded by a colonial blacksmith in Bridgewater, Massachusetts, the company was moved to Easton, Massachusetts, by his son. After a century of expansion in Easton and elsewhere, Ames began to encounter competition. Then during the Depression many of the shovel manufacturers failed. To survive, Ames acquired several other manufacturers and moved its operations to Parkersburg, West Virginia, where it operates today.[14]

The two important elements in this story are the success of the Ames Company in surviving and thus in providing employment for its people and the fact that under economic pressure it was forced to close its home plant and consolidate its operations in West Virginia. Therefore, although the operation remained active, it did not provide continuity in Easton, Massachusetts, which was its location during its previous growth period.

Summary

For a business to assess the social impact of its resource policies, it needs to look at a number of different areas. These include:

1. Any actions that change the degree of use of community capital by the business or the contribution of the business toward the cost of this capital

2. Any actions that affect the integrity and long-term viability of the business and its ability to provide continuing opportunities for employment and growth to its employees and the dependent community

3. Any impacts that result from the policies by which it allocates its profits to new investments versus payment of dividends

4. Any impacts that result from the shifts in jobs and opportunities as it reallocates its resources from one element of the business to another

---

[14]Leonard Sloane, "Ames Prospers as it Marks 200 Years," *New York Times,* 20 April 1974.

5. Any actions that affect the various franchises the corporation may have developed in the marketplace

This list, which could be further extended, is summarized in Figure 14.1 and includes most major corporate actions.

We can conclude that most major corporate actions have some social impact in that most represent current or potential shifts in resources that could affect the equilibrium between business and the surrounding society. As society changes, as markets change, and as a business goes through stages of development, corporate management must review its investment and reinvestment plans and reallocate its resources appropriately. This review and reallocation is essential to the health and survival of the firm.

As management reallocates corporate resources, it has impacts on society, which are often considerable. Balancing these impacts is necessary to avoid social costs. As a result, the level of opportunity the firm offers to employees and the dependent community must be maintained (even after resource shifts to other areas or other lines of business have occurred), actual and implied franchises to serve the public must be maintained, and profits must be used in ways that the surrounding society considers to be suitable.

This is an awesome responsibility that is not always sustainable by the corporation, even given the best efforts and intentions. And the standards to which a business should work are not well defined or comfortable, particularly in the area of profit flows. However, in this area as in others, disregarding the corporate impact and social consequences involves the risk of a serious confrontation with society.

This chapter has presented examples of the profound social disruption that occurs when a town is abandoned by its only employer, when work is shifted to another area, or when layoffs that may only be temporary are imposed. Similarly, corporate decisions on use of profits and management of its assets as it operates are being questioned.

To survive, business must make a profit; to ensure its long-term viability, it must maintain its stock of capital; to provide opportunities for its people and ease the burden of maintaining a good balance with the community, it should grow. The fulfillment of these needs solves many problems including maintenance of a satisfactory corporate impact. However, when operations must be closed and resources withdrawn, the balancing of the adverse corporate social impact becomes both more difficult and urgent to accomplish.

Figure 14.1 Social Impact of Business Resource Policies

Maintenance of capital	Use of profits
Maintenance of opportunity	Asset reallocation
Business survival	Layoffs
Business growth	Transfers
	New investments

Business resources are society's productive assets. The policies governing employment of these assets have profound social impact.

Guidelines for Managing Corporate Social Impact

In managing the social impact of business resource policies, social balance will tend to be maintained if the following guidelines are applied:

Maintenance of capital A business operates to conserve and expand its resources in order to maintain and increase the level of opportunity in its own interests and in the interests of both its employees and the dependent community.

Use of profits A business handles its profits in such a way as to minimize the economic, social, and political impact of their use, particularly the impact from any movement of profits from the business to a parent corporation or the stockholders.

Alternatives to severance When evolution of the business creates a surplus of plants, people, or community services, the firm makes a serious effort to find alternative, profitable uses for these dependent resources or, at least, to cushion the severance so that the long-term economic health of former members of the organization and the health of the community will be preserved.

Applying the Guidelines

Maintenance of capital As a firm operates, the management should, to conform to this guideline, keep aware of the trend in economic value of the asset base on which the firm depends (rather than the book value or replacement cost). If the economic value of this base is maintained and increased, the present and future viability of the enterprise is likely to be sustained, as is the source of both future career opportunities for the firm's members and employment opportunities for the dependent community. In contrast, some U.S. steel companies have not succeeded in maintaining the economic value of the asset base underlying their businesses, as new technology in the hands of others has made plants less and less competitive. Resulting shutdowns by Youngstown Steel and Bethlehem Steel, among others, have had an extremely adverse corporate social impact on the dependent communities.

Use of profits A given management may allocate a part of its cash flow to debt repayment and current business needs, another part to capital projects, and yet another portion to business research and expansion. Normally, these uses would not develop into sensitive issues, but those that might have possible social impacts, such as the choice of a controversial plant location, should be considered carefully. Other uses, such as the shifting of profits between companies and currency areas, often do have an impact. This impact may sometimes be cushioned by simple timing of the flow of funds or instead may necessitate the purchase or production of some product that can be exported and sold elsewhere without disturbing national currency balances.

Such a roundabout approach adds an extra management task but may be desirable where currency movements are closely controlled.

Alternatives to severance General Foods attempted to cushion the adjustment when it closed two obsolete Jell-O plants. The choice of duPont was to build a new plant for a new process and retrain the employees to use a community labor force that would otherwise have been idled as duPont closed an obsolete plant. (See Chapter 13 for the discussion of these two cases.) Other companies have established placement programs to aid in smooth transition of the terminated employees to new jobs. Most acts of termination and severance cause pain. In the course of managing a business, such acts are sometimes necessary. However, all sound alternatives that might lessen the adverse corporate social impact should first be examined so that undeserved severance is avoided or at least its impact reduced. Then any feasible alternatives should be put into effect wherever corporate resources permit.

Questions for Analysis and Discussion

1. List some examples of (a) business use of community capital and (b) community use of capital investments provided by private corporations.

2. Look for examples of businesses that have diversified to maintain their level of opportunity and businesses that have dissipated their capital by their failure to expand or diversify.

3. Suggest other examples where corporate reinvestment of profit is beneficial to society in the long run.

4. Find examples of both local benefit and local injury from shifts in corporate resources. How could the injuries have been minimized?

5. Give examples of corporate franchises developed by success in the marketplace. What types of franchise maintenance activities does such a position require to maintain a social balance?

For Further Information

Ansoff, Igor. *Corporate Strategy.* New York: McGraw-Hill, 1965.

Galbraith, John Kenneth. *The Affluent Society.* Boston: Houghton Mifflin, 1958.

Madden, Carl. *Clash of Culture: Management in an Age of Changing Values.* Washington D.C.: National Planning Association, 1972.

Reilly, William K., ed. *The Use of Land.* New York: Crowell, 1973.

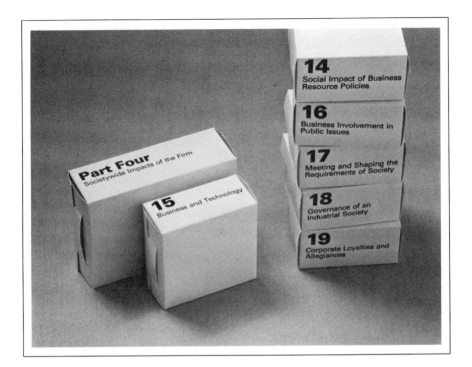

15
Business and Technology

Modern industrial society has reached a point where its hopes not only for
progress but also for survival are dependent on, among other things, advances in applied technology. This technology must be more wisely applied
than it has been in the past to avoid destruction of world ecology. The foundation for the necessary innovations is a technological pool of information
formed by advances in scientific knowledge not yet fully applied. This pool
stimulates the innovation process in those organizations dependent on continuing generation of a flow of new products and services. The pool will
need to be replenished through further advances in scientific knowledge if
innovation is to continue in the long run.

Since new technology can have profound impacts on society, the issues
of technology assessment and technology control have arisen. The impact of
new investment of resources and new innovations in goods and services is
the domain of technology assessment. This assessment is a useful new
planning tool that also could become dangerous in promoting restrictions on
new technology. Yet on some issues urgent to public safety an attempt at
technology control seems necessary.

Halting technological growth is not the answer to the problems of urban decay, education, health, and so on; we need more of the right kinds of technology. . . . *if we condemn the technologist we should also attempt to guide him.*[1]

HAROLD S. BECKER

We live in an industrial society made possible by its technology. Our standard of living is based on consumption of the wealth that is manufactured each year; almost nothing is used without manufacturing or processing. Nor do we have a choice; without modern technology, we could not feed or clothe ourselves. The Earth could support only a fraction of its present population without the technical developments that have occurred since the Industrial Revolution.

The Need for New Technology

The many ills and strains in modern society urgently require action and redress, but in many cases more new technology is required—to purify toxic wastes, make refuse biodegradable, reduce wastage of energy and scarce resources, and deal with the myriad of other technical problems society faces.

In a society that is founded on a rapidly evolving scientific base and in which the urgency of social and environmental change involves a continuing need for invention and use of new technology, each individual business firm's position and role in this wave of change become a matter for proper and necessary concern. In the first place, the concept of a wave of change is apt, in that an innovation is swept across an industry by the pressures of the moment. The early tentative part of the conception and adoption process is often slow until competitive pressures begin to favor the new development. While the germination and diffusion of the innovation that diesel locomotives represented proceeded slowly, a point in time was reached at the end of World War II where U.S. railroads needed to adopt diesels rapidly in hopes of improving the economics of their lagging transportation systems. Episodes such as the abandonment of Caliente (see Chapter 14) were not completely under the control of individual railroad managements in the face of the general pressure to improve railroad costs.

---

[1]Harold S. Becker, "Technology Assessment: Another View," *Business Horizons,* October 1973, pp. 58–60.

The Pool of Technology: Potential for Innovation

Any business has a need for new things to sell—whether new products or services. One of the ways of obtaining new products and services is by inventing them. All across industry this process of invention occurs spontaneously, but in many of the larger firms and particularly in industries where the invention process has great strategic importance, separate research departments are formed to organize the process and harness its ability to produce innovations that may make possible new products and services.

New products and services arise as the result of a need, on one hand, and a potential for development, on the other; the need is defined by the future customer, and the potential is to generate the necessary innovation that may serve to fill that need. However, a consideration of the process of organized innovation involves determining what it is that makes innovation possible and rediscovering the need for

The Firm as Viewed by Society

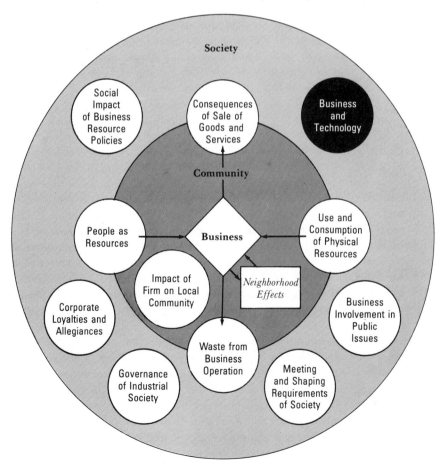

a basic source of technology on which the innovation process can draw. In other words, the frontiers of scientific knowledge must have moved far enough to define a theoretical foundation that permits the formulation of an applications hypothesis as the basis for an innovation process.

Thus, the innovation process depends, in part, on the existence of an adequate pool of technology in each appropriate area, where this pool consists of theories and concepts that have not yet emerged in the form of specific inventions. Underlying the innovation processes is an accumulation of scientific knowledge that has not been applied to its fullest extent and, thus, determines the innovation potential of the society at any given time. Since many draw from such a pool of technology, it must be replenished to maintain the potential for a systematic application of innovation processes. As advances in scientific knowledge are made, the pool is increased; as the potential range of innovations within the existing body of knowledge is explored and developed, the pool is decreased.

The individual firm's role as it relates to the evolution and application of society's technology resources can be divided into three elements. The first is the competitive response necessary to keep current with the technology applied by competitors, the second is the social impact on society of the new technology that is adopted, and the third is the innovation effort in that firm as it develops new applications from, or returns new knowledge to, the underlying pool of technology supplying the needs of society as a whole. The first and second elements tend to merge with the other corporate actions that have impacts on specific sectors of society (for example, consumers, employees, and the community) and are largely treated with the other issues affecting these sectors in the preceding and following chapters.

This chapter focuses on the third element, the relationship of the innovation processes of the individual firm to the underlying pool of technology on which society is drawing at a given time. That such a pool exists is useful information; technology can be created, used, and replaced. Since management can make decisions that affect this process of creating, using, and replacing technology, society has reason to ask about the consequences of these decisions. Thus, this area of corporate impact may require management.

Of course, some firms do not need to innovate at a level that draws on new knowledge or presses on technological frontiers. Yet elements of many businesses are dependent on technical advances. From the electronic check-out systems being designed for supermarkets to the new digital watches and pocket calculators, the availability of and the need for new technology pervade our society. All firms need to understand their relationship to the new technology frontiers, even though only a few firms are actively involved in expanding technological horizons.

Technology is a result of the basic scientific processes of conceptualization and discovery. Each fundamental advance in basic knowledge makes possible later development of that knowledge into specific applications that may be developed as useful processes and products or even weapons. For example, after the basic conceptualization of the nature of the forces binding the atomic nucleus, knowledge evolved and applications were conceived. The atomic bomb became a viable concept and the Manhattan project was born. Later came the concept of atomic power, but this led only to fission power plants.

Safer and cheaper power from hydrogen fusion will undoubtedly come but will require another basic scientific advance in the techniques for containment of the plasma of hot gases in a fusion reaction. Containment is necessary to maintain stable reaction conditions (including the necessary pressures) at the incredible temperatures of a hydrogen reaction. Since normal types of refractory materials would be vaporized, an entirely new approach must be formulated. The contributions of Einstein and others to the pool of technology were sufficient to permit development of weapons and fission power but have had to be supplemented with new basic knowledge in the practical development of fusion power.

As another example, consider the advancement of knowledge about electronic microcircuits and information storage devices that has been stimulated by the progress in the aerospace program. These advances make possible a myriad of applications of minicomputers and microcomputers in our daily lives, of which the evolution of the pocket calculators is only a humble beginning. The number of applications of this group of innovations is large but finite; eventually the potential for communication and calculation devices and so-called intelligent machines would be exhausted and innovations of such products would decrease if concurrent new advances in fundamental knowledge were not also taking place.

This gap between fundamental knowledge and the actual applications that can be conceived from it represents the pool of technology available to society at a given time. One of the issues over the activities of a given firm is whether it is acting in such a way as to have impact on this pool and, if it is, whether it is adding to or subtracting from the reservoir of technology available for the further application to the needs of society at a given time. First, this area will be examined, and then a consideration of the assessment procedures now being used tentatively to gauge the impact of new developments will be undertaken.

Innovation and Technology Consumption

By definition, technology is generated as a result of the research and development (R&D) process. However, many kinds and levels of R&D may be involved that range from the purely accidental individual effort to truly fundamental basic research. In addition, there are application and formulation efforts involved, for instance, in the production of new cosmetic products, where the focus of the effort is rapid and ingenious application of known technology and where it is unusual for any fundamentally new technology to be required. These business efforts do not deplete society's pool of technology to any significant extent, are unlikely to contribute new knowledge to it, and really do not have an impact on this technology in the course of their operation.

Among high-technology industries that have considerable interest in the maintenance of an adequate underlying pool of technology are pharmaceuticals and electronics. Wonder drugs of the 1940s and 1950s came from new knowledge of chemotherapy coupled with an awareness of microbial antibiotics as a fruitful source of therapeutically active new molecular structures. Then the number of important new products began to diminish, and the research investment for each new product began to increase exponentially beyond the extent that growth of regulation and bureaucracy could explain. The pattern is one that could parallel the exhaustion of that particular vein of technology. And industry R&D has tended to shift in search of promising new concepts for other new generations of products, with some early indications that these new areas will be found.

The electronics industry has had the impetus of the original semiconductor discovery at Bell Laboratories reinforced by both the military R&D expenditures for World War II, Korean War, and Vietnam War needs and the thrust of the aerospace effort. Technology exceeded the civilian and industrial ability to find applications, creating a base for developing large numbers of new products. Here the industry problem will come only later, if the flow of public R&D funds is not renewed. The need and self-interest of the industry will then require a sufficient investment in the generation of new technology to permit the forward momentum of new product growth and development to continue.

A corporation that is well known for successful innovation of new products is Minnesota Mining & Manufacturing, which encourages members of its organization to go into the laboratory, develop a new idea into a product, and then organize a new part of the company to produce and market it. Scotch Tape is only one example of the family of products that have resulted.[2]

The type of innovation for which 3M is known is a most imaginative and ingenious application of technology related to its families of products. It clearly draws on the current technological reservoir. Available information does not confirm whether or not 3M is also investing in one way or another in the kind of basic work that will replenish this pool. There is no requirement for this, except self-interest in assuring a continuing basis for growth through new products.

Technology Generation

In cases where innovations of a fundamental technical nature are important to the continuing success of an industry, some replenishment of the basic technological reservoir seems to be both appropriate and in line with the self-interest of the larger and more future-oriented firms. For instance, Bell Laboratories has made significant contributions to basic knowledge and, specifically, to the electronics industry, in addition to its supportive R&D role in the Western Electric and Bell Telephone systems. The Roche Institute of Molecular Biology also represents an equally fundamental endeavor created to explore critical technical areas in the field of human health. While a specific social balance is somewhat difficult to calculate, the requisite criteria for corporate impact analysis do exist, and basic research does make a social contribution.

The suggestion here is that industries dependent on R&D are likely to find that both social balance and their own self-interest call for a long-term program to at least replenish the primary stocks of technology on which their innovation processes must draw. The means of accomplishing this replenishment can suit the circumstances, and examples that come to mind include the funding of research in academic

---

[2]"How Ideas are Made into Products at 3M," *Business Week*, 15 September 1973, pp. 224, 226–227.

centers, joint R&D programs in cooperation with an appropriate governmental branch, basic corporate research departments, or business-supported fundamental research centers. These options involve different levels of funding and levels of control. The normal expression of corporate self-interest is to seek control over any discoveries that result from the research, unless it seems that a lesser degree of control will make the work either significantly less expensive or more fruitful that self-interest calls for a greater degree of openness.

Social Consequences of Discovery

If we consider innovation as an organized process based on the application of technology, then we find that the possibility of organizing the process suggests a degree of research management control over the outcome. Along with the possibility of controlling the outcome comes a responsibility for the long-term social impact of the discovery that results from this innovation process. Where discoveries have fundamental long-term social impacts (as did the telephone, automobile, or television), the ability even to attempt a research program aimed at such discovery implies a responsibility for the consequences to society when this discovery is introduced to the total social community.

The Edison electric light, the Bell telephone, the automobile, the television—each has brought profound changes in the national way of life that have had both good and bad impacts. Society has required neither individual inventors nor corporations to anticipate the nature of the social changes that will be precipitated by new inventions or products. Even though the possible need for limiting the rate of innovation has been discussed, it is not yet clear whether social science has advanced to the point where the impact of product and service innovations is predictable with certainty, even if society wishes to require it.

Many dramatic new discoveries remain to be made, and ambitious projects currently underway include plans for drilling for oil in the arctic oceans, systems for harvesting minerals from the ocean floor, plans for tapping oil shale and oil sands, geothermal power, weather control, and even airfoils to keep the inexperienced skiers from crossing their ski tips at high speeds. An amazing range of potential developments are under consideration and investigation; some are serious and feasible, and others will fail as being impractical or ill-conceived. This churning at the frontiers of applied technology, with its pain, failures and occasional dramatic successes, is the process by which our society has advanced its frontiers of applied technology and opened one new area after another.

Technology Assessment

Even though the prediction of social impacts of a particular discovery is a difficult process, and one for which the existence of specific criteria is at best uncertain, the temper of our society is turning more and more toward requiring that an effort to predict these impacts be made. Representative Emanuel Daddario is widely credited with coining the term *technology assessment*, bringing it to public attention through a series of hearings, and obtaining legislation creating an Office of Technology

Assessment that is intended to watch over the public interest in new technology impact areas.[3]

Also, among its other provisions, the National Environmental Policy Act of 1969 requires an environmental impact statement in advance of the approval of many different kinds of projects, including any major administrative action of any federal agency. Inevitably, these impact statements will evolve into a considerable assessment of the social impact, including that of existing and new technology. The Department of Commerce has created its own Office of Technology Assessment, which is focusing more on the problems of obtaining technology transfer (that is, of obtaining commercial application of available technology developed in other countries or other sectors of the economy[4]). In addition, the concept of technology assessment has spread rapidly to other sectors and has been fostered by technical and consulting groups that see its applicability and perhaps its profit potential. Books are being written on technology assessment, a society has been formed, and national and international conferences on technology assessment techniques are becoming commonplace.

All of this activity reflects a sense of need and yet there is much doubt over the validity of the basic tools. Drucker, for example, has attacked the technology assessment concept as dangerous because it attempts something that cannot be done and must inevitably lead to false conclusions and false judgment about future actions.[5] Concerns such as this are well founded but are unlikely to check the growth of the technology assessment movement.

Social change and the social consequences of discoveries have a subtlety and a pervasiveness, particularly as the higher-level consequences of a discovery unfold and as subsequent second- and third-level inventions emerge as the result of the problems and opportunities caused by the social impacts of the first discovery. It was said earlier that the social adjustment to the invention of the automobile is still far from complete. How could a technology assessment of the automobile have been done in 1900? It is clear that such an assessment could not have dealt with the increased social mobility, the impact of the interstate highways, or the toxicity of tetraethyl lead and other gasoline additives. This would have required a foreknowledge of the scope of the many additional discoveries that flowed from the first invention, as well as an understanding of the changes in social forces and lifestyles that have resulted from the new technology.

And yet a definitive technology assessment could not have been made without considering the interrelationship with other independent inventions. The impact of the automobile as a discovery has interacted extensively with that of the radio and television and with the changes brought by the rising standard of living as the Industrial Revolution has matured in the United States. Technology assessment can usefully consider the range of impacts and dislocations resulting from any given

---

[3]Francois Hetman, "Steps in Technology Assessment," *International Social Science Journal* 15, no. 3, (1973): 261.

[4]Office of Technology Assessment and Forecast, *Technology Assessment and Forecast* (Washington D.C.: Department of Commerce, 1973).

[5]*New York Times,* 8 April 1973.

development and should be carried as far as possible into the anticipation of secondary impacts and interactions with other inventions. However, the assessment must become more speculative and less definitive as the complexity of the problem expands.

A Planning Tool

Technology assessment is an exciting new discipline whose failure (in terms of any requirement for comprehensive and accurate predictions) can be forecast with confidence and yet whose steady growth seems equally predictable. Technology assessment deals with a part of the general planning problem, which continually requires forecasts of the future in the face of the fact that the future is eternally unknowable and unpredictable. Like other future predictions however, technology assessment can, if developed with a realistic awareness of its limitations, contribute usefully to the planning process in both corporations and the public sector. It can define the major possible alternatives for the future, estimate the probabilities of their occurrence, and delineate the factors potentially influencing the emergence of one rather than another. Thus, an appropriate role for technology assessment is to predict possible alternative levels of impact from any new discovery as part of the planning process.

When Monsanto developed a promising new plastic beverage bottle, the environmental and resource considerations related to its adoption and use were recognized. As part of the evaluation and introduction of the bottle, a technology assessment was performed and published, from which we include some excerpts:

> In the early 1960's, Monsanto decided to direct its technical efforts to developing a beverage container with the aesthetics and transparency of glass, but lighter and with better break and shatter resistance. . . . by 1969, sufficient progress had been made to justify a small market test with a methacrylonitrile/styrene beverage bottle, tradenamed Lopac.
>
> Concurrent with development of the technical program was the realization that the successful introduction of a polymeric beverage container, because of the numbers involved and the novelty, would have many societal and environmental impacts that required quantification. In contrast to the quantifiable performance specifications and the competitive economic calculations, societal and environmental constraints are generally qualitative—depending as they do on attitudes and value judgments which may not even exist until after the fact. What would be the reaction to a beverage container that floats rather than sinks in water? Would the discarded containers be more or less objectionable than glass or paper cups in a sports stadium? Is it better to plan to recycle these lightweight containers or to dispose of them by burning or land fill?
>
> The total environmental pollution impact from the manufacture of one million 10-oz Lopac bottles is shown in Table 3. . . . For comparison, similar data are given for aluminum or steel cans and nonreturnable glass bottles. In

Table 3. Environmental Pollution Impact per 10 Million Oz Contained

(In 12-oz cans or 10-oz one-way bottles)

	Aluminum can	Steel can w/Al top	Glass bottle w/Al cap	Lopac bottle w/Al cap
Air pollutants, lb	20,500	11,500	17,500	14,500
Water pollutants, lb	8,500	4,400	101,500	3,500
Industrial solid wastes, lb	114,000	54,000	7,000	7,600

each instance the evaluation began at the raw material source—the wellhead for Lopac and the mine for the others.

The production of aluminum cans results in the greatest quantity of air pollutants, with steel cans least. Glass and Lopac bottles are intermediate.

Production of glass bottles results in an order of magnitude increase in water pollutants over the other beverage container materials. In this instance, Lopac produces the least pollution load. In total solid waste, aluminum and steel are the major sources, aluminum producing twice as much as steel with glass and Lopac one seventh that of steel.

The energy consumed in producing a single Lopac, nonreturnable glass, steel, or aluminum container is shown in Figure 1. . . . These data show Lopac, glass, and steel containers as being essentially equal in their energy consumption while the aluminum can requires approximately twice as much energy as the other three materials. (It should be pointed out that the energy consumed in producing aluminum cans would be significantly reduced if it reflected the recycle rate now being achieved by the industry.) However, 800 of the Btu's required to make a 10-oz. Lopac container are recoverable. The emergence of systems to burn or pyrolyze solid wastes offer a practical means to recover much of the energy of combustible materials such as Lopac. Figure

Figure 1. Energy Consumed Through Manufacture of Container

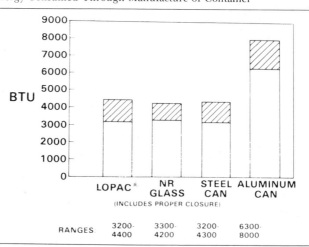

Figure 2. Energy Consumed with Credit for Recoverable Energy

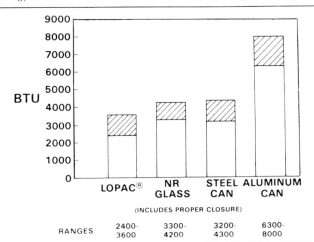

| RANGES | 2400-3600 | 3300-4200 | 3200-4300 | 6300-8000 |

2 shows the net energy demand of various beverage containers when credit is taken for recoverable energy of combustion. With this credit, Lopac is clearly the most frugal consumer of energy.

Lopac containers were added to the fuel load of a municipal incinerator at levels up to 4% and the effect on air emissions and incinerator operation was determined. Levels of Lopac containers up to 8% were burned in a package incinerator (the apartment house, institution type), under normal and overload conditions with stack gas analyzed, smoke density and particulate count noted, effect on operation recorded, and residual ash leached and the leachate analyzed.

In a properly operated incinerator, the material is almost completely consumed—stack gas composition is essentially unaffected. Under poor operating conditions, large quantities—8%—in the feed can cause an increase in smoke density. However, some gaseous emissions, such as hydrocarbons, are significantly reduced.

The cause of resource conservation is furthered by recycling materials. The Lopac container was developed as a recyclable product with significant energy savings, as shown in Figure 3. The Lopac bottle requires the least energy to recycle of any of the materials—700 Btu per 10-oz container as compared with up to 2900 Btu for a comparable glass bottle.

Since all containers will not be recycled, consideration was given to the problem of disposal. To begin with, the Lopac container is only slightly heavier than an aluminum can, 30 grams for a 12-oz Lopac bottle vs. 21 grams for a 12-oz aluminum can. A comparable steel can weighs 51 grams, and a glass nonreturnable bottle about 250 grams. Obviously, replacement of any of these materials, except aluminum, by Lopac containers will reduce the burden on the solid waste stream.

Figure 3.   Recyclability, Energy Needed to Produce Recycled Container

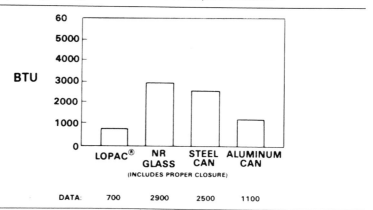

. . . Results show the Lopac container to be highly resistant to degradation, a resistance unaffected by the presence of known uv activators. In a high-microbial populated compost pile, after 116 days Lopac container material showed no signs of attack. Induced degradation was considered and rejected as a desirable objective, primarily because it would result in a permanent loss of a valuable material, degradation products that have unknown environmental and ecological effects, and a container with little or no potential for recycling.

The studies show that neither land, water, nor air pollution is increased appreciably in disposing of Lopac containers.

There is no reason to expect Lopac containers will cause an increase in the amount of litter. However, if a Lopac bottle is discarded, there will be less risk of injury to people and property, as will be discussed later.

When Lopac bottles do fragment, the edges usually are feathered and not of sufficient rigidity to cut—they bend instead. The rare, pointed, Lopac bottle fragment is less hazardous than sharp metal or glass fragments.

The effects of accidental or intentional misuse of Lopac containers was investigated. Conceivably, they might be used to fuel a fire over which food is cooked. Rats fed hamburger so cooked for four weeks showed no ill effects. Humans should be able to tolerate an occasional hamburger or hot dog cooked over a fire containing Lopac bottles.

Studies were conducted to quantify the nature and quantity of gases produced by burning or pyrolyzing Lopac containers under a variety of misuse conditions. Tests simulating campfire or fireplace burning of Lopac containers showed that to be endangered, one literally would have to stick one's head in the plume and hold it there for periods ranging to over an hour. Only if quantities of Lopac bottles are burned or pyrolyzed in a sealed room is there a reasonable expectation of harm. Animal inhalation studies, further to quantify this risk and to compare it with common household materials with historical broad exposure to burning accidents, are under way.

> While it is unlikely that anyone would eat the bottle, 10% of the ground
> material in the diet of rats for 90 days was harmless.[6]

The assessment of the Lopac container serves to illustrate additional dimensions of a problem involving tradeoffs among objective considerations, such as cost and energy consumption, and subjective considerations, such as litter in parks and damage or subsidy to various classes of business. Since alternative approaches exist to litter control and certain of the other considerations, the total problem is extremely complex and involves public policy issues likely to be under discussion for many years.

Monsanto's container program has moved forward since the technology assessment, with its family of plastic bottle products finding applications, particularly for larger soft drink bottles where the difference in weight is noticeable to the consumer. Unfortunately for Monsanto, the FDA has since decided that the technology assessment did not go far enough in exploring possible toxicity. Feeding studies with relatively high levels of the monomer from which the plastic bottles are made caused weight loss in rats. The approval of the bottles that had been granted was withdrawn, effective as of March 11, 1977, and Monsanto suspended production at three plants. Its customers have announced conversion to other materials. Because of disagreement with the FDA interpretation of the toxicity data, Monsanto set in motion legal procedures for contesting the decision in the courts, although this is likely to be a lengthy procedure, even if it should ultimately meet with success.

A Control Device

One consequence of the widespread use of aerosol spray products is the release of large quantities of fluorocarbon propellants into the atmosphere. This has caused great concern because of potential injury to the ozone layer, as discussed in Chapter 9. The injury to the ozone layer has not yet occurred, or at least not to the extent that various scientists agree that a significant change has occurred.

Thus, the moves toward restriction of this use of fluorocarbons are a pioneering application of technology assessment. They represent a social judgment that the possibility of damage to the ozone layer is large enough so that regulatory action is required. This effort is an early example of the use of a technology assessment for purposes of control.

Such social judgments are undesirable because of the fallibility of the available assessment processes. But they are increasingly necessary because of the profound potential consequences if system-level environmental damage were allowed to proceed to a measurable extent. Unfortunately, the need for such judgments is increasing, as science begins to understand at least partially the potential impact of new industrial materials on environmental systems.

It has been suggested that a public control mechanism is needed—that someone

---

[6]F. D. Wharton, Jr. and J. Kenneth Craver, "Technology Assessment in Product Development; A Case History." Reprinted from *ChemTech*, vol. 5, no. 9, September 1975, pp. 547–551. Copyright © 1975 by the American Chemical Society and reprinted by permission of the copyright owner.

should monitor new inventions such as the fluorocarbon products and prevent their introduction if the benefit to society will not be sufficient to justify the disruption. This dangerous concept has caused the opponents of technology assessment to attack it so forcefully. Given that the future cannot be predicted and that most technology assessments in the next few years are likely to be wrong in degree if not direction of impact, the consequences of an attempt to use this interesting tool as a social control mechanism are very disturbing. They immediately raise visions of Big Brother and 1984.

Regrettably, the evolution of the system of environmental impact statements required under a legislative charter dealing with the health and welfare of the nation will undoubtedly lead to some effort to use technology assessment for control of discovery, or at least for control over individual projects embodying new technologies and any new uses of old technologies that are of sufficient magnitude to require impact statements. This trend justifies the concerns that have been expressed about the procedure, and its evolution must be watched with care.

Recombinant DNA, a product of genetic research in which genetic material from different species is separated and recombined, was immediately identified as a research area where careless or unfortunate experiments could create and liberate deadly new diseases and life forms. The concern of the scientific community was communicated to the National Institute of Health, which entered the discussion and fostered the creation of a set of research guidelines that were then endorsed as a control mechanism for this type of research. Several community groups have also insisted on local guidelines. This was a case of almost spontaneous technology assessment leading to a control not yet completely tested but with hopeful indications of potential effectiveness.

In cases like those of the fluorocarbons and recombinant DNA, control over new technology seems mandatory in spite of the imperfections of the control concepts. The urgent effort should be to restrict such controls to cases of similar magnitude where a worldwide survival issue exists.

Summary

Technology assessment is a tool that appears to have significant value and the potential for becoming part of the national scene over the foreseeable future. As it matures, it will take its place among the tools for gauging corporate social impact that were discussed in Part Two. Therefore many must learn to use this tool, whether their intent is to aid its development or rebut its analyses. As a tool, it will be interrelated with the general process of assessing the rights and responsibilities of discovery for business firms and with any attempts to assess the social balance that a particular firm may have in the area of generation and use of technology.

The underlying concept of such a balance is clear: A firm may be expected to contribute to the evolution of new technology through direct or indirect support at about the same rate that it is drawing from the existing stock of technology in its development efforts. This requirement is really more a statement of business or industrial self-interest than a social dictum that will be imposed on the business community. In fact, of the various social balance areas that have been discussed, this one seems to be farthest from applying any direct pressure on the business for performance.

A much more pressing and growing issue will be the public question about the responsibilities for the consequences of discovery. In its potential role as a social control mechanism, technology assessment could threaten the right of introducing new discoveries into society, which entrepreneurial opportunity and improvements in the standard of living have depended on to a significant degree. The extent to which society may press for control over this right depends to a large extent on the perceived consequences of these new discoveries.

The general maxim introduced earlier suggests that manufacturers must have a concern over any outcome that their decision-making authority permits them to influence. In this area the consequence of a new application of technology could have a very significant impact on society. This social balance area is difficult because it is so hard to anticipate such impacts fully.

If the right of introducing new technologies is not exercised responsibly in the eyes of the public or if bad experiences with new products cause the public to react unfavorably, intervention through public technology control processes becomes increasingly likely. An example is provided by the case cited earlier involving the thalidomide disaster, where a good drug embodying new tranquilizer mechanisms turned out to cause profound damage to unborn children, as an incidental side effect. The consequences of the social concern over the thalidomide disaster had a powerful effect on the regulatory controls over new drugs that were extended above and beyond those required by the incident itself. In the same way, Chapter 12 described how the environmental contamination caused by PCBs was credited with precipitating the passage of the Toxic Chemicals Act, even though a program for phasing out PCBs was achieved by voluntary action. Similar sequences of indignation followed by new regulation are likely if the public is touched by major disasters resulting from unanticipated side effects of a product or from some other failure to assess in advance the impact of new technology in other sectors of the economy.

Thus, it becomes increasingly important that a social balance be maintained and that manufacturers attempt to anticipate at least the direct consequences of both new technology and new applications of existing technology. Then their product and market planning will reflect the degree of responsible consideration of the public interest necessary to maintain business's freedom to introduce new products and technology in the future. Figure 15.1 summarizes some of these considerations.

This chapter has dealt with technology as an underlying force that is a part not only of the social capital of society but also of the resources fundamental to industrial innovation processes. As with the use of any other resource, the need for a social balance exists. Here, however, the impact of innovations based on this technology could be profound, and concern over this potential has led to the development of technology assessment as a useful planning tool. This technique can also be used as a control tool in spite of its inherent limitations, although the control aspect should be limited to use in cases where urgent public safety issues could result from unwise applications of technology.

Figure 15.1   Business and Technology

New technology	Technology assessment
Need	As a planning tool
Generation	As a control tool
Social consequences of discovery	Technology control
Rights	Dangerous in concept
Responsibility	Justified only for global issues

Technology is a primary resource for learning to live better with the environment. Technology's rate of generation and use is critical to some industries and a major competitive issue among nations. Dangers from careless uses of technology are forcing assessment and some control. Thus the state of California now has a Department of Appropriate Technology to consider what balance of technologies should be focused on any particular social or other problem. Also, a science court has been proposed as a means for obtaining a thorough and informed airing of the pros and cons of any technical argument.

Guidelines for Managing Corporate Social Impact

In managing the social impact of the business as a producer and consumer of technology, social balance will tend to be maintained if the following guidelines are applied:

Technology   A business dependent on the long-term processes for generation of new technology develops an understanding of this dependence and seeks opportunities to encourage the replenishment of this technology.

Impact on society   A business engaged in offering goods or services based on new technology recognizes the responsibilities, which are growing but are still imperfectly defined, for the consequences of the social impacts that derive from the right to introduce new discoveries.

Applying the Guidelines

Contemporary society is irrevocably wedded to an evolving stream of technology. The increasing costs and complexity of discovery have raised serious concerns about the continuing sources of the new technology required for both correction of past excesses and continued forward evolution of a technological society. Increasingly, the adverse human, social, and ecological impacts of heedless technological exploitation have been recognized. Corporations, as the primary agents in application of technology, have reason for concern over (1) the source of new discoveries necessary to sustain the continuing flow of new products and services that specific markets require, and (2) the social impact of the new technology embodied in each new product.

Thus, a corporation such as IBM needs a role in stimulating the scientific discoveries that must underlie continuing progress in its information and data processing products, while it seeks simultaneously to manage its role as an agent of social and organizational change through the use of these products so that it will not cause undue strains or induce social resistance to these streams of development.

Questions for Analysis and Discussion

1. Suggest other industries that are dependent on technology in the way that pharmaceuticals and electronics are. Where is the new technology to support the future development of these industries being generated?

2. Find other examples of companies that have excelled in applying technology to the generation of new products and discuss the way in which these applications are organized and managed.

3. Pick a recent invention, list the social consequences of the discovery, and suggest some of the additional social consequences that will develop in the future (for example, the impact of television).

4. How might technology assessment be a favorable or unfavorable influence on the introduction of an important new discovery?

5. To what extent do you see inventors as being responsible for the social consequences of the use of their inventions? The manufacturers?

For Further Information

Baier, Kurt, and Rescher, Nicholas. *Values and the Future: Impact of Technological Change on American Values.* New York: Macmillan, 1969.

Gilfillian, S.C. *The Sociology of Invention* and *Inventing the Ship,* companion vols. Cambridge, Mass.: MIT Press, 1970.

Hottel, H.C., and Howard, J.B. *New Energy Technology.* Cambridge, Mass.: MIT Press, 1971.

Kuhn, Thomas S. *The Structure of Scientific Revolution,* 2d ed. Chicago: University of Chicago Press, 1970.

Steele, Lowell W. *Innovation in Big Business.* New York: American Elsevier Publishing Company, 1975.

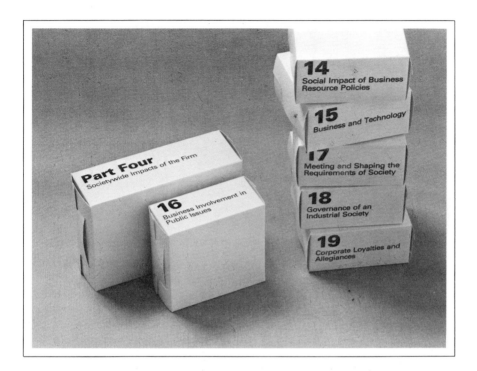

Part Four
Societywide Impacts of the Firm

14 Social Impact of Business Resource Policies

15 Business and Technology

16 Business Involvement in Public Issues

17 Meeting and Shaping the Requirements of Society

18 Governance of an Industrial Society

19 Corporate Loyalties and Allegiances

16
Business Involvement in Public Issues

Because of their position and leverage in society, most significant corporations have lost the option of maintaining silence and neutrality. Their involvement in the public forum is inevitable. The necessary flow of corporate actions and decisions as the business operates has a sufficient social impact to make impossible the old concept of the low corporate profile. In addition to the involvement that its very operation creates, the business sometimes finds that it is used as an instrument of public policy. At other times, it participates in governmental processes; again, it takes issues to the public forum or even engages in public confrontation with the government. The business may also find that others have made public issues over the propriety of its actions. In all, the potential social impact of various corporate actions and decisions is sufficient that these impacts must also be managed to maintain an appropriate business role and an appropriate degree of business involvement in public issues.

If business and labor leaders wish to steer the system in the direction they believe best, they cannot simply deplore, fume, curse and hire a Washington lawyer or lobbyist. They must get directly involved. . . . [1]

C. JACKSON GRAYSON, JR.

A business corporation, because of its obvious interaction with the public and its involvement in various public issues, must have a public face. This face may be closed if a corporation wishes to minimize its contact with the public, or perhaps it may be carefully screened through a public relations officer or some similar functionary who modulates the flow of information. At still other levels of openness, the information begins to flow both ways and have an impact on corporate and social policy. The public relations officer, perhaps supplemented by other members of the executive group, begins not only to transfer information but also to participate in a dialogue with the surrounding society. To prepare for analyzing the involvement in the public issues impact area, we must first review some of the basic types of interaction that occur and then examine the potential for social consequences, social costs, and social balance in each case. Initially, the chapter will take up the case in which business finds itself used as an instrument of public policy; then the discussion will move on to its conflicts with government, its participation in governmental processes, and the circumstances under which business processes may become public issues.

Business as an Instrument of Public Policy

It is a common experience for a business firm to learn that its actions are part of a desired and fostered pattern of some public body and find that it is being used as an instrument of public policy. Public policy is a matter for public discussion, and, thus, the assigned business role may lead to public issues. A frequent example is the public attack on corporations that act as suppliers for key defense programs. GE has been the target of several demonstrations because of the company's involvement in building jet engines for the B-1 bomber program.[2] Thus, a defense materials supplier is as much a target as the Defense Department.

In another instance Vinnell Corporation was strongly attacked for taking a Defense

---

[1]C. Jackson Grayson, Jr., "Let's Get Back to the Competitive Market System," *Harvard Business Review,* November–December 1973, p. 111.

[2]"G.E. Bomber Role Protested by Marchers," *New York Times,* 25 April 1974.

Department contract to train Saudi Arabia's national guard. The Pentagon supported Vinnell. Because of a change in U.S. policy, U.S. military personnel are doing less overseas training work, with such contracts presented as a cost-saving alternative for meeting commitments.[3] In this case Vinnell was pursuing its own direct self-interest in doing this task for Saudi Arabia. It was serving the purposes of the Defense Department, which wanted the training accomplished, but was not using U.S. military personnel. This is a very direct example of the process of using a private firm to accomplish a controversial public purpose as an instrument of U.S. foreign policy.

Other examples of this relationship might include cases where corporations have been asked by government agencies to create hiring and training programs aimed at bringing unemployables from ghetto areas and converting them, by assistance and education, into productive members of the work force. Or, as the pattern of

The Firm as Viewed by Society

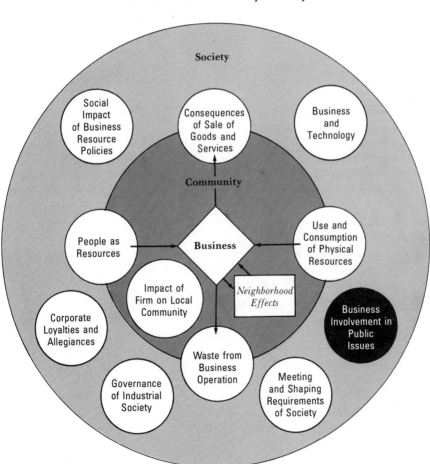

---

[3]"The Executive Mercenaries," *Time,* 24 February 1975, p. 16.

international relations has changed, various business firms have been encouraged to extend their operations into less developed nations both to help in the country's developmental process and serve as a means to the desired extension of the U.S. trade.

This role of being used as an instrument of public policy can be advantageous or can bring problems. PepsiCo, for instance, was widely envied in the role that has made it such an important bridge in developing trade in American consumer products with the Soviet Union. The envy stems from the access that PepsiCo obtained for its product in a tremendous new sales territory, together with its export franchise for Soviet vodka, which also seemed likely to bring substantial profits.

These business-government relationships do not always prove to be as beneficial as are anticipated. A few years ago Goodyear Tire & Rubber Company had reason to believe that it was being encouraged, as a matter of public policy, to participate in the project of building a tire plant in Rumania. However, when this proposed project came to public attention, it was bitterly attacked by the press and in the Senate. Goodyear found it necessary to retreat promptly. Those in government who had given Goodyear quiet encouragement disappeared equally quietly, and Goodyear was tried and convicted by the press for proposing an unwise extension of American dealings with the East European countries.

The generalization represented by these examples is that although business firms often have the opportunity to aid in implementing public policy, they need to view such opportunities with certain caution. Governmental processes work in an essentially political way; thus, the durability of a government opinion can be only as great as the public stature of the public servant who offers it. For this reason, an administrator in the middle management of a government bureau may be extremely influential in the day-to-day flow of events, may exert a significant impact on the way that the department does business, but still may have to withdraw quietly when someone higher in the hierarchy expresses a strong opinion on an issue or when outside political reactions make it unwise for a member of the administration to take a public posture.

In the interaction between business and public policy, industry trade associations may often have an influential intermediary role. Thus, a government official may wish to suggest to one of the many industry associations, such as the National Association of Manufacturers, that a program to promote more hiring of marginally employable people is in the public interest; the official may ask for industrial cooperation in a campaign to achieve this purpose. Although the government has no direct authority in such matters, often it can be influential. The association or individual company may feel a considerable obligation to comply with such a request, even if improper actions should be involved.[4]

---

[4] In his confession of illegal political contributions, Mr. Spater, then president of American Airlines, pointed out that the number of sensitive issues pending before various administrative agencies at that time had made him reluctant to refuse a direct request for funds from someone associated with the higher levels of the Nixon administration. When told that a contribution of $100,000 was expected, American Airlines contributed $55,000. Apparently, this represented the corporate judgment of the minimum amount that could be considered as a fulfillment of the request.

Of course, governmental bargaining power may be strong or weak, when it comes to influencing fulfillment of requests of this sort. Some requests for industrial assistance have been totally disregarded when the request exceeded the political bargaining power of the people or agencies involved.

The same process also works in reverse, although the leverage tends to be less. Thus, an industry trade association will be very careful to make various legislative and administrative leaders aware of the position and concerns of the group that it represents. Where these concerns are significant, they are likely to be weighed with some care before action is taken. This does not necessarily mean that the industry group has a secure line of influence. In fact, many of the efforts to oppose consumer and environmental protection legislation have been completely unsuccessful. However, these trade associations do form a convenient conduit for opinions, which are almost always considered for both their substance and their source. Therefore, such associations provide a communication mechanism that can, on occasion, allow an industry group to have significant influence on public policy in a particular area.

Because of the pivotal role that the business system plays in the economy, there is always an interface between a business firm and public policy matters. Sometimes it is in the form of the public body trying to influence industrial behavior or of industry trying to influence public policy. But, in any case, the two are closely linked and interact significantly.

Since corporate actions have such fundamental and pervasive effects on its employees and at least a portion of the community, corporate management cannot stay neutral; the fact of its actions enforce or reinforce a certain pattern of behavior. It is not surprising that unions, community groups, activists of various sorts, and most other public voices seek to influence or direct the corporate role. Thus, a few years ago a series of urban boycotts caused integration of the work forces of corporations, whose efforts in this direction were seen to be lagging, and there have been a number of bombings directed at offices of corporations because of their business dealings with South Africa or some other country held in disfavor.

Government Regulation of Business

In its extension and generalization, the public policy area moves into the larger universe of governing and being governed. In other words, a business as an individual member of the corporate community is subject to the governance of a variety of different political subdivisions, each of which has rule-making and rule-enforcing powers, and various powers to levy fees and taxes for governmental support and other public purposes. A given corporation may deal with city, county, state, and federal governments, as well as various regional authorities, such as the commission that regulates Delaware Valley pollution and water supply problems or the Port of New York Authority. A national corporation with operations in many states will normally need to deal with a tier of different governmental bodies in each location, and, when these are combined with the various state and federal administrative agencies and regulatory authorities, the number of necessary governmental contacts may increase substantially.

The business position in each case is a mixture of a normal desire to be let alone and a real interest in the way that the government is functioning. The interest in governmental activity is first of all selfish, because the tax money from the corporation and its employees is being spent by the government. Then, too, each level of government has such life-or-death power over corporate operations, even though economic and political realities often minimize such potential threats. This interest is also related to the future outlook for the business, which is definitely influenced by the kinds of regulations that are proposed and passed, the fairness and equity with which they are administered, and the degree to which business and government can work together constructively in the public interest.

Business Participation in Government

Because of the interrelationships of the interests of business and government, the actions of each become more intertwined with the actions and interests of the other. The basic relationships are of at least three types: (1) interdependencies between the business and society that are great enough to draw government interest, (2) advocacy relationships, where the business seeks a change in laws and regulations or reacts to a change proposed by others, and (3) actions related to obeying laws. As stated earlier, a corporation is and ought to be strongly constrained to obey the law on which its existence depends. The interdependencies and advocacy roles are less obvious and require further discussion.

Interdependency

Lockheed Aircraft Corporation, the nation's largest defense contractor, was almost totally dependent on defense needs, and the defense establishment, in turn, depended heavily on Lockheed. Government loan guarantees to prevent Lockheed bankruptcy were deemed to be a practical national necessity.[5] Whether this situation was the result of extraneous circumstances or bad management is not directly relevant; the government had little choice but to come to Lockheed's rescue.[6] In much the same way, the British government faced the practical necessity of keeping Rolls-Royce in operation.

The message for corporate management is that some kinds of operations are so deeply involved with the public interest that, governmental intervention is predictable if they are not managed in that interest. Concern over what was viewed as bad management at the Hughes Tool Company at a critical point in the aerospace program led to Defense Department encouragement of the group that split off to form Ramo Woolridge (now TRW), which provided a competitive source of missile systems.[7] In a similar way public concern over service caused the New York City transportation system to be taken over piece by piece by the city from struggling private companies in hopes of establishing a better operation managed in the public

---

[5]"Administration Message to Congress," *New York Times,* 14 May 1971.
[6]Harold B. Meyers, "The Salvage of the Lockheed 1011," *Fortune* 83, no. 6 (June 1971): 67 ff.
[7]C.J.V. Murphy, "Blowup at Hughes Aircraft," *Fortune* 49, no. 2 (February 1954): 116 ff.

interest. On the other hand, governmental programs to encourage private sector production of live virus vaccine for poliomyelitis and measles were largely successful, in that the companies involved supplied at competitive prices the necessary quantities of vaccine to support the desired public programs.[8]

This situation can be defined in terms of franchises. Just as the Fifth Avenue Coach Company and the Hudson-Manhattan Tubes operated on the basis of specific public franchises, Lockheed has an implied franchise on a large segment of defense work. Similarly, the drug companies offering vaccines have an implied franchise to provide these aids to public safety.[9] The community grows accustomed to receiving certain services from a given firm and may demand that they continue to be performed. Thus, New York City banks have been accused of failing to discharge their responsibility to the city every time that there has been a shortage of credit for a public purpose. Earlier, the issue had been over the need for loans to permit various kinds of urban development. In 1975 the confrontation developed because other investors were refusing to buy New York City bonds, and the banks were said to be responsible for filling the gap. Insisting on the performance of this obligation seemed easier than the pain and trauma of overhauling city operations and balancing the budget. Unquestionably, the banks do have a responsibility to the city, which could be defined as a financing franchise, and this responsibility may not always have been properly discharged.

The problem for the banks and society is to define obligations of this type clearly and realistically. The banks were being asked to convert a marginal situation into a sound one by investing money and confidence as others were withdrawing their confidence in New York City securities. A truly sound situation can be helped by recruiting support in this way, but all parties would be damaged if the banks were induced to support an unworthy situation and jeopardized their own stability.

A franchise may be formally recognized, as in the case of a public utility that is given the right and duty of supplying certain public services, usually on a monopoly basis, within a specific territory, and subject to specific regulatory control. Normally, such a company controls an essential service through a natural or created monopoly of sufficient durability that the public interest requires public regulation. Thus, Bell Telephone saw its own public utility status and anticipated the need for regulation. Most consumer franchises (for Ivory soap, Coca Cola, and so forth) do not bring a business to public utility status, unless the franchise permits an important degree of control over an essential good or service. Where the true characteristics of a public utility exist, a business will usually find that its self-interest lies in encouraging the proper degree of regulation in advance of regulation being imposed by an irate public.

---

[8]"Award for Outstanding Service for Children," *Parents Magazine,* January 1970, p. 24; Yale L. Meltzer "Pound of Cure: Social Progress Has Been Made in Vaccines and Other Biologicals," *Barron's,* 15 December 1969, p. 5; and "Polio Now Conquered," *Science News Letter,* 24 April 1965, p. 258.

[9]The President of Mead Johnson & Company has said: "One of the principal criticisms that is valid with regard to businessmen and the profit motive, however, is that too many businessmen do not understand the relationship of franchise-building to long-run profits. By franchise-building I mean creating and maintaining a favorable industry and public attitude toward your firm and your product." D. Mead Johnson, "Consultation: Are Profits and Social Responsibilities Compatible," *Business Horizons* 2, no. 2 (Summer 1959): 56.

The franchise is best defended by anticipating and defusing the issues that will result in social confrontation.

When an important franchise is not supported by satisfactory performance, a public issue is created. Just as Lockheed loan guarantees were approved and New York transit companies were purchased by the city, the government could act to maintain critical vaccine supplies if the drug companies in the private sector permitted their performance to come into serious question. However, the outcome of such public concern over business problems is not always the same. For example, the number of jobs at stake was not a large enough issue to save the SST. And the federal government has seemed disposed to intervene more quickly in rail strikes than in steel strikes, even though both have significant impact on the national economy.

Management can and should analyze the public franchise implicit in its continued operation and also any consequences that nonperformance could invoke. The potential for public issues and possible governmental intervention will provide an obvious guideline for business performance. As Alfred Sloan once put it: "The automobile industry has a tremendously valuable franchise from the United States and should respect it."[10] Immediate self-interest and a longer-term social balance requirement both call for dealing with these forces of interdependence between government and the public realistically and with the type of foresight that good management requires.

Advocacy

In its advocacy roles, as in its franchise responsibilities, business has every reason to seek its own self-interest in an intelligent and enlightened way. However, any improper attempts to influence the legislative and regulatory processes are outside the basic boundary of legal operation that any corporation in its own long-term self-interest is required to follow and outside the boundaries defined here. Within proper legislative and administrative channels, a business has a clear self-interest in speaking when its interests are at stake, either by opposing the proposals of others or by sponsoring its own program.

Obeying Laws

As discussed earlier, a business lives in a regulated environment. The intensity of this regulation, which varies depending on the particular industrial sector, is increasing rapidly in volume and scope. Today any business is in the constant presence of regulation.

A multitude of forms and reports are required for submission to various agencies. Data on employees and employment, social security information, census data, and other statistics are required. Special reports are required by particular agencies, since each regulatory authority tends to have its own pattern of information requirements

---

[10]As quoted by Lawrence I. Wood, "Social Performance of Business," *Economic and Business Bulletin* 17 (September 1964): 17.

and controls and continues to develop and expand its operational scope to fulfill its mission and the aspirations of its managers.

Thus, a most important interface with government is that through which industry gains the necessary approvals for the actions it plans to take. These may include more-or-less routine processes, such as obtaining license and registration approvals for company vehicles, requesting changes in zoning laws, or obtaining building permits. More extensive approval processes govern permission for major facilities, such as the construction of a new harbor and refinery complex to accommodate supertankers, permission to construct an atomic power plant, or approval to change the course of a river or close a city street. It is important that a business be able to handle its role in these processes well. The business should also be able to respond credibly when an authoritative government body defines new requirements, whether such action involves a new kind of environmental impact statement or estimates of a particular plant's need for specific city services over the next ten years.

The corporation, a creature of the law, is controlled by and dependent on law for its existence. Hence the corporation needs to be effective and adept in living with not only the law but also the network of regulations developed within the framework defined by the law as a means to its administration and enforcement. This coexistence represents self-interest in the most direct sense. Because it depends on the law, each corporation must operate within a legal framework whose related elements are effective and respected by the country at large. That is, the corporation controlled by the law receives only limited benefit from its necessary legal compliance unless other corporations and the public are conforming similarly to the same standards.

Submitting to Regulation: Antitrust Enforcement

One area of regulation worth special comment is that of antitrust enforcement policy. Here the Justice Department and the Federal Trade Commission are the primary enforcement agencies, although private suits between companies are not rare and other agencies sometimes also have an interest in the process. The primary authority flows from a series of statutes of which the Sherman Act and the Clayton Act are the best known.

This area of regulation is old but active, and changes in the nature of economic, political, and social processes seem to be reflected in the kind of antitrust issues that become most important and generate the greatest response. While congressional strictures against combinations in restraint of trade, monopoly, or discriminatory pricing are quite clear, the meaning of these restraints in a particular market and at a particular time and place is less obvious.

Collusion between firms is clearly banned, and mergers are closely screened for their possible creation of either a monopoly position or the base from which such a position is likely to evolve. Now any significant merger requires advance notification, to give time for a regulatory response before the actual union is consummated. Many mergers are challenged to some degree and some are undone as a result of the opposition. Thus, Kennecott Copper acquired Peabody Coal and then was forced to divest its holdings because of the concentration of mining interests. However, GE acquired Utah Minerals in the largest merger in history after the Justice Department review indicated that the merger probably would not be challenged.

A more difficult antitrust issue for both the Justice Department and corporate management to assess is the basic issue of bigness. When duPont was forced to divest its GM stock a few years ago, the government suit cited the potential for abuse that was created by giving duPont a favored position as a GM supplier because the very size of the two firms would cause such an agreement to lessen competition in those markets substantially. Currently, prosecutions against AT&T and IBM depend at least in part on whether these firms are too big relative to the effective functioning of markets and the national interest.

The issue of when a corporation is too big is an important public policy issue that seems bound to arise repeatedly until some criteria are accepted by the regulatory community and the public. IBM, AT&T, and other large corporations make a virture out of their size, and this issue has some substance. So far no economic limit to the efficient size of an organization has been demonstrated, and the large resource base of a corporate giant does allow major investments in research, facilities, and market development that smaller companies cannot undertake. But since a few of the largest corporations show a sustained ability to grow faster than the economy, their relative size within it must increase every year. At some point or at some fraction of the total national GNP, an IBM or GE would be too big, but no criteria seem to have emerged to suggest where that point really is. Since the current litigation started as a specific issue with a specific company, it may or may not advance the discussion of the general criteria that must eventually be developed.

Business Actions as Public Issues

Business does not always live in a peaceful relationship with government. Lawsuits are not infrequent, and sometimes a corporation takes an issue to the public, as Donald Cook of American Electric Power did in his confrontation with the EPA over rules for pollution control.

Business Week reports that AEP has been a pioneer in technological development to the point that it is considered to be the nation's most efficient utility. It has traditionally been a coal-based company and has moved only slowly and cautiously to nuclear power. Under the pressure of EPA regulations, it has carried out a major investment program to install electronic precipitators to control fly ash emissions from its smokestacks. Earlier, AEP pioneered strip mine reclamation projects and cooling towers to control thermal pollution of rivers before these were legal requirements. But, having committed its efforts to fly ash control, AEP balked at the requirement to install scrubbers to reduce sulfur dioxide content of the flue gases. Scrubbers are expensive to install and operate. Early installations failed to perform satisfactorily. AEP estimated that the required installation would cost $400 million initially and $110 million per year to operate. The function of the scrubbers is to cause the sulfur dioxide to react with lime to produce a calcium sulfate slurry, which itself represents a difficult disposal problem. The *New York Times* cites an AEP advertisement stating that the slurry from the scrubbers required for its power system would cover Washington D.C. 10 feet deep within five years, if it were dumped there. At any rate, the slurry is acknowledged by all to present a difficult disposal problem.

While one could argue that AEP should simply have spent the money and requested permission to increase its rates accordingly, Donald Cook, AEP's chairman and chief executive officer, took strong exception to the requirement, arguing against the tremendous waste of resources to obtain a short-term solution. He argued that the desired improvement in air quality was no more than marginally necessary and could be obtained more economically with tall stacks to disperse the flue gas better. For a long-range solution, he argued for opening western coal fields to obtain low-sulfur coal and developing pretreatment of high-sulfur coal to reclaim the sulfur and represent a more economical coal treatment process than scrubbing the flue gas and throwing the sulfur away.

In the face of EPA requirements for action, AEP filed lawsuits to block the enforcement process and started a major advertising campaign to take the issue to the public in hopes of getting the requirements amended. Cook directed the campaign personally and exchanged heated letters with EPA Commissioner Quarles, and with White House Environmental Quality Chairman Peterson. At one point, Cook appealed to President Nixon to intervene. By allocating over $3 million to advertising and engaging in a public debate, Donald Cook made a public issue over this particular requirement. He succeeded in emphasizing that scrubbers represent only a marginal technological advance but did not succeed in halting their progress.[11]

Other utilities also objected to the requirement for installation of scrubbers. None objected as openly and vociferously, even though their feelings may have been as strong. After Donald Cook retired and AEP had taken a quieter stance, the TVA continued to refuse to install scrubbers. As of early 1977, the necessary legal proceedings to determine how one federal agency goes about suing another were beginning, as EPA prepared to go to the courts to force the TVA to install scrubbers and conform to the sulfur dioxide emission standards.[12]

It is difficult to evaluate what this confrontation between AEP and the EPA accomplished. Certainly, it brought to the attention of at least some of the public the tradeoff issue of how much scarce national resources should be spent for a given gain in air purity. Thus, it represents a process, but not a victory, in which a business can publicly protest what it feels to be an unfair requirement or decision. In this process the firm occasionally succeeds, sometimes only by conditioning the evolution of public opinion that may affect some future decision on a related subject.

Cook reacted vigorously against what he considered to be an improper regulatory position. As the number of regulations and regulatory bodies increases, the chances of improper regulatory action also increases, and protests are becoming more frequent. Another recent protest is from the matchbook industry because the U.S. Consumer Product Safety Commission wants to ban mail-in coupons from paper matchbooks. LaSalle Extension University of Chicago buys 500 million coupon matchbooks each year, and other firms also use them for the same purpose. The commission is concerned that consumers may tear off the coupon and continue to use the matches. An estimated 9,000 injuries each year are attributed to matchbooks that burst into flame, and it was felt that this may be one of the causes.[13]

---

[11]"Donald Cook Takes on the Environmentalists," *Business Week,* 26 October 1974, pp. 66–74; "Donald Cook vs. E.P.A.," *New York Times,* 25 November 1974.

[12]"EPA and TVA Face Off," *Chemical Week,* 2 March 1977, p. 14.

[13]"Matchmakers Burn Over Safety Rules," *Business Week,* 3 February 1975, p. 21.

While this issue may seem to be on the border of the ridiculous, it is of vital importance to the affected businesses. The tradeoff issue is whether the hazard to public safety is really sufficient to justify the injury to the matchbook advertising industry.

These issues get into the public press not only from the business side. As stockholders, various institutions are beginning to react publicly against management actions of which they disapprove.

> Aetna Life & Casualty, a proper old insurance company with $1.5-billion in common stocks and no known radicals on its board, cast its proxies four times last year against the managements of companies in which it holds stock. Aetna supported stockholder resolutions that called for disclosing business activities in South Africa, ending investment in the South African territory of Namibia, publicizing political contributions and lobbying, and hiring an outside auditor. It will vote against management again this year whenever companies in its portfolio fail to live up to their social responsibilities, Aetna spokesmen say calmly. . . .
>
> "Our primary investment purpose is financial return," says Robert B. Nicholas, Aetna's vice-president for corporate planning. "But once you have bought a company's stock, you assume the responsibility of a shareholder."[14]

The *Business Week* article also lists eleven other institutions with similar interest in using proxy power to influence management. As institutional stockholders begin to react to social issues, corporate management must become more sensitive to these issues in seeking to avoid confrontations with large stockholders.

As a gathering point for the analysis of corporate activity and protests in appropriate areas, several groups collect disclosure information and publicize it.

> Corporations are not very happy about giving required information to the government, and they fight a continuing battle to defeat new federal or state disclosure laws and to dilute old ones. Business is unwilling to reveal much about its activities outside of that which is required by law. Part of the practice is based on sound competitive ground. Companies do not want to reveal anything to give their rivals an advantage. More often, however, in what one corporate executive termed the "warp and woof of the world in which we live," in dealing with the government or public, companies are secretive out of fear of bad public reaction or costly and restrictive government intervention. The issues involved are volatile, and what in one political climate and administration may seem harmless disclosure, could turn to civil or criminal prosecution in another climate. Thus, little information is offered to the public by most companies and specific requests are not likely to get more than a general response that is favorable to the company.
>
> To be sure, there are other routes of access to information and control of

---

[14]"Institutions that Balk at Antisocial Management," *Business Week,* 19 January 1974, pp. 66–67.

corporations. Groups to which these routes have been available have had varying degrees of success.

Since the sum of information coming from government, stockholders, employees, and consumers is not adequate to the task of evaluating corporate social impact, and the companies themselves rarely volunteer such enlightenment, other approaches seem warranted. Thus the New-York-based Council on Economic Priorities has come forward with a new book that (1) emphasizes the need for this information, (2) collects many previously published facts, and (3) coaxes an unprecedented amount of data from a large group of companies.

Its *Guide to Corporations: A Social Perspective* does not attempt to rate the performance of the companies or industries based on its information since, in many cases, too little data could be obtained for a definitive judgment. However, it does provide company profiles that include extensive data on the four social areas covered, major products, consumer brands, sales, and profit figures. And it does rate the companies on their willingness to cooperate, and the quality of data they released.

There was substantial difference in the willingness of the companies to cooperate. The ratings which follow were based on company responses to the Council's request for a core of very basic information in four social areas covered by the book. The data sought includes: pollution control expenditures (both capital and operating) and a reasonable summary of what the company is doing to improve its control of pollution; the EEO-1 form filed with the EEOC stating numbers and percentages of minority group individuals and women employed; a reasonable summary of what the company is doing to improve the composition of its workforce; and dollar totals, locations, and operating policies of any company units operating in southern Africa. The latter applies to the foreign investment section, in which a case study of operations in racially troubled southern Africa was chosen to provide some comparable statistics about the multinational aspects of business.

The Council found most companies reluctant to release some or all of this basic information. Only one of the forty-three companies studied, Weyerhaeuser Company, released all of the core data used in the compilation, and was rated "excellent." Twelve other companies were rated "good," twenty-two were rated "fair," and eight "poor." The high ratings were concentrated in the paper and airline industries. Six of the eight poor ratings, on the other hand, came from the steel industry.

Public demonstration occasionally has some impact on company policies. The Dow Chemical Company suffered substantial dollar loss in public goodwill following repeated public demonstrations against the company's production of napalm for use in the Vietnam War. The outcry caused Dow to make substantial disclosures about its war-related production and may have eventually influenced the company to discontinue its government contract for manufacture of the chemical weapon at the peak of U.S. involvement in the war.

Still, the amount of information to which the public does not have access is tremendous. As it stands, in addition to the Justice Department, EEOC, and OFCC data already mentioned, the public has no way of learning the following basic things about a corporation from any source whatsoever:

How much a company spends to lobby on federal, state, or local legislation. Current lobbying and election laws are so riddled with loopholes that corporations can effectively conceal from the public millions of dollars spent for such activities. It has also become clear from investigation of the 1972 presidential election that millions of dollars in illegal corporate campaign contributions can be concealed.

How much a company has invested in foreign countries and what impact such investment has on domestic prices and jobs, and on the politics and economy of the other countries.

Who owns a company, other than those owning 10 percent or more which must be reported to the Securities and Exchange Commission. (Even this is not entirely revealing—ownership of large corporations is often concentrated among family individuals or members of boards of directors. A number of family members or directors, or both, may each own 10 percent or less of a company but the aggregate ownership may be a controlling interest.)

Whether advertising claims made by a company are true. The Federal Trade Commission requires the manufacturers of a handful of products—such as automobiles, televisions, and tires—to file proof of their advertising claims with the Commission. However, these products are only a small percentage of those on the market.

How seriously most companies' products pollute the environment and what they are doing about the pollution they create. Data on air and water pollution from manufacturing processes is compiled at many regional, state, and local agencies, but the information can be difficult to obtain, even though it is normally public by law. The new National Pollutant Discharge Elimination System which according to the 1972 Federal Water Quality Act amendments replaced the Refuse Act permit system, has simplified this problem by making data on company water pollution readily available at regional Environmental Protection Agency offices. However, high duplicating costs may be encountered, and data is supplied by the companies and generally unverified.

As long as such gaps remain in the information pried from companies by government or other groups, American corporations will be truly accountable to none but themselves. Perhaps the Council on Economic Priorities' fair treatment and analysis of voluntarily disclosed social data presents a new and potentially effective alternative for both the companies and the public.[15]

---

[15]Lee Stephenson, "Prying Open Corporations: Tighter Than Clams," pp. 43–49. Reprinted from *Business and Society Review,* Winter 1973–1974. Copyright © 1974, Warren, Gorham and Lamont, Inc., 210 South Street, Boston, Mass. 02111. All rights reserved.

Clearly the public exposure of corporations will continue to increase, and corporate involvement in public issues will also become more extensive. It is hoped that not too many issues will occasion the kind of violent public protest evidenced by the destruction of a test tower being used to evaluate a proposed atomic power plant site at Montague, Massachusetts.

> As far as Samuel H. Lovejoy was concerned, the 500-foot-high meteorological tower erected here by Northeast Utilities as a preliminary to a planned $1.3-billion twin nuclear power plant installation was no good.
>
> So he toppled it.
>
> The deed took place in darkness, early in the morning of George Washington's Birthday. Barbed wire atop a cyclone fence was cut. Turnbuckles on one of the three sets of high-tension cables serving as guy wires were loosened.
>
> The top 360 feet of the red and white tower snapped off and crashed down among the scrubby evergreens of the Montague Plain. The instruments stopped recording, workmen at the site said, at 2:50 A.M.
>
> And the destruction has caused shock, consternation and anger among townspeople and local officials who hope that the nuclear plant will bring tax benefits and jobs to this chronically depressed area, which was once supported by small factories and cotton and silk mills.
>
> . . . damage to the tower [was] . . . estimated by the utility company as in the neighborhood of $100,000. . . .
>
> Police Chief Edward W. Hughes was upset that Mr. Lovejoy had been released after his lawyer read the bail statute to the court.
>
> "I can't understand our system of justice," he said. "A guy can do the kind of damage that Lovejoy did and walk away the same day laughing and talking like a football hero."[16]

This type of incident manifests a new public attitude, which is a cause of deep concern since it goes against the tradition of the country for due process. But attitudes are changing, and a corporation increasingly must deal with the hazard of violent protest from an aroused public.

Summary

Business gets involved in public issues because it must. As a large fish in shallow water cannot move without rippling the surface, so the corporation cannot function in society without creating ripples in the public forum. These impacts are important

---

[16]John Kipner, "Toppler of A-Plant Tower Shocks New England Town with Protest," *New York Times*, 2 March 1974. Copyright © 1974 by The New York Times Company. Reprinted by permission.

Figure 16.1   Business Involvement in Public Issues

As an instrument of public policy	Business versus government
As a participant in government processes	Business actions as a public issue
Business management of its public role	

Impact of business policies, actions, and potentials makes a conspicuous public role inevitable. This role demands management to reduce unpredicted or unnecessary conflicts and impacts and to advance the constructive programs of the firm.

enough to merit careful management. Figure 16.1 summarizes some of the dimensions of business's public involvement. The potential capabilities and powers of the corporation invite the government and others to seek corporate aid in furthering a particular public cause. Thus, business may find itself used as an instrument of public policy, and this role can be attractive, except for the higher business risk that accompanies political exposure that was illustrated in the case of Goodyear and the tire plant. The involvement with administrative and regulatory processes has assumed a lower profile, except that public issues over actions and statements at the various stages of these processes have become much more frequent than in the past. Business may enter these processes as an advocate seeking to influence tariff regulations, strip mine or oil legislation, or other actions; or business may challenge government processes directly in the courts and the public forum, as was done when various utilities opposed the EPA requirement for flue gas scrubbers. It is also possible for others to oppose business actions, in the way that the Disney Mineral King development was opposed and blocked by environmental groups (see Chapter 9).

Altogether, the range of business actions that affects public processes is so extensive that their social impact requires increasingly careful management. Wherever the corporate actions have an impact on public processes, the freedom to take such action brings a responsibility to deal with the consequences. With greater frequency, the resulting reaction to controversial corporate behavior is a public discussion or challenge because the evolution of corporate processes into the open public forum continues to develop in the pattern of the present anticorporation, antibusiness biases held by significant elements of that public.

Corporate managements will inevitably become more accustomed to a continual involvement in public issues either as the business pursues its own self-interests or as the public reacts to actual or expected business behavior. Business will necessarily become more careful with regard to the potential public impact of its actions and will increase its efforts to avoid causing social cost through corporate impact wherever possible.

This chapter has considered business involvement as an instrument of public policy, business confrontations with government, business participation in government processes, and the auditing of corporate actions and policies. Because of the importance of business in society and the impact of its actions, business is increasingly accountable to the public for the consequences of its social impacts and must consider how to balance these impacts.

Guidelines for Managing Corporate Social Impact

In managing the social impact of business involvement in public issues, social balance will tend to be maintained if the following guidelines are applied:

Public self-interest   In public processes a firm recognizes and pursues its own self-interest and cultivates an understanding of this self-interest as it relates to the social and political processes so that neither the anger of society nor its political power will be aroused.

Respect for law   A corporation obeys the law and cultivates respect for it from others.

Applying the Guidelines

A significant element in the corporate public affairs posture of many leading corporations is an attempt to recognize and make effective the proper and defensible self-interest of the business. This posture, together with the creation of special offices and departments dedicated to its achievement, is the result of bitter experience, as both inept corporate initiatives and the absence of effective response to outside attack have caused corporations to lose issues to political opponents repeatedly. The same experiences are reinforcing the importance of the law to corporations, since the law establishes clear boundaries. For example, law provides limits for the rapacity of political forces in feeding on corporate funds, which has begun to attract public attention in the aftermath of the Watergate episode.

Questions for Analysis and Discussion

1. If Congress approves a program and appropriates the funds so that a particular product becomes an embodiment of U.S. public policy, can a manufacturer be expected to participate in its manufacture? (Consider, for example, the case of GE and the B-1 bomber.)

2. When business works in partnership with government, do you feel that the political uncertainties are sufficient to justify a higher than average profit rate?

3. What do you see as the proper boundary for business efforts to advocate changes in legislation?

4. Because of the needs for confidentiality of some data, do you feel that corporations should continue to resist the requirement for more public disclosure of their activities?

5. How should corporations deal with the public tendency to break out into violent and destructive protest more often than in the past?

For Further Information

Duncan, W. Jack. *Decision Making and Social Issues.* Hinsdale, Ill.: Dryden, 1973.

Greenwood, William T. *Issues in Business and Society,* 3d ed. Boston, Mass.: Houghton Mifflin, 1976.

Perrow, Charles. *The Radical Attack on Business.* New York: Harcourt, Brace, Jovanovich, 1972.

Sethi, S. Prakash. *Up Against the Corporate Wall,* 3d ed. Englewood Cliffs, N.J.: Prentice-Hall, 1977.

Wall Street Journal. Getting Involved. New York: Dow, Jones & Company, 1972.

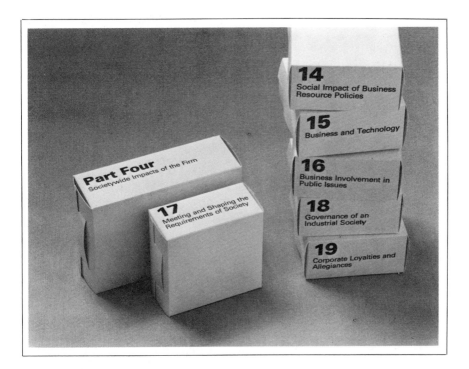

17
Meeting and Shaping the Requirements of Society

The degree of malleability and adaptability that exists between corporation and society is demonstrated in their interaction. Where the corporation must fulfill the requirements of society, it has the opportunity to consciously shape those requirements, which will be affected through its actions. Thus, management must maintain an awareness of its corporate social impact on the culture of the society through the value systems inherent in its actions, the intrinsic nature of its operations, the choice of activities it supports, and the changes resulting from its marketing efforts. The result of all the mutual impacts of the business-society interrelationship is gradual change in the basis for corporate authority. The corporation has a significant, subtle power to shape society, and society has a greater but less-used power over the destiny of the corporation.

313

When business is understood as a social system, it is recognized that business influences individuals, groups, and society at home and abroad in many vital ways beyond the economic. In fact it is a creator of norms and values.[1]

ALVAR O. ELBING, JR. AND CAROL J. ELBING

This chapter focuses on interplay and interaction, as society and corporation change under the force of their impacts on each other in the evolution of their relationship. The corporation shapes society by the manner in which it does business and the nature of the goods and services it creates. Society shapes the corporation by the nature of both the guidance it exerts and the constraints it places on the corporate process. Together they evolve toward a new cultural equilibrium that is continually shifting as the corporate and social process interact to produce new needs and new innovations.

In examining this mutual impact area, we first explore the direct corporate impact on community culture and then move on to the implications for management authority and for the power of corporation and society to shape each other in various ways.

Impact of Business on Community Culture

As a firm operates, it will have some direct or indirect impact on community culture, where the meaning of culture is taken in the broadest sense. Social balance requires that there be no negative influence on culture, although evaluation of cultural impacts is subjective and difficult. Therefore, it is necessary to define the nature of this potential impact and then describe the standards by which it can be judged. The areas of such business influence are numerous. They include community traditions, lifestyle, level of community artistic and cultural activity, many aspects of community intellectual life, and ethical and moral standards.

The very nature of a business changes the area around it. Thus, a section of Peterborough, Ontario, is different because the factory on the river bank is the Peterboro Canoe Company, rather than a textile mill. Furthermore, one major portion of the city of South Bend, Indiana, was formerly dominated by the overwhelming presence of Studebaker automobile plants. And Dubuque, Iowa, owes a part of its

---

[1]Alvar O. Elbing, Jr. and Carol J. Elbing, *The Value Issue of Business* (New York: McGraw-Hill 1967), p. 217.

nature to the requirements and community rhythms of activity generating from its meat-packing plants.

Also, the business employment pattern influences the community that develops. Where Endicott, New York (Endicott-Johnson Shoes) and Hershey, Pennsylvania (Hershey Foods Corporation) have had the stability of a long-term association with one company and a father-and-son employment tradition, communities dependent on aerospace industries (such as Bethpage, Long Island) are conditioned to a flux in employment as contracts are won and lost.

Another intrinsic feature of a business is the type of visitors and temporary residents that it brings into a community. A research and consulting firm such as Battelle Laboratories in Columbus, Ohio, or Stanford Research Institute in Menlo Park, California, attracts a steady stream of scientists and business executives from all over the world who spend a few days in the community in the course of their business. In neither case is the impact large enough to dominate the community, but

The Firm as Viewed by Society

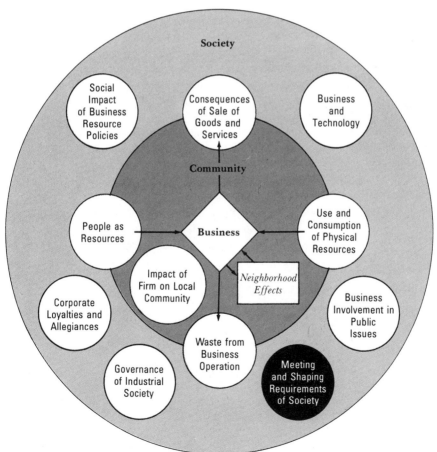

the contribution is clearly in the direction of a national and international center of business and technology. Freeport, Maine, is the home of the L.L. Bean mail-order sporting goods business, and a major influence on the town comes from the tourists and other visitors to the L.L. Bean retail store. Another type of influence on La Sueur, Minnesota (the home of Green Giant) and other cannery towns is the brief seasonal influx of migrant workers during the picking and packing season. Columbus, Menlo Park, Freeport, and La Sueur are each somewhat different in basic nature because of the type of industry that provides employment.

The direct management attitude toward a community also has important effects. Consider a small city that has among its industries the regional distribution centers for two national firms. The managers of one center are told that they will be transferred in a year or two as part of an overall company pattern and that, in the meantime, it is better not to get too involved in local affairs. The local managers of the other company are told that the relationship of the company to the community is their responsibility and that they are expected to exert a constructive local influence. Clearly, very different types of relationship with the community are likely to result.

Management attitudes toward a community can be reflected in the efforts to beautify its own facilities and those of the community. The Johnson Wax Research Tower in Racine, Wisconsin, is a classic and widely known example of the great early period of Frank Lloyd Wright's architecture. Columbus, Indiana, has public buildings designed by Saarinen, Birkerts, Pei, and other well-known architects as a result of the offer of the Cummins Foundation to pay the fees if designs by any one of a group of nationally known architects were selected by the community. This offer resulted from the management interest of Cummins Engine in increasing the architectural stature of the entire community.[2]

These examples illustrate a few of the ways that management attitude and the nature of a firm's activity can affect the community. There are other effects also. Consider the alternative impacts on the culture of the community from an influx of migrant laborers versus visiting scientists or from encouraging management to be involved in the local community versus being withdrawn from it. Because of its close linkage with business, the community must, in some degree that is proportionate to the size and importance of the business to that community, mirror the nature and style of the business enterprise in its own actions and processes.

> The contributions of the business corporation to value formation can be viewed under three rubrics: the shaping of the material environment of our society; the shaping of its symbolic environment, verbal, visual, and perhaps to a much lesser extent, auditory; and the definition of "work," and in particular, worthy achievement in work.[3]

All in all, a community becomes to a large extent an expression of the values,

[2]John H. Watson III, "Cummins Engine Foundation," 20 Company-Sponsored Foundations (New York: National Industrial Conference Board, 1970), pp. 49–50; also George Vecsey, "Columbus Indiana Grows Used to Its Fine Architecture," New York Times, 17 May 1971.
[3]Carl Kaysen, "The Business Corporation as a Creator of Values," in Sidney Hook, ed. Human Values and Economic Policy (New York: New York University Press, 1967), p. 211.

aspirations, and achievements of its businesses. Thus, the internal standards a corporation sets for itself and for the members of its organization have an influence that carries down through the work force and out into the community. A corporation whose management is involved in price-fixing, collusion, and under-the-counter business deals or builds up the weaker elements in local government through payoffs for favors sheds its standards onto the community. In the long run such a corporation must cause some shift in the value systems of any members of the organization or of the community who observe these practices. Businesses that live in the twilight of legality must have a similar negative impact on the values of those with whom they deal. Likewise, a management that works for good local government, deals fairly with its employees, and fosters good business practices can be a force for improving community moral and ethical standards.

Values, Ethics, and Standards

Whether society or the corporation created the value systems that corporate actions represent, as business activities move into the moral twilight they either create or further institutionalize a negative bias on the value system of society as a whole.

The business community has been hit with sweeping new regulations of its products and advertising by the Government, and with increasing complaints about high prices and defective merchandise by a public whose faith in the free-enterprise system, according to recent polls, has sunk to a new low. In this already embattled atmosphere, some of the big multinational firms have been targets of a highly publicized series of revelations concerning bribery and payoffs abroad. Some of the country's flagship corporations—Exxon, Lockheed, Northrop, Gulf, United Brands—have admitted funneling massive amounts of cash to officials of foreign governments and hiding the transactions from their shareholders and directors. With their ethics as well as their profits under attack, many businessmen view themselves as Job beset by a plague of boils.

Of all the tribulations, the exposure of shady foreign business practices was the most unexpected, concerning as it does a practice that has existed at least since the 1600's, when the British East India Company won duty-free treatment for its exports by giving Mogul rulers "rare treasures," including paintings, carvings and "costly objects made of copper, brass and stone." Nations like Great Britain and Sweden, whose standards of government ethics are a good deal stricter than our own, take it for granted their businessmen will pay bribes when operating abroad, especially in developing countries. "Without it," says The Financial Times of London, "business simply would not get done." The only difficulty such bribes pose for British firms, according to a recent survey by The Financial Times, is one of morale. Some British executives feel unfairly treated when comparing their own modest and highly taxed salaries with what The Times calls "the large, tax-free rewards going to an assortment of foreign middlemen."

When the facts began to unravel about a $1.25-million bribe paid by United

Brands to the former President of Honduras to reduce the tax on the production of bananas, the company's president committed suicide, its stock dropped 40 per cent, its holdings in Panama were expropriated and its tax and tariff concessions in Honduras were revoked.

Such activities are not universal. Several large U.S. multinationals, as a matter of corporate policy, prohibit foreign political contributions and come down hard on suspected bribes. Among them are RCA, I.B.M. and Bendix. W. Michael Blumenthal, president of Bendix, says his company prefers to pass up increased profits and occasionally an entire national market rather than engage in the ethical compromises and deceptions such practices necessarily involve.

If corporate bribery abroad has offended the post-Watergate morality, the companies implicated have nevertheless taken a greater share of the blame than they deserve. Bribery abroad is not exactly the corruption of innocents. Several of the incidents spotlighted by the Senate hearings smack more of protection and extortion than of simple bribery. In the most outrageous case, the chairman of the ruling party in South Korea threatened to close the $300-million operation of Gulf Oil in that country unless the company made a donation of $10-million to his party's presidential campaign. Gulf's chairman, Bob Dorsey, was able to shave the demand down from $10-million, which he considered "not in the interests of the company" to $3-million, which he said was.

The reasons multinationals must do business amid a profusion of outstretched hands go deep into the history and structure of the lands in which they operate. In much of Asia and Africa, the market economy as we know it, in which the sale of goods and services is governed by price and quality competition, never has existed. What has developed in its stead are intricate tribal and oligarchic arrangements of social connections, family relations and reciprocal obligations, lubricated by many forms of tribute, including currency. In a meeting at the Department of Defense in 1973 (a report of which was subpoenaed from the files of the Northrop Corporation) Adnan Khashoggi, one of the most successful middlemen in the Middle East, justified his enormous sales commissions—$45-million on a single deal for fighter planes—by his need to cover his operating expenses and also take care of his pecuniary "loyalties" to Saudi Arabia's royal family. Another memo explained Northrop's loss of a contract to build a communications system by noting that Saudi officials wished to help out the local agent of a Northrop competitor, one Ibriham el-Zahed. "They felt," the memo said, "that by awarding a contract to his principals, he will make enough money to pay off his debts."

In most developing countries, civil-service salaries are deliberately low—the average Indian bureaucrat makes $1,650 a year—on the assumption that people will supplement their salaries by taking money where they can find it. Where political instability is the rule, the tenure of high officials is always uncertain and often short. Bribes provide a form of retirement fund. It is considered far more patriotic to take the money from rich foreign corporations than out of one's own country.[4]

The problem for corporate management grows out of the growth opportunity from country to country. As cultures differ, standards of conduct have differed in the past. By accepting a bad standard of conduct in a given country, the multinational corporation by its size and impact further establishes and institutionalizes that pattern of conduct in that country. Then, through the internal corporate apparatus, that pattern of conduct tends to be carried elsewhere because it is almost impossible for a group of managers in the top and upper middle management of a large multinational corporation to use more than one set of ethical and moral standards in the course of their worldwide operation. In other words, if bribery and payoffs are a norm in one part of the organization, the management that is willing to do business in this way is unlikely to be able to uphold higher ethical standards elsewhere.

Obviously, the need is for worldwide standards of conduct, which will evolve rapidly as international business grows. While the precise nature of the value system that will emerge is not yet known, it is likely that it will not condone payoffs and bribery because these practices are considered unethical in so many countries and other standards would be so hard to contain and enforce.

In the aftermath of the Watergate investigation of illegal campaign contributions in the United States, the Securities and Exchange Commission has become far more vigorous in its disclosure requirements, and the public has reacted with indignation to the resulting disclosures. One of the first came from Gulf Oil Corporation, as the domestic analogue of the international payments pattern came to light.[5] Of course, the Gulf case is a good illustration only because it was one of the first major cases of this type to be exposed. The SEC disclosure requirements have shed this sort of light on a broad pattern of illegal use of corporate funds for political purposes.

The Southwestern Bell case was similar, except that the political ties were somewhat more open. In this case the corporation had entertained a member of the Missouri Public Utilities Commission on a three-day hunting trip while a decision on a rate increase was pending. Two members of the Kansas regulatory commission had apparently accepted free telephone credit cards and an expense-paid trip to Las Vegas. And, according to a dismissed Bell executive, the company had required its management group to contribute to a political slush fund.[6]

While public reaction to these scandals has been in the form of anger, the corporate reaction has been embarrassment. Some management changes have followed—at Gulf, for example. Predictably, few corporations will allow the type of illegal contributions that cause this sort of disclosure to the SEC and the public in the future. Thus, the SEC action in forcing the disclosures is a constructive forward step,

---

[4]Milton S. Gwirtzman, "Is Bribery Defensible?" *New York Times Magazine,* 5 October 1975, pp. 19 ff. Copyright © 1975 by The New York Times Company. Reprinted by permission.

[5]Kenneth H. Bacon, "SEC Testimony Tells How Gulf Oil Gave $300,000 a Year to Politicians in the U.S.," *Wall Street Journal,* 17 November 1975.

[6]"Officials Linked to Bell Scandal," *New York Times,* 2 March 1975.

so far as it constrains business behavior in a manner that seems to have met with broad public approval.

From political contributions and payoffs, it is a short step to other dubious corporate practices.

> Last week a Federal grand jury accused Bergdorf Goodman, Inc., Bonwit Teller and Saks Fifth Avenue of violating the Sherman Antitrust Act by engaging in a conspiracy to fix prices on women's clothing.
>
> The one-count indictment charged that for a five-year period beginning in the late 1960s, the three Fifth Avenue stores not only conspired among themselves to fix prices of women's ready-to-wear clothing, but also had pressured several manufacturers into forcing other retailers to maintain the same high prices. What's more, the grand jury said, the three would agree to hold clearance sales on the same day.[7]

From illegal price-fixing, it is also a short step to various unethical internal corporate practices. A *New York Times* feature indicated that in the printing industry one out of every eight dollars is tainted by bribery and that one out of every five purchasing executives in that industry is probably involved in illegal kickbacks or payments. This is a part of a white-collar crime problem that the Department of Commerce values at $40 billion per year, $7 billion of which is in kickbacks and bribes, and all of which is passed on in some way to the prices paid by consumers.[8]

Of course, workers and the public sometimes find ways of participating in these thefts also.

> Meanwhile, contractors routinely add a "pilferage number" to their costs and pass it along. So real estate buyers are footing the bill, one that totals millions of dollars each year in the metropolitan area.
>
> Capt. Aaron Goldstein of the Central National Investigation Agency, which has provided security for at least 15 per cent of the recent major construction projects in Westchester County, estimated that there are $100,000 in thefts for every high-rise building.
>
> More than eight out of ten construction thefts are committed by employees or accomplished in collusion with them, according to Raymond Magro, general manager of Pan American Investigation Service of Bronxville.
>
> "Typically," he said, "some fellows just come to work with empty pickup trucks and go home with full ones." An anonymous worker interviewed recently in the trade magazine Apartment Construction News described having stolen $50,000 worth of construction materials last year. He said he had sold them to construction materials dealers and underworld buyers and had ended the year with an extra $15,000, tax free. "Everyone steals," he commented. "We've seen builders bribe police and building inspectors."

---

[7]"Does Saks Tell Bonwit?" *Newsweek,* 21 October 1974, pp. 78–79.
[8]Jules B. Kroll, "Business Bribery Close to Home," *New York Times,* 9 November 1975.

. . . He says that builders almost never hire guards for duty during the working day, when most employee thefts take place, and that contractors virtually never prosecute when an employee is caught.

"We did an investigation for one firm that hired us because it had had a lot of theft," he recalled. "We nailed down the case. One of the contractor's men had a garage full of plumbing, fittings and other equipment. The builder said, 'We want everything returned. Thank you very much.' And that was the end of it. Now this guy is probably out there doing the same thing to somebody else."

"Builders are afraid of the construction unions," Mr. Magro contended. "I don't say that it's justified, I doubt very much that labor unions would cause any commotion. But the builders have an embedded fear of them."

Captain Goldstein, too, said, "We know how to handle those inside thefts. We could cut them way back. But the builders won't go along with us. Many times I'm told to look the other way."

A contrasting view came from Arthur Colasanto, secretary-treasurer of the Building and Construction Trades Council. He said that in 10 years he had never heard of a journeyman's being implicated in a construction site theft.

"Of course, I've heard of places being looted at night," he said, "but that's different."[9]

Public desire for further governmental intervention in control of corporate ethics is growing. A group called the Investor Responsibility Research Center suggested that corporations should develop their own internal ethical control systems to avoid outside controls. These should include a statement of practices to be avoided, controls to monitor employee behavior comparable to those some firms now use to ensure proper behavior of purchasing officers, review of senior officers by outside directors, disciplinary penalties against violators, and a sufficient flow of information to the public so that it would know that standards of corporate behavior exist and are being enforced.[10]

As suggested earlier, the corporate codes of conduct carry over into community activities. As Max Ways has pointed out, other business practices also spread and have aided in generating pressure against improper corporate practices.

Businessmen ought to notice that many expressions of consumerism offer business the sincerest flattery: imitation. Airlines, fortunately, seldom buy planes that fall as far below the seller's promise as do the meals airlines serve. Alert corporations buying from other corporations take pains to make sure that what is delivered meets the specifications of the contract. When consumers demand more accurate and more reliable information, they are following

---

[9]Ernest Dickinson, "Pilferage Rampant, and the Buyer Pays," *New York Times,* 23 October 1974. Copyright © 1974 by The New York Times Company. Reprinted by permission.

[10]Robert M. Smith, "Company Control Over Internal Ethics Is Urged," *New York Times,* 10 November 1975.

the pattern set by businessmen. This democratization of commercial practice is an instance of how business, by its very rise to a central position in the society, has stimulated the new ethical demands that now confront business.[11]

Not only is society shaped to a degree by the level of ethical or unethical practices of each of its businesses, but society is increasing its interest in what these standards are and how they are actually applied.

While it has often been argued that a business can only reflect and follow the standards of the surrounding society, this point of view is frequently attacked. The problem is that when management simply follows the local standards, the status quo is endorsed and strengthened. In other words, taking a neutral posture on important issues in a time of social stress is to assume a passive role, and management is being asked to take an active role, either for or against proposed change.

Thus, a few years ago U.S. Steel used a clear and well-established community standard as the basis for designing segregation between black and white employees in a new steel plant and then found itself under sharp public attack for opposing integration. A decision to integrate the new plant would have been equally controversial. In either case management was forced to make a choice influential in the shaping of community standards for many years. Building the old standard into a new plant was totally unacceptable to the forces demanding change, and these forces proved to be dominant legally and politically.

Support of Community Activities

Another dimension of the involvement in the community and impact on culture by a business is the type of community activities that are supported. As argued in Chapter 13, the reason for any community activity to be supported with business funds must lie in either the specific needs of the business or the unmet needs of the employee group. Therefore, if business expansion will cause a shortage of hospital beds for the community (as discussed earlier), the business should participate in the planning and fund raising, to ensure an appropriate level of contributions. In the same way a business management may encourage its employees to support music and the arts in the community and may invest some of its own funds. The investment can be justified by the need to make the community increasingly attractive for scientific staff, the overall desirability to the community of such programs, and the public relations image and advertising value to the firm of helping the community.

> The newly burgeoning interest in the creative arts reflects management's conviction that corporate property is related to the total social climate where knowledge, liberty, esthetic sensitivity and ethical responsibilities are *all* highly prized.[12]

---

[11]Max Ways, "Business Faces Growing Pressures to Behave Better," *Fortune,* May 1974, pp. 193 ff.

[12]Clarence C. Walton, "The Changing Face of a Business Corporation's Responsibilities," *Economics & Business Bulletin* (Temple University), September 1964, p. 13.

James Kuhn and Ivar Berg have commented on the pivotal nature of corporate support in the art and entertainment areas and express their concern that it may bias the culture through disproportionate support of those art forms that are most amenable to corporate purposes.

> The decisions and activities of corporate officials also influence the arts if in less obvious ways. Through their sponsorship of television or radio programs and their placement of advertisements, they favor some kinds of art and encourage them over others. Insofar as they fail to sponsor philharmonic orchestras, grand operas, and ballets as part of their effort to build up good will, familiarize their trademarks or peddle their wares, they make the widespread development and maintenance of these performing arts more difficult than the presentation of "soap operas," "horse operas," and situation comedies. They throw the immense weight of their vast resources toward one kind of art form, usually for reasons which have little to do with the art itself but that nonetheless significantly affect the relative success of the various kinds of art forms.[13]

The choice of worthwhile charities and other public activities also represents an area where a business management can render a distinct service in determining the effectiveness with which the contributions are turned into social benefits; most business managements are better able to judge this than the average small contributor. Thus, by helping the campaign of organizations that make good use of the money and avoiding corporate support to those organizations that do not, the business community can aid in improving the efficiency of these activities in serving the public interest.

Advertising and Promotion

Advertising is both a product and molder of contemporary culture. Industry's great advertising campaign to introduce the cigarette to women is often cited as a classic case.[14]

> Viewing the problem in a social framework, cigarette advertisers are recognized as a social group, and cigarette advertising as a social act and a potential creator of social norms and values. In any social act, of course, moral responsibility inheres.[15]

At the time, it was considered socially unacceptable for a woman to smoke; the

---

[13]James W. Kuhn and Ivar Berg, *Values in a Business Society* (New York: Columbia University Press, Harcourt, Brace & World, 1968), p. 61.

[14]James Playsted Wood, *The Story of Advertising* (New York: Ronald Press, 1958), pp. 375–380; also, John Gunther, *Taken at the Flood: The Story of Albert D. Lasker* (New York: Harper & Brothers, 1960), pp. 167–169.

[15]Elbing and Elbing, *Value Issue of Business,* pp. 118–119.

objective of the campaign was to double the size of the cigarette market by erasing this barrier. The art was in the insinuation of the cigarette in successive advertising campaigns without unduly offending public taste or rupturing the fabric of contemporary culture. First, a woman was shown in a scene with a man who was smoking. Then a man and woman were shown together with someone's cigarette in the ashtray. In another sequence the cigarette in the ashtray had lipstick on it. Then, as the campaign evolved further, the woman was shown holding a lighted cigarette and finally shown smoking it.

The result was a major shift in norms of behavior. Smoking became acceptable and normal for women. The tobacco industry and their agencies were very fortunate or perceptive in their timing. They felt that American women were ready to take up smoking, except for the social stigma, and through a carefully planned campaign succeeded in removing that stigma. While this transition in values might well have occurred within a few years in any case, the advertising appears to have caused it to happen earlier and more rapidly.

Because advertising has the proven power to mold opinion and shape behavior, some responsibility must be assumed by the users of such power. Clear social standards have not yet been established. However, growing restrictions on advertising claims and extension of legal liability for nonperformance of products or injury resulting from their use shows that society is becoming less tolerant of abuses of advertising and marketing power. Although social balance guidelines are not fully developed, the pattern of accountability is evolving. The emerging norm calls for fair claims and safe products that perform as advertised; advertising beyond these boundaries has provoked further restrictions that will have a profound effect as they are implemented. However, at present the social balance requirements for advertising are satisfied by fair tactics within the range of self-interest.

One example of this growth of regulation where industry self-policing failed in the judgment of the public agency involved is in the restriction on television advertising of children's products.

> Mmmm, Kemo Sabee! No more Lone Ranger rings or silver bullets?
>
> That's right, Tonto. Maybe no more Captain Video decoders, Davy Crockett T-shirts, or Sky King turquoise rings either.
>
> William Tell Overture in the background—and the scene shifts to Washington, D.C., where the cause of this consternation is revealed. On Monday, Lewis A. Engman, chairman of the Federal Trade Commission, proposed banning kid's television commercials in which prizes are offered for sending in box tops.
>
> "I also have concluded that, under some circumstances at least, the use of 'hero figures' in children's advertising may constitute an unfair practice . . ." he said.
>
> That apparently could mean that neither Hank Aaron nor Mighty Mouse could endorse cereal.
>
> Peggy Charron of the Boston-based Action on Children's Television called Engman's announcement a "beautiful first step." She looks forward to

reducing the number of minutes of commercials to which children may be exposed in one day.[16]

Chairman Engman also noted that

> A 10-month effort by the industry to devise its own new code for children's television had "yielded little, if anything."
>
> "The advertiser who chooses a child audience as the target for his selling message is subject not only to the standards of truthful advertising; he is, in my judgment, also bound to deal in complete fairness with his young viewers. In my opinion, advertising directed to or seen by children which is calculated to, or in effect does, exploit their known anxieties or capitalize on their propensity to confuse reality and fantasy is unfair within the meaning of Section 5 of the Federal Trade Commission Act."
>
> The section referred to broadly outlaws all unfair or deceptive acts or practices or methods of business competition.
>
> Mr. Engman said he was prepared "to conclude as a matter of law that the inclusion of premium offers in children's television advertising has no place in American marketing and—as I read the law—is a violation of the Federal Trade Commission Act. "The industry that relies most heavily on such premium advertising produces breakfast cereals."[17]

The American scene will change as children's premiums are banned from television. This issue touches a vein of nostalgia in many of us, as we wonder whether the restriction was really necessary. Perhaps it was. In any case it is a logical way to regulate an unchecked abuse. This is one of the reasons why it is better, in those circumstances that permit foresighted action, for the business community to choose a more moderate path of action so that new regulations for which the social forces press so strongly are not necessary.

Judging Corporate Impact

Society has established no clear standards in the area of business interaction with community culture except those conveyed by public disapproval of some corporate actions. This lack of standards complicates the management problem in assessing social balance, since real social costs must be valued subjectively by standards not yet validated by public processes.

More public interest and clearer public standards are to be expected in the future, as society's interest in the impact of business firms increases. A business seeking to evaluate social balance in this area can only judge whether the impact of its operation

---

[16]"No More Decoder Rings?" (UPI release), *Rockland County Journal News* (Nyack, N.Y.), 4 June 1974.

[17]David Burnham, "Children's TV Premiums Illegal, F.T.C. Head Says," *New York Times*, 4 June 1974. Copyright © 1974 by The New York Times Company. Reprinted by permission.

on the community appears to have a positive or negative effect. Then it must decide whether the positive effects are sufficiently clear-cut to be defensible if challenged or the negative effects are well enough defined to require remedy. Neglect of obvious needs because society's standards are still unclear is to invite a punitive social backlash at some future time.

Regulatory Controls

In other corporate impact areas, society has long since made its wishes known in the form of a growing list of rules and regulations that limit and control the way a corporation conducts its business. These rules vary from general ones that bear on all corporations to specific ones that exercise control over individual industries. Thus, at the federal level a corporation is required to file a wide variety of forms and reports for the Internal Revenue Service, the Census Bureau, the Department of Labor, the Securities and Exchange Commission (if its stock is in the hands of the public), and many others. Income, social security, property, stock registration, and many other types of taxes must be paid, and employee incomes must be reported, showing the amount of income and social security taxes that has been withheld.

Specific regulation of individual industries involves the Interstate Commerce Commission regulation of railroads and other group transport; the Civil Aeronautics Board and Civil Aviation Authority control over airlines; the regulation that several agencies impose on banks, utilities, communication, drugs, food additives, pesticides, agricultural acreage allotments and price supports; and other specific federal regulations for individual industries. The EPA has exerted pressure on specific industries in an attempt to bring all to an acceptable level of compliance. In many cases individual states have a set of corresponding regulations and regulatory commissions whose jurisdiction must also be respected. In some cases cities or regional authorities represent still another level of regulation. Taken together, these regulations represent a complex body, which have the force of law and must control corporate behavior.

Regulation of the workplace and consumer protection legislation are especially important in terms of their relationship with corporate social impact and require separate discussion. Regulation of the workplace is not new. Minimum wages and maximum hours before overtime payments are required were established by the Wagner Act; the National Labor Relations Act and the guarantee of the right to organize date from the Depression years also. More recently, new controls over working conditions and discrimination against minorities and women have been added.

OSHA

A recent and comprehensive regulation governing working conditions is the 1970 act creating the Labor Department's Occupational Safety and Health Administration (OSHA). OSHA then adopted about four thousand standards for industry to follow and was authorized not only to inspect companies for violation of these standards but also to fine violators. Some critics have found the standards vague, and the fines so low as to be ineffectual. The standards were created rapidly and have needed some revisions, and OSHA has lacked the enforcement personnel necessary to make the numbers of inspections that are required to bring the standards into general use.

OSHA has attempted to break new ground in terms of a comprehensive treatment of the exposure and tolerance standards necessary to ensure safe and healthy working conditions. By creating a new enforcement structure charged with the generation of a completely new set of standards, Congress moved far toward ensuring a complete rethinking of existing practices. Because the agency has been given broad inspection and enforcement authority and because all employees have been granted the right to call for an OSHA inspection either in their own name or anonymously, with a guarantee against reprisals of any kind, the act has had a fundamental impact on the workplace that will require several more years to manifest itself fully.

In the short run OSHA must deal with the controversy and uncertainty over the definition of safe exposure levels for dangerous materials. Unduly strict standards incur heavy costs, including shutdown of processes and elimination of jobs in some cases. Standards that are too loose allow worker injury of the type OSHA was specifically charged to prevent. Scientific evidence has not yet provided for precise determination of a standard in many cases. The approach has been to set tentative standards that represent a compromise between apparent risk and economic impact, then consider the protests and appeals, and subsequently modify the standard when appropriate.

Recent events, such as the worker injuries associated with the Kepone problems mentioned in Chapter 12, caused OSHA to shift from early emphasis on worker safety to the area of worker health, with three thousand cases of worker exposure to toxic substances reported by inspectors in one three-month period. A McGraw-Hill survey put U.S. industrial worker health and safety expenditures at $3.2 billion in 1976, representing a 17 percent increase from 1975. Thus, it appears that a substantial corrective program is under way, even though many problems in the workplace still remain to be addressed, and OSHA standards and enforcement are assured a priority on management time and attention for some years to come.

Equal Employment Opportunity and Affirmative Action

The Equal Employment Opportunity Commission (EEOC) was created to help assure compliance with the 1964 Civil Rights Act, which forbids discrimination based on race, color, religion, sex, or national origin. The Equal Pay Act of 1963 required equal pay for equal work regardless of sex, and the Age Discrimination in Employment Act of 1967 made discrimination on the basis of age (under 65) illegal. Then the Equal Employment Opportunity Act of 1972 gave EEOC enforcement powers within this comprehensive background of legislation, and the impact of this enforcement is being felt.

Affirmative action is a separate, effective antidiscrimination concept. Its origin is in the requirement that, as a condition of the awarding of any federal contract or other sale of goods to the federal government, the contractor must not only demonstrate compliance with the various laws against discrimination but include a program of affirmative action to remedy any past discrimination or other imbalance in the membership in the organization by increasing minority employment at all levels. Enforcement includes broad provisions for cancellation or suspension of existing contracts, delay in contract awards, and barriers against future bidding. While these actions are subject to appropriate appeal and review, time pressures at the point when contracts must be awarded often give enforcement officers tremendous leverage against private firms.

While the federal laws and enforcement activities are the most conspicuous, many states have enacted parallel laws and enforcement procedures and have established active, and in some cases overlapping, inspection and control programs. Thus, in addition to the EEOC and any federal agency with contracts to award, state (or even city) law enforcement agencies and governmental contracting agencies may be reviewing the major firms. Firms not involved with governmental business have felt less pressure, although EEOC and others have provided for processing direct complaints of individuals or of civil rights organizations against a particular firm.

The economic impact of EEOC enforcement is clear-cut. In 1974 an agreement with nine steel companies resulted in requiring $30 million in back pay to 34,000 male and 5,600 female workers, with $25 to $30 million in additional costs projected for the next year, and permanent changes in hiring and seniority rules. This was not an isolated case. In the last six months of 1975, EEOC actions resulted in the awarding of $50 million in additional back pay, and the number of charges of discrimination filed has risen rapidly. The EEOC case backlog has risen with the increased filing rate, however, which has caused complaints about delays in processing of charges.

The impact of EEOC and affirmative action on managements appears in several areas. In the first place, discrimination has become economically unwise, although the paths to corrective action are sometimes difficult. Second, the burden of proof has been put on the employer. This means that nondiscrimination is not sufficient in itself; beyond obedience to the law, the corporation must be prepared to prove rapidly and conclusively that it has not discriminated, since any complaint is likely to paralyze certain business processes until it can be resolved to the satisfaction of the law enforcement officer. To be prepared to prove nondiscrimination, the corporation is forced into more formal and more rigidly controlled procedures and records for all actions involving the members of its organization, from the handling of applicants and interviews to performance appraisals and salary increases.

Additionally, the EEOC activity has brought to the surface many contradictions. Seniority, for example, is a basic worker protection that can also serve to delay correction of past discrimination if layoffs eliminate junior workers who were added to give the work force the desired balance. Society must choose between these conflicting worker-protection principles, and the corporation may be caught by the uncertainty preceding any definitive resolution of such issues. Likewise, affirmative action requirements to remedy past lack of ethnic minorities or women in managerial assignments act to reduce the promotion opportunities of white males, whose discrimination complaint can then be sustained in certain circumstances. As the work force has discovered that rules can be changed, vocal activist groups may appear to challenge management actions, with the result that the management task is made more difficult and the other groups in the work force are required to become more vocal to avoid losing their rights and position.

Altogether, the equal employment opportunity and affirmative action requirements have transmuted the wise and necessary management emphasis on providing equality of opportunity for all members of the organization into a thorny, current (if not daily) issue requiring careful management of the impacts of all actions. Now even the fairest decisions may have to be defended and justified in detail against searching and perhaps even irrational charges.

Consumer Protection Legislation

The Consumer Product Safety Commission in the Department of Health, Education, and Welfare was created in 1972, and consolidated earlier programs established under the Hazardous Substances Act, the Flammable Fabrics Act, the Poison Prevention Package Act, the Refrigerator Safety Act, and the Child Protection and Toy Safety Act. The toy safety area has been an early focus of the CPSC's expanding interest and activity.

The Food and Drug Administration is one of the older consumer protection agencies. Beyond its familiar area of control over prescription and nonprescription drugs and food additives, its control over cosmetic and toiletry ingredients is being extended. Recent actions have focused on removing dangerous products from the market, and the resulting controversy over whether saccharin should be banned as a carcinogen will probably serve to clarify the extent to which the FDA role in such areas is acceptable to Congress and the public.

Meanwhile, the EPA continues to develop the administrative pattern for its Office of Toxic Substances, which was created under the 1976 Toxic Substances Control Act. While the regulatory focus will be on the myriad of toxic chemicals, the evolution of regulations will undoubtedly cause major changes in some consumer products, and consumer protection issues will establish permissible thresholds for many product applications.

The Federal Trade Commission also has taken an active role in consumer protection by pressing for truth in advertising and has gained an effective voice in determining the way that a product can be promoted. It continues to move toward clearer requirements that claims made in advertising copy be documented in advance to the satisfaction of independent authorities. Concurrently, the Consumer Protection Credit Act and the Fair Credit Reporting Act, as well as the Federal Truth in Lending Act, have increased consumer protection in this area. Financing costs and interest rates must now be specifically stated in advance. Consumer rights to cancel contracts and protest disputed billings have been established, and credit reports have been opened to inspection by the consumer, who may dispute adverse entries and require information as to their origin.

Another type of consumer protection arose through the National Traffic and Motor Vehicle Safety Act of 1966, which created what has now become the National Highway Traffic Administration, the creator of mandatory auto safety standards for cars sold in the United States.

Altogether, the nation has moved rapidly toward an elaborate set of standards for protecting consumers in certain areas and has extended this protection gradually into many new areas. Some standards of protection are mandatory, such as the now relaxed requirement that motorists wear seat belts. Other standards assist consumers in obtaining their rights under various acts such as those controlling consumer credit terms. One approach maintains the rights of the individual, while the other reduces individual freedom, although perhaps in a good cause. A key issue in the further evolution of consumer protection legislation is whether the consumer can be allowed to behave responsibly in many cases or must be protected by the government against all hazards and be permitted minimum opportunity for making an individual choice.

The Social Basis for Management Authority

One of the more subtle but no less important ways in which the corporation and society interact to affect each other is through the gradual modification in the basis for management authority and, thus, in the management practices through which this authority is exercised.

Management authority originated as the right of the owner and is now usually exercised through a board of directors that chooses operating executives and vests them with the delegation of authority to operate in the stockholders' best interest. Once, this authority had few limits. As cited earlier, Alfred Krupp was free to dismiss his employees on suspicion of political activity. He owned the company and the town, and, as owner, he had authority. The employees he dismissed had no recourse or appeal; they were fired from their jobs and expelled from the town on the basis of Krupp's absolute authority.

Many U.S. firms in earlier years acted as arbitrarily as Krupp and on the same basis. But there has been a change. Most large corporations are no longer managed by their owners, and most stockholders are distant from the actual management processes. Stockholder authority remains a real force, as evidenced by the increasing frequency of corporate takeover bids, but in many respects corporate managements have become independent of ties to individual stockholders. Rather, the managements seek to operate in a way calculated to bring collective favor from the public markets, courting the securities analysts and the investing public and trying to produce and project earnings growth patterns that will find favor and, thus, command a stock price that is a high multiple of the earnings.

The property owners' delegation of authority still exists as a primary basis for management action, although it has become less personalized than in the past and has been greatly modified by the growing body of law, administrative regulation, and public practice that defines the rights of employees and sets other boundaries on management action. Coordinate with the property owners' delegation as the basis for authority are several other authority concepts that act with it and usually, but not always, reinforce this authority.

In the first place, the employee group contributes to management authority by recognizing and obeying that authority. At least the passive consent of the governed is required for any government or management structure to operate; this is why the internal propaganda necessary to maintain this consent is such an important part of the program of any totalitarian structure.

Employee groups sometimes withdraw their acceptance of management authority. This occurs in individual areas when an inept supervisor fails to establish an effective management role. It occurs on a larger scale when a union or other representative group protests specific management actions with active support from the specified number of employees.

Management authority also accumulates as a corporation develops an operating franchise that its employees see as valuable and desirable. Thus, the employees of a shipyard may develop a strong sense of pride in the ships that they build and may accept management authority in part because it makes continuance of this role possible. As the employees see elements of public benefit and public service resulting from this role and realize the importance to their customers of continued service, the importance of the operating franchise increases. This serves as a reinforcement for management authority.

Management authority, then, is derived from (1) the outcome of the pressures of the property owners' delegation, (2) employee endorsement of this authority as proper, (3) loyalty to the operating franchise, and (4) awareness of public dependence on the corporate products or services. A pattern of modification can be traced through the change in scope of corporate authority over time. Where society used to accept the fact that corporate authority included the right to control the lifestyle and private conduct of its employees, this right to control has now been greatly curtailed. Even during working hours, when the corporate authority to establish strict dress and appearance codes was once unchallenged, changes have occurred. Today's lifestyles reflect a much wider variety in clothes, hairstyles, and standards of grooming, and corporate authority has been sufficiently restricted so that this variety is permitted in the workplace to a much greater degree than in the past.

Elsewhere, the growth of regulation is discussed. Here it is necessary only to point out that OSHA, Equal Employment, and the myriad of other laws and regulations over the workplace and corporate conduct each represent a curtailment of management authority. Decisions once made as a part of management freedom are now constrained by rules and interpretations of the law.

The essential pattern that needs emphasis is a pattern of authority based on the interaction of several forces. The nature of this interaction is continually modified by the changing needs and demands of society, and a consequence of this change is a considerable shaping of corporate behavior.

Corporate Power to Shape Society

Society is the arbiter and the business organization is the provider of goods and services. The business cannot provide goods or services that the public rejects. The Ford Motor Company learned this through bitter experience in its attempts to win public acceptance for the ill-fated Edsel. On the other hand, in the years when General Motors and Ford chose not to cultivate the market for smaller cars, the development of that market was retarded.

Eventually, through the invasion of small European and Japanese cars, the

compact car market was developed and U.S. manufacturers entered and participated. Then the energy shortage focused fresh attention on this market and
apparently stimulated a shift away from the larger, more fuel-hungry models. GM has
announced a major program to expand its participation in the compact car market.
Because Ford and Chrysler have chosen to move more slowly, this program has
stirred fresh fears that GM will increase its market share to the point of complete
dominance of the automobile market. These antitrust fears are a reflection of the
potential impact of such an extensive capital program.

By choosing to throw its resources into serving the change in consumer prefer-
ence, General Motors will, if it has judged consumer preferences correctly, make the
change to a new type of car market move much more rapidly. It will shape this aspect
of the development of U.S. society in a very real way. Its competitors will be forced to
conform in making the transition and compete on new terms, and GM might well
succeed in increasing its market advantage.

All of this is in the direction of serving consumer interests effectively. However,
there is no question that by choosing to invest in the development of this market at
this time rather than holding back as it did in the 1940s and 1950s, this corporation is
shaping the evolution of society. Corporations frequently find themselves with such
opportunities, although usually the impacts are smaller and less conspicuous. A great
responsibility goes with the power to cause such changes, and this power requires
wise use lest it be curtailed.

Society's Power to Shape the Corporation

As society makes rules, the corporation must obey. As society changes its needs, the
corporate opportunity for sale of goods and services is changed. As society changes
its norms for conduct and lifestyles, the corporation must make related changes in its
rules for and administration of the workplace. Thus, society's power to change the
corporation is profound.

This substantial power is usually utilized only in an evolutionary way. For the most
part, society reacts passively to corporate initiatives, accepting some and rejecting
others. But this does not mean that society's power is confined to a passive role.
Whenever corporate action enters the boundaries of jurisdiction of the administrative
authorities already constituted by society, that action is subject to review and
perhaps to reversal.

Whenever a corporate action is perceived as posing a threat by any constituent of
society that is sufficiently effective and vocal to direct the rule-making processes,
appropriate new laws and regulations are created and the corporate action is curbed.
Society's power over the corporation is total and unlimited but not frequently roused.
Careless use of this power is restrained by the degree to which the public perceives
corporate operations to represent profound social benefits.

Thus, while the corporation's power to shape society is subtly manifested by the
impact of its initiatives, decisions, and innovations, society's power over corporations
is much greater but usually passive. The corporate power is that of a skillful and
ingenious servant to a society that is not always fully conscious of the degree to
which it is truly master.

Summary

The theme of this chapter has been the power of the corporation and society to shape each other, as summarized in Figure 17.1. The activities of the corporation can and often do have a profound effect on community culture. First, the nature of the business contributes in important ways to determining the nature of the community, through the kind of work its employment represents, the kind of achievements the members of the organization share, the kind of activities it supports or encourages, and the ethics and value systems inherent in the business and expressed through its business practices. In addition, the advertising and promotion of each firm's marketing approach to the community encourages patterns of adoption and use of products and services, many of which represent changes in convention. Thus the cumulative impact of all of these marketing efforts is toward an evolution of the culture as new goods and new habits are adopted.

One of the ways that society shapes the corporation is through the continued evolution of the basis for management authority, as property concepts change and society's attitudes change. Another way is through its rule-making power, which is usually only slowly aroused and mobilized and, although sometimes variably influential, is very powerful.

Because a corporation is dependent on society to act as the rule maker and to provide its access to whatever portion of the total social capital it employs in its business, it has good reason for maintaining interest in and giving attention to its social impact, while showing respect for social governance functions. The corporation's impact on community culture is perhaps the most subtle of the impacts, but fundamental in its long-term importance to the relationship. Society needs the corporation for its ability to produce wealth, and so the balance must be between an adequate level of public social benefits and private corporate profits. The corporate interest is not only in creating and maintaining this balance but also in making sure that its pattern of actions cannot be misinterpreted. Society must not be misled by the antagonists of corporate activity into forgetting that society is gaining by corporate operation. The corporation must both manage its affairs well and be sure that society knows that it is doing so.

This chapter has profiled corporate actions that have impacts on values, including the impact of promoting the use of the goods and services that justify the corporate existence. Out of the interrelationship flows a continuing and, to a degree, a changing basis for management authority that can be observed as the corporation offers

Figure 17.1   Meeting Society and Being Shaped by Society

Impact on community culture	Society and management authority
Values, ethics, morals	
Corporate giving	Power to shape society
Advertising and promotion	Society's power to mold the business

A corporation must live up to society's standards and change as they change. But because of its prominent and powerful role, the firm is in the forefront in generating new change—for better or for worse.

change to society and attempts to induce society to accept it. Since the latent power of society is so much larger, the corporation needs to develop an awareness of its impacts as it shapes society and to achieve a balance that is sufficient to avoid social reprisals.

Guideline for Managing Corporate Social Impact

In managing the social impact from adjusting to and shaping the requirements of society, social balance will tend to be maintained if the following guideline is applied:

Social change   The corporate power to mold and reshape society subtly is used wisely by selecting areas where the social forces justifying and supporting the change have already been set in motion and by not encouraging any change that will be rejected by society's governance processes.

Applying the Guideline

Both the CB radio and the moped have attained a wide level of acceptance only recently. Both have the capacity for causing social change. Both devices had been available to the market for many years and had failed to achieve popularity in spite of previous promotional efforts. While good marketing may have catalyzed the current acceptance process, previous efforts had not succeeded in popularizing either product until underlying forces of social change had reached a point that permitted this acceptance.

On reaching a degree of acceptance, both the CB radio and the moped have triggered further social change and social stress. The acceptance of the CB radio has required restructuring the available band frequencies and has created new social and communication patterns (such as police monitoring of distress calls) and new social concerns (such as those arising over the report that prostitutes make dates with truckers in this way). So far, however, the social changes due to the CB radio have not raised great enough stress in society to threaten the product.

The moped has begun to receive adverse public attention because of its potential hazards. Licensing laws for vehicle and driver are being passed, and concerns for driver and public safety are leading to proposals for restricting moped use. Both the CB radio and the moped released forces of further social change, which, at least in the case of the moped, is leading to a series of restrictions on what the public views as risks and abuses. The suggestion from the guideline proposed here is that manufacturers and promoters develop an understanding of the social change processes that both permit the initial acceptance of the product and are triggered by its spreading adoption. Furthermore, these corporations have an interest in recognizing the social stress that is being created and in working conspicuously to stem abuses or draft governing legislation that may be required to obtain an acceptable social balance with minimum public abuse, minimum public anger, and minimum risk of undue restrictions being placed on any newly accepted product or service.

Questions for Analysis and Discussion

1. Find and discuss other examples of corporate impact on community culture through the nature of the business.

2. Look for examples of corporate business ethics with good or bad community impacts. What are these impacts? Discuss them briefly.

3. To what extent do you feel that corporations should conform to community ethical standards versus taking a leadership role in setting better standards? Discuss.

4. Do you see corporate advertising or corporate support of art or architecture as having any significant impact on community standards? Discuss.

5. Develop and discuss your own illustration of corporate power to shape society. What are the responsibilities attendant on this shaping?

For Further Information

Kaufman, Herbert. *The Limits of Organizational Change.* Birmingham: University of Alabama Press, 1971.

Kubler, George. *The Shape of Time.* New Haven, Conn.: Yale Press, 1962.

Powers, Charles W. *Social Responsibility and Investments.* Nashville, Tenn.: Abingdon Press, 1971.

Sutton, Francis X., Harris, Seymour E., Kaysen, Carl, and Tobin, James. *The American Business Creed.* New York: Schocken Books, 1962.

Views From the Socially Sensitive Seventies. New York: American Telephone & Telegraph, 1973.

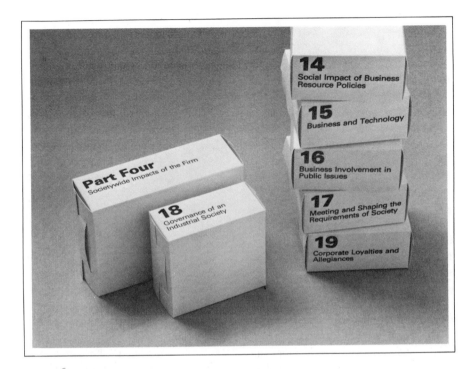

Part Four Societywide Impacts of the Firm

14 Social Impact of Business Resource Policies

15 Business and Technology

16 Business Involvement in Public Issues

17 Meeting and Shaping the Requirements of Society

18 Governance of an Industrial Society

19 Corporate Loyalties and Allegiances

18
Governance of an Industrial Society

Society has an urgent management problem in trying to govern itself in an increasingly complex industrial age. This state of affairs relates to and becomes a part of the corporate problem in judging and attempting to balance the social impact of its actions, because of the increase in important interrelationships between business and the expanding network of government regulation. Managing the regulatory interface requires a recognition of the dimensions of the governance problem as developed here, since significant changes in regulatory practice and philosophy must evolve if the economy is to survive the almost inevitable growth of regulation.

A corporation can better manage its relationship with and its social impact on society's governance apparatus if management is aware of the more rational and less rational parts of the structure, the nature of the stresses on it, and the direction in which it hopefully can be encouraged to evolve.

The true test of a good government is its aptitude and tendency to produce good administration.[1]

ALEXANDER HAMILTON ET AL.

Contemporary industrial society is in many ways a regulated society. Commissions, agencies, and other regulatory operations have been added in an attempt to make the society run better. Imperfections remain, and the national response to these imperfections is to call for more regulation. Entrepreneurs and business executives cry out against increased restraints and the expansion of bureaucracy. Yet the end is not in sight, as new clamors continually arise for government to prevent an industrial collapse or check corporate power in some new area.

The clear trend is toward more governmental involvement in the activities of private enterprise. To favor or not to favor regulation is not the question. Regulation is here and growing, but inefficiently. This chapter will argue that a new approach toward regulation is urgently needed, with (1) a shift toward governance at the system level, (2) better public data gathering on national business and economic activities, (3) imaginative development of management action and public policy alternatives, (4) a pluralistic national decision process based on public discussion leading to an informed consensus, and (5) a governance system made more responsive by appropriate economic regulation of private productive processes. The first step will be to examine some of the factors underlying the continuing proliferation of social control, and then we will consider the nature of the equilibrium between public and private interests that is most likely to serve the long-term national need. This examination will begin with the wealth-producing processes that provide the basis for this regulation.

The Corporation as the Producer of Wealth

The average level of living in the United States has risen because the amount of output from the productive sectors of the economy has increased faster than the population that consumes this wealth. But the distribution of wealth among this population, as portrayed in Figure 18.1, has become a matter for national concern. Out of the evolving pattern of social legislation since the Great Depression, a national social objective has emerged. The people of the United States seem to have adopted

---

[1]Alexander Hamilton et al., *The Federalist* (New York: Modern Library, n.d.), p. 444.

as a national goal that no individual be deprived of that minimum share of national wealth necessary to maintain a socially adequate standard of health and welfare.

This objective of guaranteeing adequate health and welfare to all has been only partially attained, and new programs toward advancing its attainment are enacted in each session of Congress. The cumulative effect of these programs has been a large shift of national resources to social and governmental activities that are not directly productive of wealth. This shift has not reduced the average level of living because the output from resources still devoted to wealth production has increased rapidly enough to compensate for this transfer of resources to social overhead.

Welfare plans, social agencies, and administrative bureaucracies do not produce wealth, regardless of their other merits. To continue shifting resources to social and governmental activities and allocating more resources to the deprived and underprivileged sectors of the society, the productivity of the remaining wealth-producing activity must increase even more rapidly. Otherwise, the additional burden of these

The Firm as Viewed by Society

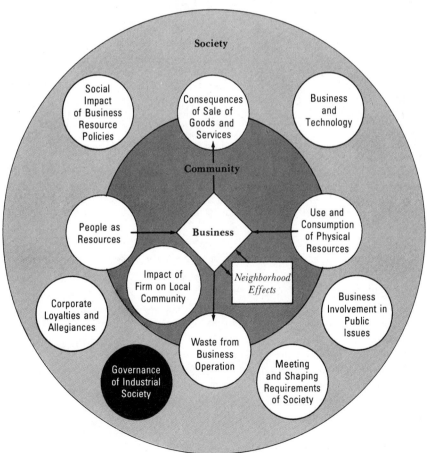

Figure 18.1 The Level-of-Living Equation

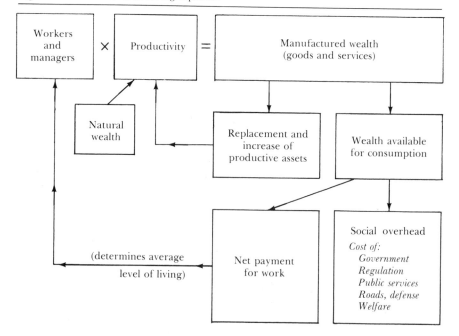

Our industrial society is almost totally dependent on current manufacture of wealth (goods and services) to provide for our needs; unprocessed natural wealth no longer represents a significant contribution. Therefore, the average living standard (level of living) depends on (1) the number of people engaged in productive activity, (2) their average output (productivity), and (3) the fraction of the wealth available as payment for work (versus the fraction devoted to support of the nonproductive members of society, cost of public bureaus and agencies, and other social overhead).

regulatory and social programs cannot be maintained without cutting living standards.

While the potential for forced reallocation among consumers has been explored, the amount of wealth available for reallocation from the wealthy is modest compared to the unfilled requirements of the needy. "Soak the rich" programs are inadequate to the need. Politically and practically, the pressure is toward increasing total wealth production, so that the sacrifice of giving more to those without wealth will not be felt by the country at large. In addition, society is beginning to require that production methods be revised, even at some extra burden on productivity, to become consistent with maintenance of a realistic long-term equilibrium with the total environment. Basic environmental limitations demand reduced pollution and more efficient use of energy. If productivity cannot be increased in spite of these added burdens, then either the average level of living or the support of social programs must be reduced.

The initiative in revising production methods and increasing the productivity of wealth must come largely from the corporations. As in the United States, all modern industrial economies use either the corporate concept of wealth management or some reasonable equivalent. That is, a modern industrial economy functions by allocating blocks of resources to an appropriate group of professional managers charged with economic and productive use of those resources toward certain defined ends. The governance problem is in obtaining the necessary supervision over the way that these resources are employed.

A U.S. corporation that produces automobiles must operate at a profit to survive, where the profit is determined (among other things) by the acceptability of the product in meeting the market needs for automobiles. In the state capitalism of a communist or socialist economy, the definitions of market acceptability of the product might be different. And the economic performance requirement might focus on achievement of a budget rather than generation of a profit. Otherwise, the automobile production management problems have considerable similarity under either state or private capitalism.

Regardless of the political structure of the state, the social needs in a modern industrial economy define the wealth production requirements, since there is no other long-term means for meeting these needs. This social pressure for wealth production creates an almost irresistible political pressure toward a social-governmental interest in the management of the wealth-producing sectors. In the United States the private corporations are the primary producers of wealth, and society as a whole shows a growing interest in how this wealth-producing activity can best serve the national welfare. The result has been more regulation.

Regulation of Wealth Production

Examination of the problem of how society may best regulate its wealth production processes reveals certain basic facts. In the first place, some overall government action is essential (1) to maintain a framework of laws to shape incentives and channel activities in desirable directions, and (2) to account for the tendency of local managements to suboptimize with regard to total system needs, even if directions and incentives have been perfectly designed by society. Suboptimization of this sort is an important consequence of effective management efforts and must be recognized and offset if it is not to become the national operating pattern.

Suboptimization

A particular management group must inevitably become absorbed in striving for the objectives it has set, maintaining the momentum of its programs, and fulfilling its own purpose in the best way possible. Any human organization focusing on a particular set of challenges and achievements must exclude most of the information that is extraneous to current problems. This is the essence of the concentration necessary for successful achievement.

The same exclusions cause a bias in perspective because concentration must lead to some restriction of outlook. While the often quoted remark, "What is good for General Motors is good for the country," drew ridicule, it revealed a narrowness in the management point of view that developed from a career of working exclusively to serve G.M.'s interests well. The necessary concentration of attention required habitual exclusion of many elements not relating to G.M.'s interests, in order to manage effectively.

In the same way, the Port of New York Authority or the Tennessee Valley Authority are vociferously attacked by critics who feel that their managers have lost sight of some aspects of the public interest. The point is not to single out G.M., the Port Authority, or the TVA but to suggest that the nature of human organizations is such that they become absorbed in their own objectives and achievements and lose touch with some elements of the larger picture. The general public interest requires that the objectives, the performance, and even the reasons for existence of these major organizations must be reviewed from time to time from some broader point of view.

Government Intervention

Although the emphasis in U.S. political and economic history is on the role of free enterprise, governmental involvement has always been significant. First, an effective free-enterprise, free-market system is only possible within the jurisdiction of a rule-making political body that will oversee the operation of such a market. Many markets are not truly free, and in many cases the governing political body has acted to restrict market freedom to shape the competitive environment. Examples include protective tariffs to check competition from outside the country, temporary monopolies through the patent system, broadcasting and utilities franchises, subsidies to American flagshipping, and fair trade and related statutes aimed at specific restraint of price competition.

On the other hand, abuses of corporate power and other private constraints of the free market have led to a long series of restrictions of a different type. Rules for corporations have been changed through legislation against monopolies, holding companies, and certain pricing and price-fixing practices. In addition, a series of regulatory commissions has been created and given authority over individual industries. Railroads, banks, and television stations are restrained significantly in their behavior by governmental bodies of this type. Thus, the United States has evolved a system in which the regulation of the wealth-producing sector by market forces has been increasingly supplemented by explicit social intervention of one sort or another.

The Regulatory Structure

Unfortunately, the U.S. structure is largely one of problem-oriented regulation that has not proved to be an efficient means of guiding problem industries to operate in the public interest. *The Monopoly Makers*, a book from the Nader group, is a searing indictment typical of the critiques of regulatory performance.[2] The prototype that emerges here is of an agency that is created to regulate in response to a specific problem, is given a charter and an industry, and is allowed to run and evolve without

---

[2]Mark Green, ed., *The Monopoly Makers* (New York: Grossman, 1973).

any significant degree of regulation of its own performance. In time agency and industry grow together, as the regulatory structure creates a group of dependent industries and as the regulatory commission increasingly must act to keep its dependent industries alive rather than concern itself with the public interest. Key problems in this regulatory structure are its focus on individual problem industries and its freedom from meaningful constraints to force regulation in the overall public interest. This indictment does not necessarily mean that the existing regulatory agencies were created in error, but it does mean that regulatory mechanisms that may once have been suitable fail in present performance. After all, our industrial society has changed fundamentally, especially in the strong growth of interdependence between its different parts.

One penalty for the progress of our society is a substantial increase in the closeness of the linkage between different areas and industries. This was illustrated dramatically a few years ago when switching errors caused a major regional electric power failure in New York and across the Northeast. Similar failures have occurred in other power networks and again in New York and have caused fresh attention to the nature of the linkages and interdependencies such networks create. However, the entire industrial economy is similarly linked in almost as direct a fashion. A transportation strike, a steel or auto strike, a restriction on petroleum imports—any one of these events causes serious disruption in the operation of the country. Our industrial economy has become so complex that it must continually be regulated to keep the components of the system in balance with each other.

Long ago it was recognized that there was no realistic alternative to governmental regulation of the money supply. More recently, control of the total level of economic activity by suitable fiscal and monetary policies has become an important role of the federal government. Increasingly, other parts of the society need the same sort of governance, except it is not clear that available mechanisms are adequate to the task. The future of our society seems pointed toward a continual escalation in the necessary degree of regulation due to its increasingly delicate and complex internal linkages, even though the clumsiness—and social overhead cost—of the present regulatory processes are imposing a serious, growing burden on the national welfare.

Public Ownership

Government ownership of utilities and other productive assets is often suggested as a means of developing the proper framework of control. Unfortunately, the virtue inherent in nationalization of a difficult private industry to solve a social control problem is limited by the same processes that create many of the difficulties in the first place. In other words, individual management groups whether in private or public corporations tend to focus on individual aspects of the national problem. They develop vested interests based on the perspective of their particular organization or agency. To put it another way, they also suboptimize by developing optimums based only on the portion of the public interest visible to a management group immersed in solving its own assigned problems.

Just as the ICC can be accused of strangling the railroads and losing sight of its public role or the Port of New York Authority can be accused of setting its own goals and objectives and ignoring the public welfare, so can a nationalized industry, such as the TVA, be accused of perpetuating itself and its viewpoints in disregard of the total national interest. Like most other corporations and agencies, none of these institutions were designed to operate as part of a national system. Each institution tends to work to fulfill its own ends to the best of the ability of its managers. Each institution works within a goal framework determined largely by the interests of the institution and its managers based on the information that is obtained. Each institution suboptimizes because its interests and information flows must be more restricted than the total span of the national interest so that it can concentrate on doing its own job well.

Stafford Beer has said: "Institutions are organizations designed for being what they are and doing what they do." This is exactly what one would expect from any human organization allowed to evolve toward its own ends without careful and continuing guidance from the total society. However, unguided evolution is no longer acceptable. Our society must redirect more of these energies if the national resources are to be adequate to the national needs.

The clear national need is that society must develop a mechanism for regulating institutions such as the ICC, the Port Authority, and the TVA, as well as the private corporations, to enable them to work in smooth coordination with each other and with the other institutions in the economy. Needless to say, this is difficult. Only political force, which is the most cumbersome and least effective of the available regulatory mechanisms, is conveniently available for the governance of a national system made up of public institutions such as the three just cited.

Regulatory Mechanism

The available regulatory mechanisms tend to be either economic or political in their function. The political mechanisms are based ultimately on the emotional commitment and active or passive support of large numbers of people. These mechanisms include both the direct demands for public action and the manipulatory bureaucracy and patronage tolerated from the established leaderships. Political force based on a public outcry for action is often required to redirect the established behavior of a corporation or other large institution.

Economic regulatory mechanisms range from tickets and towing fines to control illegal parking in cities to the substantial judgments now being levied on various U.S. corporations for failures in affirmative action compliance. Corporations are highly responsive to well-designed economic regulatory processes; for example, the Department of Labor can obtain prompt reaction from most managements to a complaint about possible unequal treatment of women in regard to pay or promotion. Having seen AT&T and several large electric utilities pay massive penalties when they lagged in compliance, most major U.S. corporations are anxious to correct errors quickly rather than risk retroactive damages and imposed quotas at the hands of the courts. If the public continues to want rapid repair of past injustices toward women, this regulatory process is highly efficient.

The same process has slackened badly in obtaining affirmative action compliance from civil service agencies and other sorts of public bodies. The difficulty arises because the economic and legal weapons that are so impressive to a private corporation have little impact on a public agency. For one agency to seek fines against another means little, and to ask the court to shut down a laggard agency is to ask it to deny the performance of the public purpose for which the agency was created. Characteristically, public bodies respond only slowly to legal and economic processes unless political force can also be invoked. Unfortunately, regulatory processes based on political force cannot be objective or even-handed in their application. Political force usually can be generated only in surges; it tends to overcorrect and then to subside until the next crisis arises.

Thus, reliance must be placed on economic processes because, by their nature, politically oriented regulatory processes offer minimum hope for the delicate and complex governance seemingly required by our society. Since the economic processes tend to work well only on profit-oriented private entities, then it follows that they would represent the optimum base for the regulatory structure. In summary, regulation works best where the regulatory body has strong legal and economic powers over a private enterprise. Therefore, the most effective regulation of a complex economy should involve maximum operation by private enterprise within a comprehensive and carefully designed regulatory framework.

This raises the next problem, the design of a suitable regulatory framework. A dangerous and faulty analogy has been drawn with state planning in some of the communist countries, where the process tends to be more political and where the state planning tends to unify many enterprises into a large bureaucracy rather than to have them operate independently under public regulation. Here the advantage of central coordination can easily be canceled by the clumsiness and potential for suboptimization of a politically oriented institutional management.

An example of the problem that the United States faces can be drawn from the experience cited by William Simon when he was charged with the start-up of the Federal Energy Office during the oil crisis in the fall of 1973. In this case it was necessary for regulatory action to commence in advance of the gathering of information about the true nature of the allocation problems that the regulatory process was designed to optimize. Even though a petroleum crisis had been predicted and could have been expected within a very few years, no public data base concerning petroleum uses and flows had been developed. Too little was known about oil supplies, inventories, and reserves, as well as about the market for petroleum products, their price elasticity, and their potential to be replaced by fuels and chemicals from other sources. The lack of information necessitated the making of arbitrary decisions that were not always correct.

Now that the nation has begun to gather the necessary details about its petroleum needs and flows, a healthy debate has been generated as to which of the alternatives for solving the petroleum shortage is most in the national interest. This sort of policy debate is in the democratic tradition of the country and should be encouraged.

Early in our history, debate of public issues was easier because less elaborate information sources were required. Now, to restore the vitality of the democratic process of formulating public policy, the necessary information must be gathered, made available to the various bodies interested in proposing public policy formulations, and the merits of policy proposals debated until a reasonable consensus has emerged and necessary legislation can be written.

What is being suggested, therefore, is the need for a mechanism where any public policy problem likely to require regulatory consideration will be supported by a publicly available compilation of necessary basic information that is developed in advance of the crystallization of the issue. From this data base various congressional, public, and private interest groups should be encouraged to develop their analyses and to present public policy proposals for discussion and rebuttal. Only then can the nation hope to define a public policy that is truly in the public interest.

Future Needs

If the productivity of the wealth-producing sector of society is to increase at a rate consistent with the requirements of the national social objectives, an active and effective governance system will be necessary. As the complexity and interdependence of the elements of society continue to increase, it becomes more and more likely that system-level intervention by the various levels of government will be required to keep various productive activities sufficiently coordinated to prevent a decrease in industrial output. Otherwise, major bankruptcies, disasters, and other sources of friction may more than consume the productivity gains of the individual industries.

A New Governance System

Governance is needed to coordinate the productivity of the independent economic sectors in the direction of the national interest. The governance system must be new because past regulation has been too narrow in focus, too uncoordinated to fit the needs of a complex industrial system, and too costly in the social overhead of its delays and bureaucratic demands. The danger is that the present system eventually will become so unwieldy that the public will lose hope and patience and will choose to sweep away existing institutions in favor of direct social control of wealth production, which, even though it may not be more efficient, will no longer have private corporations in the role of suspected or actual public adversaries.

This evolution of a new governance system is not the only alternative, but it appears more likely to offer hope for long-term gains in efficiency in regulating wealth production in the public interest than either the extension of the bureaucratic and mediocre approach to the problem-oriented regulation of the past or the political complexity of the national planning for state-owned enterprise by the socialist and communist countries. The necessary new governance system will require the following elements.

1. *Public debate from a public data base*　A large, accessible store of basic social, industrial, and economic data is needed so that public policy can be formulated after an informed and continuing public debate of alternatives as new regulations are proposed and administered.

2. *New public processes for adjusting and directing an economy*　A new emphasis is needed on the efficiency and effectiveness of regulatory processes, which can

be achieved primarily by applying economic pressures and sanctions within a legal framework that will give private enterprise maximum incentives to turn its energies in the direction of the public interest.

Many unregulated public sector activities could be returned to management by the private sector with a gain in productivity and in responsiveness to the governance process; hopefully, some of these reversions will occur.

Since planning and policy groups are not infallible or omniscient, their products must also be evaluated and audited. Given a broader data base of publicly available information about a particular issue, public interest groups such as Common Cause and the National Planning Association, special interest groups such as the American Petroleum Institute and the National Coal Association, and the various administrative, executive, and legislative staffs will generate alternatives and discuss their merits constructively. The United States has an outstanding ability to foster productive public policy discussions of this type, but the quality of these discussions has tended to decline since the days of the founding fathers because the increasing complexity of public issues has been only partially offset by the growth of reliable and timely sources of information on these issues.

An informed public debate of policy alternatives not only should be conducted initially when a regulatory need emerges but also should be continued as regulatory performance alternatives are devised. Such dialogue is crucial in determining the effectiveness of any regulatory process since effectiveness depends, first of all, on the correct regulatory policy choices. The ability to choose is enhanced after public debate of alternatives because the tendency of individual planning groups to trap themselves in suboptimization of their own points of view is counteracted.

Effective Regulatory Processes

As previously suggested, effective regulation should emphasize economic regulatory mechanisms. But within this framework are many approaches and alternatives. The public sector fixes utility and transportation rates, establishes communication and other franchise monopolies, and sets boundaries and tolerances (sulfur dioxide emission standards, radiation exposure limits) for industrial operation. The good regulatory processes are clear, objective, and significant enough to warrant and obtain effective enforcement. For example, the current debate over vinyl chloride and asbestos exposure is over the tolerance levels that should be permitted. Once this debate is completed and a clear set of standards is defined and established, enforcement and compliance will be relatively easier to monitor. This can become an effective regulation; hopefully, the real needs of public and worker safety will not have too drastic an impact on existing industrial installations.

Public utility rates are difficult because the regulatory standards have become much less clear as the rate-making process has become increasingly complex and sometimes political. The initial purpose of utility regulation was to restrain local monopoly power through public authority over pricing and terms of service. The various utilities, the railroads, and the other transportation forms have each fallen under such regulation. But rate-making authority is not only a restraint on high or unfair pricing. It also shapes resource allocations, including regional development of the affected industry and of the public sectors dependent on it. Thus, administration of rate-making authority has evolved into allocation of markets, regulation of the degree of competition, and review of operating practices down to details such as the equality of the terms on which competing airlines serve refreshments to their passengers.

The net effect is that the regulatory purpose of protecting the public has become translated into that of restraining or even assuring the rate of return of regulated industries. But the rate of return on capital is not a clear standard because it depends on operating expenses that vary in inverse proportion with management competence. And as the regulatory commissions have been drawn deeper into the morass of trying to monitor operating efficiency, the political impact of the resource allocation process has emerged to the point where much utility and transportation regulation is ultimately more political and intuitive than objective in character, in spite of the diligent efforts of the regulatory staffs.

For example, the Nixon administration was believed by many to have influenced decisions on airline route allocation. Whether or not the allegations were correct, they serve to emphasize the political nature of the process, just as the movement of New York State toward purchase of key Consolidated Edison facilities basically sprang from political considerations. Regardless of whether the decisions were right, the process is wrong because it is so far removed from simple objective measures of service to the public.

In other words, regulation is intended to achieve a public service objective, which can best follow from rational analysis of performance based on defined and accepted standards. Political processes do not work that way. They are more emotional than rational and often work from intuitive or otherwise obscure standards of performance. Thus, a sound regulatory process cannot be primarily political because that type of process does not lend itself to fair, even-handed, and consistent governance year after year.

System-Level Regulation

An important area for a public policy debate in the present is over the matter of regulatory alternatives, industry by industry, since the need to shift to a new basis is so clear. In the case of the transportation industries, it should be possible to look at the freight system and the passenger system as a whole instead of separately regulating each form of carrier. The question is to determine the public service standards that should apply and also the simplest format for their administration. If a passenger system (air, rail, highway, or water) could be defined in which the regulatory function could focus on control of the pattern of competition and leave the rate structure and operating details to market forces, the regulatory process would be vastly simplified and increased in effectiveness.

The point here is not to attempt to anticipate the conclusion of a complex study of how to design the governance system, but to suggest both the urgency of a shift to system-level regulation, rather than individual industrial control, and the need to find measurements linked to objective performance of the desired public service that can be used for control, rather than taking complex and semipolitical measures to fix prices, rates of return, and operating practices.

The desirability of regulating private enterprise is no longer the question. Regulation has been established and is proliferating at the same time that public frustration with big business is increasing. More frequently, the public looks to the government to solve its problems, including problems caused by big business. And nothing in our society ensures that its institutions will be eternal; corporations, as artifical beings created by law, could be fundamentally changed in nature and purpose by legislative changes, if the public favored such a development.

But the present free-enterprise pattern of our industrial society has brought unparalleled wealth to the country; the growth of regulation need not change these institutions fundamentally. In fact, social productivity and prosperity will be greater if they continue. The purpose, ultimately, is to look for sensitive, effective governance measures to permit public sector coordination and direction of industrial performance, where it appears that private-sector activity is most amenable to regulation in the public interest. And, although it would be more pleasant to talk about a society regulated by market forces alone, this alternative is no longer realistic in the increasingly complex and interdependent industrial society of today and tomorrow.

The objective is to encourage a greater production of wealth, without environmental damage, from the portion of national resources devoted to wealth production so that the output will be sufficient to support evolution of social programs for the less fortunate without reversing the steady increase in the national level of living. This purpose will not be met by present means, yet the nation seems to be more determined than ever to continue expanding its social programs. Thus, a new approach to regulation, to the governance of an industrial society, becomes progressively more urgent.

Regulation Problems

In the contemporary scene regulation is evolving rapidly, with new problems, new rules, new legal battles, and new problems as regulations have impacts on people and as people react to changes in their regulated environment. A few examples follow.

The Need for New Regulations

As society becomes more conscious of the delicacy of environmental balances, more new problems come to light. One problem concerns the increasing levels of dangerous pollutant chemicals in drinking water in many parts of the United States.

> The more that scientists learn about man-made chemicals in the environment, the greater the dangers to public health seem to be. Indeed most specialists in the new field of environmental disease believe that 85% of all cancers are caused by exposure to substances in the air or water. These include everything from compounds in tobacco and automotive fumes to asbestos, vinyl chloride, the pesticide dieldrin, carbon tetrachloride and chloroform.
>
> Now there is a new threat. Paradoxically, it involves chlorination, the process that most U.S. towns and cities use to kill the disease-carrying bacteria

in ordinary drinking water. When water from a polluted source, like Lake Erie or the Mississippi River, enters a treatment plant, the chlorine apparently interacts with industrial and agricultural wastes to produce chemical compounds that have been shown to cause cancer in laboratory animals.

Concern arose last year when the Environmental Protection Agency's Cincinnati laboratory found that the levels of some hazardous chemicals in polluted water—most notably carbon tetrachloride and chloroform—increased when passed through municipal water-treatment plants.

Why? The EPA found in later tests that New Orleans' drinking water which comes from the Mississippi River, contained minute traces of 66 organic chemicals, some of them known carcinogens. (In New Orleans last week, there was a rush on bottled water, and city officials announced that they would investigate the water supply further.) Actually, the link between chlorination and the formation of these chemicals was confirmed abroad. J. J. Rook, a Dutch scientist, added chlorine to contaminated river water and to relatively pure lake water. The concentration of carbon tetrachloride and chloroform rose sharply in the polluted water, but not in the sample from the lake.

Meantime, the Environmental Defense Fund, a public interest group of scientists and lawyers, was approaching the problem from a different angle. A research team compared statistics on the mortality rate of cancers of the urinary organs and gastrointestinal tract in 64 Louisiana parishes (counties). The study showed a "significant relationship" between the use of drinking water from the Mississippi and cancer deaths. The report also noted that dangerous chemicals had been identified in municipal drinking-water supplies in West Virginia, Indiana, Ohio, Nebraska and Washington, D.C.

The EPA quickly responded by ordering a two-part nationwide study of drinking-water supplies. The first phase will determine the concentration and potential effects of the various chemicals in U.S. drinking-water systems. After that, the possible sources of pollutants—mainly industrial discharges and agricultural runoffs—will be investigated, along with ways to eliminate them either at their source or in water-treatment plants.

This week the U.S. House of Representatives will consider a bill to set strict minimum national standards for drinking water. A new item certain to be on the agenda for discussion: the possible hazards of chlorination.[3]

The problem here is complex. As water is used and reused, wastes build up. Standard methods of water purification involve chlorination because of the disease-killing ability of chlorine. But when organic wastes are chlorinated, they generate chlorinated organic compounds of many sorts. These were first detected as contaminants causing false readings in chlorinated hydrocarbon assays designed to detect DDT residues. Now it is being established that many of these other compounds are equally harmful.

---

[3]"Chlorination Threat," *Time* 25 November, 1974, p. 123. Reprinted by permission from *Time*, The Weekly Newsmagazine; Copyright Time Inc. 1974.

Where the source of the original wastes is industrial or municipal, it is subject to EPA control. Where the wastes represent natural drainage from farms and fields, the problem is more complex. Even from unmolested forests, the natural water often develops a slight tan color, and most northern states have named at least one "Tea Lake" in recognition of this color. This harmless color originates from the lignins and other natural compounds that result from the decay of leaves and trees. But water thus colored is converted into a variety of chlorinated hydrocarbons and other chlorinated organic compounds if it is exposed to the chlorination step in a municipal or industrial water or waste treatment plant. Thus, even the forests of Minnesota and Wisconsin contribute to the problem at New Orleans.

As a complex problem affecting the public interest, this drinking water contamination invites and probably requires governmental analysis and intervention. The cure is unclear, since most water contains some organic wastes and since chlorination processes are so widely used. Alternatives to chlorination do exist and will undoubtedly be re-examined.

As a first step in establishing regulations in a new area, government often proposes standards. National interest, stirred by the New Orleans water problem and others like it, led to the passage of the Safe Drinking Water Act. Under the terms of the act, the EPA proposed standards for the nation's 240,000 public water supplies, thus starting the enforcement machinery. The new act left enforcement responsibility with the states, so long as standards at least equal to the federal standards are met. The EPA will monitor water quality and intervene only if a state fails to establish and enforce adequate standards.[4]

A new regulatory process has started. After permanent standards are established and put into effect and after legal or any other sorts of problems raised by the standards are resolved, the EPA will undoubtedly begin to publicize failures to meet standards and try gently to encourage adequate local programs. Public interest in the issue should stay at a high level, with intermittent agitation from consumer groups, because bad drinking water affects so many people.

Eventually, improvement in drinking water will result. Concurrently, a new regulatory sphere will become established and institutionalized. As a nation we will have purer water and a new element of social overhead in the cost of regulating its purity.

Reducing the Regulatory Burden

The cost and inefficiency of some regulatory agencies has been under attack for many years by various activist groups. On 7 October 1974 the administration signaled serious interest in regulatory reform.

> In an unusual speech for a Federal official, the chairman of the Federal Trade Commission, Lewis A. Engman, attacked Federal regulatory agencies today—specifically including the Civil Aeronautics Board and the Interstate Commerce Commission. He charged them with protecting the industries they

---

4"E.P.A. Proposes Rules for Water," *New York Times,* 17 February, 1975.

regulate in an unhealthy relationship that raises costs to the consumer unnecessarily and thus contributes to inflation.

In his major address at the fall convention of the Financial Analysts Federation, received with enthusiasm by the 325 delegates, Mr. Engman declared, "Most regulated industries have become Federal protectorates, living in a world of cost-plue [sic], safely protected from the ugly specters of competition, efficiency and innovation."

Airline competition, he said, has been relegated by the C.A.B. to one unregulated area—consumer service.

That is why the average airline commercial looks like an ad for a combination bawdy house and dinner theater," he complained.

Next Mr. Engman turned to practices of the I.C.C. New trucking companies, he said, are restricted from entering the market while rates are fixed by the carriers that are given antitrust immunity to do so.

"And what is the result? Well, when the Supreme Court held some time ago that fresh dressed poultry was an agricultural commodity under the I.C.C. act and thus not subject to regulation, the average rate for shipping it fell by 33 per cent," he said.

Mr. Engman said "private estimates" indicate that regulatory measures in transportation may cost consumers $16-billion a year.

"Dozens and dozens" of additional Federal and state regulations and strictures subvert competition, he asserted, giving some examples:

State laws against advertising the prices of eyeglasses or prescription drugs.

The Jones Act, forbidding foreign competition in the shipping business between United States ports.

The Federal Government's own "buy American" procurement preferences, which can allow domestic producers of some items to charge as much as 50 per cent more than foreign sellers.

Mr. Engman declared: "Our airlines, our truckers, our railroads, our electronic media and countless others are on the dole. We get irate about welfare fraud. But our complex systems of hidden regulatory subsidies make welfare fraud look like petty larceny."

In asking for re-examination of every regulation or regulatory policy that contributes to inflation to see if the trade-off between costs and benefits is still valid, he said, "We may well find that some of the more costly ones look a lot less attractive in a world of 12 per cent inflation than they did in a world of 3 per cent inflation."[5]

Shortly after Engman's attack on the regulatory processes the President requested a National Commission on Regulatory Reform, and serious discussion began to spread. Steps toward reform so far include sunshine and freedom-of-information

---

[5]Robert Mety, "F.T.C. Chief Calls Role of Agencies Inflationary," *New York Times,* 8 October, 1974. Copyright © 1974 by The New York Times Company. Reprinted by permission.

laws, opening certain proceedings and records to the public, and the effort to introduce zero-base budgeting. Regulatory reform has also been identified as a major interest of the Carter administration. Hopefully, interest in reform will continue at least until the nation succeeds in creating a mechanism for re-evaluating agencies and regulations from time to time. As society progresses, change is needed to cope with national development and its problems, and the present mechanisms do not adapt to new needs.

Resisting Regulation

New rules are often unwelcome and many arguments are attempted by those who wish to avoid applying them. Thus, the National Confectioners Association asked the FDA to exempt candy bars from the requirement that the net quantity of the contents be printed on the wrapper. Several public figures attacked the proposal as a means of avoiding the necessity of informing the consumer when the weight of the candy bar is decreased to maintain or improve profits.[6]

Or a rule may be enforced in a way that causes a reaction against the regulatory process, as was the case when an Illinois state agency shut down the factory whistle that Canton, Illinois, uses to time its daily routine.

> The town whistle blew here today. . . . It was further proof—if any was needed—that the end had come for the Great Whistle War, a sudden skirmish that taught the state government, a giant corporation and much of a cheering Middle West just how strong an aroused community can be when its institutions appear to be threatened.
>
> It all began on Dec. 7, a day which will live in infamy here. On that date, just three days before Canton's 148th birthday, an antinoise pollution squad from the Illinois Environmental Protection Agency infiltrated this town to measure the decibel count of the giant steam whistle on top of the International Harvester plant.
>
> Later, E.P.A. officials said that some disgruntled but unidentified residents had invited the agency in. . . .
>
> Soon after the test, the factory was told officially that its whistle, which blows seven times each weekday, might violate new noise-pollution codes taking effect next August.
>
> Not wishing to alienate neighbors, and since computers, time clocks and union washup regulations have long since eliminated any corporate need for the 61-year-old whistle, Robert Nelson, the plant manager, shut the whistle down.
>
> His decision came 45 minutes after The Canton Daily Ledger's deadline. But for news that big, the presses were held. And like Minute Men summoned in the night, Canton's residents answered the call of the silenced whistle.

---

[6]Will Lissner, "Candy Bar Makers Don't Want Weight on Wrapper," *New York Times*, 23 March, 1975.

Led by Lee Allaman, 7,000 persons—one-half the town's population—signed petitions within 48 hours. They wrote to their State Representatives. They called State Senators.

"The government," said Edward Lewis, "is into too many little aspects of life—airplane passenger searches, 'gas' and speed limits and now the whistle. Next, it'll be the churches."

The Daily Ledger called for open defiance of the state government.

In the Middle West, town whistles and sirens are common. They sit perched on top of tall poles in thousands of towns and cities, waiting to blast the noon signal or the evening curfew for teen-agers.

Over the years, the whistles become more than a mechanical message. They become a part of the fabric of life.

Watches are set by the whistle. Husbands go to work by it. Children are to be home by it. Wives start dinner by it. And here, it is said, Mrs. Clarence Hossler's deaf milkman could hear the whistle when it was about to rain and warned her not to hang out her washing.

If a town's whistle or siren blows at any unusual time, that can only mean trouble—a house or grass fire, or still worse, a tornado.

Even more alarming, however, is when a town's whistle does not blow at all.

"In our community," said Mr. Allaman, a 57-year-old township road supervisor, "you're born to that whistle, and you die to that whistle. Buildings may come and go, and that's progress. But we wanted our whistle to blow."

The factory turned the whistle back on. The Daily Ledger toned down its call to arms. There was talk of a legal variance for Canton's whistle. And everyone got back on schedule.[7]

Of course, the state agency may have been right, and noise pollution does need control. But the agency showed a singular lack of sensitivity to social processes by its sudden intervention to cause a small but significant change in the life of the community. This case is worth study, because corporate managements have so often triggered similar reactions unwittingly by their lack of sensitivity to the effect of changes on social processes in the work group or community.

Regulatory Side Effects

When regulations are established, people and industries revise their operating patterns to conform. Eventually, they come to depend on the new regulatory framework and can be hurt severely when changes are made. Thus, in forty years under the Sugar Act, a protected U.S. industry grew up. When, due to the rise in sugar prices and a changing world situation, the Sugar Act was allowed to expire, it had major impact potential. In the sugar cane areas of Louisiana, the expiration of

---

[7]Andrew H. Malcolm, "A Town Shows Its Strength by Winning War on Whistle," *New York Times,* 6 January, 1974. Copyright © 1974 by The New York Times Company. Reprinted by permission.

federal subsidies was expected to drive out many of the smaller growers. Also, this expiration left the field workers without minimum wage protection, which had been provided by the Sugar Act.[8]

Probably the Sugar Act should have been allowed to expire because it was based on a concept of sharing the U.S. market among several poor nations in times of chronic surplus and carried in its framework political and market concepts that had long since been made obsolete by change. However, the long-protected domestic industry did not become less important but actually gained importance as foreign shortages and marketing strategies caused the sudden surge in sugar prices. It is hoped that sugar prices will stabilize at a level that will permit the domestic sugar industry to continue so that the long-term impact may be minimal. Nonetheless, Congress suddenly broke an implicit commitment that had been in effect for a long time. These areas had become dependent on the Sugar Act framework and were not allowed the time to make an orderly readjustment when the rules were changed.

Determining the Future of Regulation

Governmental intervention in the daily life of people and of businesses is increasing. As argued earlier, there seems to be no alternative within the framework of our industrial society. Given that regulation must grow, the country must learn to perform the regulatory function better, which will require new thinking about the process and its outcomes. The corporations and the public have every reason to search for means of stimulating the intellectual processes of the country in hopes of encouraging constructive thought about more effective regulatory processes. Historically, the intellectual leadership has come from the more radical sectors of society, and more needs to be done to develop a broader participation in the necessary redesign of society's governance system. The antagonists of the system are vocal and effective, and one analyst suggests a studied effort in establishing intellectual leadership from the more responsible elements of society.

> If public attitudes today are a key determinant in shaping public policy, then it becomes vital to determine to the extent possible what shapes public attitudes. Obviously, no simplistic answer will suffice. Yet, after a quarter century in this public policy jungle, I am convinced of the basic and pervasive impact of the so-called intellectual class on the policy formation process.
>
> Let me offer a generalized example—the Americans for Democratic Action was founded in the late 1940s as a "political idea organization." Among its stated primary objectives, the ADA sought to function as an intellectual educational propaganda group striving to formulate comprehensive liberal positions on national issues and to translate these positions into public policy. Most practical men—that is men who live in the "real" world—tend to smile deprecatingly when ADA is mentioned. Yet, as Al Smith used to say, "Look at the record!" Nearly 70 percent of the several score domestic policy resolu-

---

[8]Roy Reed, "Trying Time for Sugar Farmers," *New York Times,* 22 June, 1974.

tions approved by the ADA in 1958 at their national convention had been written into the federal statute books by 1970. Many of the remainder, such as the Consumer Protection Agency, are today in various stages of active gestation.

These examples simply underline two fundamental points in my thinking:

The so-called intellectual class is a major and I deeply believe the dominant force in forming public attitudes and public policy in the United States today.

In the mainstream of idea formation—in the intellectual arena—business has been persistently losing because it has been persistently defaulting. As Daniel Bell the co-editor of *The Public Interest*, recently put it, "In the realm of culture, and of cultural-social issues—of political philosophy, in short—the corporate class had abdicated. The important consideration is that, *as an ideology*, liberalism had become dominant over these past decades."

I further assert that in that intellectual arena is where the *fire power which molds public attitudes* and ultimately *determines public policy is generated.*

What is needed in the intellectual mainstream—which is in my opinion the major factor in forming public attitudes and ultimately determining public policy—is effective competition. A free society, if it is to remain free, cannot allow itself to be dominated by one strain of thought. The cornerstone of a free society is rational debate. The opportunity must exist for the clash of ideas, effectively presented, to arrive at public policy decisions that will not undermine but rather bolster the foundations of our free society.

One of the elements that has contributed to the creation of a monopoly hostile to business has been, as Daniel Bell puts it, "the abdication of the corporate class."

To break this monopoly requires a calculated, positive, major commitment—one which will insure that the views of other competent intellectuals are given the opportunity to contend effectively in the mainstream of our country's intellectual activity.

There are such people.

They can be encouraged and mobilized.

Their numbers can increase.

But, that can hardly happen without reordering priorities in the support patterns of corporations and foundations—at least by those corporations and foundations concerned with preserving the basic values of this free society and its free institutions.[9]

Baroody is arguing for incisive, well-focused thinking, which represents all points of view in society, to stimulate a healthy debate over political and regulatory alternatives.

[9]William J. Baroody, "Toward Intellectual Competition," *NAM Reports,* 16 April, 1973, pp. 10–12.

Summary

The corporation is the principal vehicle of the wealth production on which the U.S. standard of living is based. The fundamental organization is the same as in any other industrial society, except that resource ownership and control and the corporate and social governance processes are progressively defined and changed according to the wishes of society. Since any individual managerial or planning group will inevitably suboptimize within a horizon delimited by the scope of its individual ability for detailed analysis, a combination of impersonal market forces and calculated interventions by the control mechanisms of the overall society represent the necessary basis for a governance process.

An industrial society becomes increasingly complex, the amount of regulation must increase, but the social overhead of the governance process should not be allowed to grow. Social overhead is already at a high level in terms of the resources absorbed in its maintenance. To allow more regulation without great increases in expenses and delay, regulatory mechanisms must become more efficient. Since the most effective governance mechanism for the economy is based on economic regulation of private processes, the direction of the shift should be toward a maximum operation of the wealth-producing processes by the private sector, with a new and more effective design for the regulatory mechanisms at the system level so that management will be more thorough but require less detail.

For society to control the governance process, the public processes for guiding government need revitalization. When the United States became independent, public debate of current issues allowed for the development of an informed consensus among the interested citizens of the country. With the growth of increasingly complicated and technical issues, this debate has dwindled because so few of the interested citizens are well informed enough about such issues to participate in a meaningful public process.

To restore this process in a time of increasingly complex issues requires better public information sources and the provision of both comprehensive analyses of complex issues and policy alternatives open for their resolution. Since it is no longer possible for each citizen to master the technology underlying each issue, the alternative is to provide competing expert studies that summarize the major points of view. Existing interest groups produce such studies now, although many are imperfect due to lack of adequate information. Thus, by organizing an adequate public information base on present and impending issues and perhaps by keynoting some of the analytical interest, the government could progress toward making the public processes for guiding the government more effective again.

The importance of these considerations to the business community and to the management of corporate social impact is in the rapid evolution of controls over business activity, where the momentum of the present growth of regulation and social overhead seems likely to burden the system to the point of rejection and abandonment. Such a prospect is reminiscent of Schumpeter's prophecy of the shift to socialism that was cited in Chapter 3. The alternative, which appears to represent the principal hope for maintenance of the private corporate structure, is a real revision

Figure 18.2 Governance of an Industrial Society

The corporation as a wealth producer	Effective regulation
Regulation of wealth production	Needs of the future
Suboptimization issue	More governance
Market forces	Less regulation
Government control	Regulation in the public interest
Public processes for governance	System-level regulation
Informed analysis	More private management
Debate and consensus	More public governance

The way our technical, industrial society fosters and coordinates the proper operation of its parts needs redesigning. Corporate self-interest dictates facilitating this redesign in the interest of operating freedom, or even survival.

of the mechanism by which society regulates economic activity. Alternatives are now under public discussion; one is the pattern that has just been suggested and is summarized in Figure 18.2.

Thus, a corporate survival issue is posed, not in the normal corporate terms of opposing the inevitable advance of regulation but in terms of the need to work positively for a constructive redesign that will aid the necessary extension of system-level regulation and will also increase the freedom to operate within it.

Due to a unique combination of circumstances, the United States at its inception was led by a very gifted and unusual group of men. Among other things they developed a new theory of government, and the U.S. Constitution reflected much of their better thinking. They built well, but not for all time, because a growing and changing society has developed new kinds of stresses and problems, which primarily revolve around the profound transition from the agricultural frontier to a mature and increasingly complex industrial economy.

Many writers have speculated on the strange fact that, after this early burst of creativity, the United States has been characterized by an absence of contributions to political theory. Now the time is at hand for some basic rethinking to develop a governance process over a modern industrial society that gives the necessary increase in social guidance to the system at a lower social overhead cost and with only the minimum necessary restrictions on the freedom of actions of individual people and corporations.

This chapter has explored the governance problem of this and any other industrial society that requires a shift to system-level regulation that is more extensive and also less involved in controlling the details of how various businesses operate. For a corporation seeking to understand its social impact, the direction is toward smooth acceptance of rational and some irrational regulation, with confrontations chosen carefully so that the energies of business and its management are devoted only to worthwhile issues and pressure is applied in the direction of needed change.

Guidelines for Managing Corporate Social Impact

In managing the social impact on society's governance processes, social balance will tend to be maintained if the following guidelines are applied:

Wealth production   As a wealth producer, and in the interest both of its own economic soundness and that of society, a firm attempts to make its productive processes as efficient in the use of materials, energy, and labor as competitive circumstances will permit.

Regulation   As a regulated wealth producer, a firm strives to build public information about and awareness of the basic issues underlying the choice of the most efficient pattern for regulating it and its industry. Thus, necessary debates over alternative governance processes can lead to wise political and economic decisions.

Applying the Guidelines

Wealth production   Through a chain of circumstances, the U.S. steel industry is no longer an effective competitor in world markets. In seeking political assistance to stem the erosion of its position in the U.S. market, the industry bargains at a disadvantage because it is not an effective wealth producer. If a public subsidy is necessary either directly or through tariffs and import restrictions, the effect will be to lower the average national level of living slightly through the need to support a weak industry. Besides serving its stockholders and the members of the organization and of the dependent communities better by being more successful in the marketplace, a corporation that is an efficient wealth producer has a beneficial impact on the society as a whole, rather than the negative impact presently typified by the steel industry. The guideline proposed would emphasize management concern with the underlying economic efficiency of its processes, even when the immediate crisis is not immediate; good management would mandate giving much attention to this area in business self-interest, as well as in managing corporate social impact.

Regulation   The airlines are a troubled, regulated industry. All parties in the current public discussion between corporations, regulators, administration, Congress, and others seem to recognize the need to recast the regulatory pattern somewhat to serve the public interest better. But the suggested regulatory reforms vary radically in scope, detail, and intent, and the underlying issues are so complex and poorly understood that a public discussion leading to a constructive process of change will have difficulty evolving. The airline industry has a strong interest in developing a broader public and legislative understanding of the industry's nature and economics so that, as the regulations are rewritten, the results are more likely to improve the position of both the industry and the public. The guideline suggested here is based on the fact, that all corporations are regulated to a significant and increasing extent and share both general and special needs to increase public understanding of the specific issues and the general regulatory process.

Questions for Analysis and Discussion

1. To what extent can you see the dependence of our society on currently manufactured wealth in your day-to-day activities? Discuss.

2. Give an example of the way a particular management group may suboptimize its decisions.

3. Can you see any alternative to the growth of regulation predicted in the chapter?

4. Discuss the different types of regulatory mechanisms. Do you agree with the premise that publicly owned enterprises are more difficult to regulate effectively?

5. Find and discuss an example where revision in the regulatory structure at national, state, or local levels is being seriously proposed.

6. Find and discuss an example of local resistance to new regulations.

For Further Information

Beer, Stafford. *Brain of the Firm: A Development in Management Cybernetics.* New York: Herder & Herder, 1972

Berle, Adolph A., Jr., and Means, Gardiner C. *The Modern Corporation and Private Property.* New York: Macmillan, 1933.

Green, Mark J., ed. *The Monopoly Makers.* New York: Grossman, 1973.

McKie, James W., ed. *Social Responsibility and the Business Environment.* Washington, D.C.: The Brookings Institution, 1974

Rockefeller, John D., III. *The Second American Revolution.* New York: Harper & Row, 1973.

Schumpeter, Joseph. *Capitalism, Socialism and Democracy,* 3d ed. New York: Harper & Row, 1950.

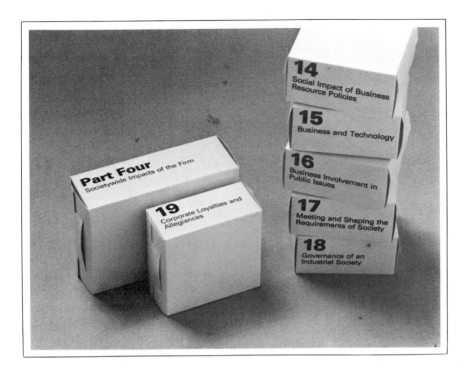

19
Corporate Loyalties and Allegiances

The question of where corporate loyalties and allegiances are most properly directed constitutes a major corporate and social issue. The issue is over which nation or level of government controls the corporation, in particular, the multinational corporation. Social balance requirements suggest the strong need for primary loyalty to be at the local level, where the corporate entity is chartered and controlled. This requirement suggests, as its implications are explored, a federated structure permitting each local corporate entity to give local allegiance to and accept full membership in the local society. First, we review the foundations from which corporate loyalties develop and the issues posed by corporate operation across political boundaries. This review leads to suggested guidelines for minimizing the social impact of corporate allegiances and for defining the degree of allegiance that the corporation is, in turn, entitled to receive from the members of its organization.

The multinational corporation will be disruptive if a political power does not develop to put the economy at the service of man, and not put man at its service.[1]

JEAN-JACQUES SERVAN-SCHREIBER

Although a corporation is a self-interested, profit-seeking economic entity, nonetheless, it operates as part of a nation or of several nations. Its employees and management are likely to be mainly from the city, the state, or at least the country in which the business is located. The corporation finds itself drawn into local affairs, in which both it and its employees have interests and obligations. It has reason for interest in national policy and may even find itself being used as an instrument of national policy.

The same process tends to occur at each plant or office in each city, state, or country in which the corporation or its affiliates are active. The interests and allegiances that are generated by each local operation will tend to conflict at the higher organizational levels of any far-flung organization. The ethics and practicalities of resolving such conflict become more urgent as transnational and multinational corporations become more important to both national and worldwide economics. This chapter will explore some of the considerations that determine the proper allegiances of and to the corporation and suggest means for their application.

The Multinational in Society

Submerged behind many of the issues discussed throughout the preceding chapters is a deep-seated concern over the role of the multinational corporations in national societies. This concern is now becoming an increasingly urgent political issue in many countries throughout the world:

1. Inherently, a corporation is based on business processes derived from market opportunities and circumscribed by resource availabilities and constraints. These business processes have boundaries derived from the nature of the markets and also the resource constraints so that a given corporation often will endeavor to extend its participation in a given business process to these boundaries. In this regard, its motivation is based on both profit and survival opportunities, because the economic

---

[1]Jean-Jacques Servan-Schreiber, as quoted by Anthony Sampson, *The Sovereign State of ITT* (New York: Stein & Day, 1973), p. 289.

and competitive strength of the enterprise is increased by such extensions. Thus the corporation becomes more profitable and better able to withstand competition from other enterprises similarly extending from other points of origin.

2. Inherently, a corporation is an artificial being that is created by law and exists only because of the law and within the limits that law prescribes. The law has sharp boundaries defined by the limits of the jurisdiction of a particular political authority.

Thus, the nature of a business often makes it desirable, if not mandatory, that a corporation operate in several different political jurisdictions. To do this, the corporation must establish a basis for its existence within each jurisdiction, often by creating a local and subsidiary corporation—in effect, thereby obtaining a fresh definition of itself as an artificial being created and governed by the laws of that particular political authority. Then, to operate as a national or transnational entity, the corporation must develop a means of coordinating the operations of these several parts under the

The Firm as Viewed by Society

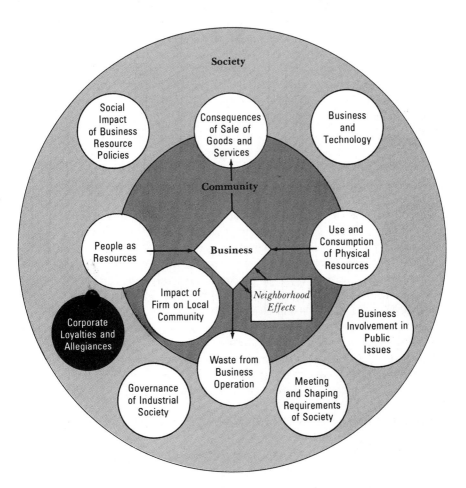

several legal codes. While this process has its complexities, most large corporations have developed workable solutions.

For society to regulate a corporation as a single unit, it would need a similar coordination between its different political authorities, which is a process that is far from possible at present. Therefore, each part of the multinational is regulated locally, usually without a great deal of coordination between the separate political authorities.

The basic conflict, then, is between the need and desire of corporations to operate in many political jurisdictions and the ability of society to regulate effectively only within individual jurisdictions. This conflict has created great concern about the proper levels of power and responsibility that the large multinational corporations should be allowed to possess, and where their political allegiances should properly reside.

One solution to the problem is to restrict corporate operations so that they can be controlled more easily. Many countries have created levels of restriction ranging from regulation of various sorts to the requirement for local equity participation or the outright nationalization of outside interests. Simple as this approach is, it violates economic reality in some cases. To operate efficiently, some businesses require a larger volume than the markets in one country can generate. Others need access to a pool of technology, where many countries can utilize the fruits of the same research and development activity. Or a business may require the integration between different stages in a complex process dependent on raw materials from several countries. In any of these three cases, a country hurts itself economically when it unduly restricts the freedom of transnational firms to operate across its boundaries.

Another solution to the control of multinational corporations would be to develop a uniform worldwide body of law and regulation. Because of the many problems of local sovereignty, full uniformity of laws between countries in today's world seems remote. Even within the United States there are many cases where it is advantageous for a corporation to locate an operation in one city or state versus other cities or states because of differences in local laws and taxes. For example, a routine consideration in the location of distribution centers is the fact that different U.S. states tax warehouse inventory in different ways.

However, the differences and difficulties in reconciling local law and regulatory structures should not obscure the real progress that is occurring. One of the functions of the European Common Market is to increase the conformity of these structures within its boundaries. And the major industrial nations show a clear tendency to adopt modifications of each other's solutions to the worst corporate abuses. Thus, antitrust processes are now developing in the European Common Market, and patent protection limiting previous abuse of foreign patents is being established in Italy. Broad and increasing similarities, at least between the structures in the major industrial countries, are definitely developing, and progress has been quite rapid in some areas. However, a truly uniform legal and regulatory pattern for all jurisdictions is not now foreseeable.

Given that corporations will operate in many political jurisdictions and will wish to continue to operate in such a fashion, the issues relevant to this discussion are those defining the way in which the corporate self interest and its necessary balance with society dictate that it should apportion its resources and allegiances across the span of its operations.

But the corporation, as an economic entity created by law and needing to maintain a relationship with the society that defines and controls that law, must look at the impact of its actions within each distinctly separate political jurisdiction. The application of the analysis developed in the preceding chapters is that the self-interest of a corporation intending to exist over the long run requires an attempt to maintain a social balance in each sector of its operation and within each separate political jurisdiction. While this balance will not always be completely possible to attain, it forms the norm toward which operating policies should be directed. To act otherwise would be to risk reprisals from any jurisdiction where social costs were allowed to accumulate, and such a risk is not consistent with self-interest over the long run.

The consequence of aspiring toward social balance within each jurisdiction is that the corporation will become an involved citizen in that area almost exactly to the extent that it operates there. A number of the more well-established multinationals seem to have adopted this general philosophy many years ago.

Controls on the Multinational

The old pattern was to identify a corporation with its home country, and to expect, if not demand, that its worldwide operations be consistent with the country's self-interest. This pattern does not conform with present-day reality in terms of the requirements for maintaining a long-term participation in the markets in other countries. If a corporation encourages and requires its affiliate in a particular country to become a participant in the local society and country, this role will not be effective unless the local management is free to act as a part of that society. That freedom cannot exist if the entire multinational is required to act in the uniform interest of the home country.

If the parent corporation does not permit its local management to act as part of the local society, local management cannot balance adverse social impacts. Furthermore, if a national government comes to believe that foreign interests may attempt to control local decisions against the local national interest, a potent argument for nationalization is immediately created.

Where political jurisdictions are numerous and overlapping, a confusing picture is created that simplifies quickly when corporate impact is analyzed on a sector-by-sector basis. For example, U.S. corporations are chartered under the laws of one state, and these laws differ. Yet they are sufficiently similar so that most corporations can relate to the national entity for some corporate impact purposes and to the state governments only where the differences in laws require unique behavior in a particular state. And, of course, many of the key impact areas concerning employees, communities, waste streams, and other elements of the operation are essentially local unless a nearby political boundary requires specific recognition and action. In summary, usually the actual corporate relationships are primarily local and national, with recognition of other governmental levels and jurisdictions whenever special requirements make this appropriate.

Thus, multinational control is based on local ties for the most part. Where some members of local societies may fear corporate economic power and where economic power often leads to strong political influence, the boundary between political influence and political power is a critical one that provides an important limit to the power of any corporation. Next the nature of that boundary will be explored.

Economic Versus Political Power

Corporate power, while real, is limited in its nature and extent. As an economic entity, a corporation often wields substantial economic power. Often it can use its economic power to influence political processes, but this corporate influence over the political process differs from political power. Political power is ultimately based on considerable popular support, whereas political influence is the ability to guide the actions of those who hold political power. Thus, politicans or elected officials will have a base of political power so long as they appear to have the support of their constituents from whom that power is ultimately derived.

Because political power is normally delegated quietly to representatives, economic power can often gain substantial control through political influence, so long as the issues do not cause enough concern to the constituency to jeopardize the political power of their representative. A large part of the art of politics is to function in such a way as to maintain a secure base of political power. As a result, the political influence of economic power will be accepted only to the extent that the political power base is not jeopardized. This limitation on economic power is quite definite and accounts for the difference in the dynamics of the use of political and economic power.

The distinction between political influence and political power is real and critical. A corporation's influence in political areas is based only on economic power. While the corporation may be a controlling force through its use of such influence, the process must be conducted subtly and must avoid at all cost any substantial confrontation with real political power based on the desires of masses of people. Through political power the rules are made; if a confrontation between economic power and political power is allowed to occur, those with the political power can change the rules to either seize the economic power or otherwise weaken its impact. This has happened repeatedly in African and South American countries.

Thus, corporate self-interest requires avoidance of confrontation with political power in each political jurisdiction where it operates except as a last resort. This self-interest greatly limits the kind of interference in government for which United Fruit was once notorious among the banana republics. It almost eliminates the potential for the great supranational corporate force that has been raised as a political specter. For example, ITT has been profiled as such a force.[2] Yet when it chose to enter the political arena in Chile to try to assure the defeat of Allende, it moved out of its position as a neutral foreign business entity looking to Chilean law for the protection of its proper interests and attempted to establish itself as a political force. Such a political force represented a potential threat to the real political power and could not be tolerated. Allende was elected and the ITT company was subsequently seized as an enemy of the state, while many other subsidiaries of U.S. companies were allowed to continue in operation.

A corporation that has economic power can exert economic influence. This

---

[2]Sampson, *The Sovereign State of ITT.*

economic influence can be converted to political influence but cannot be changed to political power. However, political influence, used with sufficient skill, can achieve effective political governance: this is its potential and its danger. The control on corporate political influence is dual. First, the means by which political influence is maintained is subject to some review. Recent progress through disclosure of improper corporate political payments forced by the SEC seems likely to lead not only to more cautious behavior by certain U.S. corporations but also to similar disclosure requirements elsewhere. Raising the awareness of this potential abuse of economic power increases both the risk and likelihood of discovery, thus reducing the incentives to use such payments.

The second and more powerful control on corporate political influence is that it cannot risk offense to the political power latent in the people. As sensitivity to corporate political influence grows, as from the Lockheed scandal in Japan, it becomes more hazardous for a corporation to attempt to maintain any improper political influence. And where many corporate battles in the marketplace can be lost in one year and won in the next, the losses in confrontation with political power tend to be more permanent. Thus, ITT in Chile and Lockheed in Japan will have to undertake a long rebuilding task if they are ever to restore their commercial stature in those two countries.

Well-managed corporations will avoid confrontation with political power except as a last resort because the corporation is so likely to lose and the loss is so likely to be large. Since this political power is local to each political jurisdiction, it forms the potent, ultimate force toward requiring a corporation to operate as a compatible, contributing entity within the local society. This political power has not checked improper corporate use of political influence in the past because the direct, local use of this power was not familiar to the people in many parts of the world. This situation has changed, and the awareness of actual and potential abuse of corporate power is growing daily. Consequently, local political power, and the corporate fear of arousing it, will be an increasingly effective check on corporate actions in the future.

The Federated Multinational

Because of the pressures for closer identification of each multinational subsidiary with the total society, the apparent direction of evolution is toward multinational federations of national companies. The parent company can maintain general coordination and ownership ties, supply technology and certain central services, and maintain bases for regional production and supply of raw and finished materials; but each affiliate will need to operate as part of the local society. The relationships will require careful definition to achieve a balance between the local needs and the needs and rights of the owners. For example, the foreign exchange problems of many countries will cause them to restrict the export of profits or the purchase of imported materials, but the local company may be able to devise an acceptable barter or other alternative form of exchange that can accomplish the corporate purpose without adding strain to the local balance-of-payment situation.

Where this federated form of multinational management develops, there will be no serious issue over national control; the control mechanism will be built into the structure. Where such a form does not develop, the multinational companies involved seem fated to lose or sell their affiliates, at least in most of the developing countries, because the local governments will not accept a foreign-dominated management philosophy. An intermediate step taken by some countries is to create the federated type of operating philosophy by forcing the sale of more than half of the equity in a particular subsidiary to local interests or to the government.

Where some governments may have national programs for coordinating and controlling the total worldwide operation of the international businesses based in their countries, this pattern is precisely the one most likely to bring reprisal, particularly in the smaller countries most concerned about foreign economic domination. Therefore, it seems clear that these control patterns must be relaxed to the level of skillful influence and guidance of a federation of subsidiaries to have a chance at continuing in the long run. As always, the risk is that a host country will attempt a partial or complete takeover of a subsidiary as a practical way to eliminate concern over excessive foreign influence.

Local Laws

The managers of foreign subsidiaries of U.S. companies can face basic contradictions between U.S. and local laws, each designed to protect the national interest. This was illustrated by the dilemma of the U.S. directors of the Canadian subsidiary of Studebaker-Worthington over trade with Cuba in 1974. Canadian officials encouraged the company to complete the sale of twenty-five locomotives to Cuba. Since the U.S. Trading with the Enemy Act barred the parent company and all U.S. citizens from making sales to Cuba, the two U.S. directors on the board of the Canadian subsidiary were concerned that they might be held responsible for a violation of U.S. law. One Canadian suggestion was that the directors could avoid the issue by resigning their directorships.[3] American directors of subsidiaries that violate the act are liable to ten years in prison and a $10,000 fine. But the corporation in question was a Canadian corporation, even though it was 56 percent U.S. owned, and the Canadian government felt that the sale in question was in the Canadian national interest. Thus, Canadians would consider an attempt to enforce U.S. law on one of their subsidiaries as constituting a violation of Canadian sovereignty by restricting a Canadian corporation from acting in its national interest. Also, it would be inconsistent for the United States to require disobedience of Canadian law, since U.S. subsidiaries of foreign corporations are required to obey U.S. law.[4]

This example illustrates a type of conflict between laws of different countries that is a continual problem for multinational corporations that must somehow live with the conflict. But underlying the problem is the generalization favoring a common corporate standard of behavior and a corporate form that grants each subsidiary the right to give primary allegiance to local laws. As such a standard continues to evolve,

---

[3]"Studebaker Unit Plans to Push Sale to Cuba Despite U.S. Trade Bar," *Wall Street Journal,* 14 March, 1974.

[4]"Trading with the Enemy," *Wall Street Journal,* 21 March, 1974.

it will aid in the reconciliation of such conflicts between national laws as represented by the Studebaker case.

Corporate Allegiance to the Local Society

A corporation managing its relationships with the local community and with local society will develop a pattern of moderating its corporate impact and protecting its corporate interests that leads to a deep and fundamental relationship with that society. A part of this relationship is with the governmental entity or entities that have legal jurisdiction over the various aspects of the corporation and the conduct of its business. Because the existence and operation of the corporation is controlled from this center, this must be a primary point of allegiance.

Other corporate needs will require other ties, but these should be managed in such a way as to avoid any adverse corporate social impact on the law-giving entity controlling the corporate existence. The widespread uneasiness and suspicion caused by local operators of foreign multinationals illustrate the stress that results when social balance has not been maintained. The trend toward expropriation and nationalization of these operations is the product of such social unrest, which will continue to grow if no efforts to provide for reassurance and balance are made.

Employee Allegiance to the Corporation

Alfred Krupp expected absolute loyalty from his employees, to the extent that they dared not even be suspected of being sympathetic toward political causes he opposed. In today's world Ralph Nader has defined the obligation of any employee to become a "whistle-blower," a person who publicly discloses an employer's illegal or fraudulent activities. The span of time between these two points of view encompasses not only several generations of industrial development but also a cultural shift from the authoritarian, semifeudal society of Germany after the middle of the nineteenth century to the democratic, even permissive, society of the United States in the present.

From this contrast comes the first conclusion: The nature of the ties between employer and employee is conditioned to a considerable extent by the legal and cultural circumstances in the surrounding society. However, the basic employment relationship has evolved with industrial development toward a basic equation that seems likely to become more prevalent in industrial societies across the world.

The basic relationship is between an individual seeking a meaningful and fulfilling career pattern with rewards that are competitive with market standards and sufficient to support an acceptable family lifestyle and an employer needing employees with accumulated experience and skills to perform necessary work. Under the best circumstances, these interests are congruent, and loyalties can be freely given and received. Under less favorable circumstances, one party's abuse of the other puts a practical limit on loyalty and allegiance.

These limits are reached when employees are required to falsify records or break the law in other ways or when the firm is defrauding customers, selling unsafe products, or behaving in other unsavory ways. In these circumstances Nader calls for whistle-blowing, and more frequently employees are taking such steps even to their personal detriment.

To Nader's list of causes can be added the more traditional abuses of the employer-employee relationship. Where pay is low, career paths are nonexistent, promotions are obtained through favoritism rather than merit, or where any of the other familiar causes of complaint may exist, employees develop little allegiance. Often their remedy has been through resignation, unionization, or protest, all of which are outside the normal bounds of allegiance and loyalty to the company.

The boundaries of allegiance and loyalty between corporation and employee arise exactly at the point where their long-term self-interests cease to be parallel. Maintaining the mutuality of self-interests is the condition that causes the organization to be most productive, and a good employer will strive to preserve it; whereas a bad employer will not. Employment contracts and legal protections on trade secrets restrain individual abuses of the employment relationship and create the obligation for ethical conduct, but the soundness of the basic fabric depends on the employer creating an employment relationship in which employer and employee share the same long-term interests. Where this is not done, the evolution is increasingly toward a situation in which employees will be encouraged by society to speak and act in their own self-interest, even where a conflict arises with their employer.

Summary

The present acute concern in society over the power of and need for control over the multinational companies seems largely to be based on an imperfect definition of the issues. Available governmental power is more than adequate to control abuses at the local level, and this is the level where control seems most likely to be effective. No government is able to truly oversee the entire operation of a giant international company, and, in fact, this is not a matter of long-term importance. The patterns of corporate behavior that are developing will increasingly require the local affiliates to behave as members of the local society and to act primarily in a manner consistent with its well-being.[5]

As this shift in behavior occurs, it will automatically limit and then eliminate this potential for abuse of multinational power in that country. This shift could be hastened by the development of a specific code of conduct, with changes in law where appropriate. This development would be in both the corporate and national interest because a more stable long-term relationship would be created between

---

[5]Ringbakk has developed a concept of structural evolution of a multinational as it ages and matures as an institution. In the final state he sees the *anational* corporation emerge, in which each national unit operates more or less independently. Thus, this is a parallel process that, for different reasons, could also contribute to the development of a federated multinational structure, as previously outlined. Kjell-Arne Ringbakk, "Multinational Corporations and Foreign Policy," in *Selected Mid-Term Problems in U.S. Foreign Policy* (Hanover, N.H.: Dartmouth College, Public Affairs Center, 1974).

Figure 19.1   Corporate Loyalties and Allegiances

Corporate loyalty	Controls on multinationals
Controlled by law	Economic versus political power
Allegiance to the lawgiver	The federated multinational
Employee loyalty	Allegiance to the local society
Careers	Corporate citizenship
Personal self-interest	Social self-interest

For survival, any corporation must function as an integral part of the society in which it is located and by which it is controlled.

business and the nation, and the risk of expropriation or repressive legislation would be reduced in the present.

It seems clear from this analysis that companies operating in more than one political jurisdiction (state, city, or country) should guide their management actions toward maintaining a social balance in each jurisdiction. One consequence, in the case of operations in different countries, will be an evolution toward a federated form of corporate structure. In this structure the local companies behave as a part of the local society and the parent company coordinates and manages the economic needs of the whole within boundaries set by the political realities of the individual countries. Some of the considerations are summarized in Figure 19.1. Thus, the major issues over control of multinational companies seem likely to fade away with time, as the more perceptive companies move toward this management form and others find themselves no longer able to operate in politically sensitive areas.

The allegiances and loyalties between corporation and employee are based on a pattern of parallel self-interests that sound management creates. Within the pattern, strong loyalties may be expected, and their boundary is not far beyond any real divergence of corporate and employee long-term interests.

This chapter has considered the foundations for corporate and employee loyalties and allegiances and for the issues between multinational corporations and governments as a means to defining the relationship between corporate and governmental roles. The corporation must give first allegiance to the rule-making jurisdiction of society that controls its local existence. As a result, corporations operating in many such jurisdictions are likely to be forced to develop an operating pattern that respects these local allegiances if an increase in the local restrictions on their freedom to operate is to be avoided.

Guidelines for Managing Corporate Social Impact

In managing the social impact of corporate loyalties and allegiances, social balance will tend to be maintained if the following guidelines are applied:

Allegiance   A corporation gives its primary allegiance to the society that makes the rules controlling its existence. In the view of that society, it must blend in as a sound corporate citizen to have hopes of long-term acceptance and survival.

Federal management A corporation with operations in many different nations or other rule-making social units encourages each subsidiary to become part of the local society. Then the corporation must manage its affairs through a pattern of corporate governance that recognizes the divergent allegiances of the several subsidiaries and develops economic and managerial unity within a framework consistent with these local ties.

Power A corporation uses its economic power and its political influence with great circumspection and discretion to avoid presenting threats to the society or confronting the political power that controls its existence.

Code of conduct A transnational or multinational corporation troubled by the suspicions of local governments and nationalist elements in their societies eases the strain of the atmosphere in which it operates by: encouraging the development of a code of conduct for local subsidiaries toward the local society and for governments toward foreign-controlled corporations, encouraging the discussion and adoption of that code, and using such a code as a guide for its own operations.

Employee loyalty A corporation expects and requires allegiance from the members of its organization within the legal scope of its business and within the personal scope of their employees' normal growth and progression as individuals. The corporation also recognizes the likelihood of unrest and defection if it should attempt to require illegal or unethical actions or actions detrimental to an employee's self-interest.

Applying the Guidelines

Multinationals A Japanese subsidiary of a foreign multinational has strong reasons for becoming as much a part of Japanese society as circumstances will permit, since few corporations without substantial Japanese equity have been permitted to operate at all. In the same way, the need to avoid even the suggestion of possibly acting against local national interests is a part of maintaining the freedom to operate at all in a number of countries. Out of this need for a subsidiary to operate as part of the local society, the parent management recognition of these local ties requires adopting a control structure that unites certain local interests within a fabric established by the underlying ownership. The long-term interests of the multinational are served by such a federated management pattern, even where local pressures have not yet made such an organizational structure mandatory. The corporate advantage to the pattern is in minimizing the risks of stress and confrontation with the various social structures within which a given transnational entity operates.

Similarly, corporate influence should be used in a quiet and proper way to advance its defensible interests and not in such a way as to risk confrontation with political power. To an extent, the present antagonisms toward multinational corporations can also be diffused more rapidly if such conduct is made more explicit through discussion, definition, and adoption of a code of corporate conduct endorsed and followed by those corporations seeking a reputation for responsible behavior.

Employee loyalty A corporation needs the loyalty of its organization's members and can obtain it and require it within the extent of the congruence of corporate and employee interests. That is, as the corporation makes an environment in which its members can invest their energy and enthusiasm, be challenged and rewarded, and thereby grow and progress in their careers, the resulting loyalty given to the corporation is far beyond that which could be required. But where inept management frustrates attempts at contribution, where rewards are not earned by performance, and where continued employment does not truly serve the individual's own best interests, society is encouraging the integrity and endorsing the rights of individuals to act in their own behalf. Now and in the future, these individuals will more frequently abandon allegiances to a corporation that does not allow the allegiance relationship to be a mutually rewarding process. This abandonment may take the form of whistle-blowing to call public attention to improper activities, the use of available resources to prepare for a better job elsewhere, or a shift of all discretionary energies and time to outside activities. The corporation controls the environment that makes allegiance from the members of its organization rewarding or unrewarding and must therefore expect them to react according to the quality of that environment.

Questions for Analysis and Discussion

1. Give examples of corporate actions that show a primary allegiance to one country.

2. In the case of the Canadian Studebaker subsidiary, do you think that the company had any other choice than to pursue the Cuban orders as directed by the Canadian government? Discuss.

3. Do you see any examples of multinational corporations acting in such a way that the issue over national control of their operations will not arise? Discuss.

4. Find and discuss examples of national restrictions on foreign corporations where the public interest may have been sacrificed to obtain local control.

5. The chapter suggests that mutual long-term self-interest is one of the major foundations of the allegiance of an employee to the corporation. Do you agree with this premise? Discuss.

For Further Information

Backman, Jules. *Social Responsibility and Accountability.* New York: New York University Press, 1975.

Nader, Ralph, Petkas, Peter, and Blackwell, Kate. *Whistle Blowing.* New York: Grossman, 1972.

Realities: Multinational Corporations Respond on Basic Issues. Paris: International Chamber of Commerce, 1974.

Robbins, Sidney M., and Stobaugh, Robert B. *Money in the Multinational Enterprise.* New York: Basic Books, 1973.

Sampson, Anthony. *The Sovereign State of ITT.* New York: Stein & Day, 1973.

Whyte, William H., Jr. *The Organization Man.* New York: Doubleday, 1956.

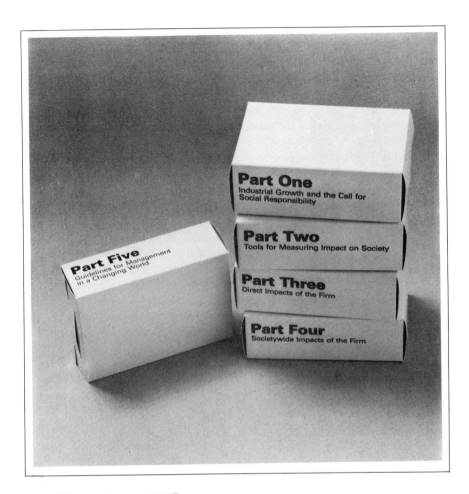

Part Five
Guidelines for Management in a Changing World

Part Four focused on the consequences of the corporate decision-making process and of the firm's actions that affect society as a whole, as opposed to those impacts directly related to the daily operation. The discussion also covered the way in which society molds the corporation and the social considerations and social processes by which society regulates itself and controls its value systems.

Thus many areas have been examined–the effect of different ways that a business can use its resources; its interest in and relation to technology; its involvement in public issues; the process by which the corporation and society change, moderate, and direct each other's evolution; the governance

375

process in today's society; and the worldwide issue of corporate allegiances. The purpose has been to weave a pattern of consequences of corporate actions at the level of the nation-system and to suggest tentative guidelines for a normative operating pattern that would maintain a social balance in each of these impact areas. This complements the material discussed in Part Three, where similar guidelines were developed for balancing a business firm's impacts on its surrounding community. Thus, a wide variety of social balance considerations have emerged. The purpose of Part Five is to provide a summary of the main threads running through this analysis, to draw conclusions from the summary, and relate those conclusions to corporate practices both now and in the future.

Chapter 20 reviews the competitive and profit implications of the major tenets underlying a social balance analysis. In Chapter 21, the problems of applying social considerations to the management of a company are discussed. This leads to a restatement of the proposed operating guidelines. Chapter 22 summarizes the major themes inherent in the social balance concept and in the management of corporate social impact. Some conclusions are presented, as well as some thoughts about the possible future evolution of the social responsibility concept and the next steps toward increasing the power and value of these ideas.

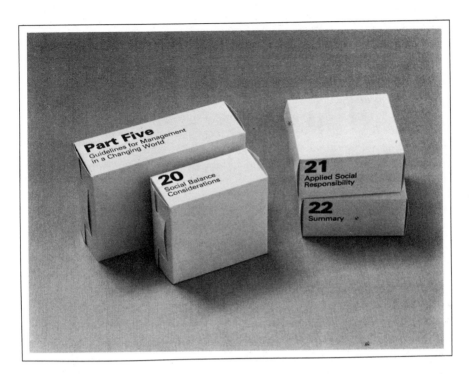

20
Social Balance Considerations

A series of basic tenets of corporate social impact management that pervade the consideration of the individual impact areas in the previous chapters will be summarized here. From this summary, considerations for operating in a true social balance with society will be developed to provide the foundation for framing corporate objectives. Then managements can minimize adverse social impact and come as close to achieving social balance as other constraints on the operation will permit.

The rule in today's world is that man's larger interest is everywhere breaking in upon his immediate short-term interest and overriding it. This applies to business. . . . This is the logic of a unifying, contracting world, where time and distance become daily shorter. . . . Because you are now more than ever dependent on your environment, . . . you will increasingly have to resolve your conflicts on the basis of what is best for society. Like it or not, the business of the modern corporation is society.[1]

ADLAI E. STEVENSON

Underlying Concepts for Management

In our analysis of the requirements for balancing the various corporate impacts on society in the many different aspects of business operation, certain concepts have occurred repeatedly; nine are summarized in the following pages. These concepts have a potential generality and a potential utility. Their identification will aid in the later portion of the chapter when we turn to relating social balance to other parameters that must be considered in setting guidelines for management action.

Responsibility Consistent with Authority

More frequently, society is beginning to ask that a corporation assume responsibility for the consequences of any decisions that its freedom of action permits it to make. The current and continuing public trend is to extend this responsibility to the various social impacts of corporate actions and include both their direct and indirect effects. There are still areas where corporations have not yet faced a specific accountability for the consequences of their decisions and areas where public standards are still evolving, so that it is a matter of individual opinion as to whether the impact of a corporate decision is good or bad. Nonetheless, the trend is clear. The need is for (1) a corporate management awareness of the social impacts of its actions, decisions, and products, (2) an expectation that, through regulation, extension of legal liability, and various sorts of public pressure, corporations will be held responsible for all adverse consequences of these impacts, and (3) a program wherever possible to balance or eliminate impacts that society judges to be adverse, preferably before the public concern reaches the white heat of indignation that often accompanies fresh extensions of society's punitive and regulatory jurisdiction.

---

[1]Adlai E. Stevenson, "Businessmen Who Think Greatly," in Dan H. Fenn, Jr., ed., *Business Responsibility in Action* (New York: McGraw-Hill, 1960), p. 156.

Social Costs

Any action of the business is likely to lead back in one way or another to costs that are being borne by society. Any significant increment to the normal operating costs of society should be identified and balanced where feasible. Insofar as possible, no social cost should be incurred without recompense in any area of the firm's operation. The alternative is to risk regulation and reprisal from society, although the immediacy of the risk varies greatly with the circumstances.

Respect for Law

A transaction must be consummated within the framework of the laws and codes established by society as boundaries for the free-market system. While transactions that violate these codes may or may not involve measurable social costs, they are automatically suspect since society has an unquestioned right to determine the parameters for free-market exchange.

The Wise Use of Natural Resources

Wherever a business is consuming scarce resources or wherever it is pre-empting a portion of the purifying capacity of the environment through its discharges, the business is drawing on nature's bounty in the form of the basic environmental resources of the society. Thus, business is being subsidized by being permitted to use the social capital in this way, even though no formal appropriation or review has ever validated the subsidy. Business has a strong interest in managing its operations well enough to minimize the likelihood that society will reconsider and withdraw such a subsidy.

Implied Continuity

Current business relationships that are allowed to continue from day to day and year to year lead to a mutual interdependence between a company and its employees, its customers, or its suppliers, although no contractual arrangement may exist. An implicit obligation to continue the relationship begins to develop and an uncushioned termination often causes social costs. Unemployment insurance covers a part of the employer's obligations in one type of termination, but most of the other components of these implied relationships have not been formally recognized. Long-term business interest is promoted by identifying and balancing each individual case to avoid accumulation of social costs.

Opportunity Costs

When a company holds close relationships over a long period of time, the existence of these relationships usually acts to take priority over other opportunities; an employee who has one job usually cannot also take another. Even part-time activities often are pre-empted by the terms of an employment contract. A distributor whose undivided attention must be devoted to a particular product line is not able to consider product opportunities offered by other manufacturers. A supplier who enters into a sales contract that absorbs the major part of the available output is cut off from the opportunity of developing other markets.

Since all arrangements of this kind originate in the mutual interest of the two parties, each relationship initially must represent the most favorable opportunity available in order for the transaction to occur. But as the relationship continues, not only is the future guaranteed by implication (as previously discussed), but also the alternative value of lost opportunities mounts and must be considered as a part of the overall balance when a firm disrupts the established patterns.

A Fair Share of the Community

The responsibilities of a business have never been limited to its employee group or to the hours of their employment. The business is a member of a community and through its taxes and other actions contributes to community support and development. Any given business should think in terms of its share of the entire community, including its own employee group, their dependents, and an appropriate fraction of the community fringe to represent the basis for defining its role in developing and maintaining community health.

The degree to which a business should be expected to concern itself with the needs of its share of the community is the degree to which society (or the specific community) has established norms for the fulfillment of these needs. Corporate participation must be limited to areas where the exercise of corporate authority is consistent with democratic processes, if the private sector of the community is to be permitted to continue independent existence.

Ethics and Culture

The business, as a part of the community, has an accumulated impact through its advertising, its behavior standards, and its effect on the appearance, health, and economic well-being of the community. Its impact is also felt through the direct contribution of its managers and its employee group. The ethics and culture of the community can be expected to show some change over time as a result of these impacts.

While each management has a responsibility for assessing and balancing this impact of the business on the community, the tools for such analysis are poorly developed. Most communities have given little attention to this area as yet, so that society's standards are still in the formative stage. As these standards develop, their direction and thrust could be conditioned significantly by business leadership.

Management of the Public Role

Any prominent corporation must have a public role because of (1) the intimate dependence of employees and community on its operating practices, (2) its stewardship of significant wealth-producing resources, and (3) its potential for creating change by shifting its resources, creating new products, or entering new markets. This power cannot and does not escape public attention; members in both governmental and public sectors ask what the corporation's motives are and where its allegiances truly lie. Therefore, the corporation cannot avoid a public role, and this role is too critical to the corporate interest to be left undefined or unmanaged.

Whether a given management will choose to be low in profile or conspicuous, or active or passive, in its public role remains to be decided by that management. It may choose a forward-looking public role, fully balancing its costs and building for a profitable long-term leadership position. It may define such a position, decide that it cannot implement it alone, and seek public subsidy, as the railroads did through attaining land grants in their westward expansion or as Consolidated Edison sought through use of public capital for expansion of electric generating capacity. Or management may choose to operate its business for the short run only and give minimum attention to social costs, expecting that it can face restriction and reprisal for degradation of the public wealth. But, whichever role is chosen, it should be a conscious and well-managed choice. The stakes are too high for the definition of business's public role to happen by default; such a development would represent mismanagement of a critical and sensitive business area.

These nine concepts are key elements in a philosophy of operation that is designed to ensure that a firm contribute to society in many areas of its operation and that it not represent a drain on social capital in any area. While there may be practical problems inherent in such a philosophy (some of which will be discussed in the following pages), the role it describes for business is both desirable and often necessary since business requires the continuing good will of society to exist. In other words, a business holds a franchise, actual or implied, and must operate in such a way that its claim to that franchise is maintained. The risk, if it defaults in its franchise maintenance, is that the franchise might be abridged or withdrawn.

The size of the risk depends on the likelihood that a problem will attract public attention and arouse sufficent public wrath to cause punitive action, as occurred when public environmental concern suddenly rose to the level where a series of new laws were passed with new agencies to enforce them and a system of regulations was established that will bring a major change in corporate behavior.

Changing Public Standards for Business Performance

Business is going to be required to change its perception, its attitudes, its goals, its organizational structure, its operating procedures. Its social responsibility is to understand what is going on in society so that it will know how those changes should be made.[2]

The discussion of the different areas of social balance has indicated that the standards of society have shifted over the years. Although business executives may complain that the rules for the so-called game of business are changed from time to time, these rules never were truly fixed. Today change is the normal condition; the steady evolution in both legal and social standards can be expected to continue.

---

[2]Emmanuel G. Mesthene, "The New Meaning of Social Responsibility," *Innovation*, no. 28 (February 1972): 5.

Many of the obligations of the business to its employees, for instance, went unrecognized in Adam Smith's day. Now these obligations have become so widely recognized, institutionalized, and accepted as a part of the routine benefits plan that proper structure of this employment package is no longer considered as a social issue. Rather, it represents a wise expression of self-interest in maintaining relations with a work force and in developing a competitive position in employee recruiting. The changes that brought present recognition of these obligations involve legislation, which has led to regulation of wages and hours, compensation, employment opportunity, working conditions, and so forth; union pressure, which has been directed to vacations, pensions, and medical plans; and other social forces. These changes will continue; consider the union campaigns for dental payment plans, and the American Chemical Society program for transferable pension benefits for professionals.

Social standards in the environmental and pollution areas had been evolving more slowly. Now with the urgency of some environmental problems and the hot focus of public opinion, it seems likely that the social requirements will shift rapidly. Once it was accepted that wastes would be dumped untreated unless good reasons were developed for forcing a given business to do otherwise. Now it has become obvious to all conservationists and many businesses that no waste stream can be discharged by anyone anywhere that will damage the environment. The real issue is over the rapidity with which necessary new standards will be applied to existing industries, since a major shift of national resources is in progress. Thus, the conversion of a paper industry's pulp mill from a massive and long-tolerated polluter of rivers and lakes to a responsible entity that takes care of its own wastes has become such an obvious step that it is suddenly hard to understand why society did not require it of industry much sooner.

In other areas where a proper social balance is a natural and necessary part of responsible operation, society has done little toward establishing standards. Business leaders have an opportunity to suggest standards as interest shifts in these directions. The challenge posed to business by social standards is to maintain social balance adequately, plan for changes as new standards are evolved (whether via legislation or social pressure), and devise programs for aiding or moving with these changes.

While the details and timing of the coming changes are more or less obscure, one direction of change is clear: Social costs will be identified more explicitly and in many cases will be converted into legal obligations of the business.

> A firm's responsibility will extend far beyond the present legal limits of the corporation. It will become legally liable for everything done in response to its demand for component parts; it will be responsible for the effects of the enabling subsystems upon the ecology and society; and accountable for the costs and other burdens attached to recycling the resulting elements of the . . . product.[3]

---

[3]Etienne Cracco and Jacques Rostenni, "The Socio-ecological Product," *MSU Business Topics* 18, no. 3 (Summer 1971): 54.

Competitive Implications

As public pressures grow, business will be expected to compensate its social costs as a part of its total cost picture. Where society has not made this payment into a legal obligation as yet, the firm that acknowledges its full cost could be placed at a competitive disadvantage in the marketplace. Thus, the question is to determine how a business should react to social balance requirements that affect its competitive position in any significant way.

John R. Commons tells how a well-framed worker's compensation law changed the accident problem. It gave individual employers, who had feared a competitive disadvantage from expenditures on employee safety, a real incentive to reduce their accident rates through a tax based on accident experience. The net result was that the extra costs to the individual employers were considerably offset by the reduced tax as the overall accident rate was cut sharply; in effect, increased profit was yielded to the employers in spite of the higher compensation payments for accidents that did occur. Once insurance rates were adjusted to correspond to actual accident experience, employers had a direct incentive to reduce these costs, and no competitive disadvantage resulted since all firms were treated alike.[4]

By creating a public agency that receives support and cooperation both from business and labor, Sweden has gone far toward the solution of unemployment problems due to plant closings and displacement of unskilled workers.

> Mobility—in skill, work and placement of employment—has become the special concern of the Swedish unions. They started and then persuaded the government to take over a nationwide agency for identifying a new opportunity, finding the employees for it, training and relocating them. This agency undertakes to find a job for anyone whose present employment is likely to terminate—which means that employers are willing to plan their manpower and to inform their men of layoffs and plant closings in advance. Instead of trying to prevent the closing down of an old plant or the phasing out of an old process, this government agency works with the employer and the workers to speed it up. If the worker needs retraining, it is being made available. If he needs to travel to look at other places to live, this, too, is being made available. If no job is available for him immediately, he is being carried. The total cost has been amazingly low, perhaps half of what unemployment insurance for these men would have cost.[5]

Although the Swedish unions took the initiative here, U.S. employers have tremendous incentives to implement similar solutions, such as the opportunity to reduce unemployment insurance payments and decrease the termination costs and social pressures generated by plant closings and layoffs.

The Kentucky Oaks Coal Company found that competitive conditions encouraged it

---

[4]John R. Commons, *Economics of Collective Action* (Madison, Wis.: University of Wisconsin Press, 1970), pp. 277–284.

[5]Peter F. Drucker, "Worker and Work in the Metropolis," *Daedalus* 97, no. 4 (Fall 1968): 1256.

to strip-mine through homes and graveyards without regard for the interests or personal feelings of the surface property owners, and Kentucky law permitted it at that time.[6] Rather than abusing the practice until public outcry forced a change, the company could have joined those seeking better laws. The resulting legislation would undoubtedly have been less burdensome in its restrictions than laws written in the heat of public wrath.

Among other things the long development of labor legislation has represented a series of steps to obtain compensation for social costs from the business that has caused them. The same pattern is evolving in the pollution area. In the long run it seems likely that all social costs must be recognized and paid by the business responsible for them. Business leaders have an opportunity to assume a strong leadership role in obtaining the kind of laws and restrictions that are most consistent with both business and public interests. If the leadership role is not exercised, the changes will still come, although perhaps more slowly, and the necessary new laws may be much more burdensome and restrictive. Competitive pressures are a poor excuse for antisocial behavior, and business leaders would be well advised to seek to have such pressures directed more positively.

> If corporations cannot deal individually with major social responsibilities because of competitive cost disadvantages, and if they are unable to cooperate in resolving such difficulties, then they logically and ethically should propose and support national governmental regulation which will remove the short-term impediments from actions that are wise in the long run.[7]

Optimal Profit Level

There is no inherent reason why social balance—or reduction of corporate impact—and profits should be linked. These concepts are separate, just as costs and profits are separate. The first question addressed here is whether a business is operated in a socially acceptable manner. If it is, then its costs (accounting and social) are fully paid. Whether it makes a profit or not is a separate consideration dependent on the market opportunity, costs, competition, and the caliber of the corporate management. Of course, whether there is a profit determines whether the firm will survive.

The management objective suggested here is the achievement of optimal profit over the long run after all costs are fairly recognized. This definition is deliberately worded to describe the greatest profit level that can be achieved at each moment without sacrificing the future profits of the business. Thus, the stream of profits is maximized over time. Achievement of this profit level requires a combination of economically focused decisions that are wise enough to generate the profit and a level of attention to the noneconomic business constraints that will ensure a

---

[6]Ben A. Franklin, "Strip Mining in Kentucky: Mountaineers Say It Kills Their Land," *New York Times,* 1 July, 1965.

[7]Research and Policy Committee, *Social Responsibilities of Business Corporations* (New York: Committee for Economic Development, June 1971), p. 46.

harmonious relationship with the surrounding society.

The meaning of *long run* is a difficult part of the definition since this concept exists individually in the minds of different management groups, is a product of their value systems, and must necessarily differ from firm to firm. These differences can become an important factor in the competitive interplay between firms.

The long-term dimension for a given management tends to be the sum of two different concepts. The first concept is that of the income stream that will be generated; this can conveniently be expressed in present worth or discounted cash flow terms. The second dimension is the value of the business as a going concern, which will be determined at any given time by its earnings, the expectations for its future earnings prospects, and the general state of the market for going businesses. By estimating the effect of its decisions on the income stream value and the value of the business, management develops the necessary tools for its attempt to achieve profit optimization over the span of time that seems most relevant. By including all legitimate costs (particularly, social costs), management can ensure the legitimacy of the resulting profit. While this statement of profitability is valid only for the time period in which that particular management maintains control, no other set of management perspectives is relevant so long as no management changes are imposed.

Social Balance as an Operating Concept

As a business firm attempts to optimize profits over the long run, it is suggested here that it should strive to achieve social balance in each area of its operation, as summarized in Figure 20.1. This balance is to be determined on a sector-by-sector basis (taking into account goods and services, resources employed, and neighborhood and broad social effects) and will involve adjusting its operation and, therefore, its costs to achieve a total social balance.

The requirement is to attain a balance in each area of operation. Efforts in one area could often lead to a definite contribution to social capital at little or no excess cost to

Figure 20.1 Social Balance Considerations

Underlying concepts	Changing public standards for
Responsibility consistent with authority	business performance
No significant social cost	Competitive implications of a social
Legal operation	balance
Wise use of nature's bounty	
Implied commitment	Optimal profit as a target
Opportunity costs	Social balance as a guide
Fair share of community costs	
Ethics and culture	
Management of the public role	

Objective: By management of corporate social impact, to achieve a social balance, thus freeing management for pursuit of enterprise profitability, which is also in the public interest.

the business, and yet in other areas social costs may be detected that are rather difficult for the business to compensate. Unfortunately, the business cannot offset gains in one area against social costs in others. The difficulty of offsetting costs in such a way is that when someone or something is injured, or resources belonging to society are dissipated, social costs are incurred. And the existence of a compensating surplus elsewhere offers no comfort at the point of the injury; an uncompensated social cost still is an abuse that will tend to fester if it goes uncorrected. When such an area of abuse finally receives the full light of public attention, it is likely to cause reaction and retribution against the offending business. Social benefits in other sectors that may be very real and may have helped other sectors of society greatly are of little interest to the individuals whose injury is represented by the social cost.

Summary

Taken altogether, the concept of social balance and its competitive implications constitute a business pattern very similar to and yet much different from that described by Adam Smith. The patterns are alike in that the economic, profit-seeking nature of the business corporation is guided in such a way as the "invisible hand" guided the entrepreneur of Adam Smith's day. The patterns differ primarily because of the change in cost concepts. The entrepreneur of the classical economists recognized only specific and identified money costs; today's corporation must make some attempt to recognize social costs as well. Yet as social costs get full recognition and become converted into legal business obligations, these patterns will tend to converge again. This will happen as: ". . . we . . . restructure our system so that the incentive to react to social costs is built directly into the foundations . . . to make the measurement of net social benefit act as real reward and penalty."[8]

This chapter has summarized nine of the key concepts underlying the management of corporate social impact and has discussed the implications of a continually changing set of standards for business performance. Then it has considered the competitive implications of a social balance, the drive for an optimal profit level, and the social balance as an operating concept.

Questions for Analysis and Discussion

1. Give examples of corporate actions that illustrate the following:

Corporate responsibility consistent with authority

Corporate balancing of any significant increment to social costs

Corporate use of and dependence on nature's bounty

---

[8]Robin Marris, "Business, Economics and Society," in Robin Marris, ed., *Social Innovation in the City* (Cambridge, Mass.: Harvard University Press, 1969), pp. 40–42.

2. Give examples of changing public standards for business performance and discuss their impact.

3. Discuss an example of a social cost that is likely to be converted into a legal business obligation.

4. Find and discuss an example of an action taken by a corporation under competitive pressure to relieve its failure to achieve social balance by seeking regulation or other public sector intervention.

For Further Information

Bell, Daniel. *The Coming of the Post-Industrial Society.* New York: Basic Books, 1973.

Drucker, Peter F. *The Age of Discontinuity.* New York: Harper & Row, 1969.

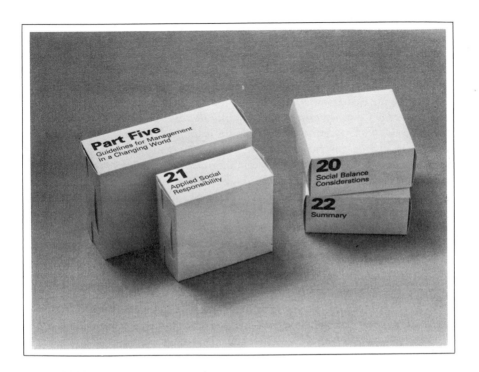

21
Applied Social Responsibility

The bridge between the management of corporate social impact and social balance and the general concept of social responsibility is critical to the conclusion of the present analysis. After dealing with some of the practical limits of this concept and the way that it might be applied, we will consider the implications of failing to achieve social balance and the need for governmental intervention in some circumstances. After summarizing the guidelines for management of corporate social impact, we will suggest the applicability of their use as normative constraints in practical operating management processes.

There is broad recognition today that corporate self-interest is inexorably involved in the well-being of the society of which business is an integral part. . . . There is increasing understanding that the corporation is dependent on the goodwill of society, which can sustain or impair its existence through public pressures on government. And it has become clear that the essential resources and goodwill of society are not naturally forthcoming to corporations whenever needed, but must be worked for and developed.[1]

RESEARCH AND POLICY COMMITTEE, COMMITTEE FOR ECONOMIC DEVELOPMENT

Social balance was defined as requiring a pattern of operation that pays all costs, both accounting and social (see Figure 21.1). In the preceding chapters the implications of these costs for different areas of the business have been reviewed, as we have traced the evolution of the conversion of certain social costs into accounting costs that achieve recognition and require payment. The current corporate social impact problem is not concerned with costs that are already recognized by the accounting system but only with the real, unaccounted costs that will go uncompensated unless a responsible management recognizes them and takes them into account in the course of routine operation.

Social responsibility is a noble concept that has been used so widely and so loosely that it has become almost impossible to define. Nonetheless, the concept has value in defining a situation in which a corporation maintains a proper respect for the society in which it is embedded, pays its costs, and recognizes its obligations.

To provide a more practical and pragmatic approach to this same area, we have dealt with corporate social impact as a specific effect of corporate operations on society. Furthermore, we have suggested that corporate social impacts be managed toward the objective of achieving social balance, that is, an objective of causing no adverse corporate social impacts. Since society benefits from the operation of the corporation when there are no specific adverse corporate social impacts, achievement of social balance puts corporate management in a very favorable position relative to its obligations to society. This position fits within many definitions of corporate social responsibility and is the sense in which the term is used in this book. *Applied social responsibility,* the term that is used for the title of this chapter, is the

---

[1]Research and Policy Committee, *Social Responsibilities of Business Corporations* (New York: Committee for Economic Development, June 1971), p. 27.

Figure 21.1   The Shift to Reporting True Profit

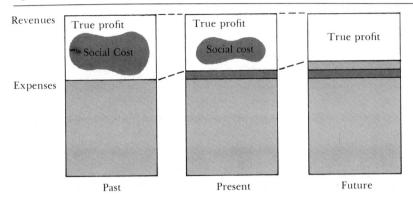

As new laws convert social obligations into financial obligations, corporations leave less social cost uncompensated, and their reported profits become closer to their true profits. The suggestion is that it is truly in the self-interest of business leaders to find means of encouraging this transition. Thus they can operate in a responsible equilibrium with society (that is, in a condition of social balance) and can then concentrate their energies on obtaining optimal levels of profit.

closest practical approach to social balance that a given corporation can manage to achieve.

Business survival depends on profits. Business managers are primarily judged by their success in generating these profits. Payment of more costs reduces profits in the short run. The pressure on business profits is usually in the short run; managers are accused of suboptimizing to show short-term profits, even on the basis of presenting accounting costs.[2]

Social balance as defined here is based on real costs and long-term self-interest of the business but will often act to reduce short-term profits through payment of costs not yet defined as legal obligations. The question is to determine how practical it may be to expect socially responsible management. The answer is that there is hope and that there are serious limitations. Both the basis for the hope and the reasons for the limitations will be explored in this chapter.

Practical Limits of Social Responsibility

Business managements are concerned with the impact of their actions on society either as a matter of conscience or out of their awareness of self-interest. The argument here is that these two constraints are the same. A proper perception of long-term self-interest leaves few problems of conscience unsatisfied, and any

---

[2]William H. Newman, Charles E. Summer, and E. Kirby Warren, *The Process of Management* (Englewood Cliffs, N.J.: Prentice-Hall, 1967), p. 712–713; also J. Herbert Holloman, "The New Meaning of Social Responsibility," *Innovation* no. 28 (February 1972): 7.

sacrifices in the present should be regained through better long-term profits than could otherwise occur.

This proposition depends for its truth and applicability on the logic of the underlying concepts that have been unfolded, as well as on: (1) The business leaders' ability to preceive their own long-term self-interest in an uncertain world, and (2) their ability to act according to this perception in the short run in a competitive world. These two points will be examined by considering the way that a business sets about determining its obligations and acting on them.

This approach to the problem of managing corporate social impact begins with a business management appraisal of the real long-term costs of its operation by means of an area-by-area review of social balance. The approach is likely to lead to identification of some areas where the business is causing costs for which there is not proper compensation. Identification of these areas represents the starting point toward taking any practical corrective action.

Each identified area of social costs might then be examined from two standpoints: (1) a careful and flexible definition of the real problem, and (2) a realistic assessment of its priority.

Defining the Problem

The reason for the emphasis on defining the problem is the frequency with which a superficial definition fails to suggest the essential factors that will provide the most effective solution. Thus, the most important single element in the problem of banning DDT was the elimination of toxic residues of chlorinated hydrocarbons from the environment as completely as possible. While this definition of the problem in terms of its essential elements did create a strong pressure for eliminating the usage of DDT, it did not preclude other solutions (such as the use of biodegradable DDT) so long as the dangerous residues were truly eliminated.

Of course, many problems have alternative definitions that reflect the value systems of the problem solvers. For instance, broad spectrum insecticides can have serious effects on the ecological balance in an area. Where this is the primary concern, biodegradable DDT is little better than the persistent kind; however, in this case the real problem is no longer DDT but the use of all broad spectrum insecticides. Under this definition, the cure is no longer related to DDT itself but to a shift to a more informed selection of insect control agents.

Another example is the suggestion by some conservation groups that use of automobiles must be eliminated or at least sharply curtailed.[3] Here many people feel that the most important single problem is to eliminate the atmospheric pollution from automobile exhausts. Whether this is approached through catalytic treatment of the exhaust, redesign of internal combustion engines, or shifting to a different propulsion system is not important to that phase of the problem. Any one of several solutions would suffice so long as the desired result is achieved. However, the solutions might

---

[3]*New York Times,* 21 February, 1970, and 27 February, 1970.

vary widely in economy and energy consumption, and the problem could have been defined in these terms instead.

Thus, both very careful problem definition and ingenuity in devising alternative solutions are needed. Many social cost problems can be transformed at little expense once the definition has exposed the basic elements so that pressure can be applied to the real issue. The earlier example of an auto body scrap process helping to eliminate unsightly automobile carcasses by making salvage profitable is an illustration of approaching a problem from a slightly different angle, thus making the expense of a direct solution unnecessary.

Some problems have several solutions; for instance, a number of urban waste problems would yield either to an economical recycling of the product itself (bottles, cans, and so forth) or a good process for recovering these products from city garbage. And some problems solve themselves (at least partially) in the process of definition; for instance, a number of successful programs for hiring handicapped workers are based on the recognition that all jobs are not the same so that the same basic hiring specifications need not be applied in all cases.

Assigning Priorities

Assignment of priority comes from the analysis required by any resource allocation decision, that is, deciding which problem in a particular category needs attention first. The considerations include the acuteness of the social problem, the chance of a low-cost or profitable solution, the expectation for public action, and the degree to which the standards for the solution have been defined.

The expectation for public action represents a practical consideration since many social costs, primarily in the employment cost and fringe-benefit areas, have been converted into direct charges to the business by laws or competitive pressures. It seems wise to look first at those likely to emerge next as direct charges. Timely business action might, by avoiding an imposed solution, lead to a more convenient or economical disposition of the problem. The automobile scrap problem serves as a good illustration; the proposed arbitrary disposal charge is neither an efficient or desirable solution but would be very likely to be imposed if such a problem remained to fester unsolved. Many other corporate social impact problems have now reached the point where social pressure will lead to regulatory action in the course of the next few years unless the problem is solved in some other way.

Except for those problems that require immediate action for business to maintain control of the solution, the natural order of priority is according to the seriousness of the cost that is being created. Within the range of not only the resources available to a business but also the acceptable alternative courses of action, many corporate social impact problems can be made to disappear at little cost once attention is focused on the problem. Unfortunately, some problems are more difficult to deal with because no standards have yet been developed for the solution. Still other problems may demand solutions beyond the resources of any business. Thus, a careful analysis of the social balance of a business followed by a realistic action program may still leave balance failures for other correction.

The Failure to Establish Social Balance

A business might have difficulty in establishing social balance in a particular area for a number of reasons, such as (1) competitive pressures, (2) inability to pay its costs, and (3) dependence on public subsidy.

Competitive pressures are a frequent cause of social balance problems and a frequent excuse for their continuance. Where costs are critical to a business and where competition between firms is reasonably ideal in the classic sense, the individual business firm may have great difficulty in shifting to a base that allows for more complete recognition of the true costs. For instance, the national minimum wage legislation represents a judgment by Congress of a necessary wage level. It was widely predicted that marginal firms would be forced to cease their operations by the additional burden of meeting these minimum wages. To the extent that this was true, the same firms would not have been able to make the same wage increase as an act of social responsibility that their competitors might make voluntarily, although not forced by law to do so.

Any broad review of corporate social balance will uncover cases where a business simply cannot afford the cost of a socially responsible action. The employers who cannot afford the cost of paying the minimum wage provide one example; Appalachian mines that cannot afford the costs accompanying the provision of proper underground mine safety provide another. Individual businesses that are struggling to exist at all will often not pay extra costs if they are given any choice about the matter.

The parallel with normal accounting practice is quite clear. To show a true profit, a business must not only pay the immediate cost of its day-to-day operation but also a fair allocation of other costs, including charges for depreciation on the capital employed in the business and depletion of any wasting assets employed. A business that cannot do this will lose money but need not shut down. So long as current costs are being paid, the owners of the business have the option of continuing to operate until the losses have depleted the capital of the business.

This is the same way that a marginal coal mine in Appalachia may continue to operate at the expense of the health and safety of its workers, thus depleting the social capital of the area. Another example is that of a manufacturer that continues to operate by paying substandard wages and depleting social capital as a consequence of forcing its employees to live at the scale that these substandard wages permit. In such cases the business is operating by means of a public subsidy in the amount of the depletion of local social capital. Clearly, society should review the merit of such a subsidy and legislate accordingly.[4]

Another type of social balance problem is that of the business that depends on other types of public subsidy. With the subsidy, the business can show both a profit

---

[4]"I think we should have a concept of social bankruptcy, where the company is thrown into receivership. If a company can be thrown into bankruptcy because it's not paying its bills, why shouldn't it be thrown into bankruptcy for making thousands of people sick and destroying other people's property without compensation, which is what contamination and pollution do. . . . Why should we accept bankruptcy if the market does it and not when it's done by a conscious and fairly applied implementation of a social cost test?" Ralph Nader, as quoted by Eileen Shanahan, "Reformer: Urging Business Change," *New York Times*, 24 January, 1971. Copyright © 1971 by The New York Times Company. Reprinted by permission.

and a satisfactory social balance; without the subsidy, the picture is different. A subsidy can be a proper public act, and the business need not be held accountable for its value. An example might be the decision of the Atomic Energy Commission to encourage private firms to enter into the reprocessing of the uranium fuel elements for atomic power plants. Toll schedules were set high enough to permit a profit to the processor; the AEC rationalized this subsidy on the basis that, as nuclear power plants become more common, the volume of reprocessing would rise to the point where these contractors could become profitable on a true accounting basis.[5]

Accidental subsidies must be considered with more care. Where a business has utilized the opportunity of dumping untreated wastes or the opportunity to mine and sell a major quantity of a scarce resource, it seems likely that sooner or later the public will review this subsidy to see whether society is receiving full value. A recent example was the growing pressure and finally the elimination of the subsidy received by the oil industry from the federal government through liberal rules for depletion accounting. A business receiving public subsidy would be wise to act on the assumption that it will someday be required to show that value is being returned in proportion to the value received from society.

Recognizing Costs That Industry Cannot Bear

Some social costs are beyond the means of a particular business. If they were converted into recognized accounting costs and charged to the business, the only result would be to put the business out of operation. This may be desirable in the case of some businesses, such as those not able to pay a realistic minimum wage; however, in many other cases these costs represent part of a larger problem. For example, when the textile industry was driven out of New England by its inability to compete, both the industries that moved and those that failed incurred large social costs. Communities were crippled, largely without recompense, by the loss of major employers in areas where alternative employment was not readily available.

Not all of the firms that moved were in desperate straits financially. Some were still strong and perhaps should have done more to cushion the shock of their departure. In some cases, managements were even accused of a deliberate effort to move out of the community quickly in order to leave deep-seated problems behind—for instance, to shift to a low-wage area and leave a strong union stranded in an employerless town. But even if these firms had addressed their responsibility more seriously, their resources would have been inadequate to balance the social costs completely.

The point is that the troubles of the textile industry represented a singular shift from an outmoded industrial pattern into a new system of modern mills better located geographically. The initial attraction of low wages was a factor that was adjusted with time. Without excusing the failure of the strong firms to play their proper role, it is quite clear that the weak ones could do nothing at that historical

---

[5]"AEC Approves Construction of Private Atom Plants," *Business Week*, 12 May, 1956, p. 140; "Reprocessing Package Cuts Fuel Costs," *Chemical Week*, vol. 82, 10 May, 1958, pp. 31–32; "AEC Sifts Process Routes to Low-Cost Fuel Recovery," *Chemical Week*, vol. 82, 14 June, 1958, pp. 39–40.

point. The problem was too large; some governmental intervention would have been a necessary ingredient to ensure a smoother transition from the textile industry in New England to the electronics and other types of industries that have developed more recently.

The Appalachian coal areas represent another case in which the economic problem has become too big for many of the individual employers to deal with effectively. The current mine safety legislation is expected to put hundreds of small coal mines out of operation. By all reports, this is as it should be; these mines appear to be too dangerous to be operating. However, the effect of this action will be to create one more wave of layoffs and unemployment in an area where the principal sources of employment (primarily coal mines) have reduced their requirements repeatedly. Already the fringe portion of the population, which must be substantially supported by those who are gainfully employed, has become too large for local employers to handle alone. New England textile problems of a few years ago and today's Appalachian problem are two examples of major areas where the government has a role in guiding and aiding the process of change, so that business can rise to a better level of payment of its true costs without leaving undue hardship in the community.

Guidelines for Managing Corporate Social Impact

Returning to the question of how social balance can be achieved through management of corporate social impact, we find that it is now possible to summarize the logic of the approach and then suggest guidelines for management action. These guidelines were introduced in successive chapters in Parts Three and Four as the different direct and societywide corporate impact areas were considered.

These guidelines are normative and are intended to suggest ways of maintaining social balance. They are neither legal requirements nor are they likely to be made into law. However, it is important to remember that the consequence of failing to achieve social balance is an adverse social impact and probably a social cost. If the social cost should become a matter of public concern, regulation and reprisals might well result. Maintenance of social balance is in the corporate self-interest in that it increases the freedom of the corporation to pursue its own ends—hence the suggested guidelines.

The Sale of Goods and Services

In the sale of goods and services, social balance will tend to be maintained if the following guidelines are applied:

Merchandise quality   On the whole, goods and services fulfill the expectations of the purchasers.

Service   Reasonable requirements for after-sale and continued support of routine use patterns are met.

Safety   Goods and services are free of danger and unexpected side effects in normal use, attempt to ensure the safety of predictable types of product misuse, and do not cause unacceptable environmental aftereffects from the goods and services or their packaging.

Impact of new products When goods and services that change lifestyles and cultural patterns are introduced and promoted, an effort is made to minimize disruption and resentment and, thus, to avoid future challenges from society concerning the right to introduce such goods or services.

Use and Consumption of Physical Resources

In the use and consumption of physical resources, social balance will tend to be maintained if the following guideline is applied:

Conservation A firm whose operation is using or consuming scarce resources develops an understanding of the role of these resources in the total social capital, both in actuality and in popular belief, and manages its operations with a sensitivity that minimizes the chance that its right to use these resources will be restricted or withdrawn.

People as Resources

In the use of people as resources, social balance will tend to be maintained if the following guidelines are applied:

Value given and received Each member of the organization receives fair compensation (including adequate provision for dependents and for old age benefits), works under conditions that do not impair health now or in the future, and in return is expected to deliver full productive energy during the time allocated to the job.

Opportunity Meaningful tasks, challenging career paths, and equality of opportunity to pursue these tasks and paths are maintained with minimum possible disruption.

Waste from the Business Operation

In the management of waste from the business operation, social balance will tend to be maintained if the following guidelines are applied:

Pollution Wastes discharged from the business operation do not cause any measurable detriment to the environment.

Building dumps Wastes going to land fill or ocean dumps, or otherwise making permanent use of surface area, have social consent for this dedication of land or ocean resources; nevertheless, such discharges are best minimized or avoided in anticipation of increased dumping costs and restrictions.

Resource waste Energy and resource content of waste streams are minimized by recovery or recycling as an operating economy, which provides a means of reducing environmental burdens in anticipation of further social pressure toward more careful resource use.

Impact on the Local Community

In the management of impact on the local community, social balance will tend to be maintained if the following guidelines are applied:

Dependence   A firm recognizes the degree to which it is dependent on and served by the health of its surrounding community and encourages this health wherever and however possible.

Fair share   A firm operates in such a way that it and its employees support their fair share of the costs of community services, including those used by the business and needed by both the employees and the fringe of the community.

Neighborhood effects   A firm recognizes its own effect on the nature and character of the neighborhood around the operation and minimizes adverse effects insofar as possible.

Business Resource Policies

In managing the social impact of business resource policies, social balance will tend to be maintained if the following guidelines are applied:

Maintenance of capital   A business operates to conserve and expand its resources in order to maintain and increase the level of opportunity in its own interests and in the interests of both its employees and the dependent community.

Use of profits   A business handles its profits in such a way as to minimize the economic, social, and political impact of their use, particularly the impact from any movement of profits from the business to a parent corporation or the stockholders.

Alternatives to severance   When evolution of the business creates a surplus of plants, people, or community services, the firm makes a serious effort to find alternative, profitable uses for these dependent resources or, at least, to cushion the severance so that the long-term economic health of former members of the organization and the health of the community will be preserved.

Business and Technology

In managing the social impact of the business as a producer and consumer of technology, social balance will tend to be maintained if the following guidelines are applied:

Technology   A business dependent on the long-term processes for generation of new technology develops an understanding of this dependence and seeks opportunities to encourage the replenishment of this technology.

Impact on society   A business engaged in offering goods or services based on new technology recognizes the responsibilities, which are growing but are still imperfectly defined, for the consequences of the social impacts that derive from the right to introduce new discoveries.

Involvement in Public Issues

In managing the social impact of business involvement in public issues, social balance will tend to be maintained if the following guidelines are applied:

Public self-interest In public processes a firm recognizes and pursues its own self-interest and cultivates an understanding of this self-interest as it relates to the social and political processes so that neither the anger of society nor its political power will be aroused.

Respect for law A corporation obeys the law and cultivates respect for it from others.

Meeting and Shaping the Requirements of Society

In managing the social impact from adjusting to and shaping the requirements of society, social balance will tend to be maintained if the following guidelines is applied:

Social change The corporate power to mold and reshape society subtly is used wisely by selecting areas where the social forces justifying and supporting the change have already been set in motion and by not encouraging any change that will be rejected by society's governance processes.

Society's Governance Processes

In managing the social impact on society's governance processes, social balance will tend to be maintained if the following guidelines are applied:

Wealth production As a wealth producer, and in the interest both of its own economic soundness and that of society, a firm attempts to make its productive processes as efficient in the use of materials, energy, and labor as competitive circumstances will permit.

Regulation As a regulated wealth producer, a firm strives to build public information about and awareness of the basic issues underlying the choice of the most efficient pattern for regulating it and its industry. Thus, necessary debates over alternative governance processes can lead to wise political and economic decisions.

Corporate Loyalties and Allegiances

In managing the social impact of corporate loyalties and allegiances, social balance will tend to be maintained if the following guidelines are applied:

Allegiance A corporation gives its primary allegiance to the society that makes the rules controlling its existence. In the view of that society, it must blend in as a sound corporate citizen to have hopes of long-term acceptance and survival.

Federal management A corporation with operations in many different nations or other rule-making social units encourages each subsidiary to become a part of the local society. Then the corporation must manage its affairs through a pattern of corporate governance that recognizes the divergent allegiances of the several subsidiaries and develops economic and managerial unity within a framework consistent with these local ties.

Power A corporation uses its economic power and its political influence with great circumspection and discretion to avoid presenting threats to the society or confronting the political power that controls its existence.

Code of conduct A transnational or multinational corporation troubled by the suspicions of local governments and nationalist elements in their societies eases the strain of the atmosphere in which it operates by: encouraging the development of a code of conduct for local subsidiaries toward the local society and for governments toward foreign-controlled corporations, encouraging the discussion and adoption of that code, and using such a code as a guide for its own operations.

Employee loyalty A corporation expects and requires allegiance from the members of its organization within the legal scope of its business and within the personal scope of their employees' normal growth and progression as individuals. The corporation also recognizes the likelihood of unrest and defection if it should attempt to require illegal or unethical actions or actions detrimental to an employee's self-interest.

These guidelines, which were developed chapter by chapter, are intended to define an operating pattern in which no adverse corporate social impacts occur. These guidelines are intended as normative statements that can aid management in seeking social balance. A social balance analysis of corporate impacts on society would then lead to identification of problem areas where a balance does not exist, assignment of priorities, and establishment of an action program. While some of the necessary solutions may be difficult and may even require the intervention of other forces, many problems are easily solved once they are clearly recognized.

Where a social cost problem challenges the profitability of a business, economic pressures may prevent balancing of the corporate social impact without governmental intervention. As with most other issues important to society, laws must be wisely designed, enacted, and enforced before the needs of society will be recognized above self-interest in the majority of cases. It is in the interest of a business caught in such economic pressures to work for enactment of the laws and regulations necessary to permit it to act responsibly rather than to endorse its default by inaction.

Where the social costs can be converted into objective costs and can become part of the cost structure of the businesses in a particular industry, the corporate social impact problem ceases to exist; only the normal problems requiring good management remain. Many of the needs of the employee group have been resolved in this way. The entire complex of costs related to pollution and respect for the environment appears to be in a formative stage that should lead to a similar shift to an objective cost basis. As such a shift becomes practical, business has an important interest in both hastening the application to prevent competitive inequities and guiding the necessary regulations to make them as practical and functional as possible.

Where the lack of objective standards makes social balance impossible to define precisely at the present time, a business is well advised to create subjective standards of its own, attempt to work in accordance with them, and thus aid in evolving fair community standards.

Problems that affect an entire industry or a whole region may require governmental intervention for solution. Where a marginal industry is operating by mining the environment, governmental intervention is the direct and effective way to initiate the problem's solution. Where such an industry is not profitable, so that the social costs it is incurring represent, in effect, a subsidy that is keeping the business in operation, society as a whole must decide whether the good of the whole justifies the subsidy. Then it should change the rules under which these businesses exist either to provide a sounder social basis for the subsidy or to cut it off and allow the businesses to disappear or reorganize.

The long-term outlook is for continuing evolution of a pattern that predates Adam Smith. That is, through its governmental units, society must make the rules within which the business community operates and must change these rules as necessary for the general good. The firms that are not profitable must be eliminated by competition or made profitable (and responsible) by appropriate subsidies and changes in the rules.

In the light of this outlook, social responsibility can be redefined as a requirement for management recognition of areas where real business costs have not yet been made into enforceable legal requirements. Where the emerging requirements are already perceptible in objective terms, corporate action is clear-cut. In areas where social standards are unclear and requirements are subjective, business management can only be encouraged to establish and follow standards that will aid in the development of proper public standards for competitors and community.

Responsible Business Management

The preceding analysis now permits a summary of rules for the operation of a socially responsible firm.

1. The purpose of the business is to make a profit; its managers should strive for the optimal profit that can be achieved over the long run.

2. No true profits can be claimed until business costs are paid. This includes all social costs, as determined by detailed analysis of the social balance between the firm and society.

3. Where social costs are found in areas where no objective standards for their correction yet exists, the managers should strive for a correction based on standards that, in their judgment, ought to exist and should simultaneously encourage the individual involvement of the firm's members in developing the necessary social standards.

4. Where competitive pressure or economic necessity precludes socially responsible actions, the business should recognize that its operation is depleting social capital and, therefore, represents a loss. It should attempt to restore profitable operation through either better management, if the problem is internal, or by advocating corrective legislation, if society is suffering as a result of the way that the rules for business competition have been made.

At the present time, many annual reports mention social responsibility, and some companies claim to have established socially responsible operations. Extensive corporate programs have been reported, which are guided by serious and ongoing experiments with several types of social audits. These activities have some obvious merits and represent constructive progress. However, these activities are only sound where a clear plan guides the nature and extent of corporate social involvement. In other words, the challenge from Milton Friedman and others is a real one; each management must be prepared to justify that the stockholder's money is not being diverted to projects beyond the self-interest of the business, however broadly defined. And each management needs an index by which to assess the adequacy of its activities, so that it can claim the respect of society and enjoy reasonable freedom from unexpected reprisals for uncompensated social costs.

The purpose of the present analysis is not to discredit current corporate efforts, which are praiseworthy and represent healthy progress for the most part, but to suggest the social balance concept as a management tool that will help in determining the proper boundaries of a corporate social program based upon the actual corporate impacts on society, as summarized in Figure 21.2. Thus, the social balance concept and the various guidelines for applying it could serve to augment social audits and various other management tools as a means to a more effective total program. In addition, it could serve, to permit, almost for the first time, the extension of effective management techniques to the management of the business-society interface.

Summary

In terms of the concepts we have presented, social responsibility is possible to define and, within certain limitations, practical to administer. Primarily, the limitations result from the lack of community standards and the existence of conflicting economic pressures. Business self-interest calls for leadership in establishing corporate performance standards and in advocating any necessary changes in rules and regulations so that economic pressures will work in the public interest and will not prevent responsible business operation. In the absence of such leadership, the public tends to translate corporate defaults into authority over and responsibility for the accepted ills.

Corporate social responsibility deserves to be an issue in the current business scene because the controversy it stimulates serves both to focus attention on the social costs that are still not adequately balanced and to call for leadership in finding the means to balance these costs. Business self-interest requires business leadership in seeking the public good and balancing its social costs as an alternative to more radical changes toward social control of the business system.

This chapter has related management of corporate social impact to achieve a social balance to the concept of social responsibility. Also, it has summarized guidelines for management of corporate social impact in a pattern that can lead to applied social responsibility as a management process for approaching social balance in actual corporate operations.

Figure 21.2   Corporate Social Impact Areas

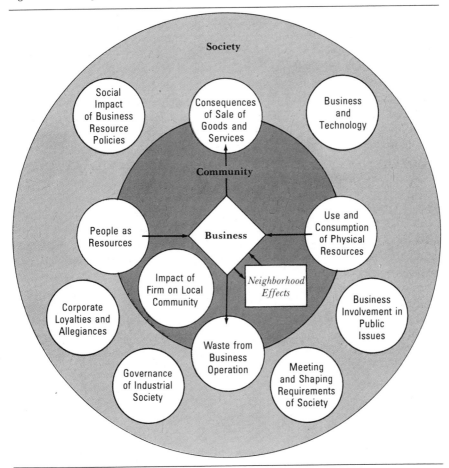

Questions for Analysis and Discussion

1. Discuss the practical limits of applying corporate social impact and social responsibility concepts in terms of a specific example.

2. Illustrate the way in which redefinition of a current problem could open new routes to solution and discuss the social balance implications of this process of redefinition.

3. Find and discuss a current social balance failure problem in relation to some of the possible solutions.

4. Among the suggested guidelines for management of corporate social impact, which do you think will be the easiest to apply and accomplish? The most difficult? Discuss your reasoning.

For Further Information

Anshen, Melvin, ed. *Managing the Socially Responsible Corporation.* New York: Macmillan, 1974.

Drucker, Peter F. *Management: Tasks, Responsibilities, Practices.* New York: Harper & Row, 1974.

Hargreaves, John, and Dauman, Jan. *Business Survival and Social Change.* New York: Wiley, 1975.

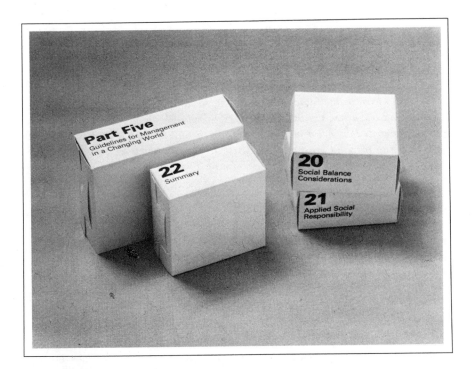

22
Summary

The preceding has completed the analysis of corporate social impact and the development of tentative guidelines for its management. What remains is a brief recapitulation, a statement of conclusions, and suggestions for further study.

Competition and its purpose are not individual, but social. It is a game played under rules fixed by the State to the end that, so far as possible, the prize of victory shall be earned not by trickery or mere self-seeking adroitness, but by value rendered. It is not a mere play of unrestrained self-interest; it is a method of harnessing the wild beast of self-interest to serve the common good. . . . It is not a natural state, but like any other form of liberty, it is a social achievement, and eternal vigilance is the price of it.[1]

JOHN BATES CLARK

This book has traced the origins of the social responsibility and social cost concepts and their interrelationship. It has proposed the thesis that if a business pays the full costs of its operation, including social costs, its social responsibilities are fully discharged and it is free to compete and pursue its own self-interest in the marketplace.

Social cost measuring techniques are still evolving, and avoidance of social costs is more important than paying for them. Therefore, this book proposes the concept of social balance as an aid to management in avoiding adverse impacts on society as a result of business operation. Social balance is defined as an operating pattern in which the operation of the business does not cause depletion of any significant element of social capital.

As we applied the social balance concept to the various aspects of business operation, our analysis assumed society's point of view. It considered individually the impact of the goods and services produced by the corporation, the impact of resource consumption, and the firm's impact on employees, the community, the environment, and society as a whole. In summarizing this impact, we can identify society's requirements for:

Corporate responsibility consistent with authority

Compensation for all significant increments to social costs

Operation in accordance with the law of the land

Recognition of the use of nature's bounty

Recognition of the implied guarantee that the future will be like the present

Recognition of the cost of lost opportunities

Concern for a fair share of the community

---

[1] John Bates Clark, *The Control of Trusts* (New York: Macmillan, 1912), pp. 200–201.

Consideration of the business impact on ethics and culture

Adjustment to the changing public standards for business performance

Intelligent management of the public role of the business

Competitive pressures might occasionally require a business to work for legislation or other legal creation of uniform standards for business performance in order to implement some social balance requirements. However, the general concept of social balance appears to be consistent with the management objective of obtaining an optimal profit level over the long run.

Thus, guidelines for socially responsible business management are proposed. These guidelines are based on a social balance analysis but recognize the need for further development of social standards in some areas. They also recognize the need for government legislation or regulatory intervention in order not only to permit adequate correction of some social costs in a competitive environment but also to deal with major social problems beyond the resources of individual business firms.

Conclusions

1. The manner of defining social responsibility through the concept of social balance and the management of corporate social impact used in this book largely resolves the conflict between the profit motive and the needs of society. This is adequate as a theoretical resolution, but further work is needed on the practical application of these concepts in some social balance areas.

2. A practical set of guidelines for management of corporate social impact to maintain a social balance has been proposed.

3. This analysis has led to several suggestions for the way in which governmental intervention can make social balance and socially responsible operation easier and can contribute to the general good by promoting greater effectiveness in the workings of the industrial system. In addition, the book has recognized the need to modify the present conceptual basis for governmental intervention in order to devise a less burdensome regulatory framework, which will be able to serve the public interest more efficiently.

4. Limitations on the objective application of corporate social impact and social balance concepts were recognized in areas where objective community standards for responsible action are not yet developed. Although subjective and imperfect standards must be used for the moment, a constructive role was identified for business firms to develop appropriate standards, attempt to apply them, and thus aid the community in evolving its own standards.

5. Practical limitations on the expectations for socially responsible operation of individual businesses were recognized where legislative changes may be necessary to minimize the competitive penalty of balancing social costs.

Suggestions for Further Study

1. Clearly, more work is needed on the measurement of social cost and the development of the social audit. Even though the primary technique proposed in this

work is based on cost avoidance rather than measurement, some social costs are inevitable and the entire social cost issue will become easier to manage once measuring techniques are developed. The difficulties in this area were also recognized, but with many diligent workers now studying this area, progress in the next few years seems likely.

2. Better techniques for turning social costs into accounting costs are needed and will follow directly from perfection of social cost measuring methods. In some cases the solution to a social problem serves also to define the measuring techniques. For instance, those obligations for employee welfare that have been incorporated in fringe-benefit packages now have a well-defined actuarial cost. In the evolving pollution area, however, society seems more disposed to follow a social balance type of approach, that is, to say that pollution beyond a certain standard is unacceptable and that the business must either find a way of meeting the standard or cease its operation. In other social balance areas a broadly acceptable definition of the social balance problem and the measuring techniques are likely to be developed simultaneously.

3. Case studies showing the application of social balance analysis of corporate impacts to individual businesses are needed to further develop the value and limitation of the conclusions presented here.

4. Available statistics for relating the role of one business to the total community, which was developed as the idea of assuming the fair share of the community, are deficient. Better data sources are needed, particularly on the composition and variability of the fringe population group. As these data become available, they will also allow refinements of the concept of this fringe group and of the techniques for working with it effectively.

Recommendations

1. Socially responsible business management (within the framework of the definitions we have used) is clearly possible. The reasons for demanding it are sound. The issue is the provision of appropriate compensation for social costs incurred. Public pressure for such responsibility should be continued and increased.

2. More effort should be made to promote and spread an understanding of both the kind of social balance that a profit-oriented business can be expected to maintain and the areas that remain outside its resources or obligations.

3. National study of low-profit business areas should be undertaken to see what kind of public intervention will be necessary to obtain a higher standard of social responsibility in the face of profit pressures. This review is likely to identify businesses whose present operational pattern cannot be permitted by society in the long run (such as the unsafe coal mines in Appalachia) and, thus, may aid in identifying root causes of a few of the social and poverty problems that cause so much national concern.

4. The need exists for a broad review of the industrial system in the United States to see how the free working of the private sector could be further encouraged in a way that would serve the general good, including socially responsible operation, more vigorously and effectively.

5. Fresh study is needed of the public regulation of business enterprise from the standpoint of the analysis developed in this book to look for better ways to balance public good and private incentives and to look for existing regulatory processes that may impede development of more effective public service. Since the role of business enterprise in our society is to produce needed goods and services at minimum cost, the regulatory environment should be reviewed and revised until it offers a sufficient balance of incentives and constraints to encourage continued evolution of the free enterprise system in the direction of the public interest.

Important Terms and Concepts

Fair share of the community Any given business should foster the development and maintenance of efficient and adequate community services. The contribution of the firm and its employees to the total community need should be fairly proportioned, using the ratio of the employee group (plus dependents) to the total employed population (plus dependents) to estimate the firm's share. The firm also encourages employee participation in developing and maintaining a healthy community. *(See p. 232)*

Corporate social impact The direct or indirect effect of any specific corporate action on society or its individual members. *(See pp. 124, 127, 391)*

Fringe of the community Individuals neither in the work force nor dependent upon a member of the work force. These include the unemployed, the unemployable, public charges of all types, those retired from a nonlocal firm, and people of independent means. *(See p. 235)*

Implied continuity An implicit commitment that the future will be a smooth continuation of the present. Employees expect their jobs to continue, customers plan to repurchase familiar brands (or to obtain needed parts and services), suppliers look for repeat orders, and governments expect tax revenue to continue. *(See pp. 140, 185, 240, 379)*

Nature's bounty   The basic environmental resources of the society. Wherever a business is consuming scarce resources or pre-empting a portion of the purifying capacity of the environment through its discharges, that business is drawing on nature's bounty. *(See p. 202)*

Opportunity costs   Income or achievement lost through alternative employment not pursued, mobility not permitted, initiatives not exercised, or frustrated potential for promotion and growth. *(See pp. 189, 240, 379)*

Optimal profit over the long run   The greatest profit level that can be achieved at each moment without sacrificing the business's future profits. Thus the stream of profits is maximized over time. Achievement of this profit level requires a combination of wise economic decisions to generate the profit and a level of attention to the noneconomic constraints on the business, insuring a harmonious relationship with the surrounding society. *(See p. 384)*

Social balance   The point at which, at each interface of business and society, society is gaining at least as much as it is losing as a result of the business's operation. *(See p. 118)*

Social capital   The collective stock of society's wealth including the holdings of businesses and individuals. This includes not only physical wealth, but also the state of health and welfare of people. *(See p. 118)*

Social costs   Costs (in a true economic sense) that have not been recognized and attributed directly to the firm, and thus are left to be borne by the society as a whole. These costs become a measure of the problems that corporate social responsibility must offset or avoid if it is to be properly discharged. Ideally social costs should be avoided, because of the difficulties in calculating and offsetting such costs. *(See p. 84)*

Social responsibility   The avoidance of social costs in the course of the business operation. As a socially responsible business firm attempts to achieve optimal profits over the long run, it must achieve social balance in each area of its operation. *(See pp. 76, 124, 391)*

True profit   The profit remaining after all business costs are paid, including all social costs as determined by a detailed analysis of the degree of social balance between the firm and society. *(See pp. 76, 390)*

Index